George E. Moran

Moran's Dictionary of Chicago and its Vicinity

With Map of Chicago and its Environs

.

George E. Moran

Moran's Dictionary of Chicago and its Vicinity
With Map of Chicago and its Environs

ISBN/EAN: 9783337182366

Printed in Europe, USA, Canada, Australia, Japan

Cover: Foto ©Andreas Hilbeck / pixelio.de

More available books at **www.hansebooks.com**

BOSTON, MASS.

THE HOTEL BRUNSWICK, on Boylston Street, corner of Clarendon, is one of the grandest and most handsomely furnished hotels in the world. It is in the center of the fashionable "Back Bay" District, and opposite the Society of Natural History and Institute of Technology, on Boylston Street, and Trinity (Phillips Brooks) Church, on Clarendon Street. Just across Copley Square are Museum of Fine Arts, New Public Library, New Old South Church, and Art Club; and only a few minutes' walk from the Central, Arlington Street, and several other churches, public buildings, and the Public Garden.

ADELINA PATTI ^{AND}_{THE} KIMBALL PIANOS

FROM ADELINA PATTI, "THE QUEEN OF SONG."

CHICAGO, December 16, 1889.

W. W. KIMBALL CO., Chicago, Ill.

Gentlemen: It gives me great pleasure to testify to the merits of the New Kimball Piano. It has a wonderfully sweet and sympathetic tone and supports the voice in a most satisfactory manner.

Sincerely yours,

Adelina Patti Nicolini

WAREROOMS, KIMBALL HALL,
243-253 WABASH AVENUE, NEAR JACKSON STREET,
CHICAGO.

ESTABLISHED 1879

ARTISTIC

& MECHANICAL

Electrotyping

ENGRAVERS

By all Modern Proceses

WOOD ENGRAVING

Half-Tone & Photo-Zinc Relief-Line

Etching

Bretsnyder Engraving Co.

179 181 CLARK ST. CHICAGO

BALD HEADS

I WILL TAKE contracts to grow hair on head or face. No cure, no pay. No pay until you have a full growth of hair. Call and be examined free of charge. Should your head be shiny and glossy, and the pores closed, do not call, as you will be only taking up my time, for in such cases there is no cure. If you can not call, write to me.

For sale by all druggists in the United States outside of Chicago.

PROF. G. BIRKHOLZ,

Room 1011, Masonic Temple,
CHICAGO.

Parties writing for information, mention Moran's Dictionary of Chicago.

-

MORAN'S

Map of Chicago

AND SUBURBS.

1893.

George E. Moran

MORAN'S

Dictionary of Chicago

AND ITS VICINITY,

WITH

MAP OF CHICAGO AND ITS ENVIRONS.

AN ALPHABETICALLY ARRANGED DICTIONARY, COMPRISING ALL OF THE
INTERESTS THAT CONTRIBUTE TO CHICAGO'S GREATNESS.

COMPILED BY

George E. Moran.

GEORGE E. MORAN,
PUBLISHER AND PROPRIETOR,
208 AND 209 HERALD BUILDING,
CHICAGO, ILL.
1893.

[new ed.]

F 5 0

.5

PREFACE.

The idea of this little book was suggested to the publisher on seeing a copy of "Dickens' Dictionary of London." The subject-matter has been gleaned from all available sources. This explanation will be sufficient to indicate that there is no claim whatever of originality made by the publisher. That the book will prove of value and of the greatest convenience to the citizens of Chicago, and strangers as well, is the only excuse for its appearance. We think that a careful examination of its contents will suffice to prove its superiority over other publications which claim to cover the same ground.

It is an Alphabetically Arranged Dictionary of Chicago. In other words, everything of a public nature is correctly located and briefly described under its appropriate name, and may be easily found by turning to the proper letter. For instance, the Auditorium will be found among the "A's;" the Stock Yards among the "S's," etc.

The book is not an advertising scheme in any sense of the word. Advertisements do appear, but never in disguise, and in their proper places.

It is possible that errors may appear, and subjects which should be noticed are omitted. However, in future editions, the work will be made as nearly perfect as possible. With this brief preface, it is launched forth by the Publisher, who is determined that it shall live to serve its purpose to the utmost.

THE PUBLISHER.

LETTER OF ENDORSEMENT

From the officials of the Columbian Exposition.
Their opinion of this book.

•

WORLD'S COLUMBIAN COMMISSION

OFFICE OF THE

Director-General of the Exposition.

CHICAGO, ILL., U. S. A., Sept. 23, 1892.

MR. GEORGE E. MORAN,
    Publisher "Moran's Dictionary of Chicago,"
        Suite 208 *and* 209 *Herald Building, City.*

    *Dear Sir: We have examined with great care your publication,
" Moran's Dictionary of Chicago," and find it a most desirable
work, both in conception and execution. It is more than the ordinary
Guide Book, and seems to contain all of the information about
Chicago which ought to be within the reach of the intelligent,
inquiring visitor. We are particularly pleased at the manner in
which you have handled the subject of the World's Columbian
Exposition, and it has given us a great deal of pleasure to verify, as
far as possible, what you have to say on this subject. We are glad
to know that the " Dictionary " is meeting with the success it so
thoroughly merits.*

            Very truly yours,

        MOSES P. HANDY,
           Chief of Dept. of Promotion and Publicity.

        JOHN T. DICKINSON,
           Secretary World's Columbian Commission.

        GEORGE R. DAVIS,
           Director-General of the Exposition.

MORAN'S

DICTIONARY OF CHICAGO

AND VICINITY.

Abandoned or Lost Property.—If left on any of the numerous street-car lines of this city, is carried to the nearest down-town office and left there for identification, a reasonable length of time, and then disposed of by public sale. All articles left in public halls or places of amusement, or on the streets, dropped by owners or thrown aside by criminals, are transferred to the officer in charge at the City Hall, under the direction of the Inspector of the Central Detail. It is wonderful where such an odd collection of sundries could all come from. These, too, are kept until no hope remains of their being reclaimed, when they are sold to make room for the constantly accumulating stock.

Abattoirs.—It is many years since the municipal ordinances allowed any animals to be slaughtered save at the stock yards. As the stock yards and packing houses are inseparable, see *Union Stock Yards.*

Academy of Music.—This theatre is located on the West Side, on Halsted Street, near Madison Street. The interior decorations, including the vestibule, are in rich and artistic designs, a blending of harmonious browns, olives, Molichile greens, relieved by crimson, gold, and silver, that presents a charming effect. The curtain is a portraiture of numerous excellently executed figures representing a scene entitled, "Rewarding the Bull Fighter," and is one of the handsomest found in Chicago theatres. The seats are comfortable, the heating and ventilation perfect, and the management provides only first-class attractions, a new company being on the boards every week during the season. This house is now christened H. R. Jacob's Academy.

Academy of the Sacred Heart.—Located at the corner of State Street and Chicago Avenue, affords excellent educational advantages to the young of Chicago. It is conducted by the Sisters, who inculcate in their young lady pupils the principles of correct habits that fit them for the duties of life.

Advertising Agencies.—There are a number of these agencies in the city, several of them doing a very extensive business and affording a facility for the judicious placing of advertisements, which is in many cases

(5)

of no small value to advertisers. Reputable advertising agents undertake to maintain an established credit with all the newpapers throughout the United States, and to procure the prompt insertion of an advertisement, without any extra charge for the service rendered; which service consists of quoting the price, printing or writing as many duplicates of the advertisement as may be required to furnish one to each paper to be used, forwarding the copy for insertion at their own expense for postage or messenger service, and examining the papers to see that the advertisement appears when and in the manner that it ought to. If errors or omissions occur, it is their duty to notify publishers at their own expense for labor, postage or messenger, and to see to it that the publisher of the paper actually does the specified service for which the advertiser contracted. They are paid for their services by a commission from the newspaper upon the price of the advertisement obtained by them. When it is desired to place a large line of advertising, or to advertise in papers likely to reach a special class of readers, the advertising agency has facilities which enable it to indicate the periodicals most likely to effect that purpose, and to procure from them a special rate for the advertisement in question. Estimates are readily furnished on application, and the real strength of the agency lies in its ability to obtain the greatest concessions from publishers' rates. Of course such a system is open to abuses, but when dealing with reputable agencies the advantages derived will be found to outweigh these, and care should be taken in this, as in all other matters, to deal only with reputable houses. At these agencies, files of all the newspapers in the country are kept, and strangers are courteously allowed to refer to them in case of necessity. Lord & Thomas, Randolph Street, near State, receive fully 1,000,000 newspapers through the mails each year. This firm also publishes a newspaper directory which contains an accurate list of all the newspapers and periodicals in the United States, now numbering no less than 18,536, of which 1,700 are daily papers, and 13,420 weeklies.

African Methodist Episcopal Churches.—The following list gives the names of those in Chicago:

Bethel, Third Avenue, near Taylor Street.

Quinn's Chapel, Fourth Avenue, near Van Buren Street.

St. Paul's, Dearborn and Twenty-ninth Streets.

St. Stephen's, 682 Austin Avenue.

Aldermen.—The Board of Aldermen exercises the entire legislative powers of the city. It is composed of sixty-eight aldermen, or two from each of the thirty-four wards. One alderman is elected from each ward on alternate years, and the term for which he is elected is two years. They have power to enforce, pass, and repeal city ordinances, subject to the approval of the Mayor, and to pass resolutions over his veto by a three-quarters vote. They meet at their own pleasure, usually once a week, but occasionally at greater intervals, in their room or hall, fourth floor of the City Hall. The aldermen are compensated with a per diem for actual services, the total of which will average about $15,000 per year. One of the duties of the Mayor is to preside at the meetings of the council, or Board of Aldermen.

Alhambra Theatre. — Corner of State Street and Archer Avenue. Take State Street cable cars. This beautiful theatre has a seating capacity of 2,500, aside from twelve boxes. It was opened in 1890 by Miss Emma Juch, the prima donna, and since then it has become very popular under the management of H. R. Jacobs. It has no less than twenty-eight exits, by which the house can be emptied in less than five minutes. The grand entrance is on State Street, and there is another entrance on Archer Avenue, both leading into the main foyer, which is located in a spacious court. The Alhambra is thoroughly modern, and with very few exceptions it is unequaled as a large, handsome theatre. It was evidently designed as the home of light and grand opera. The interior is of Moorish design. the colors a happy combination of salmon and shrimp pink. The stage is 48 feet deep and has an opening of 28 feet. The stage arrangements are all that money could obtain or the demands of the age suggest. Its location makes it exceedingly convenient for those who reside on the South Side.

All Souls' Church.—Unitarian, at the corner of Oakwood Boulevard and Langley Avenue. The present pastor, Rev. Jenkin Lloyd-Jones, is considered, on account of his eloquence and success, one of the leading divines of Chicago. The church is very handsome architecturally, and has a large congregation.

Amateur Dramatic Societies.—The amateur drama in Chicago meets with but little success, and Thespic societies are not very numerous. The only dramatic clubs which are really worthy the name are connected with the more prominent social organizations. The Carleton Club, of the South Side, has a dramatic auxiliary of real merit, whose performances are most noteworthy. Several well-known members of the stage have graduated from the Carleton.

Amateur Photography.—The camera fiend is quite numerous in Chicago, and there is quite a number of really talented amateurs. A photographic contest, such as is often conducted under the auspices of the New York weekly papers, would be a great incentive to the development of amateur work, and the idea is worthy of notice. The light and sky of Chicago are very favorable to good photography.

Ambulances.—Every one of the thirty-five patrol wagons in the police service is so equipped that it may be used as an ambulance in case of need, while two regular ambulances are kept always ready for use. Within a few minutes after an accident, a patrol wagon can be brought into service, and the victim speedily transported to the nearest hospital.

American Association of the Red Cross.—Has a branch in Chicago located in Central Music Hall.

American District Telegraph.—Main office, No. 501 Pullman building; numerous branches located all over the city. This company derives a large revenue from Chicago, and its active messenger boys are ever in demand.

Amusements.—Probably no city can boast of a greater variety of amusements, theatrical and otherwise, than Chicago. During the summer months, when most cities are almost destitute of sources of enjoyment, the visitor can still find a variety of resorts open to selection, while the winter offers more and better attractions than any other city in the country. There are more than twenty theatres, four museums, and a number of concert halls, but few of which are closed during the summer. For those interested in athletic and other sports, Chicago is a veritable paradise. There are five enclosed base-ball parks within the city limits, several cycling clubs, and several first-class billiard halls. Two race tracks also offer enjoyment to the devotees of the turf, and there are half a dozen boat clubs located on the Lake Front.

Within recent years Chicagoans have been favored with the leading attractions of theatrical and musical art, and have shown themselves both liberal and appreciative. Whatever is popular in London, Paris, or New York, is soon produced in Chicago, while many new plays make their first appearance here.

Anarchy in Chicago.—The metropolis of the Northwest is the product of honest, untiring men who came here to acquire homes, and having obtained their wish, they are raising families to follow in their footsteps. Anarchy was an imported weed, sown and fostered in its growth by a few reckless, footloose individuals who had nothing to lose, and whose wild, restless spirits craved strife, and blood even, to drown their disturbed consciences. The visiting strangers from all the world who intend to honor the Columbian Fair with their presence, need have no fear of this red-headed dragon. It received its final quietus on the 11th day of November, 1887, when four of the ring-leaders in the anarchist outbreak were hanged in the county jail. There has been neither rattle nor hiss since; and it is nearly six years since there has been any riotous demonstration in our streets. There never was any movement with strength enough to be dignified as revolutionary. The disturbance was simply the frothing of a few dangerous leaders who aspired to be Robespierres and Marats, and a great crowd of spectators who simply wanted to see. This little group could have been suppressed long before the crisis, if the municipal executive had seen fit. Chicago's workingmen are not, and never were, anarchists. Within the last eight years the spread of building and loan associations, by helping the wage laborers to own their homes, has increased many hundred-fold the immunity from anarchy and its teachings.

Animals, American Society for the Prevention of Cruelty to,—Was organized through the efforts of Mr. Henry Bergh, in 1866, in New York. It has extended a system of branch organizations to all the large cities of the Union. One of the most flourishing branches is in Chicago. Its object is to enforce the laws preventing cruelty to, and protecting animals of all kinds, but especially draft beasts, who are more exposed to the ignorant brutality of their drivers. The police are bound to make arrests in its behalf, when asked by any person who is willing to make complaint before a justice of the peace. Its accredited agents have power also, as special police, to arrest offenders guilty of cruelty to their animals on the public streets. Many of our prominent business houses allow complaints to be forwarded by their telephones to the main office, 242 Wabash Avenue. They have ambulances for conveying injured animals through the city in any case where there is any chance for recovery. In 1873 they established a paper called the "*Humane Journal*," which is still fighting for the cause in whose interest it started.

Annexation.—Previous to 1889, the business men of Chicago who lived in the suburbs and traveled back and forth to their business in the city, often wondered why the municipal advantages their taxes helped to procure those living within the limits could not be extended to themselves at their homes. Finally, permission in due form was obtained from the Legislature and submitted to a vote of the people. Thus the towns of Cicero, Hyde Park, Jefferson, and Lake, and the City of Lake View, on the 29th of June. 1889, were annexed to the City of Chicago. From about forty-four square miles, her territory increased by this peaceful conquest to 128.24 square miles, extending from north to south not less than twenty miles, and on an average, seven and one-half from east to west. The Supreme Court handed down a favorable decision as to the validity of the law in October, 1889. In 1890, South Englewood, West Roseland, Washington Heights, and Gano, were added to the annexed territory. In 1835 Chicago claimed 2.55 square miles. In 1891 she is responsible for the good government of 181.70 square miles, of which 5.14 square miles are covered with water, and 176 56 are in condition t ₂ be improved as may be needed. The city fathers have cut this area up into thirty-four wards, varying in size from thre -quarters of a square mile to twenty-seven square miles. The various annexations increased the resident population by 239,607, but as they were all really citizens before, the increase was simply a legal fiction, for, while they lived in the annexed territory, their brains and money had built the central city. (See *Territorial Growth*.)

Anshe Maariv Cemetery.— This is a small cemetery used by a Jewish congregat on. It is located at North Clark Street and Belmont Avenue. Take Evanston Division of Chicago, Milwaukee & St. Paul Railway, or North Clark Street cable line.

Apartment Houses.—Within the past ten years the efforts made to induce people of moderate means to live in apartments and abandon boarding-houses and hotels, in which a large proportion of the population had theretofore resided, has met with a marked degree of success. The first proposition of the kind met with great opposition, the majority of people being unable to distinguish between an apartment house and a tenement house. The prejudice was overcome in a great degree by the fact that the first buildings erected were of an expensive character, and the rents of the "flats," as they are commonly called, placed at a figure within the means of the wealthy alone. When people were found willing to pay for a suite of rooms, the rent usually demanded for a first-c'ass residence, a demand was created for similar accommodations at cheaper rents, and several hundreds of these buildings are now distributed over the city, and others are constantly being erected. Apartment houses in the city, as a rule are divided into two suites on each floor, consisting of a parlor or drawing-room, dining-room, kitchen, bath-room, and from two to four or more sleeping-rooms, most of the sleeping rooms being lighted and ventilated from a shaft running through the house from the basement to the roof. The more expensive "flats" have a passenger elevator and a door-keeper; the others have not. All, however, have elevators for coal, wood, ashes, marketing, and similar freight. All have also a private hallway, and these two advantages are usually accepted as marking the line between a tenement - house, where family necessaries are carried up and down stairs and it is necessary to pass through one room to enter another, and an apartment house or "flat." Many of these houses, even of the more modest class, are finished in hard-wood, and have mirrors, gas fixtures, electric lights, and mantels of an artistic and even elegant character as fixtures. Stationary wash-tubs are placed either in the kitchen or in a laundry in the basement or top floor. The houses where a man servant is not stationed at the door to receive visitors, always have a bell, a letter-box, and a name-plate within the vestibule for each apartment. Above these is a speaking-tube, and after ringing the bell and announcing one's name through the tube, the occupant is able to open the door by an electrical device and allow the visitor to enter and pass to the flo r occupied by the person he wishes to see. More expensive apartments have a general reception-room and a man servant to announce the visitor. The rents of these apartments range from $2,000 to $300 p r year, dependent on their size, elegance of finish, and the location of the apart-ment and the house. Those in the neighborhood of the Lake Front are the most expensive.

Apollo Club.—A musical organi-zation, of which Prof. W. L. Tom-lins, the well-known vocal director, has long been the leading light.

The club has its headquarters in Central Music Hall, and gives fre-quent concerts, which are considered notable events in the musical world.

Architectural Features.—The most untruthful thing that could be said of Chicago would be to charge monotony to its architecture. No city in the world, not even New York, presents so wide a variety in design, material, or construction. Perhaps the very diversity has leaned somewhat toward the *bizarre*. All uniformity of outside appearance is lost in the personality of the builder, who may desire a house modeled up-on one in any of the four quarters of the globe. We have the Renaissance,

the modern French, the Greek, Roman, Italian, Gothic, Tudor, and not by any means the least, the Chi-cago Construction. Our material is granite from New England and Nova Scotia; marble from Vermont, Illi-nois, and Wisconsin; bricks from Wisconsin, Illinois and Indiana; iron from Pennsylvania and Ala-bama, and whatever is used any-where can be found as a part of this cosmopolitan city. Iron and glass are much used, but the style belonging to Chicago by right, and called the "Chicago Construc-tion," is a framework of iron, bolted together and standing upright, with-out resting upon the walls at all, but upon a foundation of grout, crossed by bars of railroad iron. The roof rests directly upon this framework, and not upon the sides. The walls are then filled in with terra cotta tiles of any desired color and shape. This form of building is used in the high buildings of from fifteen to twenty stories, which will, in time, quadruple Chicago's floor space. Not-able examples are the Auditorium, the Rookery, the Chamber of Com-merce, the Masonic Temple, the Wo-man's Temple, and the Unity Build-ing. Many more are yet unfinished, or projected. In the business quarter, Marshall Field's wholesale building, the Board of Trade, the Post Office, the Wisconsin Central Rail-road station, and the Rialto Build-ing, all exhibit peculiarities that fit them for their use. It is certain, however, no matter how the build-ing appears on the outside, the inside will be particularly adapted to get the utmost service from both the owner's labor and his employ(s'. In the residence quarters, no man builds a house like his neighbor, but to suit his own taste and wants. It is a cus-tom, very largely indulged in during the summer time. to gather upon the broad, high steps, with or without porches, but the steps and the porches are as varied in design and build as the houses themselves. On the North and South sides, within sight of the lake, can be seen the most varied architecture of the homes. On the West Side the boulevards are claiming more and more attention in this direction. It is impossible to give anything more than a few hints about a subject so varied in feature and infinite in form. One must indeed be very hard to suit who could not find something to please in the architecture, the construction, or the material of Chicago's buildings.

Armour Mission and Free Dispensary. — Located at Dearborn and Thirty-third streets is a very handsome building of pressed brick, with stone copings. The institution has been in operation about five years, and contains a commodious auditorium for church services, several Sunday-school class-rooms, lyceum, kindergarten-rooms, reading-rooms, bath-rooms, etc. Mr. Joseph Armour left a sum of money to establish a philanthropic institution, and Mr. Philip D. Armour having added largely to it, the present mission was erected. It is supported entirely by Mr. Armour, Mrs. Armour looking after the kindergarten, in which she takes great interest.

Artistic Furniture. — In nothing, perhaps, is the influence of art so well measured as in the improvement of designs in furniture. The modern idea is not only to look pretty, but to add to the comfort and rest of those who use. Our furniture warehouses and salesrooms contain full lines of all designs, from the Gothic to the modern. We have immense buildings on the South and West sides devoted to the exhibition of rich hangings, elegant furniture, and

the rarest bric-a-brac. Our supplies are drawn largely from Grand Rapids, Mich., acknowledged as leading the world as a furniture manufacturing point. But we gather from all sources, East or West, and will undertake to import any variety, from any point, whether it be tapestry from Damascus or Farther India; rugs from Persia; furs from Russia, Siberia, or Alaska; onyx slabs from Mexico; carvings from Germany, Switzerland, or France, or anything else from the manufactories of our own country. In no city of the Union could a contract for furnishing a house from the cellar to garret be filled so quickly and completely, to the artistic satisfaction of the buyer, as in Chicago.

Art Galleries. — Aside from the galleries connected with the Art Institute, there are no public collections. One or two of the most prominent art dealers have considerable space, well lighted and fitted up for the exhibition of any noted work in which they may have an interest. Chicago is promised, and through the exertions of the patrons of the Art Institute will undoubtedly get, an art hall on the Lake Front, in connection with the Columbian Exposition. The plan is to make this permanent. If the designs are carried out, then Chicago will have an art gallery worthy of the name.

Art Institute. — The Art Institute, which so long made its home at the corner of Michigan Avenue and Van Buren Street, is to have a magnificent abode. A permanent Art Palace is now arising on the lake front, and the Institute, aided by the Directory of the World's Fair, will become the richest and most powerful artistic center in the land.

The various collections and classrooms of the Institute will occupy the greater part of the new building, and literary, architectural, and social clubs will divide with the studios of noted artists the remainder of the space.

There will be two large audience halls, each of 3,500 capacity, and thirty smaller rooms of a capacity ranging from 300 to 750 feet.

Like all buildings designed for similar purposes, this was the inspiration of the generosity of men whose money and leisure have given scope for the growth of public spirit. The amount invested in building is estimated at nearly $2,000,000, while the value of the art collections in its possession for use runs up to a half million. The patrons of the Art Institute, when they travel, are always in touch with their protégé. They come home laden with spoils drawn from the four quarters of the globe. In 1890 the Institute was enriched by some fine samples of carved ivory, which supplements some Japanese carving loaned to the Institute. The popularity of this institution is attested by the total number of visitors, 66,926, for six months. The average of visitors on Saturday, admission free all day, was 669; for four hours on Sunday, 855.

Artistic Silverware.—It is conceded that the United States has no competitor in the world in the production of artistic designs and elegant workmanship in silver. All Chicago's prominent jewelers carry large stocks, and will take orders for any original design. While we have no large manufactories as yet, we have firms who will do work as perfectly and promptly as any others in the country, whether East or West.

Art Schools.—The principal art school of Chicago is connected with the Art Institute, and located in the Art Institute building. A large number of students, many of whom come from other cities, attend the various classes, and have free access to the galleries and collections of the Institute. Instruction is given in drawing, painting, sculpture, and architectural designing.

Art Stores.—There are a dozen stores in Chicago where an artist can obtain anything he might need in the line of his work, and twice as many who carry smaller and more miscellaneous stocks, but who will always gladly fill orders for their customers. The most prominent stores are on the South Side, within two or three blocks of the crossing of Madison and Wabash. Not only can materials be obtained here, but also originals and copies of paintings, lithographs, and prints of the best work. An hour can easily be whiled away in them.

Ashes and Garbage.—Presumably ashes and garbage are removed by the carts of the Street Cleaning Department, but they are taken away so irregularly and infrequently at present that they constitute one of the greatest annoyances to the residents and the visitors of the city. Long rows of unsightly boxes and barrels filled with ashes and garbage often adorn the curbstones of the finest streets of the city for days at a time, and their contents, which are at the mercy of every wind that blows, are scattered about the streets and deposited in the eyes and upon the clothes of every passer-by. When the carts do not pass regularly, complaint should be made to the Street Cleaning Department, City Hall, but this has heretofore been found of little avail. No vegetable or animal refuse ought, under any circumstances, to be mixed with the ashes. Garbage should always be first dried under the kitchen fire and then burned, a process which is slowly coming into general use. Ashes should be placed on the walk in a galvanized iron cylindrical vessel and should be taken away by the public carts in the early hours of the morning, and the empty vessels removed from the sidewalk before the hour of 7 A. M. When this reform will be accomplished, however, remains an unanswerable query. For the public disposal of large quantities of garbage unmixed with ashes, a number of properly adapted and suitably located crematories appears to be the best means at present that could be adopted for the city. There is a most serious objection to permitting the garbage of a great city to be removed to any place where it may be used to feed animals designed for human food, because investigations by sanitary scientists demonstrate that animals so fed become unfit for domestic use. If not consumed in some manner it may breed disease.

Ashland Block.—The new Ashland Block, which is located on the northeast corner of Clark and Randolph streets, is one of the most imposing structures in the city. It is sixteen stories in height and the top of the cornice is 200 feet from the sidewalk. The building is of steel construction and fire-proofed with tile and brick. The walls are of red pressed brick with terra-cotta trimmings. The exterior style of architecture is Renaissance, while the general style is in accordance with modern Chicago office buildings. The main entrance is on Clark Street and is in the form of a semi-circular arch with an elaborate Roman effect. There are seven elevators. The first three floors are designed for large business establishments, while the other floors will be used for offices. The entire cost of this splendid building is $650,000.

Ashland Club.—A West Side social organization, located at the corner of Washington Boulevard and Wood Street; one of the leading clubs of the city, both in membership and accommodations. The club house is very large, with all modern conveniences, dance hall, bowling alleys, billiard room, etc. No intoxicating liquors are sold on the premises. The membership numbers about 400.

Assets of the City.—It will be observed by the following statement, based upon the most accurate data, that the corporation of Chicago is solvent, in fact, in a flourishing condition:

	Cash Value.
Water Works	$50,000,000
Sewers	11,000,000
School Property	11,000,000
Police Property	844,000
Fire Property	2,500,000
Public Library	232,000
Street Lamps	750,000
Electric Light Property	2,000,000
Real Estate	1,000,000
Buildings	2,000,000
House of Correction	1,000,000
Total	$82,326,000
Liabilities—Bonded debt	13,554,400

Making a total net value of city property	$68,780,600
Assessed valuation of real and personal property	$219,354,386.00
Total amount of levy for city purposes	4,397,087.36
Revenue for licenses	3,000,000.00
Total annual income of the city from taxes, water, licenses, fees, and other items	$25,000,000.00

Associated Press.—It was in 1849 when the leading daily papers of New York City discovered that there was more money in the coöperative collection of some classes of news than in the chance of an occasional "scoop." As dollars were worth more then than now, it added to their income to be able to obtain, for six or seven papers, matter that cost only one price, or divided the expense by seven. When the league had grown strong, the scope of the gathering was increased to cover all news. From the first, no new member could be admitted to the combination without unanimous consent. As a new-comer could never obtain this, the Associated Press has been denounced again and again in newspaper columns and on the floor of Congress, as an unjust and profitable monopoly. As time went on, the newspapers of various cities formed associations depending upon the parent association, and governed by the same laws. In Chicago this franchise was held originally by the *Tribune*, *Times*, *Inter-Ocean*, *Staats Zeitung*, *Journal*, and *Daily News*. Some of the other papers have now limited contracts, which permit their receiving the news at a fixed price. The association "swaps," or sells its news to other associations all over this country and Europe. Nothing worthy of telegraph attention can escape its notice, no matter how obscure the quarter in which it happens. It has successfully resisted all attempts at competition in the gathering and distribution of news. It has passed into a proverb, that no journal can succeed outside the pale of the Associated Press. The anomaly of its existence is, that it has no capital stock; is not a corporation, in the usual sense of the word. It takes a cool $250,000 to buy a membership, so that its total good-will can be named at about a couple of millions. The Association has its office in the Western Union Telegraph Company's buildings, Broadway, corner of Dey Street. The telegraph company grants it special contracts in the use of its wires. There is also a National Press Association using the wires of the Atlantic and Pacific Telegraph Company, at 145 Broadway, with offices in Chicago.

Asylums and Benevolent Institutions. — Chicago has never been niggardly in its charities. The voluntary subscriptions to charity and charitable institutions in this city annually, is estimated at over three million dollars. This does not, however, include hospitals, nor reformatory institutions.

AMERICAN EDUCATIONAL AND AID ASSOCIATION.—This is better known as the Children's Home Society of Chicago. The churches in this city all have local boards. These are in constant communication, through the Superintendent of the Association, with a thousand other local boards throughout the country. A needy or homeless child is reported at once to the executive, and, if necessary, is received in the temporary homes at Englewood or Aurora, and remains there until some home needing a child can be found, to which the waif is transferred. Voluntary contributions cover the whole expense. The cost per child, of assisting in the work of making a good citizen, is less than $50. Nearly two thousand children have found thus good homes during the last eight years. They are now averaging a child per day. The office is located at 230 La Salle Street.

ARMOUR MISSION. — This grand charity is due to the bequest of $100,000 from the late Joseph F. Armour. It was established in November, 1886, at the corner of Butterfield and Thirty-third streets. It can be reached by State Street cable cars. Philip D. Armour was designated by his brother as trustee of this fund, and he has given it the same energetic management which has so prospered his own business. Whatever was needed to make it a success in every respect, he has added from his own resources. The present institution represents $1,000,000. The Armour Mission is a legal corporation, which owns not only the Mission itself, but 194 flats, called the Armour Mission Flats. The income from the renting is devoted to the maintenance of the Mission. The last addition to this institute is a manual training-school. Race, creed, nor any other distinction are not a bar to admission into the Mission. It is a part of Mr. Armour's creed that as the "twig is trained so is the tree inclined." He expresses the utmost satisfaction at the outcome of this work, so peculiarly his own. The Mission building is constructed solidly and thoroughly of pressed brick and brown stone. The woodwork is of polished oak. A creche, or day nursery, is fitted up on the first floor, which contains also the kitchen, day-room, kindergarten-room, reading-room, dispensary rooms, of which there are four, coal and furnace cellar, bath-rooms, and closets. The second floor has the main audience-room, pastor's study, officer's room, library, spacious halls, and two large side rooms, used for Sunday-school purposes or for small gatherings. The third floor is taken up by a large, handsomely fitted lecture-room. The main audience-room, with its adjuncts, will accommodate about 2,500 persons. There is a large pipe-organ here, and every accessory from stained-glass windows to admirable, acoustic properties combine to make this the most beautiful room of its kind in the city. The school has enrolled 2,000 members, with an average attendance of over 1,400, an increase over last year of about 200. Nothing has

been left undone that could conduce to the success of the enterprise. This includes the publishing of a monthly paper, called the *Visitor*, used for gratuitous distribution.

BETHANY HOME. — Founded to care for old persons and the children of working-women. Can be reached by Madison Street cable. It is on West Monroe Street, No. 1029.

BUREAU OF JUSTICE.—Located at 149 La Salle Street. It was started in 1888. Its design is to secure justice for the helpless, man, woman, or child. It is supported by the contributions of the best business men of Chicago. It employs leading legal talent, and has accomplished much in defense of the unprotected. In 1890, it had in court 325 cases, of these it won 300. This amply demonstrates the necessity for an institution of this kind. It is a most efficient instrument for the recovery of small wage claims, withheld under various knavish excuses, and a proportion of one case lost to thirteen won, speaks most highly of the justice of the claims urged.

CHICAGO CHILDREN'S HOSPITAL. —This is designed as a charitable mission for infirm or crippled children of poor and destitute parents. It is supported by voluntary subscription. Its location is 214 Humboldt Boulevard.

CHICAGO DAILY NEWS FRESH AIR FUND.—Even Chicago's busy journalists find time to do much for their unfortunate fellows. The beneficent work under the charge of the Chicago Daily News Fund is one that meets with much deserved favor from all classes of our citizens, from the laboring man who freely gives his dime, to the millionaire who donates his hundreds. In 1889 a great step was taken in the erection of a permanent sanitarium for the special benefit of infants and young children, at

Lincoln Park, which can be reached by the Clark or Wells Street cables. The design of the building was intended for solidity and endurance, no money was spent on ornamentation or elaboration, every point conduces to the main feature, use. The building is wholly over the water, standing on a large floor, supported by piling ninety feet wide and extending into the lake 200 feet. The great roof, and its projecting eaves covers almost eighteen thousand square feet. Over all this space, swing infants' hammocks, they being the chief beneficiaries of this charity. Broad verandas and an extensive court opening to the air and lake, supply accommodations for older children and the attendants or mothers. All the necessary offices are at the shore end. From a large reception-room, the guests pass to the office of the physician-in-charge, for examination, and such medical attention as may be needed. They are then registered, and the matron assigns them to trained nurses who see they have the necessary floor space, hammocks, chairs, food, etc. The room of the matron communicates with both the office and the surgeon's quarters. Critical cases that sometimes must be kept over night, find in the matron's room a suitable dormitory. This group of rooms are all on the right of the entrance. On the left we find the kitchen, pantries, store-rooms, and north of these are bath-rooms and closets. The connection with the park is by a broad bridge, with an easy slope for the baby carriages. Older children can find plenty of amusement in the park, while their younger brothers and sisters are drinking in the life-giving breezes of Lake Michigan. The total cost of the building and furnishing was over twelve thousand dollars, for which the *Daily News* made itself responsible, until such time as the generous

citizens of Chicago, should transfer the burden upon their own shoulders. The South Side Sanitarium is, at the present, a summer resort for the babies, located at the foot of Twenty-second Street. A huge pavilion tent, 54x84 feet, covers the hammocks in which the little ones swing, and fill themselves with the bracing oxygen of the blue expanse of waters. A kindergarten is also carried on to relieve the mothers from the care of the second or third size of children they can not leave at home alone. In connection with these expressions of thoughtfulness for the poor we always have with us, there is still another branch of summer work known as "The Country Week," in which co-operative human sympathy is made available to permit the toiling poor, the children first, to enjoy a few days in the country during the heated term. In this movement are combined the contributions of our own citizens; the reductions of railroad fares, and the generous hospitality of the "country cousins," in Indiana, Illinois, and Wisconsin. This charity gives over a thousand persons, a chance yearly, to escape the horrors of the "heated term" in the slums. It has also often happened that children going into the country thus, have been adopted, into homes of plenty and health. For all this bountiful work the *Daily News* stands sponsor, and receives contributions from any generous hand at 123 Fifth Avenue.

CHICAGO FREE KINDERGARTEN ASSOCIATION is doing an immense work in this city. Twenty-three hundred and twenty-seven children were enrolled in 1890. Counting all items of cost, the expense per child is about $5.00 a year. Young ladies interested in the work have received diplomas and certificates to the number of sixty-nine. The active staff of workers numbers 101. The effort of the Association is to bring the workers and the mothers together for the best training of the children. The paper issued by the Association, the *Free Kindergarten*, is rapidly increasing its circulation. It is a quarterly, and contains a record of the work constantly going on. This is a proof of increasing interest.

CHICAGO NURSERY AND HALF ORPHAN ASYLUM.—Situated on Burling Street, south of Center Street. The money passing through the hands of its managers annually, reaches a total of about $20,000.

CHICAGO ORPHAN ASYLUM.—The Cottage Grove Avenue cable line will carry you to 2228 Michigan Avenue, the location of this most deserving institution. While under Protestant management, it never inquires concerning the religious preferences, of those needing its help.

CHICAGO POLICLINIC.—Either line of the North Side cable, will take you into the neighborhood of 174 and 176 Chicago Avenue. There is no institution of greater merit in the city. All sorts of diseases are treated free of charge to the sufferers. At the first, intended simply as a means of succor to the destitute, a sort of mission, it has developed into a clinical college where post-graduate courses in medicine and surgery are obtainable. The buildings now have accommodations for two hundred. The Faculty not only donate their services but pay their own bills for material used in their practice. The attendance on the clinics will average 150 daily. The latest addition is a department of Orthopedics. About twenty of Chicago's most distinguished physicians are on the roster of the Faculty.

CHICAGO RELIEF AND AID SOCIETY.—This exists by special charter of the legislature of 1857. It occupies its own building on LaSalle

2

Street, between Lake and Randolph. It received a large portion of the surplus of the world's contribution, when the fire of 1871 had swept over the city. It has been often criticised for its methods, whether justly or not is not for us to say. From its reports, one would infer that the most crying waste is among the abject poor. It handles in its work yearly about $40,000.

CHURCH HOME FOR AGED PERSONS.—Number 4327 Ellis Avenue. Can be reached by Cottage Grove Avenue cable line. This institution is in a flourishing condition and doing a good work.

CONVALESCENTS' HOME.—Just organized with an admirable management. Will undoubtedly make itself heard from, in the future.

DANISH LUTHERAN ORPHAN'S HOME.—Situated in Maplewood on the Wisconsin Division of the North-Western Railroad.

ERRING WOMAN'S REFUGE—On Indiana Avenue, between Fiftieth and Fifty-first Streets. It can be reached by Indiana Avenue car on the Wabash Avenue cable line. This institution dates back to 1865. But it was not until 1890 that the present building, which cost $60,000 and will accommodate 100 women, was opened to the public. The ground cost $11,000. It is built of red brick and limestone, with all necessary conveniences and appurtenances. The third and fourth floors are devoted to dormitories and bathrooms. On the fourth floor are two lock-ups lined with corrugated iron. This is an improvement on the underground dungeon, for a refractory inmate would hesitate before flinging herself from the fourth story out of spite. This is considered one of the best managed institutions in the city. From 14 to 20 is the usual limit of the ages of the inmates and as a rule they are of the ignorant, hard-working class, to whom life has always been a harsh task-master. They come to the Refuge by various routes, a great many from the justice courts, although there is no law on the statute books, which authorizes either commitment or reception by the Refuge. If they desire, a writ of *habeas corpus* will at any time release them. The aim of the management is to restore them to themselves and to teach them house-work, plain sewing, and dress-making, the appeal being made to their moral and religious natures. From 10 A. M., to 4 P. M. daily are visiting hours.

FOUNDLING'S HOME. — Situated on Wood Street, corner Ogden Place, Madison Street cable line. Dr. Shipman, stirred to the depths of his sympathetic nature by his professional experience, and by the report of the coroner, "that at least one infant a day was found dead from exposure;" in 1870, opened his home for the reception of the little waifs, in no way desiring or expecting it to become a public charity; but the papers spoke of it as a charge belonging to the ocean of life surging about us. From the first, the Doctor and his good wife, believing that God had promised to be a father to the fatherless, trusted their needs and wants in His hands. Little by little, under the most remarkable exhibitions of faith answered, the supplies have come. One development after another has unfolded, until the present well-appointed building, holding 112 inmates, is the result. The Home still depends on voluntary contributions; but it is so widely known that the fears of starvation and freezing no longer oppress it. Some of the brightest minds in the West have been saved to the country by its agency. During the daily visiting hours, visitors are most cordially welcome.

GERMAN OLD PEOPLE'S HOME. — Altenheim is in Harlem, ten miles west of the Court House, can be reached by the Wisconsin Central Railroad. This is the pet charity of the best German people in the city of Chicago. It is most ample and convenient in all its arrangements, and is most admirably managed. The grounds are beautifully laid out, and nothing is omitted which can possibly make the lives of the elders committed to its charge as pleasant as possible.

GOOD SAMARITAN SOCIETY. — The Industrial Home of this Society can be reached by a Lincoln Avenue car, at 151 Lincoln Avenue. It operates under a special charter. Its design is to provide a place where worthy but destitute women and girls can earn an honest and respectable living, until such time as they can be provided for elsewhere. They are supplied with money necessary to pay car fare, but nothing more. It depends upon the contributions of the benevolent for its support. Its motto is to help those who will help themselves.

GUARDIAN ANGEL ORPHAN ASYLUM. — A German institution, under the management of the Roman Catholic "Poor Handmaids of Jesus Christ," situated at Rosehill.

HEBREW CHARITY ASSOCIATION.— Notwithstanding the slanders of their maligners, no people are more just or charitable than the Hebrews. Their ostentation in giving may be less; but it accomplishes all that could possibly be done. This is particularly the case in this city, where all their brigades of charity work are massed into one division, each helping all, and all each. The receipts of the last Hebrew Charity Ball, given in Chicago under the auspices of this Association, were $12,000.

HOLY FAMILY ORPHAN ASYLUM. —A Catholic home on Division Street, corner of Holt.

HOME FOR INCURABLES.—Cottage Grove Avenue cable line to Ellis Avenue, corner Fifty-sixth Street. Mrs. Clarissa C. Peck filled her life full of noble deeds and in her will left $500,-000 for the founding of this institution which is for her an enduring monument, living in the hearts and lives of those whom it benefits and blesses. A Board of Trustees from some of our most active and honorable business men have carried the work on to its present completeness. For six years, in which interest accumulated, the action of the Trustees was delayed. The buildings and grounds cost $107,000 and there was left $600,000, the income from which is more than sufficient to meet all running expenses and to increase the building fund, to be ready when additional facilities for its work shall be needed. The full capacity is 125. It started with thirty-three inmates from a similar Home at Lake View, which was then closed. It is theosophical in its invitation to the suffering, receiving them without distinction of race, creed, or color. When possible the friends are asked to pay a monthly stipend, but from the destitute nothing is asked. A candidate for admission must be incurably afflicted with some disease of which the Trustees are final referees. The ailments most frequent are paralysis and rheumatism; the majority of the former. If not able to walk, invalid chairs are provided, by which they can change place and position at will, in their own rooms or through the long corridors and wide verandas, where bright glimpses of sunshine upon the green lawn and gay parterres of bright flowers, bring momentary surcease of pain to weakened limbs and dimmed eyes. Visit-ors are always welcome at the visiting hours.

HOME FOR SELF-SUPPORTING WOMEN.—An Indiana Street car will take you to 275 and 277 Indiana Street, a home for women or girls who are willing to work, whether employed or not. It throws its protecting arm about those who otherwise would be all alone.

HOME FOR UNEMPLOYED GIRLS. —Market, corner Elm, North Side, reached by North Market Street car. Under the management of the Roman Catholic "Franciscan Sisters." It takes care of girls who may temporarily be out of employment. It is very generously supported.

HOME FOR WORKING WOMEN.—Reached by North Clark Street cable, at 189 East Huron Street. It is managed by an association of women and men, who know from experience the need of such homes. The design is to give wage women a chance for a comfortable resting place, at a cheap rate, and wholesome cleanliness, and if she should be thrown out of work, by sickness, would not feel that she was likely to be thrown into the street. From the first of July to January, 1891, 327 enjoyed the benefits of the Home. It is the intention of the managers to make it not an institution but a genuine home in the best and truest sense.

HOME FOR THE FRIENDLESS.—Wabash Avenue cable to 1926 Wabash Avenue. Chartered in 1858. Takes care of 200 inmates on an average. From a weak and humble beginning, it has grown and prospered until its income, including the Crerar bequest, is now $21,000 per annum. During the last ten years, an army numbering 20,167 of women and children has continuously filed through its welcome portals. It is theosophical in its work, as it makes no distinction of race, creed, or color. The only question is whether the applicant is needy, and for the time being needing a friend's help. It matters not whether they are deserted wives and mothers, or abandoned children; assistance, material and moral, is freely tendered, including rest, good food, encouragement, sympathy, and advice for the future. During its life it has found permanent homes for 734 children "legally surrendered" to the Home by their parents. Any woman but a drunken one can find shelter here temporarily, if she has no money to pay for her lodging elsewhere. The Humane Society sends most of their waifs here, when found abandoned by their parents. If under nine months, a child is not received. Visitors between the hours of 10 A. M. and noon, and 1 and 4 P. M., are always welcome.

HOME OF INDUSTRY.—A Van Buren Street car will take you nearly to 234 and 236 Honore Street, where Michael Dunn, a reformed criminal, who had spent the best thirty years of his life in penal institutions all over the world, holds out a helping hand to those tempted as he was tempted. He was born and reared an English criminal. He commenced his prison life when seven years old on conviction for petty larceny. At thirty he had been in prison a half dozen times and in several of the English penal settlements. Finally he was sent to America to get rid of him. He continued his criminal careers here, until about ten years since, when, having reformed himself, he attempted to better the class he had left. His life has stamped its impress upon his face, but those who are working with him to enable "prison birds" to change their plumage have not the least question of his complete and thorough reformation. It was Dunn's idea to provide homes for discharged criminals,

so that the pressure of hunger or cold should not drag them back into the old ways. He has established refuges in New York, San Francisco, Chicago, and Detroit. The average time for which they stay in the Home is about two weeks. In connection with the Home a broom factory is run, so that each may do what he can toward self-support. The income from this source does not cover running expenses, and therefore it must depend largely upon charity. The rules are necessarily quite strict and rigidly enforced. From the records kept, drink is the cause, in most cases, of their downfall. Many who enter the Home go out reformed and renewed, and continue to be useful members of society.

HOME OF PROVIDENCE.—Calumet Avenue, corner Twenty-sixth Street. Can be reached by Cottage Grove Avenue cable. Intended to care for and protect young women. Managed by the Sisters of Mercy, whose hospital adjoins.

HOME OF THE AGED.—Very few of the business men of Chicago have not received a visit from a couple of "Little Sisters of the Poor," soliciting alms of any amount, no matter how small, for the Home of the Aged, which they are thus able to maintain at the corner of Harrison and Throop Streets. The structure is a plain, commodious building of brick. It is always full of inmates, in age ranging from sixty to 100 years. The sisters in asking alms, simply state who they are. If denied, they merely go away and come again some other day. They are never out of humor, but always grateful for whatever is bestowed.

HOUSE OF THE GOOD SHEPHERD.—Under the management of the Sisters of the Good Shepherd. It is a haven and house of refuge for fallen women who desire to lay hold again upon a pure life. It is far-reaching in its usefulness.

MARGARET ETTA CRECHE KINDER-
GARTEN.—Wabash Avenue cable to
2356 Wabash Avenue. Mothers
who are obliged to work for a living
leave their children here to be cared
for by this broadest of all the city's
charities. The average expense of
taking care of a child here is about
$5.00 per year. Beside the nursery
a kindergarten is carried on. It depends upon the charitably inclined
for its maintenance.

MASONIC ORPHANS' HOME.—Carroll Avenue, corner Sheldon, looks
after thirty children and is supported by voluntary contributions
from city and State.

NEWSBOYS' AND BOOTBLACKS'
HOME.—At the present this is located at 1418 Wabash Avenue, and
can be reached by the Wabash Avenue cable. This charity is now over
twenty-one years old. It began as
the Chicago Industrial School. It
was not long, however, before it as-
sumed its present purpose and name.
It was the very first organized effort
to aid the helpless children of this
city. It is intended to provide a
comfortable Christian home for
newsboys, bootblacks, and other
homeless, unprotected boys, and, if
possible, to find them homes in the
country, or employment in the city.
The doors of the Home are never
closed to anyone requesting shelter
or food; but to cultivate independence and foster self-help fifteen
cents is the price of breakfast, supper and lodging. This the boys call
paying their "banner." Provision
is made by which destitute boys may
earn immediate living expenses by
selling the *Newsboys' Appeal*, a small
paper published in the interests of
the home, or else they are loaned
funds to buy a small stock of daily
papers.

The Home is by no means self-
supporting, still no appeal is made
outside for charity. Previous to the
fire, a lot on Quincy Street was given
to the Home, upon which a small
building was erected. After the
fire, by funds from the Relief and
Aid Society, a building of brick was
built. Some years later this and the
lot was sold to Marshall Field & Co.,
for commercial purposes, for $50,000.
When the Board of Directors can
find a suitable location within their
means they propose to use this fund
in building a suitable home. This
sum is now on interest, and the
Home is supported by the investment in charity of our business men,
who are satisfied with the security of
" He who giveth to the poor lendeth
to the Lord."

The laws of the institution are few
and easily understood, and intended
simply to promote the well-being of
the boys. It is the design of the
management to take a wise, kindly,
personal interest in every one of the
thousand or more boys who are
sheltered there every year. An
accurate record is made of every boy
who comes to the institution. These
pathetic records are full of the
effects of the grasping greed of sel-
fishness. Many of these boys have
parents, or legal guardians living,
but they have either turned the boys
adrift, or abused them to the utmost
limit of human endurance, until they
have cut adrift for themselves.
Four evenings in the week there is a
night school in session from 7:30 to
9:00, which the boys are required to
attend, and if deemed best, means
for other instruction is arranged for.
The chief aim of the Home is to
bridge over the chasm between absolute destitution and some kind of
permanent employment, and thus
prevent the boys from becoming
criminals. The directors communicate constantly with the Humane

Society and other like organizations, and thus know a good deal about homeless boys. This is the only place in the city where a boy can go and clean up and be sure of getting a clean shirt. Partly worn garments are always acceptable. A second-hand shirt is always preferable to a new one, for if it is new the boys are likely to realize on it, for they consider a fellow a "jude" who wears anything that can be sold for cash. The matron has done much to help the boys to become workers in the world in steady positions, and she says it is a fact that when once a boy has felt the pleasure of independent self-support, as a rule, he never recurs to street life from choice.

OLD PEOPLE'S HOME.—Indiana Avenue on Wabash Avenue cable to Thirty-ninth Street. About thirty years ago a hard-working seamstress had saved a little money and bought a home on Third Avenue. She found herself rapidly drifting into the contingent of "old maids." Kindly of heart, as are all of her guild, she conceived the design of starting some home that might lighten the suffering and worry she saw and felt on every hand. Having advised with her pastor, her first effort was a small frame house near her own, where a few indigent old ladies could be cared for. In a short time the public began to take an interest in "Samantha Smith's Charity." Then their quarters became cramped, and Miss Smith dedicated her own home and its entire furnishings to the use of the institution, which was transferred bodily, at once, to the new quarters. Miss Smith was matron for quite a number of years, and then retired. Then the Home was removed to Indiana Avenue, near Twenty-sixth Street. After the great fire the Relief and Aid Society donated $50,000. This was used as the beginning of a home

at their present location, which has been improved and enlarged to its present condition. The help from the Relief and Aid Society was given on condition that the name be changed to "Old People's Home," thereby opening its privileges to old men as well as old ladies. The Relief and Aid Society hold twenty rooms for their protégés. Old men are not admitted, and when arrangements are made for them it will be in a separate building, where there can be a chance for outdoor work. The John Crerar will added $50,000 to the funds of this institution. Sixty-eight inmates occupy the building. The rooms of the Relief and Aid Society being free, are always full. Anyone else, after a rigid examination, a probation of six months, and an entrance fee of $300, may become an inmate. If, after probation, they are deemed unsuitable, they are charged $3 per week, or $78, and the balance, $222, is returned. The candidate must be at least forty-five years of age and with no visible means of support. If children are living who can support her, she is not eligible. The office of matron is by no means a sinecure. A noteworthy fact is that the youngest matron in the city has charge of the oldest people.

PIONEER AID AND SUPPORT ASSOCIATION.—This is an association for the support of the families of the anarchists who were hung or sent to the penitentiary for instigating the Haymarket riot.

SCHOOL FOR DEAF AND DUMB.—Situated at 409 May Street, on West Side. Managed by the nuns of the Holy Heart of Mary, and maintained by the Ephpheta Society. It is conducted by a board of lady directresses, who have given much time and attention to the work. Four experienced teachers take care of fifty deaf mutes.

SERVITE SISTERS' INDUSTRIAL HOME FOR GIRLS.—Van Buren Street car or Madison Street cable to 1396 Van Buren Street. This Home aims to protect and train girls who have no homes, or whose homes may be unsuitable. Controlled by the Servite Sisters of Mary.

SOLDIERS' HOME FUND.—This is a balance of $70,000 left from the great Sanitary Fair which monopolized, during its existence, Chicago, and the whole country soon after the War of the Rebellion began. A rest, or home, was then established with the money raised, where Northwestern troops moving to the front could be fed and housed if necessary. The sick and wounded, dragging their weary bodies homeward, could also find here rest, medicine, and refreshment. For this work an old hotel at N☉. 75 Randolph Street, sufficed. The association was incorporated and the ground where the Roman Catholic Orphan Asylum now stands was at first acquired. The city was canvassed by ladies for $1 subscriptions, and a big amount was raised that way. One lady, Mrs. Bristol, canvassed not only all the North Side, but extended her quest into a number of the suburban villages. After a while the Thirty-fifth Street property was sold, a block of land bought in South Evanston, and a house built with part of the proceeds. Some of the balance was loaned on North Side property, and the remainder went into a mortgage on a State Street block in the neighborhood of Archer Avenue. Both of these mortgages were foreclosed, and the association is yet the owner of the State Street property. The North Side real estate was closed out advantageously, and the money received was put out at interest. After the Government established Soldiers' Homes there was no further need for a private institu-

tion of the same kind. So the property has been converted and arranged to serve as a relief fund. This fund has not decreased, neither has it increased, because the entire increment has been used to help those worthy of relief. It costs the fund $100 a year for the services of a clerk and a room to make the disbursements in. They pay monthly to sixty or seventy-five pensioners about $300. Mrs. Bristol is still the disbursing officer, and at the rooms of the Chicago Relief and Aid Society gladdens her *clientele* on the last Saturday of each month to the amount of from $2 to $10 each, the maximum limit.

ST. JOSEPH'S ASYLUM FOR BOYS.—On Crawford Avenue, between Belmont Avenue and Diversey Street. Reached by Milwaukee Avenue cable.

ST. JOSEPH'S HOME.—A 12th St. or Blue Island Ave. cable will carry you to 409 May Street, on the West Side, the location of this institution. Its principal object is to afford the protection of a home to respectable young girls out of employment, until such time as they can secure positions in offices. The terms for board vary with location of room, from $2 to $5 per week. Quite a number of young ladies employed down town have private rooms in the Home, preferring the restful quiet offered here to more stirring quarters elsewhere. The building is conveniently and comfortably arranged for over 200 persons. It is self-supporting.

ST. JOSEPH'S ORPHAN ASYLUM.—Maintained by the Sisters of St. Joseph, at the corner of Lake Avenue and Thirty-fifth Street. Can be reached by Wabash Avenue cable.

ST. JOSEPH'S PROVIDENCE ORPHAN ASYLUM.—Located at Pennock, a suburban station on the Chicago, Milwaukee & St. Paul Railway, running out of Union depot, on the West Side. A little rise in a prairie farm of forty acres is used as a site for a building capable of holding, without crowding, 180 boys. The house is steam-heated, and furnished with all the appointments necessary to comfortable living and proper training for such a large section of young America.

ST. PAUL'S HOME FOR NEWSBOYS. —An institution at 45 and 47 Jackson Street. Similar to the Newsboy's Home, it is intended to care for the boys of Catholic parents. Quite a large number are taken care of here.

UHLICH EVANGELICAL LUTHERAN ORPHAN ASYLUM.—Started in 1867 by ladies belonging to St. Paul's Church, in a small cottage on La Salle Avenue, corner Ontario Street. Incorporated in 1869, its larger building on Clark Street, between Garfield and Webster avenues, was rented later on, but this was engulfed in the Great Fire. The orphan inmates were first sheltered at Lake View, and then were boarded at the Chicago Nursery and Half Orphan Asylum, at 175 Burling Street. The ladies had $8,000, the Relief and Aid Society put up $20,-000. Twelve lots were bought at the corner of Burling and Center streets. On these the building now stands.

WAIFS' MISSION.—Undertakes the care of homeless boys at 44 State Street. The management are very active and zealous in their efforts for the homeless ones, but are very much cramped by the smallness of their present quarters. But it is to be presumed that the charitable heart of Chicago will not long allow so important a charity to languish for want of assistance.

YOUNG LADIES' CHARITY CIRCLE. —Is composed of sixteen young ladies who have organized themselves for the purpose of independent charity work where it shall seem to be most needed. They have no stated location.

Athletics. — Athletic sports of every kind flourish and find support and patronage in Chicago. Several gymnasiums, of which the most noted are the Ahetnæum and the Y. M. C. A., afford opportunities for muscular development, while the athletic clubs of all varieties are almost innumerable. There are about 400 organized base-ball clubs in Chicago, seven or eight boat clubs, and several prominent cricket organizations.

Cycling is a most popular amusement, and nearly 2,000 wheelmen are enrolled among the different bicycle clubs of the city. There are a large number of hunting and fishing clubs, nearly all possessing tracts of land near the city limits. Tennis finds many devotees, and several excellent courts are largely patronized during the summer. In the winter there are frequent exhibitions of boxing and wrestling, numerous foot-ball games, and a great variety of out-door sports, which the mild climate renders possible.

Many athletes keep in training at hand-ball courts, while the club men and their friends find sport and exercise in "in-door ball."

The recently organized Chicago Athletic Association, which occupies a magnificent building on Michigan Avenue, has a membership of 1,500, and bids fair to become the most powerful athletic society in the country.

Auctions.—The number of people who, like Mrs. Toodles, have a passion for attending auctions in search of "bargains," is very large, and hence, although mock-auctions have been suppressed, in a great measure, there are still many ingenious swindles perpetrated under the guise of auction sales. The mock-auction occasionally crops up on Clark, West Madison, and Halsted streets, but one must be extremely simple to be lured into one of these shops, and their victims, therefore, are usually green and uneducated countrymen or foreigners. Mock-auctions are commonly carried on in a small shop, carefully darkened by filling the windows with various kinds of ostensible merchandise, and tenanted chiefly by the proprietor and his confederates, who keep up a lively bidding, till some unwary passerby is seduced into entering, and speedily "stuck" with some worthless article at a fabulous price. Should the victim find that he is called upon to pay too dearly for his folly, he may escape scot free by stoutly denying that he has made any bid, calling in the police, or, perhaps, showing fight. In most cases, however, the victim prefers to pocket his loss and his mortification together. There is a kind of a sale of a less distinctly fraudulent description, but still anything but bona fide; which takes place sometimes in auction rooms, but more frequently in private houses which are hired for the purpose, and is worked upon this plan: The household goods offered are usually vamped up, or originally manufactured for the purpose, but are advertised and announced as the property of some family "declining house-keeping" for some reason or other, but which is always ostentatiously made known. However great a bargain the innocent purchaser may think he has secured, a short time will invariably serve to show him his mistake. The custom of introducing a portion of these articles into a genuine sale by irresponsible auctioneers, also prevails to some extent. Indeed, if one attend a legitimate sale, held by responsible auctioneers, he will find himself but little better off. As a buyer, he will be opposed by a mob of "dealers" in second-hand goods and brokers, all in league with each other either to crush him altogether or run him up to the highest price that can be screwed out of him. As a seller, he will find the same combination exerting all their skill to secure the knocking down of each lot to one of their own gang, the articles afterward being divided among themselves, and the profits of the transaction secured by a private sale. The only chance for a novice, when selling, is to get some friend to watch the sale and bid up to a fixed reserve price on each article from a marked catalogue, and when buying to make up his mind as to the highest price he is prepared to pay, and never, under any circumstances, to allow himself to be coaxed or irritated into exceeding that figure in his bids. At the best, however, the novice will do well, and make money by saving it, if he keeps away from auction sales, especially of household goods, where the boarding-house mistresses and dealers usually have it all their own way. Auction sales of books and works of art are in the hands of two or three reputable dealers, with well-known places of business, and fair treatment may be expected, and is usually received. There is a class of auction sales of pictures, where the articles offered are mostly glittering daubs expressly manufactured for the purpose, and calculated to deceive the uninitiated.

Auditorium.—The building which bears this name, while it is the private property of a corporation, the people have adopted as their own. A few rich and enterprising citizens own the stock ; but the people, rich and poor—all classes and all creeds—have a share in this public institution. They glory in its grandeur, and would bear arms in its defense. When private individuals rear temples, over the shrine of which *pro bono publico* is implied, if not inscribed, they must not complain if the same public regards the institution as its own. This building is not alone the common property of Chicago, but it has likewise been appropriated as a political temple by the great parties of the Union. In this grand Auditorium, located as it is in the very keystone of the Union, every State and district

building, ten stories, is 145 feet; tower above main building (8 floors), 95 feet; lantern tower above main (2 floors), 30 feet. Total height, 270 feet; weight of entire building, 110,-000 tons. Exterior of building, granite and Bedford stone; interior, iron, brick, terra cotta, marble, and hardwood finish. There are 17,000,000 brick, 50,000 square feet of Italian marble, Mosaic floors containing 50,-000,000 pieces of marble, 800,000 square feet of terra cotta, 175,000 square feet of wire lath, 60,000 square feet of plate glass, 25 miles of gas and water pipes, 230 miles of electric wire

CHICAGO AUDITORIUM BUILDING

may meet in the person of their representatives, and make presidents. It is the shrine of music, art, and the drama. It is also large enough, generous enough, and broad enough in its policy to cover any sect or creed, or a convention of all denominations, and the voice of its unequaled organ would drown the chants of one and sound the praise of all.

There is certainly no other structure in America that equals the Auditorium. It is located on Congress Street, Michigan and Wabash avenues, having a total street frontage of 710 feet. The height of the main

and cables, 10,000 electric lights, 11 dynamos, 13 electric motors for driving ventilating apparatus, 4 hydraulic motors for driving machinery, 11 boilers, 21 pumping engines, 13 elevators, and 26 hydraulic lifts for moving stage platforms. The building cost $3,200,000. Ground was broken January, 1887, and it was completed February, 1890. The building includes:

THE AUDITORIUM. — Permanent seating capacity over 4,000; for conventions, etc. (for which the stage will be utilized), about 8,000. This department of the building contains the most complete and costly stage and organ in the world. Recital Hall seats 500. The business portion consists of stores and 136 offices, part of which are in the tower. Tower Observatory, to which the public are admitted (25 cents for adults, 15 cents for children). United States Signal Service occupies part of the seventeenth, eighteenth, and nineteenth floors of the tower. These departments of the building are managed by the Chicago Auditorium Association. The Auditorium hotel has 400 guest rooms. The grand dining-room (175 feet long), and the kitchen, are on the top floor. The magnificent banquet hall is built of steel in trusses, spanning 120 feet over the Auditorium. (See *Auditorium Hotel*.)

The idea of the construction of a great building of this character was first made public before the Commercial Club, in an address by Ferdinand W. Peck, the originator of the enterprise, May 29, 1886. The necessity of just such a building to house political conventions and for exceptional entertainments, was recognized, and Mr. Peck received unlimited encouragement and substantial support.

The dream has been realized. It is certainly the most popular if not the most useful building in this city. It can not be described in this work; a volume would not do it justice.

Auditorium Tower.—One of the grandest views from any artificial elevation in the world is to be had right here in Chicago, from the tower of the great Auditorium building. Thousands have already ascended the eminence and viewed the grandest of modern cities, and yet the fact that so fine a view is to be had from the balcony of the upper tower is comparatively unknown, even to people living within the city. A bird's-eye view of this eminence reveals some strange and interesting things. Men and women below appear like dolls, and dogs like mice. Michigan Boulevard like a long white tape or thread, with its thousands of vehicles and pedestrians, and Wabash Avenue with its many trains of cable cars, Lake Michigan and the Lake Park and basin, are among the chief objects of interest. The sight that meets the eye is indeed a study and the effect most pleasing, instructive and entertaining. Neither St. Paul's in London nor St. Peter's in Rome offers so fine a view of modern architectural magnificence as opens up to view here. The smooth and rapid elevators take you to the seventeenth floor, from which you ascend a flight of stairs which takes you to the roof of the main tower. From thence you go still higher, led by an iron spiral staircase, till you reach the upper tower balcony. On a clear day Michigan and Indiana shores are clearly visible to the naked eye. And last, but not least, is the view by night. The myriads of lights of every description all over the city, in every direction as far as the eye and glass can reach, scattered and in clusters, and in long double rows, threading either side of the streets and avenues, are a charming and fascinating sight that reminds you of the fables of the Arabian Nights and Aladdin's Cave. Then add the moonlight, and the enchantment is complete. The public is admitted to the tower, a small fee being charged for the service.

Austin. — A western suburb of Chicago, about seven miles from State Street, with a population of nearly 5,000. A most pleasant village, and a desirable residence district.

Austro-Hungarian Cemetery.—Located at Waldheim, ten miles from the City Hall. Take train at Grand Central depot via Chicago & Northern Pacific Railroad. Train leaves at 12.01 P. M., daily, including Sundays, running direct to the new cemetery station immediately adjoining Waldheim, Forest Home, and Jewish cemeteries. (See *Waldheim.*)

Auburn Park.—This charming suburb is located on the Chicago, Rock Island & Pacific Railway, nine miles south of the center of the city. Population, in 1892, 4,000, composed of the best business and professional people, and their homes are among the best within the city limits. The property on which this suburb stands is owned by Messrs. Eggleston, Mallette & Brownell, one of the city's largest and most responsible real-estate firms. Upward of a million dollars has been invested in laying out wide and beautiful streets and other improvements. The suburban train service on the Rock Island and the Chicago & Eastern Illinois railroads is all that could be desired, and makes Auburn Park easily accessible to the heart of the city; and it would be well for those seeking a good location to call on the gentlemen whose names are mentioned above. Their offices will be found in the Tacoma and Royal Insurance buildings. A reference to Moran's Map of Chicago, which will be found in the front part of this book, will acquaint the reader with the precise location of Auburn Park.

Bakeries.—There are nearly 700 bakeries in the city, several employing from 200 to 300 hands each. Many of the larger bakeries have lunchrooms attached, and cater to a large patronage.

Bankers' Club.—Composed of the leading bankers of the city, meets quarterly for the sole purpose of enjoying a social interchange of friendships.

Banking Capital.—The aggregate capital of the national banks in the city, as per official returns made on February 26, 1891, was $17,646,645, and their surplus fund amounted to $10,272,579. The capital stock of the State banks amounted to $9,252,000, and their surplus funds to $5,023,123. This does not include private banks and bankers.

Banking Institutions, National.—There are three kinds of banks in Chicago: State, private, and national. The latter are supervised by the United States laws and Government. All private and State banks are under the laws of the State. The national banks report to the State Auditor. The State and private banks report to nobody. The capital of the Chicago national banks at the close of 1890 was $16,100,000. This, added to the $8,352,000 in the State banks and the $1,148,000 in private banks, makes the banking capital $25,602,000. The report of the Comptroller of the Currency for 1890 shows that Chicago is gaining swiftly on the Eastern cities in its struggle for leadership as a money center. Chicago handles now seven per cent. of all the checks and drafts in the country. New York still is ahead, but it is only a neck. Illinois ranks as second of the States in the amount of drafts made, and New York fourth, Massachusetts being first. There are twenty-four national banks now doing business in this city.

The New York *Financier*, reviewing Chicago's financial business at the close of 1890, said : " The bankers of the country think New York's banking business is large, and that the percentage of increase of deposits during the period mentioned (the six years preceding this statement) is, or ought to be, larger than elsewhere, *but this is a mistake so far as the percentage of increase is concerned, for Chicago beats New York by over 125 per cent. on New York's increase.* This is a remarkable difference, *and means that Chicago's commerce, so far as bank deposits show it, is growing twice and one-fourth as fast as New York's.* Everybody knows that Chicago is one of the phenomena of the country, so far as its development is concerned, but few are aware of the remarkable speed shown by the figures of our tellers. Even Boston's growth of banking during the six years mentioned is far outstripped by Chicago. It does look as if the "Hub" was going West. Chicago's percentage of increase exceeds Boston's by 30 per cent. upon Boston's figures, in spite of the big manufactories in New England. Philadelphia, too, whose population is now slightly exceeded by Chicago, is away in the rear in the percentage of increase, as Chicago's figures exceed Philadelphia's by 44 per cent. On the deposits of its national banks for 1890, Chicago increased its business during the past six years 46 per cent., or $50,152,348 upon $108,178,165 deposits. New York increased during the same period about 20 per cent., or nearly $89,000,000 on $431,000,-000 deposits. Boston increased about 36½ per cent., or $49,800,000 on nearly $137,000,000 deposits. Philadelphia increased about 32 per cent., or about $30,500,000 on $98,-600,000 deposits.

The following are the names and capital stock of Chicago's banks:

NATIONAL.

American Exchange, Monadnock Building, southwest corner Jackson and Dearborn streets; capital, $1,-000,000.

Atlas, Union Building, southwest corner Washington and La Salle streets; capital, $700,000.

Bankers', Masonic Temple, northeast corner Randolph and State streets; capital, $1,000,000.

Chemical, 85 Dearborn Street; capital, $1,000,000.

Chicago, southwest corner Monroe and Dearborn streets; capital, $500,000.

Columbia, Insurance Exchange Building, 218 La Salle Street; capital, $1,000,000.

Commercial, southeast corner Monroe and Dearborn streets; capital, $1,000,000.

Continental, Insurance Exchange Building, 218 La Salle Street; capital, $2,000,000.

Drovers', 4207 South Halsted Street; capital, $250,000.

First, northwest corner Monroe and Dearborn streets; capital, $3,-000,000.

Fort Dearborn, Adams Express Building, 185 Dearborn Street; capital, $500,000.

Globe, 240 La Salle Street; capital, $1,000,000.

Hide & Leather, southeast corner Madison and La Salle streets; capital, $300,000.

Home, 184 West Washington Street; capital, $250,000.

Lincoln, Clark and Michigan streets; capital, $200,000.

Merchants', 82 La Salle Street; capital, $500,000.

Metropolitan, The Temple, southwest corner Monroe and La Salle streets; capital, $2,000,000.

National Bank of America, The Temple, southwest corner Monroe and La Salle streets; capital, $1,000,-000.

National Bank of Illinois, 115 Dearborn Street; capital, $1,000,000.

National Bank of the Republic, southwest corner La Salle and Quincy streets; capital, $1,000,000.

National Live Stock Bank, Union Stock Yards; capital, $750,000.

Northwestern, Rookery, southeast corner Adams and La Salle streets; capital, $1,000,000.

Oakland, 3961 Cottage Grove Avenue; capital, $50,000.

Prairie State, 110 W. Washington Street; capital, $200,000.

Union, northeast corner Adams and La Salle streets; capital, $2,000,000.

United States. See Columbia National.

STATE.

American Trust & Savings, northwest corner La Salle and Madison streets; capital, $1,000,000.

Avenue Savings, Thirty-first and Michigan Avenue.

Bank of Commerce, The Temple, southwest corner La Salle and Monroe streets; capital, $500,000.

Central Trust & Savings. 155 Washington Street; capital, $200,000.

Chicago Trust & Savings, 130 Washington Street; capital, $500,000.

Commercial Loan & Trust Co., 115 and 117 La Salle Street; capital, $500,000.

Corn Exchange, The Rookery, southeast corner La Salle and Adams streets; capital, $1,000,000.

Dime Savings, 104 and 106 Washington Street; capital, $100,000.

Division Street, 309 East Division Street; capital, $20,000.

Garden City Banking & Trust Co., northwest corner La Salle and Randolph streets; capital, $500,000.

Globe Savings, Monadnock Building, southwest corner Jackson and Dearborn streets; capital, $200,000.

Hibernian Banking Association, Ashland Building, northeast corner Clark and Randolph streets; capital, $222,000.

Home Savings, 184 West Washington Street; capital, $5,000.

Illinois Trust & Savings, The Rookery, southeast corner La Salle and Adams streets; capital, $2,000,000.

Industrial Bank of Chicago, corner Twentieth Street and Blue Island Avenue; capital, $200,000.

International, 110 La Salle Street; capital, $500,000.

Jennings Trust Co., 185 Dearborn Street; capital, $500,000.

Merchants' Loan & Trust Co., southeast corner Dearborn and Washington streets; capital, $2,000,000.

Milwaukee Avenue State, 409 Milwaukee Avenue; capital, $250,000.

Northern Trust Co., Chamber of Commerce Building, southeast corner La Salle and Washington streets; capital, $1,000,000.

Prairie State Savings & Trust Co., 110 West Washington Street; capital, $200,000.

Royal Trust Co., 167 Jackson Street; capital, $500,000.

State Bank of Chicago, 154 Lake Street; capital, $500,000.

Union Trust Co., 133 Dearborn Street; capital, $500,000.

West Chicago Bank, Ogden Avenue and Twelfth Street; capital, $50,000.

West Side Bank, 502 West Madison Street: capital, $50,000.

FOREIGN.

Bank of Montreal, The Temple, southwest corner Monroe and Dearborn streets.

Scandinavian Exchange. See Central Trust & Savings.

RESOURCES OF CHICAGO STATE BANKS.—The last report of the State Auditor regarding the State banks, showed that their condition so far as their resources were concerned, indicated a total of $55,091,940.

FIRST NATIONAL BANK, was incorporated in 1863, with a capital of $100,000. Its first corps of officers were: E. Aiken, president; E. E. Braisted, cashier; on the death of Mr. Aiken, in 1867, Samuel M. Nickerson was elected President, a position he held till 1891, and was then succeeded by Lyman J. Gage. In 1868, Lyman J. Gage was appointed cashier. For many years past he this bank's enormous business. The bank went through the panic ordeal of 1873 with flying colors, increasing the public confidence in the strength and stability of its resources, and in the wisdom and honesty of its management. In 1882 the charter of the bank expired. It then went into liquidation, paying for each $100 of its stock $294. This without taking into account the dividends paid upon

FIRST NATIONAL BANK, DEARBORN AND MONROE STREETS.

has been vice-president. The building occupied by the bank stood at the southwest corner of State and Washington streets, before the Great Fire of 1871, but was engulfed in that "ocean of flame." The building was immediately rebuilt, and the bank occupied it until it was able to control for itself its present elegant and commodious structure, which was designed and built especially for the rapid and accurate transaction of its stock from time to time, which always averaged ten per cent. per annum. In the place of the old bank, a new First National Bank obtained charter number 2,670. This succeeded to the business of the old bank. It has a paid-up capital of $3,000,000. Mr. Gage is president and Mr. R. J. Street, cashier. Not only is the First National Bank the soundest and largest bank in Chicago, but it is ahead of all other financial institutions in the United States. Its present officers are Lyman J. Gage, president; J. B. Forgan, vice-president; R. J. Street, cashier; Holmes Hoge, assistant cashier. Its resources are: Loans and discounts, $16,697,052.16; overdrafts, $5,607.66; United States bonds to secure circulation, $50,000; United States bonds on hand, $45,850; other stock, bonds, and mortgages, $930,900; bank building and other real estate, $650,000; due from other National banks, $2,408,123.79; due from State banks and bankers, $2.019,480.09; checks and other cash items, $2,109; exchanges for clearing house, $1,757,328; bills of other banks, $350,000; fractional paper currency, nickels, and pennies, $8,183.22; specie, $5,620,833; legal-tender notes, $1,750,000; redemption fund with U. S. Treasurer (5 per cent. of circulation), $2,250; due from U. S. Treasurer, other than 5 per cent. redemption fund, $23,000; total, $32,320,716.92. Liabilities: capital stock paid in, $3,000,000; surplus fund, $2.000,000; undivided profits, $1,072,124.19; dividends unpaid, $576; individual deposits subject to check, $11,779,049.50; demand certificates of deposit, $956,960.21; certified checks, $279,424.61; cashier's checks outstanding, $563,672.50; due to other National banks, $7,719,876.34; due to State banks and bankers, $4,949,033.57; total. $32,320,716.92.

CHICAGO NATIONAL BANK, is located on the southwest corner of Dearborn and Monroe streets. This institution was organized on the second of January, 1882. Its present officers are: John R. Walsh, president; H. H. Nash, vice-president; William Cox, cashier; F. M. Blount, assistant cashier. Resources: loans and discounts, $4,275,510.59; overdrafts. $1,615.09; U. S. bonds to secure circulation, $50,000; other stocks and bonds, $270,636.93; due from

other National banks, $1,252,089.92; due from State banks and bankers, $144,339.96; exchanges for clearing-house, $262,306.25; bills of other banks, $46,000; fractional paper currency, nickels, and pennies, $843.06; specie, $1,135,000; legal-tender notes, $300,000; U. S. certificates of deposit for legal-tenders, $210,000; redemption fund with U. S. Treasurer (5 per cent. of circulation), $2,250; due from U. S. Treasurer, other than 5 per cent. redemption fund, $21,700; total, $7,972,291.80. Liabilities: capital stock paid in, $500,000; surplus fund, $500,000; undivided profits, $66,810.88; National bank notes outstanding, $45,000; individual deposits subject to check, $5,078,676.50; demand certificates of deposit, $714,625.40; time certificates of deposit, $41,535.77; certified checks, $86,908.25; cashier's checks outstanding, $76,864.34; due to other National banks, $536,765.02; due to State banks and bankers, $325,105.64; total, $7,972,291.80. Ever since its organization the Chicago National Bank has taken high rank as one of the leading financial institutions of the country.

Baptist Churches.—The membership of the Baptist denomination in Chicago numbers about 10,000. The following are the names and locations of the churches:

Central Church, corner Halsted Street and Belden Avenue.

First Church, South Park Avenue, corner Thirty-first Street.

Second Church, corner Morgan and West Monroe streets.

Fourth Church, corner West Monroe Street and Ashland Avenue.

Immanuel Church, Michigan Avenue, near Twenty-third Street.

Memorial Church, Oakwood Boulevard, near Cottage Grove Avenue.

Centennial Church, corner Lincoln and West Jackson streets.

MACHINERY HALL.

South end of the Park, midway between the shore of Lake Michigan and the west line of the Park. 500 x 850 feet. With Machinery

AGRICULTURE BUILDING.

Near the Pier on the lake shore. 500 x 800 feet. Cost, with annexes, $1,000,000. Architects, McKim, Meade & White, New York.

North Ashland Avenue Church, North Ashland Avenue, near West North Avenue.

Western Avenue Church, corner Western and Warren avenues.

Millard Avenue Church, Lawndale.

Providence Church (colored), 15 North Irving Place.

Tabernacle, 354 and 356 Wabash Avenue.

Dearborn Street Church, Dearborn, corner Thirty-sixth Street.

Olivet Church (colored), Harmon Court, corner Holden Place.

Englewood Church, Englewood and Stewart avenues.

Bethany Church, Lock and Bonaparte streets.

Hyde Park Church, Hyde Park.

Scandinavian Pilgrim Church, Carpenter, corner Ohio Street.

First German Church, Bickerdike, corner West Huron Street.

First Swedish Church, Oak, near Sedgwick Street.

Second Swedish Church, Butterfield, near Thirty-first Street.

Bethesda Church (colored), Thirty-fourth, southeast corner Butterfield Street.

Humboldt Park Church, Humboldt, corner Cortland Street.

La Salle Avenue Church, La Salle Avenue, near Division Street.

Second German Church, Willow Street.

German Baptist Mission, Wentworth Avenue and Twenty-ninth Street.

South Chicago German Church, South Chicago, Ninety-second Street.

Colehour German Church, South Chicago, One hundred and Sixth Street.

Trinity Baptist Church, West Ohio, near Robey Street.

Baptist Hospital.—The Baptist Hospital Association, recently incorporated with a capital stock of $1,- 000,000, will establish and maintain a hospital in Chicago.

Bar Association.—A society of members of the Chicago bar, the objects of which include the elevation of the profession, the preservation of a dignified and upright judiciary, high morality in practice, and the promotion of all needed legal reforms.

Base-Ball.—The level ground, and large number of vacant lots, renders Chicago peculiarly the paradise of the base-ball player. Within the city limits there are now six enclosed ball parks, three of which are the property of the National Base-Ball League, and three belong to the City or Amateur League. The National League Club, of which James A. Hart is president, and A. C. Anson, manager and captain, plays alternate games on the South and West sides, and is very largely patronized. The City and Boys' League teams play on Sundays, and before large gatherings of spectators. Besides the professional teams there were, by a recent computation, 415 uniformed amateur nines in the city, whose contests, on Saturdays and Sundays, monopolize every vacant lot of sufficient size to accommodate the players. Chicago is, in fact, considered so rich a field for base-ball harvests, that the American Association will probably locate a club here in the near future, with a probability of considerable profit during the World's Fair.

Baths (Public.)—Although public baths have for years been "a long-felt want," but little progress has as yet been made toward their establishment in Chicago. There are two "natatoriums," one on West Madison Street, and the other on North Clark Street, and the owners receive a large income from the natural desire of young men for swim-

3

ming as an athletic exercise. As the use of soap is not permitted in these establishments, they can hardly be classified as "baths," and do not fill the need by any means. Frequent agitation has been made in the City Council, and Chicago will doubtless have a complete and satisfactory system of public baths at no distant day.

Baths (Turkish).—The Turkish bath, as an agent for the reduction of flesh, or the restoration of vitality, is very popular in Chicago, and the larger hotels have excellent bath-parlors connected with their establishments. The baths of the Palmer House, Grand Pacific, and other hotels, are well patronized, and prove sources of considerable profit.

Beer is fast superseding all other beverages except water in the affections of the people of Chicago. The first place where lager-beer was made in this country is said to be Philadelphia, but Chicago now stands in the van in the consumption, if not in the production, of beer. During 1890 the output of the Chicago breweries was 2,500,000 barrels of malt liquor. The brewers have grown wealthy, and their breweries, which are scattered over the city, are buildings of fine appearance and colossal size. There are forty-three within the city limits, with an aggregate capital of $11,500,000, employing 2,200 persons, producing a product of $12,790,000 annually. The malt-houses, which are an auxiliary to the breweries, are thirty-two in number, with a capital of $6,000,000, and an annual product of $4,400,000. There are 600 persons employed in the malt-houses. During the same year the imported ale, beer, and porter, in value reached the sum of $50,329. The beer saloons of the city number at the present time (1891) 5,782, and are to be found on nearly every square and business street.

The revenue derived by the city for granting licenses to these liquor houses for the year 1890, aggregated the respectable sum of $3,072,729.08. Large quantities are sold in all the public gardens and music halls, on all the excursion boats and at the resorts in the vicinity. The uniform price is five cents a glass. It is delivered in bottles at private residences for about 75 cents a dozen, the bottles to be returned, and a deposit made upon them by strangers. Imported beer costs about double the above price. In the spring the new beer is sold, and is called "bock beer." Its advent is announced by the appearance in the windows of the saloons of a pictorial representation of a bucking goat. *Lager-bier* means storage-beer, and is presumably brewed in the fall and kept until spring in cold vaults, the first taken out being called "bock," possibly because it is very "heady." This is the old theory, but in this age, beer, like every other commodity, is made to order in the shortest possible time. The beer you drink to-day may have been Lake Michigan water and malt until a very recent date. Certainly it is brewed with neatness and dispatch by what is frequently termed the Great Chicago Beer Trust.

Beggars.—Chicago is no exception to the rule that the streets of every large city are more or less infested with beggars. They abound principally in public places and often select the streets through which persons must pass in going to and returning from places of amusement or public resort, in which to ply their trade. Unfortunately, they are too frequently rewarded by considerable gains for their clever insight into human nature, since men, and particularly young men, prefer bestowing a trifle upon them to enduring their importunities when in company with a lady. The impostership of street beggars is the one rule to which there has been as yet no exception. If you have a desire to relieve the distress of any worthy object, by inquiring of any clergyman, or of the Overseer of the Outdoor Poor, 33 West Washington Street, near Canal, you may find plenty of opportunities, but in the streets you will find only professional and shameless beggars who levy *ad valorem* dues on personal weakness. To give to them is worse than foolish, since by so doing you encourage them in their assaults upon others. When appealed to in the streets, a short, sharp "No!" will usually suffice to rid you of your beggar; but if he persists, threaten to hand him over to the first police officer, and he will leave you at once. To remarks from shabbily dressed men like, "Excuse me, sir, but I—" or, "May I speak to you a moment, sir?" reply "No" decisively, and before they get any further, as this is the prelude to some tale as touching as it is untrue. Householders should positively forbid their servants to allow any beggar inside the basement doors under any pretext whatever, as they are very often the "pals" of thieves, and while they may not steal themselves, they quickly inventory the place and gauge the strength and fastenings to the doors and windows for the information of thieves. The great number and wide scope of the charities of Chicago (see *Benevolent Societies and Institutions*) leave no excuse for mendicancy, and it is the duty of every police officer to arrest any person found begging in the streets.

Bennett Free Dispensary is under the management of Bennett Medical College.

Bennett Hospital, 511 State Street, is run in connection with Bennett College.

Beth Hamedrash Cemetery. —Located at Oakwoods, Sixty-seventh Street and Cottage Grove Avenue. Take Cottage Grove Avenue cable line, or Illinois Central train, foot of Randolph or Van Buren streets. (See *Oakwoods Cemetery*.)

Bicycling.—There are, on a moderate computation, 10,000 cyclists in Chicago, of which number over 4,000 are members of organized cycling clubs. The level streets, the asphalt boulevards, and the pleasant roads of the suburbs, offer unequaled facilities to the wheelman, and the cycling population is continually increasing. The Chicago bicycle clubs are social as well as athletic organizations, with handsome club houses and every facility for enjoyment in winter as well as in summer. Of these clubs, the best known and largest are:

Chicago Cycling Club, corner of Lake Avenue and Fifty-seventh Street.

Cook County Wheelmen, No. 218 Leavitt Street.

Douglas Cycling Club, No. 586 West Taylor Street.

Illinois Cycling Club, 1068 Washington Boulevard.

Æolus Cycling Club, Milwaukee Avenue.

Lake View Cycling Club, Lake View.

Lincoln Cycling Club, 235 La Salle Avenue.

Oak Park Cycling Club, Oak Park.

Pizen Cycling Club.

Washington Cycling Club, 650 West Adams Street.

Many ladies of Chicago are devotees of the wheel, and on pleasant days the boulevards are alive with their trim figures and their speedy "safeties."

The great annual event of Chicago cycling is the Pullman Road Race, held every Decoration Day, when the leading wheelmen ride from the Leland Hotel to the Hotel Florence, at Pullman, the winners receiving numerous and costly prizes. So great is the general interest taken in this race, that 100,000 people are estimated to have lined the course during the contest of 1891, which was won by "Dick" Barwise, of the Chicago Cycling Club.

Billiards. — Amateurs of this game, who are strangers in Chicago, would do well to remember that billiard sharps, as well as billiard tables, abound in every quarter of the city, and should therefore be wary of nice young men who want to bet a trifle on the game. Whenever this is done, the stranger's game is apt to improve marvelously at critical moments. Tables are to be found in all the principal hotels and restaurants, and at many places devoted exclusively to that purpose and drinking. The Collender and Brunswick & Balke Co. tables are the best. The usual charges are 50 cents an hour.

Bill-posting. — As blank-walls and board-fences decrease in number, the bill-poster becomes a more and more important factor in Chicago business circles — at least in those circles where showy advertising is considered an essential element of success. There was a time when anybody could post bills, but now the business is almost entirely in the hands of a few persons, and woe to the man who has the temerity to hire an outsider! His bills, if they are put up at all, are covered up so quickly by others that it would be difficult to establish that they were there at all. Once in a while regular bill-posters have a disagreement among themselves, and they wage bitter war by each destroying—generally at night—the bills put up by the other; but as a rule they work together in harmony, and divide custom on some regular plan. The theatres have bill-boards of their own, placed on the principal streets in front of premises, the owners of which give permission, generally in consideration of a stipulated number of "dead-head" passes. Windows in which lithographs are displayed are paid for, as a rule, in the same way. Owners of vacant lots and builders of new houses very often turn an honest penny by letting out the privilege of posting bills on the fences, or on the piles of brick, to some particular bill-poster.

B'nai Abraham Cemetery.— Located one-half mile south of Waldheim, and about ten miles from the City Hall. Take train at Grand Central depot via Chicago & Northern Pacific Railroad. Trains leave at 12.01 P. M., daily, including Sundays.

B'nai Shilom Cemetery.—Located on North Clark Street and Graceland Avenue. Take North Clark Street cable line or Evanston Division of Chicago, Milwaukee & St. Paul Railway.

Boarding Houses are the homes of a large number of the permanent as well as transient population of Chicago, and are of as many grades as there are ranks in society. People living in tenement houses not infrequently "take boarders" in their cramped and dirty apartments, and from this basis boarding houses rise in size, style, and price to the superb houses in the fashionable avenues, where every convenience and luxury of a first-class hotel may be obtained. The boarding houses of the laborer and mechanic may be passed over, and the next grade are the houses occupied by the vast army of clerks and salesmen and saleswomen employed on small salaries all over the city. The rates of board in these houses range from $5 to $10 a week, according to the location of the house and the room occupied. Three meals a day—breakfast, dinner, and supper—are furnished, and the table is the same for all, variations in price being based solely upon the apartments occupied. Some of these houses are not distinguished for cleanliness. The traditional frowzy and slatternly servant girl waits on the door and is omnipresent at meal time. The meals are, as a rule, composed of coarse food, poorly cooked and served. The stranger who, for economy or other reasons may desire to patronize one of these houses, will find them in great numbers a few squares from the business center in almost any direction, indicated always by a slip of paper pasted on the side of the doorway, on which is written, " Furnished rooms with board." On entering he will find in each a parlor of severe aspect and an oppressive air of shabby gentility. In almost every section of the city there are boarding houses where handsome rooms and a good table may be had at prices ranging, for one person, from $10 to $50 a week or more, the price being still graded on the room, so that if two persons occupy one room the price is materially decreased. Strangers or others engaging board would do well to carefully avoid engaging their rooms longer than from week to week, as the presence of disagreeable people or other contingencies frequently make it desirable to change, and an arrangement for a longer term is almost sure to result in trouble. Americans are exceptionally fond of hotel life, and at all of the hotels there are a large num-

ber of permanent boarders who obtain a concession of from 30 to 50 per cent. from the rates charged to transient guests. Added to the people who live in boarding houses and hotels, there are many who live in lodgings and take their meals at restaurants and clubs. Particulars in regard to these are given under appropriate heads. Persons who live in boarding houses are subject to many annoyances from the presence of disagreeable co tenants, and strangers in the city will do well to make it a rule not to make acquaintances among their neighbors, nor to accept invitations to accompany them about the city. References as to character and responsibility are usually given and required in the better class of boarding houses, but strangers who are unable to furnish these, if of respectable appearance, are admitted upon payment of their board in advance. In winter an extra charge of from 50 cents to $2 is made for fires in rooms. Gas is not charged for, nor attendance; but it is well to have all these things stipulated in advance. Many boarding houses also take lodgers, the taking of meals in the house being optional. This, however, is the exception and not the rule.

Board of Education.—The public schools of Chicago are under the management of a Board of Education, whose quarters are on the third floor of the City Hall Building. The Board, formerly composed entirely of gentlemen, now includes several ladies in its membership, and represents both political parties about equally.

Board of Trade.—That powerful parliament of Chicago business, the Board of Trade, had no existence to befit recognition as a substantial thing before 1856, but the grain dealers, live-stock dealers, commission merchants, jobbers, and manufacturers had been slowly educating each other to organic trade during the preceding eight years, the incipient organization dating in 1848. A zeal was manifested, the passage of declaratory resolutions seeming to have been the favorite exercise. At the present day it is amusing to read with what simplicity the Board of Trade was called in special meeting

BOARD OF TRADE, JACKSON, HEAD OF LASALLE STREET.

meeting was called March 13, 1856, officers elected, by-laws adopted, and a room rented at $110 per year, and it was resolved to hold daily meetings. For some time considerable to protest against the removal of the toll collector's office to another place on the canal, on grounds of conserving the prosperity of Chicago. In April, 1850, that Board terminated its unchartered existence, the members re-organizing under the general statutes of Illinois on the 8th of February, 1849. Thus arose the present Board of Trade, of which Charles Walker was the first president. At its organization the annual dues were fixed at $3. From that period to 1856, the Board of Trade was frequently in session, discussing public measures, applauding eloquent harangues, ridiculing strange ideas, and interchanging all the blunt, frank, and hearty offices of western good-fellowship. But this body of men could not overcome the habit of feeling that the time spent on "'Change" was in derogation of the stern exactions of real business, a fact demonstrated in a manner rather ludicrous, by providing, after ample and convincing discussion of the expediency of the measure, for a daily entertainment of ale, cheese, crackers, etc., to be spread by the secretary, as an inducement of attendance. This was first adopted in 1853, and worked very favorably. It was thought safe after a while to discontinue a practice which exposed the Board to some badinage, but experience quickly proved that the refreshments could not yet be spared, and in 1855 the hospitality of the Board was revived with great popularity—too great, indeed, as persons not members participated in such numbers that an official was constituted to keep the door against bibulous and hungry visitors. But ere long the Board began to develop a clear sense of its important position, and with the year 1856 its permanent organship of systematic trade may be dated. The influence of the Board, however, from the respectability of its membership and the magnitude of the business represented, had long been salutary. The Canadian Reciprocity Treaty of 1855 was in a great degree shaped by its counsels; the substitution of weight, denominated by bushels, for measuring bulk of grain; the adoption of a rigid and just system for the graduation of qualities of lumber, grain, and other produce, and for the inspection of these and other merchantable articles, are among the principal fruits of their earlier usefulness. But in a greater or less degree many matters of public interest were forwarded by the agitation, discussion, and resolution of the Board. Of such interest are the bridge wharves, harbor dredging, lighthouse, improvements of the Illinois River navigation, and especially navigation of the St. Lawrence and the lakes. At one time—and very early—an attempt was made to supply the felt want of bank facilities, by a great bank with a capital of $5,000,000, which was advocated at that time with considerable zeal. The boldness of this project in 1853, when the aggregated commerce of the port was but $30,000,000, is one of the most striking events of that time at Chicago. The eighth annual meeting of the Board of Trade was held at the Tremont House on the 7th of April, 1856. This meeting disclosed self-sufficient interest, and thence forward the institution was an assured one. Forty-five new members were elected. Before the end of the year memberships had largely increased, and a suitable building was projected for a merchants' exchange. Daily meetings were held, and an offer of a building site on the corner of Clark and Washington streets, at $180,000, was promptly accepted. From some cause, probably a subsequent sense of extravagance, this engagement was not consummated, and the Board found, and was long content to occupy, satisfactory quarters on the corner of South Water and La Salle streets at $1,000 per annum. Until 1856 this body was a mere embryo, for a Board of Trade that can be induced to assemble, after often-tried experience, only by crackers, ale, etc., can not be personified otherwise than as a child *in utero*. One railroad had been partially complete and was open far enough to prove what railroading could do when the Board first organized as a legal body corporate in 1850. This road was at once the earliest and the only exclusively local railroad enterprise ever set on foot by Chicago. By the time the Board acquired a self-sufficient footing (1856), Chicago, in early but demonstrable prospect, was the greatest railroad center of the West. Yet it is a fact, that until that prospect had become an actual realization there was not so much as a serious recognition of the great builder of the city. For all shown by the records of the Board of Trade previous to the time (1859), when the body accepted the invitation of Missourians to attend the festivities of the opening of the Hannibal & St. Joseph Railroad, one might infer that there had never been such a thing connected with Chicago. With some prudent and sensible regulations of detail, such as equalizing charges for handling goods, substituting weight for bulk in reckoning grain in bushels, etc., the minds of members seem to have alternated amongst ill-defined and illusory plans for supplementing St. Lawrence navigation, and for dredging, clearing obstructions, etc., from the Illinois River for steamboats. For the sake of the harbor there was a good deal of petitioning of Congress, the Legislature, and the City Council, of appointing inexpert committees to sound the mud, and measure the sand-bars, but the receipt of cattle and hogs had become three times, and those of grain twelve times, as great in 1856 as they had been in 1850, before the Board seems to have suspected the railroads of having been the means of bringing them.

While from Boston to Baltimore the feeling was quickening for intimate passenger and commercial connection across the mountains and over vast spaces, and line upon line actually opened, the Board seems to have felt steam navigation to and from St. Louis as a paramount object, sending committees thither from time to time, attending conventions at Peoria, and occupying its sessions at home with prolonged discussions, conducted in the main by experienced Fourth-of-July orators, candidates for office, or known visionaries. When the commercial crash of 1857 came, the Board had an opportunity to distinguish itself by the wisdom of its councils, but inspiration seems to have been reserved for the two greater occasions of four and fourteen years later. There is small record and less memory of any noteworthy relief it was able to afford. In a word, the principal use of the Chicago Board of Trade, almost up to the Rebellion, was to develop the present body, and it is enough that its mission was well performed. The first salaried officer appears to have been a superintendent, at $1,500 per year, who should look after the interests of the Board. This was in 1857, since which date the daily meetings have always been well attended. The initiation fee was $5. Daily telegraphic reports of the Eastern markets were received and actual trading commenced. In 1859, arrangements were made for quarters on South Water Street, to which the Board removed the next year, continuing to occupy them till the erection, on the corner of Washington and La Salle streets, of the buildings destroyed by fire, on the site of the magnificent structure which was erected after the fire, and which was subsequently pulled down to make room for the present celebrated Chamber of Commerce Building

CATHEDRAL HOLY NAME,
COR. STATE AND SUPERIOR STS.

UNITED STATES GOVERNMENT BUILDING.

(which see). In April, 1860, the twelfth annual meeting disclosed 625 names. The most notable event of the Board this year was its earnest, prompt, and for the time, effectual remonstrance against the abrogation of the Canadian Reciprocity Treaty. In April, 1861, the membership was 725. The report of the Chief Inspector of Grain was elaborate and lucid, reviewing the preceding year, during which there had been shipped 1,603,920 barrels of flour; 15,835,-053 bushels of wheat; 24,372,725 bushels of corn; 1,633,237 bushels of oats; 393,813 bushels of rye; 226,534 bushels of barley; a grand total, reducing flour to its equivalent of bushels of wheat, of 50,481,862 bushels of grain. The packing season, ending with that year, there had been packed 34,624 cattle and 271,805 hogs; total, 306,429. The season beginning in that year (1861), 53,763 cattle packed; 505,691 hogs; total, 559,454. So vast were the figures of a trade which, considered as large, was hardly ten years old. But they have since multiplied many fold. The patriotism of the Board was fully tested during the war; and among other things, $10,000 was appropriated for a military organization, which was known as the Board of Trade Battery. To even outline the history of the Chicago Board of Trade from that time would fill volumes, and there is only space here to indicate what it is to-day. The Chicago Board is now a world-renowned commercial organization. It exercises a wider and a more potential influence over the welfare of mankind than any other institution of its kind in existence, tor it practically regulates the traffic in breadstuffs the world over. Its transactions are of far more importance to humanity in general than are those of the Exchange of London, the Bourse of Paris, or the Stock Exchange of New York. The volume of business transacted on the floor of the Chicago Board of Trade annually is amazing; the fortunes made and lost within its walls every year, astonish the world. The membership of the Board of Trade is now about 2,000, nearly all young men full of the genuine Chicago spirit.

The magnificent building now occupied and owned by the Board of Trade is located at the south end of La Salle Street, in the square bounded by Jackson and Sherman streets, and Pacific Avenue. The structure is of granite, 175 feet wide and 225 feet deep. The main hall is 144 feet wide, and 161 feet deep; height of ceiling 80 feet ; tower 322 feet to the top of the ship and 237 feet from the ground to the lookout balcony. The largest clock in the United States is located in that splendid tower. This structure, which is an ornament to the city, was commenced in 1882, and completed in 1885 at a cost of $1,800,-000. A visitors' gallery is provided for ladies and gentlemen, and a special gallery for ladies who have no escort. The members of the Board will obtain tickets for their gentlemen friends or correspondents, giving them the entrée to the trading floor, providing they reside out of the city. The members can be reached through an official who is stationed outside of the south door of the trading floor, access to which is had by the elevator at that end of the building. The prices of corn, wheat, pork, etc., are given by three dials which are placed on the south gallery. These indicators are moved by electricity and are entirely under the control of the official reporters. The clearings of the Board of Trade for the year 1889 reached the enormous amount of $55,463,080.75; for the year 1890, $86,617,157.25, or in other words, an increase of more than $31,000,000 over the preceding year. At this rate, who will predict the amount of speculation on the floor of this now famous Board ten years hence ?

Boating. — The usually placid waters of Lake Michigan offer great advantages for boating, and several prominent and popular boat clubs are located along the shore. Of these clubs, the best known are the Catlins, Chicago Canoe Club, Tippecanoes, Chicago Yacht Club, Evanston Boat Club, Delawares, Iroquois, Quintards, Social Athletics, Farraguts, Ogdens, Pullmans, and Lincoln Park Yacht Club. Boating in the parks is also a popular amusement, while fatal accidents are very infrequent.

The annual event in boating circles is the "Chicago Navy Regatta," a series of races for all classes of boats, held off the shore of Lincoln Park.

Bogus Lots. — There are over 2,000 lots in Cook County 7½ feet front by 40 feet deep, with a 2-foot alley and a 5-foot street. In addition to their diminutive size, they lie under water about twenty-three miles from the court-house, and six miles from any railroad, in section 19, town 37, range 13, a locality where drainage can never be successfully accomplished. This lot swindle was perpetrated by one Scott and his accessories, under name of "The Boulevard Addition to Chicago." This is the only downright swindle of the kind known in Chicago for years. No doubt other dealers have flattered themselves that they were cheating their customers badly by shoving remote and unpromising lots upon them, but so rapid has been the development of the city and its surroundings, by new railroads and otherwise, that the buyers of bad bargains have, by holding on, come

out gainers, in spite of their own stupidity.

Books of Reference. — The number of books about Chicago giving information and location are legion. The City Directory, published by the Directory Publishing Company, and two business directories by two large publishing houses, may be taken as the standard authority on this line. Besides these are three or four "élite" directories which contain the names and addresses of the "swell" people, used for sending out invitations, and similar purposes. All respectable drug stores keep a copy of the City Directory for free consultation by those who desire. There are two or three "medical registers." To these must be added a host of lesser guides and descriptions of the city, more or less compactly put together for the convenience of the sojourner in this mighty city. We have also a "Postal Guide," published by the post office, containing the arrival and departure of the mails, and post-office regulations, etc. In addition to these, reliable and accurate maps of the city and county are for sale in all the book stores.

Book Stores. — The book stores of Chicago are quite numerous, and derive an immense revenue from a large literary population. All the new and noted books of every author are sure to find a ready market in Chicago, and a number of mammoth book stores has become a necessity. A. C. McClurg's great store, on Wabash Avenue, is the greatest book emporium in the city.

Brentano's, on Wabash Avenue, and the Western News Company, on Randolph Street, are the headquarters for periodical literature, while Ivison, Blakeman, Taylor & Co. supply school books to a vast section of country.

Boot-blacks.—Chicago s t r e e t boot-blacks are as a rule an exceedingly noisy and importunate class. Formerly the native *gamin* took kindly to the business, but of late years he has begun to retire slowly before the invading hosts of Italian youth. A male stranger will do well to have his boots polished before starting out on a walk, if he does not wish to be constantly greeted with a loud and imperative, "Hey, shine!" at every corner. The 'boys' ordinary charge for a "shine" is five cents, but if any one of them is asked about the price after the job is done, the demand is very apt to be twice as much. Hence never ask, but always take it for granted that five cents is the right sum to give. Boot-blacks, generally colored, are to be found in all hotels and barber shops, but these invariably expect not less than ten cents.

Boulevards.—The system of boulevards under control of the several boards of Park Commissioners, contemplates a continuous driveway of thirty-eight miles around the city, taking in the chain of parks, from Lincoln on the north to Jackson on the south. Much of this mileage has been improved in a substantial manner, and Drexel Boulevard, especially, has been made the scene of a floral display along its two miles of roadway. The great boulevard lines are broadly marked on all maps of Chicago, and every eye must have become familiar with the outline. At the far southwest is Gage Park, twenty acres; at the far northwest corner is Logan Square, four acres. The boulevards on the South Side are Grand, Drexel, Oakwood, and Garfield, under control of the South Park Board, whose jurisdiction also embraces Michigan Avenue from Jackson Street to Thirty-fifth Street. On the West Side the park boulevards have seventeen miles of frontage, from a connection on the south with the South Side park improvements to the north with the Lincoln Park improvements. The authority of the West Side Board has also been extended over Washington and Jackson streets, west of Halsted Street, and over portions of Ashland Avenue, Twelfth Street, and Ogden Avenue. The Lincoln Park Commissioners are to complete the grand boulevard connection by a broad thoroughfare westward to Logan Square, and it is contemplated to extend their authority over some North Side street for a direct connection with the center of the city, thus completing the circuit. All this great achievement has been the work of less than twenty years. What dreamer shall reveal to us the glorious scenes which these parks and boulevards will present in another twenty years, when Chicago, with her vast population, will have put them under the highest improvement and best utility?.

Bric-a-Brac.—To presume to advise professional collectors, or experienced amateurs, would be worse than useless. Whatever they know, they have, in almost all cases, dearly paid for. The well-informed stranger in these matters will find a field where he can pick up quite a number of antiques and curios among the shops scattered throughout the city where pawnbrokers' unredeemed pledges are sold. If one desires to purchase, or simply to look, in his sightseeing, at bric-a-brac, he will find himself welcome in various establishments, where there are on exhibition collections of great beauty and variety. One of the most unique collections is at Gunther's candy store on State Street, which is worthy of a visit from any stranger visiting the city.

Bridewell, or House of Correction.—This is practically a prison for the incarceration and punishment of those who violate the city ordinances, and for offenders who do not deserve a term in the penitentiary. It is located in the southwest portion of the city, or to be exact, at South California Avenue, near West Twenty-third Street. Take Blue Island Avenue cars. Chicago has no particular reason to be proud of this prison, nothwithstanding the fact that it cost to date about $1,500,000. It is managed by a superintendent, who is appointed by the Mayor. Of late years, the arrival of prisoners per year will average 9,000, of whom seven-eighths are male. The prisoners do about $60,000 worth of work per year, and the chief industries of the place are a huge laundry and brick making. The county prisoners are also sent here. For this service the city receives thirty cents per capita, daily. The superintendent has succeeded in securing 1,300 volumes, the voluntary contribution of the citizens, as a nucleus of a library for the benefit and instruction of the inmates. The younger inmates of both sexes, during their stay, also receive a daily course of instruction from a competent teacher. These new features of prison life at this institution are calculated to improve the mental and moral condition of the inmates, and thus, so far as circumstances will permit, making the institution in deed as well as name, a House of Correction.

Bridges.—There are nearly fifty bridges across the Chicago River, nearly all of which open to permit of navigation. Several of these bridges are worthy of notice, especially those at Adams, Lake, Wells, Rush, Madison, and Jackson streets. Although these bridges can be turned very rapidly, great complaint is made of the delay caused to street travel and traffic by their opening, and their abolition is contemplated, in which case river navigation will be by means of barges.

Bucket Shops is a term applied to places outside the Stock Exchange and Board of Trade, where stock gambling is carried on in a small way, by the aid of the quotations furnished by the instruments of the Gold and Stock Telegraph Company. This is gambling pure and simple, since not a share of stock changes hands, a formality carefully preserved in the regular exchanges, although it is generally understood to be simply an ingenious way of "whipping H. S. M. around the stump." A large blackboard is erected on one wall of the bucket shop, and on this board are displayed figures of the latest quotations of all the principal stocks and provisions. Two young men are constantly engaged in changing these figures in obedience to the mandates of a third, who sits at the instrument and announces the fluctuations. On a row of benches and chairs in front of the board sits a crowd of men and boys, watching with all the gambler's eagerness the changing quotations. At an office at the end of the room stock privileges are sold, as small a sum as $5 being accepted. When a stock rises or falls in price enough to wipe out the margin paid, the account is closed. On the other hand the speculator presents his privilege and collects his money and profit, less a small percentage for brokerage. The habitues of these rooms are broken-down stock brokers and speculators, and young men and boys. Many once wealthy men, ruined by stock gambling, may be seen, seedily dressed, hurrying about these places, unable to resist the fascination of the street, and many boys are lured on to ruin by venturing their employers' money. At one time there were a great many of these places in the city, but by a concerted action on the part of the Board of Trade and the recently enacted law, most of them have been driven out of the business.

Building Department, City Hall.—The Commissioner of Buildings is a feed office. The commissioner is nominated by the Mayor and confirmed by the Board of Aldermen. The department supervises the erection of new buildings and additions to old structures, within the city limits. All plans for buildings must be filed with and approved by the Building Department before a permit is granted. It also inspects the condition of buildings with reference to their safety, and has the power to order torn down or repaired all dangerous buildings, and to see that proper means of escape from buildings, in case of fire, are provided. The extent and character of the work done in the city, under the authority and supervision of this department during the past year, is in excess of any like period in the history of Chicago. From 1876 to 1889 there were erected in the city 87,042 buildings, covering a frontage of 172 miles, costing $176,460,779, being an average of 3,087 buildings per year for twelve years, an average of fourteen and one-third miles of frontage and an average cost of $14,705,065. The least number of buildings erected in any one year was in 1878, with a frontage of about six miles. The least expenditure was in 1879. The largest transaction for the same period was in 1888. Number of buildings, 4,958; twenty-two miles frontage; expenditure, $20,360,800. During the year 1889, the number of structures erected was 7,590, covering over thirty-four miles of street frontage and costing $31,516,000.

During that year many noted buildings were erected and completed, among the latter the great Auditorium, and also forty-one churches. The imposing public and private structures built, range from six to twenty stories in height and cover extensive ground area. Building during 1890 showed a still greater increase. The totals revealed the issuance of 11,544 permits for 263,-377 feet or about 50.1 miles of frontage, at a cost of $47,322,100. This showed an increase over 1889 of 52 per cent. in the number of permits, 45 per cent. in the amount of frontage covered, and 19 per cent. in the cost of buildings. Total number of buildings erected from 1876 to January 1, 1891, 56,240; total cost, $255,298,-879; total frontage, 256 miles. These figures do not represent the buildings that escaped the fire in 1871 or the buildings erected from that period to 1876, and it represents only those buildings erected in the annexed portions of the city, since the date of annexation, which is a very small percentage of the whole. It is impossible at this time to give the figures for 1891, but they will greatly exceed those of any similar period in the history of the city. The fees of the Building Department will now reach about $40,000 per year; expenditures about $35,000.

Building Permits 1891.—The building operations of the first half of the year 1891 compare favorably with the operations of the corresponding period of last year. The record of permits show a gain both in frontage built up and in aggregate value of buildings. During the first six months of the year application was made for permits to build 6,068 buildings, to cover a frontage of 149,177 feet, and at an estimated cost of $22,877,000. During the corresponding period of 1890 permits were issued for 5,840 buildings, to cover a frontage of 132,461 feet, and to cost $21,445,000. The gain is in 228 buildings at an estimated cost of $1,632,000. These figures show that during the half year ending June 30, permits have been issued for the improvement of twenty-eight miles of frontage.

Burr Mission.—This institution is located at the corner of Twenty-third Street and Wentworth Avenue. It has for its object the religious and secular education of the poor.

Business Colleges.—There are several first-class business colleges in Chicago, and an excellent commercial education can be obtained at comparatively little expense. The most prominent among the business colleges are:

BRYANT & STRATTON'S BUSINESS COLLEGE, Wabash Avenue and Washington Street. This is one of the leading commercial schools of the country, and has nearly 700 students.

CHICAGO BUSINESS COLLEGE, 45 Randolph Street; about 300 pupils. A thorough and conscientious school of business training.

CHICAGO ATHENÆUM, popularly called "The People's College," is located in the splendid building at 18 to 26 Van Buren Street. With a first-class curriculum, the Athenæum is destined to become one of the most noted educational institutions of the nation. About 800 students are usually in attendance.

METROPOLITAN BUSINESS COLLEGE, corner Michigan Avenue and Monroe Street, with 500 pupils, ranks very high as a commercial school.

SOUDER'S BUSINESS COLLEGE, 276 West Madison Street; a first-class institution with about 100 students.

Calumet Club owns the building they occupy, which is on the corner of Michigan Avenue and Twentieth Street. Here is a wealthy club, whose membership includes prominent men of all careers, but mostly business men. The main dining hall has a capacity for seating 300 guests at table at one time; besides, there are three private dining rooms, which can be thrown into one grand salon, if occasion required.

Calvary Cemetery.—The burial place for the dead of Catholic faith, contains some hundred acres of beautiful ground on the Lake Shore, north of the city about ten miles, and is reached by the Chicago & North-Western Railway. The grounds are beautifully improved. There are many very handsome monuments denoting the resting place of former residents of Chicago, and the plats of ground surrounding them are kept in a high state of cultivation. There is a large green-house in connection with the cemetery. This burying-ground was consecrated in 1861. The interments have exceeded 25,000. Trains leave the Wells Street depot daily for the cemetery.

Canadian Club is composed of Canadians and their descendants, and such as they may elect.

Carleton Club.—Located at the corner of Thirty-eighth Street and Vincennes Avenue, in a handsome and capacious building. The Carleton is a very popular club, its dances, indoor ball games, and dramatic entertainments being social events of much note and merit.

Cathedral of the Holy Name. —This, one of the most substantially built of all the Roman Catholic churches in Chicago, is located on the corner of Superior and North State streets. It is built of stone after the plan best suited to such structures; planned for the needs of a live, earnest-working congregation. It has been recently renovated, and its interior re-decorated with all those adjuncts to harmonious thought, and pious contemplation, for which this denomination is famous all over the world. There is at present no church interior in the city which is so soul-inspiring to the devout worshiper, or that suggests so forcibly to the seeker the glories of the heavenly home he desires, as the Cathedral of the Holy Name.

Caxton is a twelve-story building at 356 Dearborn Street. The lot on which it stands has a frontage of eighty feet on Dearborn Street, and a depth of sixty-seven, running back to Fourth Avenue. It is owned by George B. Harris, of Salem, Mass., and leased for ninety-nine years by Mr. Bryan Lathrop and Mr. W. C. Reynolds, who jointly put up the building. This is of steel construction with brick walls. On the front are two tiers of bay windows, each equi-distant from the north and south ends of the building. The building, which was completed in May, 1890, cost about $225,000.

Cemeteries.—The cemeteries of Chicago will compare favorably with those of any of the older cities. There are many attractive views in these quiet Cities of the Silent, and there is much in the way of sculpture. The early places, say up to 1843, have been abandoned, and the deposits all removed to the newer and present grounds provided by the several cemetery associations of the city. The cemeteries are mentioned under their proper names, which see. They are :
Anshe Maariv Cemetery.

Austro-Hungarian Cemetery.
Beth Hamedrash Cemetery.
B'nai Abraham Cemetery.
B'nai Shilom Cemetery.
Calvary Cemetery.
Cemetery of the Congregation of the North Side.
Chebra Gemilath Chasadino Ubikar Cholim Cemetery.
Chebra Kadisha Ubikar Cholim Cemetery.
Concordia Cemetery.
Forest Home Cemetery.
Free Son's of Israel Cemetery.
German Lutheran Cemetery.
Graceland Cemetery.
Hebrew Benevolent Society Cemetery.
Moses Montefiore Cemetery.
Mount Greenwood Cemetery.
Mount Hope Cemetery.
Mount Olive Cemetery.
Mount Olivet Cemetery.
Oakwoods Cemetery.
O'haney Emunah Cemetery.
O'haney Scholom Cemetery.
Rosehill Cemetery.
Sinai Congregational Cemetery.
St. Boniface Cemetery.
Waldheim Cemetery.
Zion Congregation Cemetery.

Cemetery of the Congregation of the North Side.—Located at Waldheim, ten miles from the City Hall. Take train at Grand Central depot via Chicago & Northern Pacific Railroad. Trains leave at 12.01 P. M., daily including Sundays.

Central Homeopathic Free Dispensary provides medical attendance free to the poor.

Chamber of Commerce Building.—The thirteen-story high Chamber of Commerce Building on La Salle and Washington streets was completed in January, 1891. Its total cost was in the neighborhood of $2,000,000. The building is notable for its magnificent interior court, reaching from the main floor to the skylight. Around the court are the galleries upon which the offices open. The interior is finished in marble and iron work of ornamental design. Nine passenger and freight elevators are provided and kept constantly busy with the thousand or more tenants. Brick, stone of a light color, iron, and steel were used in the construction of this magnificent structure. The site is historical as that of the old Chamber of Commerce Building, so long occupied by the Board of Trade. It is immediately opposite the City Hall and Court House. This trio of buildings form a massive, grand, and imposing scene that is hard to equal in any city.

Channing Club has rooms 135 Wabash Avenue, and has for its object the interests of the Unitarians

Charity Organization Society helps the able-to-work but out-of-employment class to be self-sustaining, and thus in a great measure put an end to street begging.

Chebra Gemilah Chasadino Ubikar Cholim Cemetery.— Located on North Clark Street south of Graceland Cemetery. Take train on Evanston division of the Chicago, Milwaukee & St. Paul Railway, or North Clark Street cable line. (See *Graceland Cemetery*.)

Chebra Kadisha Ubikar Cholim Cemetery.—Located on North Clark Street south of Graceland Cemetery (which see). Take train on Evanston division of Chicago, Milwaukee & St. Paul Railway, or North Clark Street cable line.

Cheltenham Beach.—Is a watering place, twelve miles south, with hotel accommodations, where many spend their time during hot months.

Chess Playing.—Chicago can boast no corporated chess clubs. That there is a considerable interest in this conflict of skill, is evident from the attention manifested whenever there has been a test of ability by noted players. There has been an effort made from time to time to organize a club, but it has never reached completion, perhaps because we have no business men who have leisure enough to give the game the requisite time. There are two or three resorts where there are opportunities to both see and play the game. More than this, there are quite a goodly number of skillful lovers of the game in Chicago.

Chicago Avenue Church.— With its crescent tower and belfry, is a striking piece of architecture very noticeable on the North Side. It is an independent church, and with its gallery and auditorium seats two thousand persons.

Chicago Bar Association.— Meets in room 71, County Building.

Chicago Bethel. — Is at Randolph and Desplaines streets.

Chicago Bible Society.—Derives its main importance from its affiliation with the American and Foreign Bible Society, whose headquarters are in New York City. The Chicago headquarters are at 49 Ada Street, where all correspondence can be addressed.

Chicago Club.—Own the building they occupy, which is on Monroe Street, between State Street and Wabash Avenue. The interior is elegantly designed, superbly furnished, and is the social resort of its wealthy and fashionable members.

Chicago College of Physicians and Surgeons occupy a splendid stone building, erected in Queen Anne style of architecture. It

After assuring its readers that a large portion of the population of Chicago had "deserted," and that the merchants, such of them as had anything left to transfer, were "transferring their business to St. Louis," it added: "No doubt the people of Chicago will struggle earnestly

COLLEGE OF PHYSICIANS AND SURGEONS, WEST HARRISON AND HONORE STREETS.

is just opposite Cook County Hospital, Harrison and Wood streets.

Chicago Doomed.—After the Great Fire of 1871, there were many tears wasted over the fate of Chicago. This, from the oldest and most influential of the New Orleans papers, is a specimen of the copious draughts.

against their adverse fate, and that a new city will arise speedily from the ashes of the old one; but it will never be the Carthage of old. Its prestige has passed away like that of a man who turns the downward hill of life; its glory will be of the past, not of the present; while its hopes, once so bright and cloudless, will be

4

to the end marred and blackened by the smoke of its fiery fate."

If the croakers will flock here on the occasion of the World's Fair, they will discover that Chicago is possessed of Phœnix-like characteristics to a degree greater than their philosophy ever dreamed of.

Chicago, History of. — The City of Chicago has been regarded as one of the marvels of the age. Her rapid growth and her stately magnificence have been the astonishment of the world. Her early history, when contrasted with her wealth and grandeur at the present time, becomes of peculiar interest.

Chicago is situated near the head of Lake Michigan, and has an elevation of 591 feet above the sea. It is situated upon both sides of the Chicago River, a slow stream, which, at a point a little over a half mile from the mouth, is formed by the junction of two streams or branches, one flowing from the northwest and the other from the southwest. The river and branches divide the city into three natural parts, legally known as the South, North, and West divisions. The South Division includes all the territory east of the South Branch and south of the main river. The North Division includes the area east of the North Branch and north of the river; while the West Division includes all that part of the city west of the two branches. From 1681 to 1795, during the time of the French possession, and after its cession to England, very little is known of Chicago or the surrounding country. After the declaration of peace between the Colonists and the English, the latter by intrigue stirred up the border Indian warfare, which became general in the Western States, and continued until 1795, at which period, having been effectually chastised by General Wayne, the chiefs of the several tribes of Indians by his invitation assembled at Greenville, Ohio, and there effected a treaty of peace, which closed the War of the West. Among the numerous small tracts of land where forts and trading-posts had been established, then ceded by the Indians to the United States, was one described as follows: "One piece of land, six miles square, at the mouth of the Chikajo River, emptying into the southwest end of Lake Michigan, where a fort formerly stood." Here we have an account of the *first land trade* of Chicago—the first transaction in that line of business which has at times distinguished Chicago above every other city of the nation— the first link in the chain of title to thousands upon thousands of transfers that have been made of the soil thus parted with by the Indians. When the first settlers of Chicago began to congregate and erect their cabins, with the view of forming the nucleus of a town, the point selected as the most available for village purposes was the tract on the West Side, at the junction of the North and South branches, and at first called Wolf's Point. In addition to the few buildings that were standing in 1818, we have only to mention this group at Wolf's Point, two or three buildings on the South Side, between the point and the fort, and the Miller House on the North Side. This house was built of logs and used as a tavern. A little above its mouth on the North Branch was a log-bridge, which gave access from that quarter to the agency, but the center of attraction was at Wolf's Point. Here, too, was another tavern, the school-house and church, as well as the store. On the South Side the most prominent object of interest was the tavern kept by Mr. Elijah Wentworth. North of this house was an oblong building which had been erected by Father Walker, a missionary of the Methodist church, for a place of worship and for a school-house. This log tabernacle was the meeting-house of the town. The Wentworth tavern was the headquarters of General Scott, when he came to Chicago with the troops for the Black Hawk war in 1832. The next building south of the Wentworth House was the residence of James Kenzie. Next to these were the log cabins in which resided Alexander Robinson, and here occasionally resided Billy Calwell, whose wife was the wild daughter of an Indian chief, and her presence did not always hallow his wigwam with the sanctity of peace. There were several more primitive houses occupied by members of the Kenzie, Beaubien, and Harmon families. In the year 1804, the United States erected Fort Dearborn upon the south bank of the river, just east of the present Michigan Avenue. Mr. Kenzie and his son John H., Indian traders, were the only white residents until the war of 1812, when the post was abandoned. The small garrison, in attempting to escape, were captured by the Pottawatomies and massacred at a point now represented by Twelfth Street and Michigan Avenue. In 1816, 'the fort was rebuilt and the Kenzies returned, and the fort served for many years as a resting place for emigrants passing to the West. The inhabitants did not exceed half a dozen families, until, in 1827, Congress made a grant of land to aid in the construction of a canal to connect the waters of Lake Michigan with those of the Illinois River. In 1829, the State Legislature appointed a commission to mark out the route of the canal, and a surveyor arrived to mark out the town. Besides the garrison, at that time, there were eight families, engaged mostly as Indian traders, in

the place. With a hard and protracted struggle by numerous individuals, and especially by Daniel P. Cook, Esq., who was at that time representative in Congress, and from whom Cook County was named, an Act was passed by Congress, March 2, 1827, granting to the State for the construction of this work "each alternate section of land five miles in width on each side of the proposed canal." We make mention of these facts because it was from this Act of Congress the State acquired the title to those lands which have formed the basis for many of its most important financial transactions; from which originated the titles to the valuable canal lands, on which a large portion of the city is built—on which, too, villages, towns, and cities have sprung up all along its line.

In the autumn of 1829, commissioners authorized the laying out of the "Town of Chicago," on the alternate section which belonged to the canal lands lying upon the main channel of the river and over the junction of the two branches. The first map of the original town of Chicago, by James Thompson, bears date August 4, 1830. This was the first beginning of Chicago as a legally recognized place among the towns and cities of the world—the first official act of organization, which must accordingly be dated as its birth or real starting point, and the town was comprised within the limits of what are now known as Madison, State, Kinzie, and Halsted streets, or about three-eighths of a square mile. Hence this city with a population of 1,250,000—the leading mart in the world for grain, pork, and other things—arrived, on the 4th day of August, 1891, at the precocious maturity of sixty-one years. In 1831 Cook County was organized, embracing in addition to the present

CHICAGO RIVER, LOOKING WEST FROM WELLS STREET BRIDGE.

county the territory which is now known by five other large and populous counties. The prospective work on the canal was attracting population, but in 1832 the cholera visited the incipient city and was very severe. In 1832 the first public religious worship was held in a log hut erected for that purpose. The tax-list for 1832 amounted to $148.29. Lake Street was laid out the same year. In 1833 the settlement had increased enough to have a post office and a weekly mail, and late in the year the *Chicago Democrat*, a weekly paper, was started by John Calhoun. On the 10th of August the voters of Chicago held an election to determine whether they would become incorporated, and to elect trustees. Every man voted and the number of voters was twenty-eight, some of whom are now living; the levy for city taxes in 1834 was $48.90. In 1834 the number of voters had increased to 111, and a loan of $60 was negotiated for public improvements. In 1835 the number of voters had increased to 211. In 1836 the town applied to the State Bank for a loan of $25,000 and was refused. In 1837 the Legislature incorporated the City of Chicago and in May following, Hon. William B. Ogden was elected Mayor of Chicago. Thus on the first Tuesday in May, 1837, fifty-four years ago, commenced the City of Chicago, which then contained a population of 4,179. At the present time (1891), school census, the population is fully 1,250,000. This has been the extraordinary growth of this wonderful city.

The natural line of the site of Chicago was but a few feet above that of the lake, and there was no drainage, and in seasons of rain the surface was covered with water. In the winter of 1855-6 the city ordered a change of grade, raising the height of the carriage-ways an average of

eight feet. This placed the lower or ground story of each building several feet below the level of the street; but the inconvenience was rapidly overcome by raising all the buildings— brick, stone, and wood—up to the level. All the large buildings, including many hotels, business blocks, warehouses, etc., were raised by means of screws from their foundations a height of from six to ten feet, and new foundations built under them. This secured deep, dry cellars and admitted of a thorough system of sewerage. The city ordered an effective dredging of the harbor, and the clay thus obtained served to fill the streets to the new grade. For several years while this process was going on, the passage of Chicago streets was a work of trying difficulty to pedestrians. The expense was great, but was cheerfully borne by the property-holders. Then commenced the work of permanent improvement in the city and how far they had progressed may have been seen before the Great Fire, and is again apparent since her re-building. Certainly no city in the world has so wonderful a record as has Chicago; and the great conflagration of October, 1871, which almost entirely obliterated the city—from which but few cities would have recovered in a century—only seemed to demonstrate the indomitable energy with which Chicagoans are possessed. Within a period of two years from that time, we find that Chicago was again shining with redoubled splendor and eclipsing her palmiest days. Where stood wood and brick, when the city was destroyed, now are reared stately commercial palaces of marble, stone, and iron.

Chicago Hospital for Women and Children is at Paulina and West Adams streets. Women and children of the respectable poor receive medical attention, and nurses are trained.

Chicago Literary Club

has a suite in the Portland Block, 184 Dearborn Street, and is composed of some of the most distinguished literary gentlemen in the country. The club has an auditorium in which such matters as may be interesting, are discussed. The club gives an annual entertainment at one of the theatres, and an anniversary banquet, usually at one of the principal hotels.

Chicago Mechanics' Institute,

next to the Rush Medical College, is the oldest organization in this city. It was chartered in 1843. Its object is the diffusion of knowledge, among the mechanic classes, by means of lectures, class instruction, and a circulating library. It had a valuable library which was destroyed by fire in 1871. For the past nine years it has done all its educational labors through the Chicago Athenæum. The course of instruction includes reading, penmanship, arithmetic, algebra, geometry, and bookkeeping, and a complete course in freehand and mechanical drawing. The average number of pupils for the past three years has been 140. Ample testimony is borne to the useful service which this institute renders the working classes. It deserves the friendly support of all manufacturers, and of architects, builders, and lithographers who seek skilled draughtsmen.

Chicago Musical College.—

This institution was established in 1867, and was the pioneer of schools of music in the West. During these twenty-four years the college has granted, after thorough examinations, such honors as diplomas, teachers' certificates, gold and silver medals, to over 1,000 pupils, among whom will be found many of the noted musical celebrities of the age. The location of the main college—it has branches in various parts of the city—is in the great Central Music Hall, corner State and Randolph streets. At the head of the faculty is a name well known both in musical circles and generally—it is that of Dr. F. Ziegfeld, who was a graduate from the Leipsic Conservatory in 1862. The course of instruction of the college includes all branches of a complete and symmetrical musical education that is equal to any that can be had anywhere.

Chicago Nursery and Half-Orphan Asylum.—

855 North Halsted Street, cares for children of poor women while looking for employment, or that are employed. A small sum is charged.

Chicago Orphan Asylum

is located at 2228 Michigan Avenue, and is under Protestant management, but children of all creeds are admitted.

Chicago Yacht Club

has a club-house at 189 Michigan Avenue, and a superb fleet of yachts owned by its members, some of which are very handsome craft and very fast. This club has done much to keep up the interest in yachting in the West.

Children's Charity Globes.—

This is a new and original device of the Fresh Air Fund management. From spring to autumn these glass charity globes will be found in almost every public place, and if you feel disposed you can make any contribution you please, dropping the money into a slot through which it falls into the globe. At regular intervals this money is collected and the amount goes to the Fresh Air Fund, which has for its object the sending of certain needy classes into the country for a summer vacation. These classes are : First, working girls and boys ; second, mothers with infants ; third, sewing and shop girls. The *Daily News* secures invitations for these from among its subscribers who live in pleasant country places. The railroads charge half rates, or make other reductions, and give special attention to those wearing the country week badges. The *News* arranges all details. When the work was begun in 1887, only 461 were sent out. Last year 1,749 were sent out, at a cost of $2,837.90, or $1.62 for each.

Chicago Opera House.—This splendid place of amusement is located in the Chicago Opera House Building, a magnificent ten-story structure, S. W. corner of Clark and Washington streets, opposite the Court House, in close proximity to principal hotels and convenient to railroad depots and street-car lines. Mr. David Henderson is the lessee and sole manager. The opera house, built in 1885, for Mr. Henderson, was constructed with the idea of giving the most lavish productions of spectacular extravaganza that have ever been seen in America. The first of these productions, entitled "The Arabian Nights," was launched six years ago, and each year since has witnessed a successful production upon a scale unsurpassed in the theatrical annals of America. These pieces include "The Crystal Slipper," "Bluebeard, Jr.," "Sinbad," and "Ali Baba." So widespread a reputation have these pieces acquired that the Chicago Opera House must be stamped as the leading theatre west of New York, and, indeed, no theatre in New York, during the last ten years, can show anything like the enterprise and achievement of this house. The American Extravaganza

Company is the name of the organization identified with the Chicago Opera House which has produced those plays. It is the custom to play this Company not less than six months during the year in Chicago. During the other six months the organization visits all the large cities from San Francisco to Boston, and in this way it has acquired a national reputation. The six months during the absence of this company is filled up with the strongest attractions from Europe and America. The house is the largest theatre in Chicago, seating over 2,000 people; it is fireproof, magnificently decorated, and in all its appointments, upon the stage and in the auditorium, it has few equals in America.

Cholera.—Chicago has been visited by cholera on three occasions —in 1832, in 1849, and in 1873. In every instance the disease was imported. This dreadful disease first came to Chicago by way of Quebec, where it had been brought by an emigrant ship from Europe early in the year 1832. During the Black Hawk war the disease broke out among the troops of General Scott, who came out to the war by way of the lakes, and caused such mortality and panic among the troops as to prevent their arrival until after the war was ended. This war also brought quite a number of immigrants to the city, and the scourge made dreadful havoc, both in the garrison of Fort Dearborn and among the citizens.

The first Board of Health was established in 1843, and a hospital erected outside the city limits for persons attacked with cholera or other infectious diseases. Another ordinance of this time gave the supervisor authority to order every male person in the town over twenty-one years, to perform sanitary labor in cleaning the streets and alleys, and a failure to perform this duty or provide a substitute was punishable by a fine of $5 for each offense. The cholera gradually spent its strength under these precautions, and by 1835 was pretty well eradicated. The fright caused by its appearance in the city, and the agitation that followed, resulted in one good at least. Under an act of the Legislature, passed February 11, 1835, the town trustees organized a board of health. Another important result of the agitation was the establishment of cemeteries outside the corporate limits. Two cemeteries were laid out. The South Side cemetery was located at what is now the crossing of Twenty-third Street and Wabash Avenue. The North Side cemetery was located on what is now Chicago Avenue, close to the lake shore. The rapid growth of the city soon necessitated the vacation of these cemeteries, and a new site was chosen between the present North Avenue and Asylum Place.

The city charter, granted March 4, 1837, provides for the election annually of three commissioners to act as a board of health. During the summer of 1838, the laborers on the Illinois and Michigan Canal were attacked by a strange disease that caused great mortality. This disease, for want of a better name, was called "Canal cholera," as many of the symptoms were like those of the real Asiatic cholera. As fast as the men died of this disease, their remains were sent to Chicago and thrown along the roads near Bridgeport. The citizens were afraid to touch the bodies for fear of infection, and they were often allowed to lie a long time without burial. In 1849, cholera made its appearance again, accompanied by the small-pox, and there were many spasmodic efforts made to improve the sanitary condition of the city. The streets and alleys were in a filthy condition, the river had become very foul, and the sewerage did not keep pace with the needs of the rapid growth in population. This state of things was gradually improved by the introduction of a general system of vaccination and the adoption of isolated hospitals for small-pox and other infectious diseases. The exposure incident to the Great Fire, and the after-crowding together of large numbers of people in barracks, again caused a great increase in the mortality. In 1873 the cholera again broke out in Chicago, but better sanitary arrangements prevented its spreading to any great extent. The only districts that were seriously affected were those where dense populations of foreigners had congregated, and where proper sanitary measures could not be enforced.

Next to cholera, small-pox has been the disease that has given the sanitary officers the most trouble; but a system of isolation and, of late years, compulsory vaccination, has resulted in pretty effectually stamping out this loathsome disease.

As the city grew, and its sanitary needs became more urgent, additional powers were conferred from time to time upon the sanitary department, and the force of sanitary officers was increased to meet these needs; not, however, without much and repeated urging, which generally came from the physicians and the press of the city.

Chop-Houses, where a first rate chop may be obtained by the lover of a "grilled bone," are almost as rare in Chicago as hens' teeth. This is possibly due to lack of demand, for it must be admitted that what Americans know about a chop or grill would make but a few lines. What Americans recognize as a chop is a bone denuded of all meat except

CHICAGO
OPERA
HOUSE

S. W. Corner Clark and Washington Sts.,
is the most popular theatre in the

World's Fair City

•

**IT IS HERE THAT THE GREATEST ATTRACTION
OF THE SEASON**

"ALI BABA"

**ENTERTAINED CHICAGO THEATRE GOERS FOR
TWO HUNDRED AND SIX NIGHTS.**

•

The Chicago Opera House plays only
the leading attractions of America
and Europe.

(For Description, see Page 55.)

MR. DAVID HENDERSON, MANAGER.

a mouthful of tough, stringy cartilage at one end, possibly hidden in a scallop of white paper, and without taste or nutriment. The chop proper is an inch and a quarter thick, cut from the loin, bounded by firm, white fat, with a good, large tenderloin, juicy, tender, and rich. A nice chop, a baked potato, a little watercress, English pickles, and plenty of bread, make a meal fit for a king. Nice broiled kidneys, porterhouse steaks, Bass' ale, porter, or stout, Scotch ale, "arf 'n arf," drawn from wood and served in pewter, are also adjuncts of a first-class chop-house. The great trouble with our people, as far as this particular supply is concerned, is that there is not enough demand for it, or the effort would have been made long before this to furnish the supply. And the heart rarely. longs for what it has never seen.

Christian Churches.—The following is a list of the names and locations of those in Chicago:

First Church, West Jackson Street, corner Oakley Avenue.

West Side Church, Western Avenue, southwest corner Congress Street.

Central Church, Indiana Avenue, corner Thirty-seventh Street.

Churches.—Every denomination of Christians is represented in Chicago, and the stranger need be at no loss where to go on a Sunday, unless it be from the difficulty of making a choice among so many. There are at this time 397 church buildings in the city, varying in seating capacity from 200 to 2,000, and averaging about 600 or 700—about 250,000 altogether. With few exceptions, these churches are supported mainly from pew rents and voluntary subscriptions. They all depend on their regular congregations, but strangers are welcome at all times, and will be cheerfully provided with seats, so long as there are any vacant. On Sunday, services in the Protestant churches begin in the morning generally at 10:30; in the afternoon at 3:30, and in the evening at 7:30. The Roman Catholic churches on that day celebrate high mass and vespers at about the same hours. Such of the churches as are noteworthy, architecturally or otherwise, are described under their own heads, while a list of those of each denomination is given under the name of that denomination, except a few scattered ones, which may be found under *Churches, Miscellaneous.*

Church of the Messiah was organized on June 29, 1836. It is built of stone, with the entrance through the basement of the massive tower which forms the corner on Michigan Avenue and Twenty-third Street. It is the pioneer of the Unitarian churches in this city, and the main structure, together with the memorial chapel, make it one of the handsomest architecturally.

Cigars.—There are nearly 1,300 cigar stores in Chicago, nearly all of which are marked by the conventional wooden Indian sign.

Citizens' Association has room 35, Merchants' Building.

City Hall.—The City Hall Building occupies, together with the County Building, the block bounded by La Salle, Clark, Randolph, and Washington streets, and stands upon the site of the first court-house built in Chicago. The present structure was commenced in 1877 and cost about $1,800,000. It is a handsome and imposing building, of a semi-Grecian style of architecture.

The machinery of municipal government revolves in the City Hall, and all the departments thereof can be found on the different floors. In the basement are located the offices of the Health Department, Central Police Detail, and fire alarm service; on the first floor are the city collector's room, water office, police headquarters, the Mayor's office, and the offices of comptroller and city clerk. On the second floor are two court

as in other large cities, have a method of transferring each other's checks all at once. Each bank has a clearing-house clerk. These men have charge of all the checks deposited up to 12 o'clock, noon. They are listed and taken with the checks to the clearing house, where, under the direction of the manager of the clearing house, each bank receives

CITY HALL AND COUNTY BUILDING.

rooms and the Department of Public Works; the third floor is tenanted by the Law Department, Board of Election Commissioners, and the Board of Education. The public library and the council rooms occupy the fourth and last story.

Clearing House Association. —All reputable banks of Chicago,

its own checks. If it receives more checks than it pays, then it is in debt to the clearing house and must make its balance good, but if the reverse, then it receives the balance due it, under the same regulations. These balances must be paid in legal tender or gold. Under this arrangement, there is no difficulty in the collections, nor risk in sending out a messenger to collect the various amounts. The system in use in Chicago is so perfect that, although the transactions through it have been enormous, no difference nor erro: exists in any of its records; neither has any bank, while a member of the association, sustained any loss from any other bank which was also a member.

Like all other clearing houses of the country, Chicago sustained nobly its share in helping the great civil war to a favorable and honorable peace. During financial panics it has become more and more the fashion to uphold and sustain each other's hands, and thus prevent the loss which must come from the inevitable loss of confidence which so surely follows. The clearing house is specially fitted up for its particular uses, and quiet accuracy and dispatch are the principal characteristics. Chicago's clearings rank next to New York's, although Boston has fifty-one banks and there are but twenty-one in Chicago. There is no question but that her business really ranks her as the second city in the country in business transactions and financial affairs. The total clearings of Chicago for 1890 were $4,093,145,904, an average per month of $357,782,159, and an increase over the clearings of 1866 of over three billions of dollars. Nothing is so striking a proof of the rapid increase of Chicago's wealth as this statement.

Clubs.—They are not as numerous in proportion in Chicago as they are in New York and London; but notwithstanding the fact that several clubs have died from inanition within a few years, the increased membership in desirable clubs seems to indicate that club life is growing in favor in Chicago. The following is a list of the principal clubs,

particulars in regard to which will be found under their separate heads:

Acacia, 105 Ashland Avenue Boulevard.

Æolus Cycling, 174 Evergreen Avenue.

Argo, extreme end of Illinois Central Railroad pier, foot of Randolph Street.

Arlington, 355 La Salle Avenue.

Ashland, 575 Washington Boulevard.

Calumet, Twentieth Street and Michigan Avenue Boulevard.

Carleton, 3800 Vincennes Avenue.

Chicago, Michigan Avenue and Van Buren Street.

Chicago Athletic Association, 125, 126, 127 Michigan Avenue.

Chicago Ball, 108 Madison Street.

Chicago Cycling, Fifty-seventh and Lake Avenue.

Chicago Literary, Art Institute Building.

Chicago Tennis, 2901 Indiana Avenue.

Club Litteraire Francais, 45 Randolph Street.

Columbus, 43–45 Monroe Street.

Cook County Wheelmen, 218 South Leavitt Street.

Douglas, 3518 Ellis Avenue.

Douglas Cycling, 586 West Taylor Street.

Farragut Boat, 3016–3018 Lake Park Avenue.

Germania Mænnerchor, Germania Place and North Clark Street.

German Press, 106 West Randolph Street.

Hamilton, 21 Groveland Park.

Ideal, 531–533 Wells Street.

Illinois, 154 Ashland Avenue Boulevard.

Illinois Cycling, 1068 Washington Boulevard.

Indiana, 3349 Indiana Avenue.

Irish-American, 40 Dearborn Street.

Iroquois, Columbia Theatre Building, 110 Monroe Street.

John A. Logan, 466 La Salle Avenue.

Kenwood, Forty-seventh Street and Lake Avenue.

La Croix, 467 Lincoln Avenue.

Lakeside, 3140 Indiana Avenue.

La Salle, 542 West Monroe Street.

Lincoln Cycling, 1 Ogden Fro· t.

Marquette, Maple Street and Dearborn Avenue.

Minnette, Campbell Avenue and Monroe Street.

North Shore, 1835 Wellington Avenue.

Oakland, Ellis and Oakland avenu· s.

Ottawa, 401–403 Orchard Street.

Phœnix, Thirty first Street and Calumet Avenue.

Press, 131 Clark Street.

Progressive, Forty-third Street and Evans Avenue.

Sheridan, Forty-first Street and Michigan Avenue.

Standard, Twenty-fourth Street and Michigan Avenue Boulevard.

Union, Washington Place and Dearborn Avenue.

Union League. Jackson Street and Custom House Place.

University, 116–118 Dearborn Street.

Walton Place Tennis, North Clark and Locust streets.

Washington Cycling, 650 West Adams Street.

Washington Park, South Park Avenue and Sixty-first Street.

West Chicago, 50 Throop Street.

White Chapel, 173 Calhoun Place.

The·athletic, base-ball, gun, and sporting clubs are very numerous, but they are purely local and social organizations, in which the stranger would not be interested.

Coal Exchange.—The Chicago Coal Exchange is located at room 635, 225 Dearborn Street, and the Anthracite Coal Association occupies rooms in the same building.

Cold Storage Exchange, The Chicago.—The corner-stone of the Chicago Cold Storage Exchange, which, when completed, will be the largest cold-storage warehouse in the world, was laid November 13, 1890. It is located just west of the river, between Lake and Randolph streets. It has a dock frontage of 385 feet, and the same frontage on the alley between the river and Canal Street. The building is divided in two parts, with an arcade between the two. Under this arcade the St. Paul, Pennsylvania, and other railroad tracks are run. A traffic-way is constructed over the tracks, and facing it and Lake and Randolph streets will be stores for produce merchants. The structure is thoroughly fire-proof, being constructed of stone, iron, terra-cotta, and brick, the frame being of steel. It is ten stories high, and will be furnished with all appliances for the handling of merchandise requiring cold storage. The land on which it stands is worth $716,000, and the building will cost $1,120,000 and the refrigerator apparatus $565,000. The total cost will therefore be more than $2,000,000.

Colleges.—Chicago is rapidly advancing as an educational center, and the colleges, mostly situated in the adjoining suburbs, hold a high rank as institutions of learning. Within a few months the new Chicago University will be opened, when the lakeside city will rank with Yale, Harvard, and Princeton. The principal colleges of Chicago and vicinity are:

LAKE FOREST UNIVERSITY.— Twenty-eight miles from the city. Denomination, Presbyterian. Attended by over 300 students, including the young ladies at Ferry Hall Seminary.

LEWIS INSTITUTE.—Not yet completed. To be modeled after the Massachusetts Institute of Technology. This institute will probably be merged into the Chicago University.

KENWOOD INSTITUTE FOR YOUNG LADIES.—A very fashionable boarding school, located at the South Side suburb of Kenwood, on the Illinois Central road.

MORGAN PARK FEMALE SEMINARY.—Located at the suburb of Morgan Park, on the Rock Island Railroad. Educates a large number of young ladies, both from Illinois and other States.

NORTHWESTERN UNIVERSITY.—Located at the pretty village of Evanston, twelve miles north of the city. This is the leading college of Illinois, and contains nearly 2,000 students, with 113 professors. Chartered in 1851, and opened in 1853, this university has ever maintained a high standard of education, and is justly considered the banner college of the Northwest. There are classical, philosophical, and scientific courses; medical, legal, and theological departments, and a well-attended female seminary. No college in the country affords a more thorough course of studies, or more pleasant, refined, and moral surroundings.

NORTHWESTERN PREPARATORY SCHOOL.—Auxiliary to Northwestern University, and attended by 700 students.

UNIVERSITY SCHOOL.—Located on the North Side, at Elm Street and Dearborn Avenue. Undenominational, and an excellent preparatory school for college courses.

UNIVERSITY OF CHICAGO is located on the six blocks between Ellis Avenue, Greenwood Avenue, Fifty-sixth Street, and the Midway Plaisance. This site was partly the gift of Marshall Field. John D. Rockefeller presented $2,600,000 to the new college, and $5,000,000 was raised by the Baptists of Chicago. With this princely sum, a college will be erected and maintained, which will be second to none in the country.

Columbia Theatre.—This is one of the most popular amusement houses in Chicago. Its capacity is over 2,800. The interior decorations are on a most elaborate scale, and the whole theatre, external and internal, is a model of artistic attractiveness. The entrance is through a spacious and elegantly decorated vestibule, the walls and ceiling of which are covered with unique and original designs, and the wainscot is of tile and mosaic work. This popular theatre was opened in 1880 with Shakespeare's "Twelfth Night," Robson and Crane respectively as *Sir Andrew Ague-cheek* and *Sir Toby Belch*. It has always been a first-class playhouse, only the higher-grade performances being permitted, and its stage has been occupied by all its leading stars and combinations. Located on the southwest corner of Dearborn and Monroe streets. Proprietors, Al. Hayman and Will J. Davis.

Mr. Al. Hayman is also proprietor of the Baldwin and California theatres, San Francisco; the Marquam Grand, Portland, Ore.; the new theatres at Seattle and Tacoma; the Columbia, Brooklyn, and the New Empire of New York. He is also managing the attractions for a score of other theatres. Mr. Will J. Davis is also proprietor and manager of the Haymarket Theatre, this city, and gives his personal attention to the local management of the Columbia.

NORTHWESTERN UNIVERSITY, EVANSTON.

(62)

Commercial Club. — Is composed of a limited number of representative business men, whose desire is to further the commercial interests of the city, and for social intercourse, as well as to entertain commercial magnates from other cities when in Chicago.

Concerts.—In some of our large cities, in the East especially, there are a number of people, or sets of people, for whom it would be "bad form" to attend an opera or a theatre, but they can not deny themselves the luxury of attending concerts. In Chicago this splitting of hairs is not so excessive, and the people are fully as fond of music as in any other city in the world. Chicago is never left in the cold when a concert troupe are making up their route. The finest musical talent in the country is attracted here, and our home talent is not one of mean dimensions. Our music halls are ample for the largest audiences, and superior talent is always warmly welcomed. The day for snubbing Chicago, because she attended strictly to business, and had little leisure for the cultivation of the finer nature, is past, and the World's Columbian Exposition will undoubtedly demonstrate to outsiders, what we already know, that music is just as highly appreciated in Chicago as elsewhere in the world.

CONCERT SALOONS.—As distinguished from concerts proper. In the one the music is the important feature; in the other the sale of liquor is the incentive, and the music is simply secondary. In Chicago, there are two classes, one where music is used as an attraction, while one sits to drink his glass of lager; but the class which is feared by all good citizens, include the "dives" and worse, where music, and an execrable excuse at that, is used to entice the young and foolish, where liquor and

painted harlots drag swiftly and fiercely down the awful road, whose end is moral debauchery and physical destruction. No respectable person likes to be known as a frequenter of any of these places. The women are without attractive beauty, completely unsexed, and deplorably ignorant. A discordant, heavily-pounded piano shrieks in its awful distress. The liquors are of the vilest, and the women insist upon being treated constantly to colored water, which their dupes pay for as the best brandy. They are not a nice place for a stranger to enter, and are constantly watched by the police.

Concordia Cemetery.—Is beautifully laid out, and highly improved, and is the burial place of the Evangelical Lutheran churches' dead. It is nine miles west of the city. Take train at Grand Central depot via Chicago & Northern Pacific Railroad.

Condemned Meat.—It is unlawful to sell meat in Chicago that is unfit for food. There is a meat inspector in the service of the Health Department, and he, with his aid, keeps a close surveillance over the Union Stock Yards, the Bridgeport district, South Water Street, and the Fulton Street wholesale market. During the year 1890, this officer condemned 3,072 hogs, diseased; 723 quarters of beef, bruised; 244 sheep, diseased; 283 calves, emaciated and too young; 15 pork hams, bruised, and 363 cattle, diseased, making a total of 936,418 pounds. It may be well for certain persons to read Section 1453 of the municipal code of the City of Chicago. It is as follows: "That no diseased or sickly horse, cattle, swine, sheep, dog, or cat, or other animals, nor any that have been exposed to any disease that is contagious among such animals, shall be brought into the City of Chicago."

Section 1490 of the municipal code reads as follows:

"That no person shall bring into the city, or keep therein for sale or otherwise, either for food or for any other purpose or purposes whatever, any animal, dead or alive, matter, substance, or thing which shall be or which shall occasion a nuisance in said city, or which may or shall be dangerous or detrimental to health."

These ordinances should be rigidly enforced, and would be were it not for the interference of the State Live Stock Board, who claim the right under the State law to ship to the city diseased animals. They have exercised that alleged right in direct violation of the city ordinances. They have brought to this market, ostensibly for rendering purposes, cattle suffering with very dangerous contagious diseases, and permitted others to do so. The practice is very reprehensible. That the carcasses of such cattle have been frequently sold in our market for human food, there is no doubt. Several of the butchers of such cattle have made affidavits that such was the case; one of the members of the State Live Stock Board has confessed that during the past years thousands of cattle affected with that dreaded disease, actinomycosis, have been driven from the Stock Yards, slaughtered, and their carcasses sold on the market for human food. It is an infamous business, and persons who engage in it deserve the most severe punishment that can be inflicted.

Congregational Churches.— The following is a list of those in Chicago, with their locations:

First Church, corner Ann Street and Washington Boulevard.

Union Park Church, southwest corner Ashland Avenue and Washington Boulevard.

New England Church, Dearborn Avenue and Delaware Place.

Plymouth Church, Michigan Avenue, between Twenty-fifth and Twenty-sixth streets.

South Church, corner Drexel Boulevard and Fortieth Street.

Bethany Church, corner Superior and Lincoln streets.

Tabernacle Church, corner West Indiana and Morgan streets.

Clinton Street Church, corner South Clinton and Wilson streets.

Central Park Church, Forty-first, corner Fulton Street.

Western Avenue Chapel, West Polk, corner Idaho Street.

Lincoln Park Church, corner Garfield Avenue and Mohawk Street.

Jefferson Church, Jefferson.

Oakley Avenue Mission, corner West Indiana Street, near Oakley Avenue.

Leavitt Street Church, corner Leavitt and West Adams streets.

Englewood Church School, corner Eighty-fourth Street, Englewood.

Lawndale Church, Lawndale.

Bethlehem Chapel, corner Center Avenue and Twenty-first Street.

California Avenue Chapel, 1256 West Van Buren Street.

Church of the Good Shepherd, 3207 South Ashland Avenue.

Church of the Redeemer, School Street, near Evanston Avenue.

Immanuel Church (colored), Dearborn Street, south of Twenty-ninth Street.

Lake View Church, Lill Avenue, corner Seminary Avenue.

Northwest Chapel, Powell Avenue, northwest corner Cherry Place.

Pilgrim German Church, Indiana Street, near Oakley Avenue.

South German Church, Ullman Street, corner James Avenue.

Union Tabernacle, South Ashland Avenue, corner Twentieth Street.

Warren Avenue Church, Warren

FINE ARTS BUILDING.

North ra portion of Jackson Park, with the south front facing the lagoon. 320 x 560 feet. Architect, C. B. Atwood.

ILLINOIS BUILDING.

Avenue, southwest corner Albany Avenue.

Welsh Church, South Peoria Street, near West Jackson Street.

Consuls.—All of the great foreign powers are represented by consuls or consular agents in Chicago. The addresses of these will be found below, under the names of governments by which they are accredited. Foreigners visiting Chicago are entitled to the advice and protection of the consuls of their Government in the city, and those who have no consul located here will usually be well treated by the consul of some government adjacent and friendly to their own. By consulting with the consul of their government on all matters of moment, foreigners will frequently avoid being swindled.

Argentine Republic, 83 Jackson Street.

Austria-Hungary, 78–80 Fifth Avenue.

Belgium, 167 Dearborn Street.

Denmark, 209 Fremont Street.

France, 78 La Salle Street.

German Empire, room 25, Borden Block.

Great Britain, room 4, 72 Dearborn Street.

Italy, 110 La Salle Street.

Mexico, room 30, 126 Washington Street.

Netherlands, 85 Washington Street.

Sweden and Norway, room 1, 153 Randolph Street.

Switzerland, 65 Washington Street.

Turkey, 167 Dearborn Street.

Convent and Parochial Schools.—The parochial schools of Chicago furnish education to nearly 46,000 children, and certainly save an immense expense from the public school funds. About 1,000 teachers are employed.

The Hebrew schools contain about 600 pupils, the Lutheran some 7,000, and the Catholic over 35,000. Many of the Catholic schools contain as many children as the largest public schools, the Holy Family schools, at the corner of Twelfth Street and Blue Island Avenue, educating 4,500 pupils.

The parochial schools have been often attacked by the advocates of the public school system, but seem to hold their own nevertheless, and apparently furnish almost as thorough an education as the schools under the management of the Board of Education.

Cook County Hospital.—Is located on the square bounded by Wood, Harrison, Lincoln, and Polk streets. Take West Madison cable car-line. This institution is for the benefit of the poor and is one of the largest and most perfectly appointed hospitals in this country. It is under the management of the County Commissioners, and is supported by the tax-payers.

Cook County Insane Asylum. —Is a magnificent group of buildings located in Cook County and affords every facility for the care of those unfortunate enough to be placed there.

Cook County Jail.—The criminal court and jail buildings are on the North Side. They occupy the east half of the block bounded by Michigan Street on the south, Illinois Street on the north, Dearborn Avenue on the east, and Clark Street on the west. Take North Clark Street cable cars. Cook County's criminal court occupies the upper part of the building. The jail is a massive structure built of brick and iron. The entire plant was erected in 1873 at a cost of $375,000. At present the quarters are cramped and a new and larger jail is sadly needed. It was in this jail

5

that four of the anarchists were executed and Louis Lingg, "The Tiger," suicided by exploding a dynamite cartridge in his mouth. There are a number of murderers and other desperate criminals in this jail at all times. The prison is connected with the court room by a walk known as the "Bridge of Sighs."

Cooking Schools.—There are a few of these useful institutions in Chicago, but not nearly enough to fill the want of culinary education. There is a "kitchen garden" at the Huron Street school, where cooking classes are held afternoons; there is an excellent cooking school on Michigan avenue and another at the south end of the Lake Front Park. The trouble with these schools is, that domestics can not afford to pay the fees for instruction, while the upper class ladies regard the cooking classes merely as amusement.

Coroner.—The County Coroner has an office in the basement of the County Building, and employs a large number of deputies.

Fatal accidents occur daily, and the coroner and his subordinates are kept busy most of the time.

The position is a lucrative one, the fees mounting up to large proportions. During 1890 there were 1,478 coroner's inquests, and 290 post mortem investigations.

County Clerk's Office.—On the first floor of the County Building. The County Clerk is elected by popular vote and receives a good sized salary and numerous perquisites, making the office both desirable and important. A large force of clerks is employed in this office.

County Officers.—The officers of Cook County are: A county treasurer, a recorder of deeds, a sheriff, a county clerk, and clerks of the county, probate, circuit, superior and criminal courts. There are also numerous minor officers and subofficials, some paid by fees and perquisites, and others directly by the county.

County Treasurer.—The County Treasurer of Cook County collects both city and county taxes. The Treasurer's offices and the various departments connected therewith, employ a clerical force of at least 100, and the expenses of the office amounted to $131,527 during the past year. The Treasurer's office is located on the second floor of the Court-House, and the scene presented there during the month of May, when the taxes are due and paid, is exciting. Tax-payers, aside from having the burden of taxes, are compelled to stand in line for hours before they can reach the counter and contribute their portion of the $16,139,966.55. Those figures represent the special assessments for improvements ($5,686,726.14), and the state, county, and school tax levy of 1890. The County Treasurer, who is elected for a term of two years, collects all of these taxes and disburses them to the city, State and county, each of course receiving the portion it is entitled to under the law.

Court-House and City Hall.—The process of evolution through which the Court-House Building has been carried in Chicago, commencing with "the estray pen" and ending with the present elaborate joint structure belonging to the city and county, forms one of the interesting chapters in Chicago's history. It is also a matter of interesting history that there was a very vigorous "kick" on the part of the County Commissioners who had the "estray pen" built, that the cou-tractor had not complied with the terms of the contract, and he was forced to accept $12 as his compensation instead of $20, which was the original price stipulated.

The real estate upon which the present building stands was acquired by a grant of twenty-four canal lots from the State to Cook County, the proceeds from the sale of which were to be used in the erection of public buildings. Sixteen of the lots were sold and the remaining eight were set aside for a public square and have been utilized ever since as the site of public buildings. This grant was made early in the year 1831, and soon after the act of January 15, 1831, providing for the organization of Cook County. The first Board of Town Trustees, who were elected August 10, 1833, when the then town of Chicago was incorporated under the act of 1831, met Wednesday evening of each week at the house of Mark Beaubien, who was one of their number. In December, 1833, the old log jail was built on the northwest corner of the square and took the place of the old "estray pen", which was thought not to be in keeping with the growing importance of the young city. During the fall of 1835 a one-story and basement brick court-house was erected on the northeast corner of the square opposite the site of the Sherman House. The basement story was occupied by the county officers, and the upper story, which was the court room, was capable of seating 200 persons. After the incorporation as a city, which step was taken March 3, 1837, the new city for several years rented quarters wherever they could find suitable accommodations. One of the " city halls" of those days was what used to be known as the "old saloon," which stood at the southeast corner of Clark and Lake streets. The

name "saloon" was merely a corruption of the French word salon, as there was no liquor sold on these premises. This building was regarded as almost a prodigy of architectural beauty and is often referred to by old settlers as being the largest and most beautiful hall in the West at that time. In this hall took place some of the stirring political discussions of that time. It was there that Stephen A. Douglas made his first speech in Chicago. The first building owned by the city and used for public purposes, was the Market Building, which was built in the center of State Street. It fronted forty feet on Randolph Street and ran north toward Lake Street 178 feet. It was built of brick and stone, was two stories high and was erected at a cost of $11,000. This building was first occupied November 13, 1848. In 1850 the Common Council agreed to unite with the county in the construction of a combined court-house and jail in the center of the public square. This building was completed in 1853 and cost $111,000. In the basement was the jail, the city watch house, jailer's dwelling-rooms and sheriff's office. The most of the city offices and the armory were on the second floor. The common council chamber was on the third floor, opposite the court-room. This building was swept away in the great fire of 1871.

After the fire of 1871 the Mayor took up temporary quarters at the corner of Ann and Washington streets. At a meeting of the council November 11, 1871, the Madison Street police station, northwest corner of Union Street, was designated as the temporary headquarters of the city government. Work was at once commenced upon the construction of the new City Hall on the lot at the southeast corner of Adams and La Salle streets, and by January

1, 1872, the building afterwards known as the Rookery was completed and occupied by the city authorities. There they remained until 1885. This building was only intended as a temporary affair, and in the fall of 1872 the city and county had conjointly advertised for plans for a new city hall and court-house. The work was commenced on the present joint structure in 1877, but owing to many delays it was not ready for occupancy till January, 1885. J. J. Egan was the architect. The two buildings cost in the neighborhood of $4,000,000. The city's share was about $1,600,000, and the county's $2,400,000. The dimensions of the present structure are: Outside length on Clark and La Salle streets, 366 feet; outside width on Washington and Randolph streets, 128 feet, and its height to the cornice is 126 feet. It is the most striking and handsomest structure in the city.

Cragin is a manufacturing village, and is northwest from Chicago only a few miles. A large factory for the manufacture of sleighs, and one for manufacturing tin and sheet-iron ware, are located here.

Cricket.—The English inhabitants of Chicago can enjoy their beloved sport as well as in Old England, as there are half a dozen cricket clubs in Chicago. On pleasant days these clubs engage in their favorite game, usually at Garfield Park and the Wanderers' grounds, and play in a manner worthy of Albion itself. The most prominent cricket clubs of Chicago are, the Chicagos, Pullmans, St. Georges, Wanderers, and Garfields. All these clubs are banded together to form the Chicago Cricket Association, whose annual banquets are great events to true English sportsmen.

Criterion Theatre is on the North Side at the corner of Division and Sedgwick streets. The seating capacity is 1,700, and its furnishing, decorations, and equipment are of the very best. It presents to its patrons legitimate drama, light comedy, and burlesque. C. S. Engle, lessee, Alf Johnson, manager. This house has a large neighborhood patronage.

Cronin Murder.—One of the most notorious and mysterious of all the remarkable events which have made Chicago world-famous. Dr. Patrick Cronin, a bachelor physician who enjoyed a large and profitable practice on the North Side, was decoyed from his office, 540 North Clark Street, on pretense of his services being needed by a sick person, on the evening of May 4, 1889, at 7 o'clock. He was taken to the Carlson cottage, 1872 Ashland Avenue. Here he was brutally assassinated. As he was in the habit of coming and going, and had no immediate relatives to be anxious about him, his absence did not make any particular stir. About a month later his naked body was found in a cess-pool on Evanston Avenue, Lake View, about two miles north of the Carlson cottage. For reasons which seemed plausible, suspicion was directed toward certain members of an oath-bound society, of which the doctor was a prominent and active member, known as the Clan-na-Gael. The testimony was all based on circumstantial evidence, but it was considered strong enough to send P. O'Sullivan, an ice merchant; Daniel Coughlin, a member of the detective police force, and a laborer, Martin Burke, by name, to the penitentiary for life. Much indignation was expressed during the developments of the trial that a political society should thus audaciously attempt to

discipline one of its members, regardless of the laws of the country, no
matter how he might have offended
those with whom he was associated.

Curling Club.—The Scotch residents of Chicago, and many Americans, greatly enjoy the winter sport
of curling, and the Chicago Curling
Club has a very large membership.
Matches are played at Lincoln Park,
where a curling rink has been built.

**Deaconess Institute a n d
Hospital** is a charitable institu-
tion of the Swedish Evangelical
Lutheran Church.

Dead Animals.—During the
year 1890, the Health Department
caused the removal of 9,661 dead
horses, 143 cattle, and 14,458 dogs,
making a total of 24,262 dead
animals. These bodies found their
way into the tanks of the Union
Rendering Company. The expense
to the city for this service was
$13,381.08.

Deaf Mutes.—Contrary to the
general class of speechless unfortu-
nates, the deaf mutes of Chicago are,
as a rule, quite comfortable and able
to care for themselves. There are
several schools for their instruction-
mostly situated on the West Side,
and almost every deaf mute of
scholastic age is in receipt of daily
tuition. As a result, the deaf mutes
are a cheerful and contented class,
and enjoy life so well as even to
marry among themselves.

The principal institution for the
instruction of this class of unfor-
tunates is located at Jacksonville,
215 miles south of Chicago, on the
Chicago & Alton Railroad. Average
number of people on the rolls, about
600. This is a State institution, and
the annual appropriation for maintenance about $120,000. A school
for the deaf and dumb is located at
409 May Street, West Side. It is
conducted by the *religieus* of the
Holy Heart of Mary, and supported
by the Ephpheta Society. The
average number of deaf mutes in the
school is about fifty, and four
experienced teachers are employed.

Decorative Art, Society of.
—Demand always brings an attempt
at supply that will be supplemented
and improved in proportion to the
urgency of the demand. So when
the busy workers of the city were
ready to rest in the homes their labor
had won for them, the no less busy
women strove to make those homes
inviting by all the aids of proportions,
color, and harmony of furnishings.
This brought them to the need of
studying the subject of art decoration. The ladies seized the shortest
route by organizing a Society of
Decorative Art, whose objects, briefly
stated, are to lead artists in any particular line of work; to master completely
the details in that line, and thus
give a commercial value to their
reputations; to assist the unsuccessful
in finding some practical and profitable outlet for their labor; to open
classes in various styles of decorative
work; to found a circulating library
of all published works relating to
subjects bearing either upon decorative art or design, for the benefit of
persons interested who can not have
instruction or the use of museums
or exhibitions in any large city; to
become the connecting medium between importers and manufacturers
and consumers, incidentally receiving
orders from both private parties and
dealers for all articles of household
art, such as decorative china,
cabinet work, carvings, draperies,
embroideries, pottery, and tiles; to
develop also the lost art of needle-
work and to adapt it to the requirements of the present day in the
matters of house furnishing and

decoration. The society has succeeded beyond its most brilliant expectation, and is to-day in a flourishing condition. Its future seems well assured, for the taste of our citizens is rapidly growing along the lines indicated. The time is not far off when Chicago will have not only the strongest and highest office buildings, but the most elegant and tastily furnished homes. The latter results are due to such ladies as Mrs. Potter Palmer, Mrs. D. Wilkinson, Mrs. J. Y. Scammon, and many others. Mrs. Scammon is now president, and the headquarters are at 200 Michigan Avenue.

De La Salle Institute.—A splendid commercial high school, erected through the efforts of the Christian Brothers, at the northeast corner of Wabash Avenue and Thirty-fifth Street. The building has been erected during the past year at a cost of $112,000.

Democratic Clubs.—There are two Democratic Clubs in Chicago whose influence is felt in the directing of political matters, not only in city affairs, but also throughout the State and the nation. It is very largely to their influence that Illinois is counted to-day among the uncertain States in the national contests.

IROQUOIS CLUB.—Is located in the Columbia Theatre Building, at 110 Monroe Street, in the center of the business district. Organization completed October 4, 1881. While it is called the silk-stocking Democracy, it does not neglect the social amenities of life, nor hold itself aloof from the rest of the political camp. Its quarters are very spacious and handsome, and fitted up with all modern comforts of club houses. It is the leading club in the city, and counts

on its roster the names of the most prominent and influential believers in the Jeffersonian creed. Its influence is not only local, but national. When it entertains, nothing is wanting to make the banquet a success throughout. The expression of ex-President Cleveland, which has passed into a popular proverb, "A public office is a public trust," was first uttered at an Iroquois Club banquet. Membership in the neighborhood of 1,000. The annual dues and entrance fee are very reasonable.

WAH NAH TON CLUB.—This is the Tammany Democratic club of this city. It contains within its membership a large proportion of the most active and efficient workers in the party here, not only those who can move promptly and successfully on the opposition, but who can plan campaigns and direct their execution. Their ranks hold congressmen, judges, bankers, newspaper managers, and all are keen, active, sturdy business men. Without doubt, it has all the material necessary to rival, and even surpass in discipline and united, harmonious action, the foremost political club in the world—Tammany. The Republican party has need to look to its laurels.

Dentistry Colleges.—There are three first-class dental colleges in Chicago, where excellent instruction is given in the art of scientific torture. The Chicago College of Dental Surgery is at No. 122 Wabash Avenue; the Northwestern College of Dentistry, at 1203 Wabash Avenue, and the American College of Dental Surgery, at 78 State Street.

Department of Public Works.—Situated on the first floor of the City Hall. This department is in charge of bridges, sewers, streets, and improvements in general, and, while sometimes crippled by lack of funds, is usually efficient and satisfactory.

Department Stores.—During the last decade the facilities of street cars and great numbers of suburban trains have favored the growth of department stores in connection with the retail dry goods and notion stores in the business center, on State Street and Wabash Avenue. Thirteen firms employ about 10,000 persons in the busy season within the walls of thirteen retail establishments, in the proportion of two males to three females, and including a great proportion of boys and girls. The department stores are crowded at all hours of the day, which proves that a large proportion of female housekeepers have an abundance of time to buy their supplies at a great distance from their dwelling places. Clothing, wearing apparel, furniture, jewelry, books, and other goods are sold in immense quantities in a comparatively small territory of the business center, furnishing employment for one-fifth of the total number who work for retail trade in the whole city.

Distances in Chicago.—Chicago is twenty-four miles from north to south, and from five to eleven miles from east to west. When the city streets were laid out, certain thoroughfares were located at exact distances from each other. Thus, from State Street to Halsted Street is one mile; from Halsted Street to Ashland Avenue, one mile; from Ashland Avenue to Western Avenue, one mile, and from Western Avenue to West Fortieth Street the same distance. With her enormous area, and the long journeys from point to point of interest, Chicago may truly be called " A City of Magnificent Distances."

Distances to Other Cities, Tabulated.

CITY.	DISTANCE FROM CHICAGO— MILES.	TIME, H'RS.
Albany	837	30
Atlanta	795	25
Boston	1,039	32
Baltimore	853	27
Buffalo..........	539	18
Cincinnati	306	11
Cleveland.........	356	12
Cairo.............	365	13
Denver..........	1,059	32
Detroit...........	285	7
Dallas	991	29
Evansville........	338	11
Ft. Wayne........	148	5
Galveston.........	1,151	37
Harrisburg	714	21
Indianapolis	183	7
Kansas City......	458	15
Louisville....	323	11
Los Angeles	2,265	100
Minneapolis......	420	13
Milwaukee	85	3
New York........	911	26
New Orleans......	915	28
Omaha	498	20
Philadelphia......	822	24
Pensacola, Fla....	972	31
Portland, Ore....	2,466	74
Portland, Me......	1,155	40
Pittsburg........ .	468	16
Rochester, N. Y..	609	20
San Francisco.....	2,450	83
St. Louis	283	10
St. Paul	409	14
Savannah.........	1,088	36
Syracuse	687	24
Seattle	2,361	69
Salt Lake City....	1,566	50
San Antonio, Tex..	2,347	70
Toledo	243	7
Tacoma, Wash....	2,321	67
Tampa, Fla.......	1,578	77
Trenton	854	29
Utica, N. Y... ...	730	26

DIS—DRA 72

CITY.	DISTANCE FROM CHICAGO— MILES.	TIME HO'RS
Washington.......	811	26
Wheeling, W. Va..	468	13
Wilmington, Del..	886	30
Worcester, Mass...	1,218	36
City of Mexico....	2,600	120

Dog Fanciers.—There is the usual proportion of persons in Chicago, that exists in any large city, who feel more trust and confidence in a dog than in a human being. These, in the ratio of their love and respect for the four-footed friends, desire pure blood and handsome breeds. The bench show of dogs and cats, and other pets, but principally dogs, has become one of the annual attractions of the city, and will be likely to be as long as the old Exposition Building, where it is held, remains on the Lake Front. If that should be demolished "The Dog Fair" will undoubtedly find some other home. It is no uncommon thing to see young dogs of special breeds exposed for sale "on the curb" where the "bulls and bears" of the Board of Trade congregate after trading hours. There are two or three houses who deal exclusively in pets of all kinds, birds, monkeys, rabbits, guinea pigs, fish, squirrels, and anything that pertains to their keeping or training. They fill orders at short notice for any kind of a dog.

Dogs.—There are about 30,000 dogs in Chicago which have received proper licenses at the City Hall. Probably twice as many more canines are never taxed, making a very numerous dog population.

The life of a Chicago dog is not enviable. If unlicensed, death is his portion at the hands of any policeman; if duly numbered and tagged, he must be muzzled whenever he is allowed upon the street. His chief enemy is the dog catcher, who gathers in all unmuzzled dogs without mercy or distinction and takes them to the "dog pound," where, if not redeemed or sold, they are put to death by suffocation.

Many wealthy Chicagoans keep valuable and high-blooded dogs, and the annual Chicago dog show is always a fashionable event.

Douglas Monument.—Located between Cottage Grove Avenue and the lake. Take cars to Thirty-fifth Street. Opposite Woodlawn and Groveland parks, on the grounds of the Chicago University, which, together with the two parks, were donated by Hon. Stephen A. Douglas, whose family mansion occupied the vicinity near the eastern terminus of Douglas Avenue and Woodlawn Park, stands the monument to this distinguished gentleman. The mausoleum containing his remains is of granite, and the shaft towering 104 feet above this is also of granite. Surmounting the shaft is a bronze statue of Mr. Douglas—very life-like. At the corners are four bronze female figures inscribed "Illinois," "History," "Justice," "Eloquence." The marble sarcophagus in the crypt bears on its side the following: "Stephen A. Douglas, born April 23, 1813. Died June 3, 1861. Tell my children to obey the laws and uphold the Constitution."

Drainage Canal.—The Sanitary District of Chicago has been organized under laws passed by the General Assembly of Illinois. A drainage commission was appointed with powers equal to those exercised by the county and municipal governments. These powers embrace the borrowing of an enormous amount of money upon the credit of the people owning property in the district to be affected by the carrying out of the scheme, the condemnation in land, the digging of canals, the construction of dams, dykes, docks, etc., and the general management of the drainage system of the district known as Chicago River to Lockport, Ill., with a capacity to carry not less than 10,000 cubic feet of water per second, for the improvement of low water navigation of the Illinois and Mississippi rivers, as well as to afford sanitary relief for Chicago. The General As-

DOUGLAS MONUMENT.

the Desplaines Water-shed. These laws contemplate a navigable waterway not less than 160 feet wide, and not less than eighteen feet deep across the "Chicago Divide," from Lake Michigan at or near the mouth of the sembly also passed a joint resolution asking for coöperation, on the part of the United States, in the construction of a channel not less than twenty-two feet deep from Lake Michigan to Lake Joliet, and thence fourteen feet deep to La Salle, from which point the Illinois River is to be improved by dredging in another channel in conjunction with a water supply from Lake Michigan. The resolution asks that these works be so designed as to permit future enlargement to a greater capacity, plainly foreshadowing the plan of a navigable waterway to the Gulf of Mexico. The project of a water-way via the Mississippi to the Gulf of Mexico is one of vast commercial importance, and it is hoped that it may be undertaken on such a scale, and designed in such a manner, that it may develop progressively until deep water to the Gulf is achieved. Then will be realized the dream of Gallatin, Clinton, and Morris, of a water-way from the Hudson River, via the lakes and the Mississippi, to the Gulf of Mexico. Such a line necessarily crosses the "Chicago Divide." There is now before Congress a bill for the construction of a ship canal, with a depth of twenty feet, for navigation into Lake Ontario, which would extend deep water 150 miles nearer the Atlantic. We are justified in anticipating that a deep water-way will at some time be extended to the Hudson on the east, and to the Gulf on the south. The advantages of such a communication would be incalculable, and whatever is done should be done in harmony with this great policy. There is, moreover, a question of large local importance involved in a channel of the depth of twenty-two feet, which is nothing less than a harbor for deep-draught vessels of twenty feet, for which lake improvements are now in progress. Should a channel of the proper width be provided, it may be made to serve a harbor purpose, and gradually draw to itself the deeper commerce of the future without infringement of vested rights. The headquarters of the Board of Trustees of the Sanitary District is in the Rialto Building, rear of the Board of Trade, Pacific Avenue. They are nine in number, appointed in conformity with the law. Of course the present great object of the canal is to dispose of Chicago sewage, and to accomplish this end an expenditure of at least $20,000,000 will be required. The work is now being actively pushed along the route chosen by Engineer Worthen. It is as follows: Starting from the west fork of the South Branch of the Chicago River, in Bridgeport, following the Ogden ditch to Ogden dam, where the route crosses the Desplaines River, then following the west bank of the Desplaines River to Joliet. In one or two places, where there is too great a curve in the river, it leaves it for a short distance. Again, it runs in the river at places, but never crosses over, always running on the west bank. It will be several years, however, before the new drainage channel can be made available as a huge sewer.

Dramatic Agencies.—These establishments are kept up by men who act as brokers in making engagements between actors and managers of theatres and theatrical companies, and they are to be found in and about Clark Street. It is more than probable that while they are useful in a business way at times, they still exert a pernicious influence upon the stage from an artistic standpoint. Agents are human and their likes and dislikes too often do injustice both to actor and public. Their charges vary from three to ten per cent. for their various services, and upon the prompt payment of these, and other like requirements of the agents, more than upon their abilities, actors now depend for engagements. The sidewalks adjoining these agencies are filled with idle actors during the summer months. In other words, the place is sort of a theatrical "slave mart."

Drexel Boulevard.—(Formerly Grove Parkway) is the result of the action of a meeting of the property owners along its borders from the railroad track at Forty-first Street to Washington Park, held about the time (1870) the initiative was taken on the park improvements, to take into consideration the proposition of the South Park Commissioners to purchase the right of way for a thoroughfare from Egan Avenue to the entrance of Washington Park at Fifty-first Street Boulevard. The purchase was made, the owners receiving sums made up of prices which averaged $4,000 per acre. It is 200 feet wide from beginning to end, the breadth being divided as follows: Fifteen feet of sidewalk, forty feet of roadway at the sides of the planting place in the center which is ninety feet wide. The Avenue l'Imperatrice, Paris, is the model for Drexel Boulevard. In the building and ornamentation of the two they are exactly similar. The Avenue l'Imperatrice is considered the finest street in the world. Drexel Boulevard is devoted to the exclusive use of pleasure, all traffic over it being forbidden. The ornamentation of each block is dissimilar. Forest, flower gardens, shrubbery, etc., alternate, and the walks are shaped in divers winding courses. The material of the walks is hard blue clay, the drives of gravel on a compact graded surface, the sidewalks of asphalt and stone, and the gutters are formed by concave slabs of slag, an imperishable material. The swell of the planting surface is considerably above the driving grade, giving a prominent and beautiful appearance. Trellis work, rustic seats and bowers, fountains, etc., are features interspersed through the whole length. At the intersection of Drexel Avenue is a magnificent bronze fountain, presented by the Misses. Drexel, of Philadelphia, in memory of their father, after whom the boulevard was named. On each side of the boulevard, throughout its entire length, the property holders have placed, four feet inside of the fence, lines of stately elms. A uniform building line of forty feet is established through the entire length of the boulevard, giving a clear, open space of 280 feet. Within these building lines are to be seen some of the handsomest mansions and prettiest villas of Chicago. At the head of the boulevard, a few steps from the Cottage Grove Avenue cable line, is the "Cottage," from which phaetons start at intervals through the day for a circuit of the south parks. The many attractions of this now famous boulevard attract thousands of sightseers annually.

Drinking Fountains.—A good system of drinking fountains is greatly needed in Chicago. At present there are only a few hydrants, excepting those in the parks. John R. Drake has determined to erect a fine fountain in the open space between the City Hall and the County Building, and his example might be followed by many other rich men.

Drives.—The finest drives of Chicago are upon the boulevards, a list of which is given under that heading. Every facility in the way of horses and vehicles is very easily obtainable.

Dry Goods.—There are over 500 dry goods stores in the city. Of these the most prominent are, Mandel Brothers', James H. Walker's, Gossage's, Carson, Pirie, Scott & Company's, Schlesinger & Mayer's,

Marshall Field's, Siegel, Cooper & Company's, "The Leader," "The Bee Hive," and "The Fair." These great stores, which employ armies of workers, are situated along State Street and Wabash Avenue.

Eden Musee.—Located on Wabash Avenue, near Jackson. Mainly an exhibition of wax works, with an amusement hall attached. The wax figures are remarkable works of the kind, and very true to life.

Elections.—The April and November elections in Chicago are events of great interest, as the two great political parties are about equally divided in the city, and the balance of power alternates frequently. The city election takes place in the spring, and the struggle for mayoralty and aldermanic honors is most enthusiastic. In the fall the county election occurs, and another spasm of political energy dominates the city and county. Formerly, frauds were quite frequent at Chicago elections, but stringent laws have now removed this dishonesty. The Australian ballot system has been recently made the legal voting method, and its results in Chicago will be watched with much interest. The elections of Chicago are under the supervision of a Board of Election Commissioners, whose rooms are on the third floor of the City Hall.

Electric Club.—The Chicago Electric Club is a social organization, with a membership composed almost entirely of men connected with electric occupations. The rooms of the club at 103 Adams Street, are elegantly furnished, and are the headquarters of some of the most cultured and successful business men of the city.

Electric Fountain.—The great electric fountain in Lincoln Park was presented to the Park Commissioners by Mr. Charles T. Yerkes, President of the North and West Side Street Railway Companies. This fountain was made in Paris. When in operation the water assumes all the colors of the rainbow, made so by concealed electric lights. It is an unique attraction to the park, and a delight to all who see its unequaled splendor. Take North Clark Street cable cars.

Electric Lights.—Chicago's experience with electric lights is entirely satisfactory and fully demonstrates that the city need be no longer at the mercy of a remorseless gas trust. These figures tell the story, and should be attentively studied by those who are in the least interested in an improved and superior form of illumination: Nine hundred arc lights are now in operation, and they have displaced 3,621 gas lights, the latter costing $20 each per annum, or a total cost of $72,420.00. The present cost of operating 900 arc lights at $83 each per annum is $74,700.00, or $2,800.00 in excess of the amount paid for the gas they displace. The aggregate volume of light furnished by 3,621 gas lights, at twenty candle-power each, is $72,420, or $1 per candle-power per year; the aggregate volume of light furnished by 900 arc lights of 2,000 candle-power each is 1,800,000 candles, or a trifle over four cents per candle-power per year. The city pays $72,420.00 for 72,420 candle-power of illumination of gas, and $74,700 for 1,800,000 candle-power illumination of electric light; deducting the amount paid for gas from the amount paid for electric light we find the city pays an excess of $2,280.00 for the latter; by deducting the number of candle-power furnished by 3,621 gas lights from the candle-power furnished by 900 arc lights, we find that for this excess of $2,280.00 the city receives 1,727,-580 candle-power of illumination.

The electric lights of the city are now being operated under a disadvantage, owing to the fact that we are lighting only a portion of several districts, and the proportionate cost is necessarily greater than if all of one or more than one district could be entirely lighted, as the land, buildings, stations, engine, and dynamo power and subways must be provided for the entire district and only a portion of them used. The same argument will apply to cables and operating. As an instance, 300 lights can be operated by the help required to operate 108 lights at station No. 8; the only additional cost necessary to be incurred is coal, carbon, and trimming. This will apply in the same proportion to the other districts.

The city has expended since 1887 (when introduced) to January 1, 1891, for electric light construction and maintenance, $556,877.72. There are four power houses located in various parts of the city using engines with a total of 1,925 horse-power, generating electricity sufficient for 3,850 arc lights of 2,000 candle-power each. At this date about 1,000 arc lights, or less than one-third of the capacity of the plant, are used. As rapidly as possible the entire city will be illuminated with the light of the age, and it should be.

Electric Railways.—The only successful electric roads now in operation are through the old suburbs. The Cicero & Proviso Street Railway Company operate a system of electric cars by an overhead wire, and have so far met with great prosperity, the line passing through several beautiful suburbs, and being very popular. Another electric road is in operation in South Chicago, and runs its cars at a speed of twenty miles an hour. Other roads are planned for different parts of the city, and "the model community," Pullman, already has a line in operation which is to be connected with the South Chicago road.

Elevated Railways.—Several elevated railways are almost completed, and more are projected, to be ready for use in 1892.

The Lake Street "L" road is nearly finished, the question of a terminal, and of western branches, being not yet settled. This road will be patterned after those of New York.

Between State Street and Wabash Avenue, on the South Side, a splendid "L" road is being constructed, and will be finished before the opening of the World's Fair. This railway will be one of the finest in the country.

Other roads are projected for Milwaukee Avenue and Randolph Street, the former of which will be operated by electricity

Elevators, Grain.—The grain elevators, now so monumental of Chicago's commerce, had reached, up to 1851, no more imposing ingenuity than that by which a mule was stationed on the roof of a warehouse, by whose traction the lift was effected. In the year named, the first steam elevator was erected. These, however, are to be taken rather in the mechanical sense, as the separate business of storing grain for the trade was of gradual and later development. At present the total capacity of Chicago's twenty-eight huge grain elevators is 28,675,000 bushels. The separate capacity of these elevators is from 500,000 bushels (the smallest) to 2,000,000 (the largest). They are located in close proximity to the river and railroads, enabling vessels and cars to load and unload direct. These huge structures can scarcely be regarded as ornamental, but they serve a most useful purpose—and to that purpose, as much, if not more than anything else, Chicago may attribute her marvelous growth. Some of the larger elevators cost $500,000, and 12,000,-000 feet of lumber was consumed in their construction. They are about 155 feet in height and as many in length. It requires 100 employés to run a grain elevator, and 1,000 horse-power engines, costing $50,000, to drive the ponderous machinery. The "marine leg," a feature of these elevators, is a device ninety feet in length, vertical, consisting of an endless belt in a movable leg, to which belt are attached buckets capable of carrying eighteen pounds each. The elevator is carried on guides, and will lift sixty feet, taking grain from the hold of the largest vessel at the rate of 10,000 bushels an hour; with the "marine leg," vessels holding 50,000 bushels are unloaded in five hours. One of these elevators loaded a propeller with a cargo consisting of 95,000 bushels of corn, in one hour and twenty-five minutes.

Englewood.—A former suburb of Chicago, now within the city limits, and an integral part of the metropolis. Englewood is south of the old limits (Thirty-ninth Street) on the Rock Island and Chicago & Eastern Illinois Railroads.

Episcopal Churches.—The following is a list of the names and locations of those in Chicago:

Bishop of Diocese of Chicago, Rt. Rev. William E. McLaren, D. D., D. C. L.; office, 18 South Peoria Street; residence, 255 Ontario Street.

All Saints', 757 North Clark Street.

All Saints', Ravenswood.

Cathedral SS. Peter and Paul, Washington Boulevard and Peoria Street.

Calvary, Western Avenue and Monroe Street.

Christ, Sixty-fourth Street and Woodlawn Avenue.

Church of Atonement, Edgewater.

Church of Our Saviour, Lincoln and Belden avenues.

Church of St. Clement, State and Twentieth streets.

Church of St. Philip the Evangelist, Archer Avenue and Twenty-fifth Street.

Church of the Ascension, La Salle Avenue and Elm Street.

Church of the Epiphany, Ashland Avenue, corner West Adams Street.

Church of the Good Shepherd, Lawndale Avenue and Twenty-fourth Street.

Church of the Transfiguration, Prairie Avenue and Thirty-ninth Street.

Grace, 1445 Wabash Avenue, near Sixteenth Street.

St. Alban's, State Street, near Thirty-ninth Street.

St. Andrew's, Washington Boulevard and Robey Street.

St. James', Cass Street, corner Huron Street.

St. John's (South Chicago), Commercial Avenue and Ninety-second Street.

St. Peter's, 1532 North Clark Street.

St. Stephen's, Johnson Street, near West Taylor Street.

St. Thomas' (colored), Dearborn Street, near Thirtieth Street.

Trinity, Michigan Avenue and Twenty-sixth Street.

MISSIONS AND CHAPELS.

Advent Mission, West Madison Street, near Albany Avenue.

Chapel of St. Luke's Hospital, 1430 Indiana Avenue.

Douglas Park Mission, Home for Incurables, Ellis Avenue, south of Fifty-fifth Street.

Mission of Nativity, West Indiana Street, near Lincoln Street.

Sisters of St. Mary Chapel, 2407 Dearborn Street.

St. James' Mission, Elm Street.

St. Michael's and All Saints' Mission, 4333 Ellis Avenue.

Trinity Mission, South Halsted and Thirty-first streets.

Episcopal Churches (Reformed).—The following is a list of the names and locations of those in Chicago:

Christ Church, Michigan Avenue and Twenty-fourth Street.

St. Paul's Church, corner Washington Boulevard and Winchester Street.

St. Matthew's Church, Fullerton Avenue, corner Larrabee Street.

Emmanuel Church, corner Twenty-eighth and Hanover streets.

St. John's Church, corner Langley Avenue and Thirty-seventh Street.

Grace Church, Girard, near Milwaukee Avenue.

Trinity Church, Englewood.

Tyng Mission, Archer Avenue, corner Twenty-first Street.

Trinity Church, Maplewood.

Erring Woman's Refuge.— Indiana Avenue and Thirty-first Street, is for the protection of women who desire its benefits and those that are placed there by lawful authority.

Estimates and Apportionments.—Chicago's rapid growth, requiring a constant outlay for improvements, has always kept the expenditures of the city well up to the receipts. The following was the statement of the City Treasurer on the 10th of January, 1891:

Balance in Treasury, January 9th..................$733,791
Received January 10th..... 45,780

Total..................$779,571
Warrants drawn January 10th................... 16,059

Cash on hand and in Bank.. $763,512
Other assets, bonds, accounts, etc., on hand were:
Four per cent. water bonds ordered issued..........$875,280
Amount sold............. 284,780

On hand.................$590,500
Three and one-half per cent. issued to retire city 7s.... $934,000
Sold... 237,200

$696,800
There were also on hand $3,000 of bonds credited to the Police Life and Health Fund and also $32,000 of Jonathan Burr bonds. Bonds on deposit, as guarantee for street paving by the Barber Asphalt Co, amounted to $18,000, and $1,220 was credited to the Harrison and Tree funds for medals. The estimated expenses of the city for 1891, partly on World's Fair account, are put between $15,000,000 and $16,000,000.

Evangelical Association of North American Churches.— The following is a list of the names and locations of those in Chicago.

GERMAN.

First Church, Thirty-fifth Street, corner Dearborn Street.

Second Church, Wisconsin Street, corner Sedgwick Street.

Sheffield Avenue Church, Sheffield Avenue, corner Marianna Street.

St. John's Church, Noble, corner West Huron Street.

Harrison Street Church, West Harrison Street, corner Hoyne Avenue.

Humboldt Park Church, Humboldt Park.

Seventh Church, West Adams, Street, corner Robey Street.

Salem Church, West Twelfth Street, corner Union Street.

Evangelical Lutheran Churches.—The following is a list of the names and locations of those in Chicago:

DANISH.

St. Stephen's Church, Dearborn, corner Thirty-sixth Street.

ENGLISH.

Church of the Holy Trinity, 398 La Salle Street.

Grace Church, Larrabee Street, near Belden Avenue.

Wicker Park Church, North Hoyne Avenue, corner Le Moyne Street.

GERMAN.

Bethlehem Church, Paulina Street, corner McReynolds Street.

Emanuel Church, Brown Street, corner West Taylor Street.

St. Jacob's Church, Garfield Avenue, corner Fremont Street.

St. John's Church, Superior Street, corner Bickerdike Street

St. Mark's Church, Ashland Avenue, corner Augusta Street.

St. Matthew's Church, Hoyne Avenue, between Twentieth and Twenty-first streets.

St. Paul's Church, Superior Street, corner North Franklin Street.

St. Peter's Church, Dearborn Street, corner Thirty-ninth Street.

St. Stephen's Church, corner Wentworth Avenue and Twenty-fifth Street.

Trinity U. A. C. Church, Hanover Street, corner Kossuth Street.

Trinity West Chicago Church, 9, 11, and 13 Snell Street.

Zion Church, West Nineteenth Street, near Halsted Street.

Gnaden Church, South Halsted Street, corner Twenty-seventh Street.

NORWEGIAN.

Bethania Church, West Indiana Street, corner Carpenter Street.

Bethlehem Church, North Centre Avenue, corner West Huron Street.

Evangelical Church, North Franklin Street, corner Erie Street.

Our Saviour's Church, May Street, corner West Erie Street.

St. Paul's Church, North Lincoln Street, corner Park Street.

St. Peter's Church, Hirsch Street, corner Seymour Avenue.

Trinity Church, West Indiana Street, corner Peoria Street.

SWEDISH.

Evangelical Lutheran Mission Church, 280 North Franklin Street.

Gethsemane Church, May Street, corner West Huron Street.

Immanuel Church, Sedgwick Street, corner Hobbie Street.

Salem Church, Bushnell Street, near Archer Avenue.

Tabernacle Mission, corner La Salle and Thirtieth streets.

Evangelical Lutheran Churches (Independent).— The following is a list of the names and locations of those in Chicago:

Church of Peace, North Wood Street, corner Iowa Street.

Evangelical Reformed (First German) Church, 181 Hastings Street.

First Church, Augusta Street, near Samuel Street.

Evangelical United Churches.—The following is a list of the names and locations of those in Chicago:

First German, St. Paul's Church, Ohio Street, southwest corner La Salle Street.

Fifth German, St. John's Church, Cortland Street near Seymour Avenue.

Fourth German, St. Peter's Church, Chicago Avenue, corner Noble Street.

Second German, Zion Church, Union Street, northwest corner West Fourteenth Street.

Sixth German, Bethlehem Church, Diversey Street, corner Halsted Street.

Third German, Salem Church, Twenty-fifth Street near Wentworth Avenue.

Evanston.—This is no longer a town; it has grown to be a charming little city, with water-works, gas, electric-light plants, extensive sewerage system, miles of graded and paved streets, fine churches, palatial residences, a bank, and the grandest campus of educational building in the western country. The Chicago, Evanston & Lake Superior and the Chicago & North-Western railways have each a handsome railroad station within one hundred feet of each other, and trains arrive and depart continually.

Exchanges.—The Exchange, known only by this title, is situated just within the entrance to the Union Stock Yards. In this are the offices of the commission men, who really transact the live stock business of Chicago and the great West that stretches to the Pacific Ocean. They, with the modesty which is so noticeable in Chicago business men, style themselves receiving shippers, but they are really merchants whose traffic in cattle supports whole States. Besides this important massing of similar interests under one roof where buyers and sellers can be in constant touch, we have a Lumbermen's Exchange, where the interests of men engaged in the lumber manufacture and sale are considered at certain hours. There is also a Builders' Exchange, where manufacturers of brick and building stone can come in contact with the great contractors who are covering

Chicago's broad acres with twenty-story buildings. There is also a Coal Exchange, a Grocers' Exchange, etc. None of these are in complete possession of a building, as are the cattle princes, but their places of meeting are amply sufficient for all their needs. It is not necessary to include the Grain & Provision Exchange, which assumes to itself the title of "Chamber of Commerce," nor the lesser "Chicago Stock Board," for they are described elsewhere.

Excursions.—The true Chicagoan is very fond of frequent outings in the surrounding country, or upon the Lake, and excursions of every kind are numerous throughout the summer. Several lake steamers are maintained for excursions to St. Joseph and other lake towns, while the railroads have an enormous business on Saturdays and Sundays.

Eggleston. — If not the most prominent this is certainly the most beautiful suburb of Chicago. It is located in close proximity to Englewood on the line of the Chicago, Rock Island & Pacific Railway, which, in connection with other roads and street car lines, affords rapid transportation to and from the city. All of the modern improvements calculated to adorn a suburban town and make it desirable for a home will be found there. Messrs. Eggleston, Mallette & Brownell, one of Chicago's oldest and most reliable real-estate firms, own this property, and it is due to them to say that their enterprise and exceptional judgment have made the name of Eggleston exceedingly popular. Many of the prominent business men and representative Chicagoans are erecting magnificent homes here. The school facilities are exceptionally good, the churches numerous, and the society first class

6

in every particular. Eggleston has this advantage: It is locat(d on a ridge, which gives it the b st drainage system to be found in Cook County.

Eggleston is prominently located on Moran's Map of Chicago, which will be found within the covers of this book. The broad and beautiful thoroughfares in Eggleston are generally taken advantage of by those who indulge in carriage riding, and who are fortunate enough to h▴ve their homes in this vicinity. Eggleston is but thirly minutes' ride by rail from the very heart of the city, making it very convenient for Chicago business men who prefer suburban homes.

Express Companies.—It would certainly be advisable for the foreign visitors who are to throng our streets, in 1893, to give a little attention to the business methods of those intrinsic factors of our commerce, the great express companies. Their complete and responsible system for the rapid and safe transmission of parcels, goods, orders, or money, either by ordinary methods or by telegraph, or the making of collections and the execution of various commissions, is unknown and uncomprehended in foreign countries.

AMERICAN EXPRESS COMPANY.— The American Express Company is far ahead of all its competitors in the amount of the business it transacts. It employs, in Chicago alone, 120 agencies, 150 wagons, over 400 horses, and nearly 1,200 men in handling its consignments. This army of men and material is simply for local conveyance and does not include the lines of rail and water-way that make up its communication with all parts of the world, and by which it receives, and forwards, and delivers, merchandise, bonds, valuables, and money; undertakes the collection of drafts, notes, dividends, coupons, bills, and other similar paper; issues money orders; will deliver any amount of money by telegraph, or execute any responsible or delicate commission with accuracy and dispatch. This Company's routes extend over 50,000 miles of railway. It has over 6,000 agencies in the United States, Canada, and Europe. Fast express trains are run especially for its use between New York, Boston, and Chicago, at the latter point they connect with mail "fliers" bound for the farther West. These arrangements enable the Company to guarantee faster time, lower prices, and complete responsibility for loss or damage, thus putting it ahead of its competitors as a medium for convenient, expeditious, and satisfactory transportation. The American Express Company will send money to or from any one of its 6,000 agencies as swiftly as the lightning can perform its task. If one desires to telegraph money, they deposit the money at the office where they happen to be, and the Company, by telegraph, directs its agent at the specified destination to deliver the amount, so paid, to the consignee. There is no extra charge for the delivery to the residence or place of business. For this service the American Express Company charge from 5 to 25 per cent. less than is usually charged by telegraph companies, who never offer to deliver the money. There are European offices of the Company at Messrs. Thomas Meadows & Co., 35 Milk Street, London, England; 13 Water Street, Liverpool; 51 Piccadilly, Manchester; 10 Hanover Street, Glasgow; 4 Rue Scribe (under Grand Hotel), Paris; E. Richards, 1 Rue Chilon, Havre; A. Huni, Bordeaux; N. Luchling & Co., Bremen and Hamburg, Germany; Kennedy, Hunter & Co., Antwerp, Brussels, and Charleroi;

Salomans & Stevens, Rotterdam; Alfred Lemon & Co., Florence, Leghorn, and Rome; John White, Genoa, Italy; Fratelli Pardo di Guiseppe, Venice.

In addition to this method of rapid transmission, the American Company issue money orders in any amount from one cent up. These are issued from any agency, and are payable at any one of their 6,000 offices in this country or in Europe. They afford a method of transferring money by mail, excelling the Government's in absolute security. The design of the commission department is to increase the facilities by which the Company's patrons are served, in obtaining goods, and in giving attention to other business matters needing careful and prompt attention, the commissions paid amounting in every case to much less than the cost of personal attention and loss of time. Orders for any description of merchandise can be sent to any agency of the Company. The agents will purchase of the dealers, with discretion born of experience, and the goods will be returned with the utmost promptness. If the amount of the purchase does not exceed $5.00 the Company will take the risk of advancing the amounts, thus saving remitters the expense of stationery, postage, and C. O. D. charges and personal trouble. In purchasing goods from irresponsible or unknown parties, all danger of loss can be avoided by ordering through this Express Company. Orders can also be telegraphed for goods, without an extra charge, beyond the cost of the telegram. Besides ordering and purchasing goods, this department will pay tax bills, gas bills, redeem articles in the hands of the "uncle" of the three golden balls, collect baggage at railway stations or hotels, secure seats at theatres, sleeping-car berths, state-rooms and passage on ocean steamers, performing with intelligent discretion, any legitimate and proper service. It can be inferred that any business commission relating to the World's Columbian Exposition of 1893 can be safely trusted in the hands of the American Express Company's Order and Commission department.

Express Offices, Location of.
—The companies doing an express business in Chicago, are:

The Adams Express Company, 189 Dearborn Street.

The American Express Company, 72 Monroe Street.

Baldwin's European & Havana Express, 187 Dearborn Street.

Baltimore & Ohio Express, 89–91 Washington Street.

Northern Pacific Express Company, 81 Dearborn Street.

Pacific Express Company, 89–91 Washington Street.

United States Express Company, 89–91 Washington Street.

Wells, Fargo & Co.'s Express, 154 and 156 Dearborn Street.

The United States, American, and Adams occupy their own buildings, the last two comparing most favorably with the other magnificent structures of Chicago's business center. The Pacific and the Baltimore & Ohio carry on their business jointly with the United States Company, and occupy the latter's building. The Adams Express Company does the majority of its business in the East, and the Wells-Fargo Company in the West. The Baltimore & Ohio is satisfied with covering the Baltimore & Ohio system of roads. The Northern Pacific works in the same way over the Northern Pacific route, but the American and the United States, as their names indicate, cover the whole country.

Brink's City Express is the

oldest and most reliable company transferring trunks, packages, etc., throughout the city.

PRICES FROM CENTER TO CARD LIMITS.

On packages, 10 lbs. (when delivered at office)...... 10 cts.
(Call and Delivery)....... 20 "
One trunk ... . 25 "
One barrel (not to exceed in size and weight a barrel of flour), each......... 25 "
Sack of potatoes, less 200 lbs., each................... 25 "
One baby cab.........25 to 35 "
One barrel sugar, cement, salt, or sewing machine.. 35 "
Typewriter, 25 cts., and stand 35 "
Barrel or box from freight (200 lbs. or less, not bulky), 35 cts.; jar butter ...... 25 "
One barrel, or sack, with one or two small packages (as starch boxes) ......40 to 50 "
One barrel oil or liquor...... 50 "
One barrel of syrup......... 75 "
Stoves.............50 cts. to $1.50

MERCHANTS' PARCEL DESPATCH. —Makes a specialty of delivering goods, both for the merchants and the express companies, when the destination is beyond the limit of their regular wagon-routes. All these methods of local delivery are supplemented by numbers of smaller concerns, who will check luggage, when taken from the house, to be re-checked at the station to which it is taken.

Eye and Ear Infirmary, The Chicago.—Is located on Groveland Park Avenue. Advice and medicine are furnished free of cost to the poor afflicted with diseases of the eye and ear.

Fairs.—Since the fire of 1871, the great annual fair event has been the exposition held in the building erected for it on the Lake Front. Much interest has been exhibited

from year to year, both in the arrangement of the exhibited articles and the attendance. This has been supplemented, of late years, by a cattle-fair. During the winter season there are always a great many private and charity fairs, of importance only to those most directly interested. But the World's Columbian Exposition in 1893 will be the standard of comparison for all fairs likely to come to Chicago in the future. Not only to Chicago, but it will, undoubtedly, "break the record" for all the world's accomplishments in this line.

Farragut Boat Club owns a beautiful club house, and is one of the most influential in boating circles in this country. Some of the crews and individual scullers from this club have captured honorable prizes in their contests with the pick of other clubs and associations.

Fencing.—The manly and graceful exercise of fencing is not very popular in Chicago, but quite a number of the "400" are patrons of the foil nevertheless. The Chicago Fencing and Boxing Club, so-called, gives its attention almost entirely to the latter sport, and Col. Thomas Monstery is almost the only noted fencing master in the city. The Colonel, although over seventy years of age, is still devoted to the sword, and has given instruction to a great number of young Chicagoans, including many ladies.

Finance Department, Office City Hall, has control of all the fiscal concerns of the corporation. The Comptroller at the head of the Department receives a salary of $5,000 per annum, and occupies a desirable position under the city government from a political standpoint. A Committee of Finance, consisting of eleven aldermen, appointed by the President of Council, look after and investigate the business of this department. The Comptroller, though not a custodian of public money, is supposed to know just where it is, what the city's resources are, how its credit stands, etc. The bonded debt of the city of Chicago on the first day of the year 1891, was $18,545,400. Five millions of this amount was the bonds for the World's Fair; the balance was for municipal, sewerage, river improvement, water, loan, and bonds of the annexed towns. The City Treasurer's report for the fiscal year ending December 31, 1890, showed a balance on hand January 1, 1890, of $1,786,596.49. The receipt, from all sources for the year 1890 was $23,109,979.25. Expenditures for the same period were $24,329,020.42. It will thus be observed that it costs the City of Chicago about $25,000,000 per year to keep up the efficiency of her various departments. The Police Department requires not less than $2,182,199.82; the Fire Department is an item that aggregates the respectable sum of $1,314,857.43; the public schools cost $1,784,506.18; the water fund, $3,022,145.42. The general taxes of 1889 put into the city treasury $6,221,524.66; water fund, $3,40,796.18; special assessments for improving streets, etc., $4,898,714.35; licenses, $3,072,729.08. The above are only a few of the important items in the receipts and expenditures. The city has many other sources of revenue and her opportunities for expenditure are almost innumerable. Notwithstanding this the city's current obligations are met with promptitude, and the heavy sums required for the monthly pay rolls are provided for on the first day of each month. The taxpayers are justly sensitive on the subject of assessment and taxation, especially

when there is a question of increasing the burden upon property owners. The City Council is the authority responsible for the amount of the annual tax levy. The Finance Department is accountable only for the application of the sums appropriated according to the terms of the annual bill, on the vouchers and accounts duly certified by the heads of the different city departments. That the present system of city valuation is obsolete and absurd is manifest by the figures given here, viz.: Valuation of City of Chicago, 1890: The assessor's valuation, as fixed by the Board of Equalization, is as follows: Real estate, $170,553,854; personal, $48,800,514; total, $219,354,368.

Fire Department.—Headquarters, City Hall; Fire Marshal and Chief of Brigade, J. D. Swenie; salary, $5,000. The Fire Department of Chicago has an acknowledged reputation for excellent management and practical efficiency. This arm of the city service now consists of 917 men and officers, 65 steam fire engines, 21 chemical fire engines, 87 hose-carts, 26 hook-and-ladder trucks, 1 water tower, 3 fire boats for river and harbor service, 90 apparatus stations, 390 horses, and an extensive and well equipped repair shop. As an auxiliary to the department there are 1,800 stations, provided with necessary instruments and thousands of miles of wire, by which alarm of fire may be communicated instantaneously to all parts of the city. The Fire Alarm and Electric Department of the city is a bureau of the Fire Department central office, located in the basement of the City Hall. This branch of the service, always important, and conspicuous for its efficiency, is becoming more so as electric science advances. The operation of this department is one of the interesting features of the city. There were 3,733 fire alarms during 1890, an increase of 838 over the previous year. The total value of property involved was $95,147,058; the total loss was $2,047,736; the total insurance was $44,083,330.

The perfect training and discipline exhibited by the men and horses is an interesting sight to strangers. The engine houses within easy access of visitors are located as follows: No. 1, 271 Fifth Avenue; No. 10, 82 Pacific Avenue, near Board of Trade; No. 13, 19 Dearborn Street, near bridge; No. 37, river fire boat, foot of La Salle Street; No. 40, 83 South Franklin Street.

Firemen are retired on half pay after continuous service of twenty years. They also have a benevolent society which cares for disabled members and the widows and orphans of members.

The total valuation of the real estate occupied by the Fire Department is (1891) $334,475. The cost for maintaining the Fire Department for the year 1890 was $1,314,-857.43.

Fire Insurance. — The strong competition between the insurance companies doing business here forces down the rates to a very low point, notwithstanding the efforts of the Board of Underwriters to maintain a standard rate. The least exposed risks in dwellings can be insured for about 25 cents per $100. Rates on business risks vary so widely that not even an approximate average can be made. By a late rule of the Board of Underwriters, all policies must be written by brokers regularly in the business, to whom only commissions are paid. This method does away with much annoyance, and fixes responsibility on known parties, in case of any trouble. It was one of

the hardest lessons taught incidentally by the great fire of 1871, that insurance in companies of poor standing is dear at any price.

Fire Insurance Patrol.— Established by the Underwriters of the city in 1871. The object is the protection of property, merchandise, etc., and the recovery of salvage from burning buildings. There are four Fire Patrol Stations, located as follows :

No. 1—176 Monroe Street.

No. 2—16 Peoria Street, West Side.

No. 3—19 Dearborn Street.

No. 4 — Forty-third Street and Centre Avenue.

There are thirty-six men and officers in the service, commanded by a superintendent. The horses and men are trained to perfection, and the operation of responding to an alarm is an interesting sight. Fast horses and light equipments are employed, and the salvage corps of the patrol service is generally first at a fire, and they save a vast amount of property annually.

Fire of 1871.—It is not our intention to give here a full account of the great conflagration of October 8, 9, 10, 1871, by which the whole central portion of the city, and so much of the residence portion as embraced the homes of nearly 100,000 people, were reduced to ashes, in a more literal sense than had ever before happened on any such scale since the creation of the world and its habitation by man. The story fills a volume itself.

The calamity broke upon the city on the night of the 8th of October. Three or four weeks preceding that date had been very dry, and during the week immediately preceding there had been much dry hot wind from the southwest. On the night of the 8th, which was Sunday, this wind was blowing at a fearful rate. On Saturday night there had been a very disastrous fire in the southwest quarter of the city, burning over several acres of wooden buildings, and figuring in the next morning's journals as the most extensive fire in Chicago since the early part of 1867. This was forgotten, however, in the hundred times more disastrous conflagration which followed. unprecedented, and which the fire department—a brave, but badly officered, organization—was utterly unable to check. The condition of the department was simply that of complete impotence, so impetuous was the gale in its action upon the flames, and so much like a tinder-box had that part of the city become by the drying process of the preceding days. The fire swept onward so rapidly that it overwhelmed and

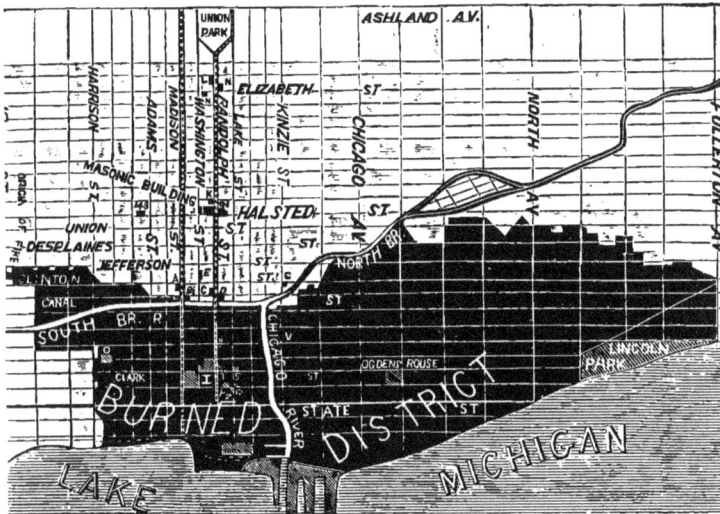

PLAN SHOWING BURNED DISTRICT.

By all accounts the great conflagration had its inception a little after 9 P. M. of the 9th, in a shanty on De Koven Street, one of the many hundreds of such shanties which abounded in that neighborhood. The origin of the calamity is with equal unanimity attributed to the source which has become famous in this connection — the upsetting of a lamp by Mrs. O'Leary's ill-tempered cow. The flames spread with a rapidity quite consumed two of the five steam fire-engines set to oppose its progress, and it spread to right and left so fearfully that it crossed the river simultaneously at two points a quarter of a mile apart, both of which points were reached in less than three hours from the first inception of the fire at a point three-quarters of a mile distant in a straight line. In three hours more it was burning at points nearly three miles apart, and was making sure of everything, combustible or otherwise, that lay between them. By this time the flames had reached the business center of the city—say the quarter bounded by Adams Street, La Salle Street, the main river, and the lake— it had accumulated much more than furnace-like intensity of heat, and the air was so charged with brands and cinders borne along by the hurricane that even the most thorough-built structure offered little resistance to i s progress. Edifices which had been built " fire-proof " went with the rest. The Court House, which stood somewhat isolated upon its square, offered no resistance; its walls crumbled; its precious archives, including every vestige of a record of titles and court proceedings, were licked up without ceremony by the flames; and the great bell in the tower sank down and melted in the ruins, pealing, as it went, its last alarm. The peculiarity of the conflagration was that its combustion seemed to be perfect; there were none of those vast volumes of smoke which we are accustomed to see roll forth from buildings attacked by the flames, there being always much matter comparatively incombustible in every building. In this case everything in the line of the conflagration went as if it had been saturated with coal oil beforehand; the fact being that while the intense heat of the general conflagration had licked up every drop of moisture which the scorching sirocco of the last few days had left, the wind that was blowing at the moment converted the whole territory round about into one vast blast furnace, from which nothing escaped unconsumed.

The fire department was early mustered out for service, and could interpose no obstacle to the remorseless progress of the flames. If their skill and exertion had been never so great, however, it would not have availed long ; for at three o'clock in the morning the house of the engines, which pump from the lake the city's supply of water, caught fire, and the engines were quickly disabled. The reservoirs had been exhausted ; hence, as soon as the pumps ceased to work, the hydrants ceased to yield when eagerly resorted to by hundreds of householders in defense of their homes. The scene attendant upon this deluge of flame will be left to the imagination of the reader ; it can not be described. No pen could convey any adequate idea of the sights, the sounds, the misery, the terror, the sudden consternation, the frantic rushing, the manifold examples of sublime heroism, the still more numerous instances of base cowardice and desperate villainy, which that terrible night and agonizing day succeeding witnessed. The inhabitants, as a rule, were not prone to take alarm, and many who had been gazing for hours upon the scene from a distance, failed to see that their own homes were doomed as well, and to take the measure of self-defense called for by the emergency. This was especially true of the people of the North Division, where the ruin was most complete ; where not only ninety-nine dwellings in every hundred were destroyed, but where also the loss of life and of household goods was the most serious. This was owing chiefly to the cause mentioned, and the rapidity of the fiery stream was not its only dangerous property. It advanced as a skillful general would push his army through an enemy's territory, throwing out separate columns, and pouncing down far forward when and where least expected ; by which means the poor victims found themselves surrounded by flames before dreaming of its near approach. Thanks, however, to the straight, broad, open streets of Chicago, nearly all of them thoroughfares, the loss of life through this means was less than it would have been in almost every other city. The stampede to the west side of the river was at one time so great that a crowd of people, attempting to cross Chicago Avenue bridge, and unable to cross as rapidly as they poured into that thoroughfare from all sides, was overtaken by the fiery demon, and some forty or fifty of them perished in attempting to reach the next bridge to the north. The number of deaths from burning which came to the knowledge of the authorities was about 150, and the most intelligent estimates obtainable, those of the coroner and county physician, place the total number of deaths, during or immediately following the fire, and caused by it, at 300. Estimates of the material losses by the fire differ greatly, according to the basis of reckoning, and the appraisal of values, always arbitrary. A few things are certain: There were 2,100 acres of land burned over, nearly all of which area was thickly covered with buildings; there were nearly 18,000 buildings destroyed, of which about 2,400 were stores and factories, and there were but few short of 100,000 rendered homeless by the calamity. The district burned over is bounded on the south by Taylor Street (to the river) and Harrison Street (from Griswold Street, east), on the west by Jefferson Street to Harrison Street, and thence north by a line working eastwardly to and along the South Branch; thence north by west along up the North Branch and streets which are nearly a prolongation of Desplaines Street; north by an irregular line losing itself on Lincoln Park, near Fullerton Avenue, and east by Lake Michigan. The extreme length of the burnt district is three and three-quarter miles, and its greatest width a little over one mile. The total losses were calculated at $192,000,-000, exclusive of indirect damage, evidences of indebtedness, or such personal effects as were not marketable. The public buildings burned included the Custom House and Post Office; $2,130,000 in money was destroyed. They also included the Court House, with all of its archives, $1,100,000; the Chamber of Commerce, $284,000; the Central Police Court and jail (called the Armory), two other police stations, and seven engine houses. The destruction of sidewalks (121¾ miles) involved a loss of nearly $1,000,000. There were eight bridges burned down, worth $2,000,000. The great Central and Southern depots were burned down, the latter of which has been rebuilt at a cost of about equal to both the former structures. Among the hotels burned down were the Sherman, $360,000 (since rebuilt at $600,000); the Palmer, worth $250,000 (succeeded by the grand Palmer House, not on the same site, worth $1,250,000), and the Tremont, worth $200,000 (since rebuilt at $500,000). Among the theatres was Crosby's Grand Opera House, then the finest in America, which had just been refurnished at a cost of $80,000, which had never been seen in its new garniture by the public. The number of buildings burned down was 30 per cent. of all in the city; their value at least 50 per cent. Of grain, 1,642,000 bushels, or 26 per cent. of the amount in store; of lumber, about the same per cent., namely: 67,500,000 feet, and 2,000,000 laths and shingles; of mercantile stock and properties, the loss reached 80 per cent. of the whole. The total calculable loss of property was $192,000 000, after allowing $4,000,000 for salvage on foundations of buildings; this estimate does not include the shrinkage of real estate values, which was thought to amount to 30 per cent. of the marketable values the day before the fire, or $88,000,000 in all. There was a large loss to the mercantile in-•terests by the interruption of trade consequent upon the destruction of stock and of business facilities, was estimated at $10,000,000, or 8 per cent. net profits on $125,000,000 worth of business. Taking all these facts into consideration, and declining to reckon in the temporary depreciation of real estate as part of the losses endured, we must still place the grand aggregate not very much below $290,000,000, the fact being that there were a great many sources of losses not reckoned in footing up this $290,000,000, one of the most serious of which was the enhanced cost of living and doing business consequent upon the sudden destruction of urban and coöperative facilities, forcing the people back upon more primitive ways and less comfortable belongings, while at the same time enhancing their expenses; also scattering trade and population to the three ends of the city, and thus necessitating a vast amount of cartage, porterage, and messenger service.

To relieve the suffering caused by the fire, the country contributed $4,-200,000 in cash and millions of dollars' worth of provisions. To-day there is no vestige of the terrible ordeal remaining; the burnt district is covered with a class of buildings superior in every respect to those destroyed.

Fires.—Fires in dwelling houses originate more frequently from imperfect flues or foul chimneys, and from carelessly allowing window-curtains to come in contact with gas-jets, than from any other causes. A little care will prevent them. In case of a fire from any cause, dispatch a messenger to the nearest fire-alarm box, on which will be found the location of the key. In case the location of the box is not known, or in any case should a policeman be encountered, he will send the alarm. The time which elapses before the arrival of the firemen should be used to collect portable valuables, and the creation of draughts by opening doors and windows should be avoided. If the fire has not obtained strong headway when discovered, let the water run into the bath-tub and basins, and use all available vessels with which to dash it upon the flames. Never admit strangers until the arrival of the police.

First Baptist Church.—This is one of the oldest church organizations in Chicago, dating back to October 19, 1833, when the Rev. Allen B. Freeman, who was its first pastor, organized it with only fifteen members. The edifice occupied by the congregation of this church to-day, is one of the handsomest pieces of church architecture in the city. Rev. P. S. Henson, D. D., is pastor. The church is located on South Park Avenue, corner Thirty-first Street.

First Methodist Episcopal Church would be a very difficult one to find, if the stranger who desired to attend services started out to look for the usual style of building indicating a church edifice. In 1857 the congregation erected a business block in the very heart of the city, Clark and Washington streets, devoting the ground floors to stores from which •they receive a handsome revenue, and using the upper portion as their church, except a small part devoted to offices, which brings them an additional good revenue.

First Presbyterian Church, with its graceful spire, is another of the striking pieces of church architecture that are to be seen in Chicago. This church was organized in June, 1833, by the Rev. Jeremiah Porter, with twenty-six members. To-day it is one of the most popular and extensive church organizations in the city. The charity work emanating from its members, particularly through its lady members, is felt in many quarters, especially in the Presbyterian Hospital, an institution that all churches of this denomination take great pride in. The First Church is located on Indiana Avenue at Twenty-first Street, and the Rev. John H. Barrows is pastor.

Fishing.—Good angling is almost restricted to the lake, where about the only fish to be caught is the yellow perch. Within easy distance, however, are many rivers abounding in finny prey, and fishing excursions are quite numerous.

Fishing Clubs.—Most of the fishing organizations of Chicago are also shooting clubs. Of those which devote much of their attention to angling, may be mentioned The English Lake Hunting and Fishing Club, headquarters at English Lake, Indiana; Fox Lake Shooting and Fishing Club; Fox River Fish and Game Association; Minneola Fishing Club, headquarters at Fox Lake; and the Union Fishing and Shooting Club, also with headquarters at Fox Lake.

Floating Hospital Association.—Provides lake excursions for sick children and others of the poor.

Flowers.—Street venaers of flowers are to be found located at prominent and frequented spots along State Street, Wabash, Michigan, and other avenues.

In summer, when flowers are plentiful, and consequently low-priced, children with a board full of nosegays and boutonnières infest the street corners, vending their wares for five cents a bunch. In winter, however, the price of boutonniers is increased to ten cents. Florists' establishments are to be found in numbers in the principal South Side business districts. Most of the florists act as middlemen, purchasing their flowers from the growers and arranging them in order. The price of flowers varies very much with the seasons, being as a rule cheaper in June and most expensive at holiday time, when the demand is greatest. Bouquets command an average price from $3 upward, and baskets from $5 upward. Window gardening has been increasing in popularity during the last few years, and the result is a vast improvement in the general appearance of the city. Window boxes full of bright, fresh green, relieved by bits of color, now flourish in front of the principal hotels and restaurants as well as many private houses. The prettiest boxes are those made of tiles set in a frame of dark wood, which may be had at very reasonable price. Frequently plants can be purchased at the Haymarket (which see).

Forest Home Cemetery is located about nine miles west of the City Hall, on Madison Street, on the bank of the Desplaines River. It contains eighty acres, and was once a pleasure resort park. It is beautifully situated and laid out with exceptional taste. This cemetery joins Concordia Cemetery, and the interments in both now number about 15,000. Take train at the Grand Central depot via the Chicago & Northern Pacific Railroad.

Fort Dearborn.—An irregular shaped pyramid of hewn logs, covered with a gray coating of dust and festooned with cobwebs, piled beneath a frame shed in Jackson Park, is all that remains of the oldest and most historic house in Chicago. The rough square timbers, with the marks of the pioneer woodman's ax yet upon them, once made the officers' inches square by the gallant troopers of Company F, Third United States Infantry, Captain Hezekiah Bradley commanding. The stockades—thick, heavy, pointed wooden palings—had been set round about the new fort. The block-house, with its quaint, overhanging upper story and windows that served also for port-holes, was completed and stored with provisions

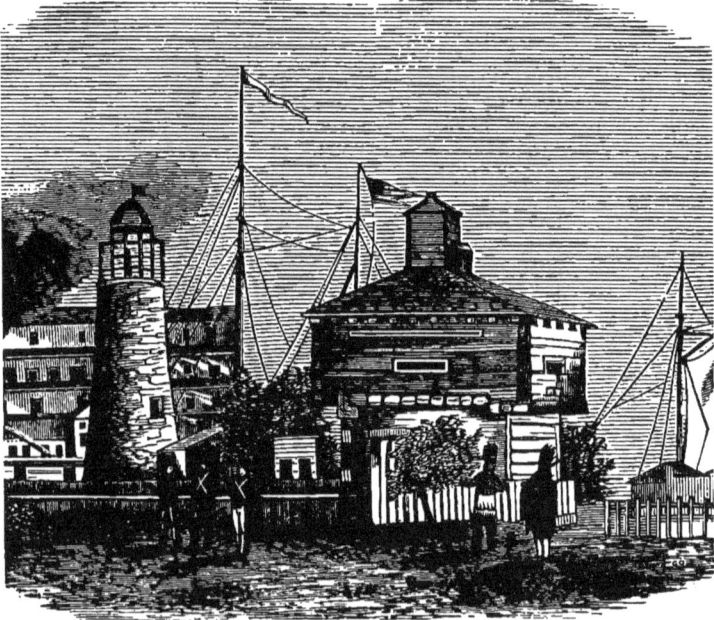

FORT DEARBORN.

quarters of old Fort Dearborn. The trees from which they were hewn grew along the North Shore, where now stand the palatial residences of some of Chicago's wealthiest citizens. The house was built in 1816. The beeches, and poplars, and oaks which composed its walls were chopped down and hewn into beams eight against a siege by the murderous Foxes and Pottawatomies. The barracks and officers' quarters were prepared and fitted up with such furniture as the wild prairie camp afforded. This was the second Fort Dearborn. The first had been burned by the Indians after the awful massacre of 1812, when half the garrison

and all the non-combatants, including women and children, were mur-
dered on the Lake Front at a point
about where Twelfth Street now is.
There, amid the tangled swamp-grass
and the bushes, half buried in the
sand drifts, the bodies, or rather
bones, of the massacred lay till Captain Bradley and his men came
thither in 1816 and gave the remains
decent burial. The fort was the
center of the social life of the settlement in those days, and the officers'
quarters were the focus, so to speak,
of the fort. Many a pleasant evening was passed within the walls
formed by the pile of logs now
awaiting architectural resurrection in
Jackson Park. The guests were
men and women whose names have
become historical in Chicago. Jean
Baptiste Beaubien and his sons and
daughters, John Kinzie and his
family, Jonas Clybourn, Dr. Van
Voorhis, Gordon I. Hubbard, Antoine Dechamps, Antoine Quillette,
and others of Chicago's first families.
Within sight of that fort the Indians
slaughtered many a prisoner, until
the banks of the Chicago reeked
with the settlers' blood. Within the
small rooms formed by these logs
were gathered, May 18, 1831, a
frightened, cowering crowd of
women and children, These had
fled in mortal terror from the outlying settlements to escape the toma-
hawk and scalping-knife of Black
Hawk's murderous band of red-
skins. It was just after the awful
massacre by the savages at Indian
Creek, and a friendly Pottawatomie
gave the settlers of Naperville warn-
ing that the scalping parties were
almost upon them. All fled to Fort
Dearborn, the women and children
in wagons, the men following at
a considerable distance to repel the
savages, should an attack be made.
In this old house, too, Gen. Winfield
Scott had his headquarters during
the fearful month of July, 1831,
when the cholera broke out among
the troops in the fort, destroying
ruthlessly those whom the fortunes
of the Indian warfare spared. From
the narrow windows General Scott
saw the dead borne by the dying to
the temporary graveyard on the lake
shore, at where Madison Street
would now meet the water, were it
extended to the shore. The fort
was occupied by officers, soldiers,
and Indian agents until May, 1837.
After that date it was no longer
used as a military post. In 1857,
the grading of a street necessitated
the removal of the old fort. The
re ic was purchased by Judge Henry
Fuller, who removed it to a place,
then far in the country, but now
known as the corner of Thirty-third
and State streets. Here the building
was re-erected and for a long time
served the purpose of a store. In
1887 the house was purchased by
Ossian Guthrie, Henry E. Weaver,
and Wardell Guthrie, and by them
presented to the South Park Commissioners, upon condition that it be
removed to South Park and preserved. In time it will be re-erected
in the park named.

Fort Sheridan.—The labor
troubles of 1886-7, which resulted in
many disturbances and several riots,
caused many of Chicago's prominent
citizens to petition the general Government to establish a military post
near the city. It was desirable to
have a sufficient force which could
be summoned in case of emergency.
The result of the movement in Chicago was the purchase of 500 acres
of land located on the Milwaukee
division of the Chicago & North-
Western Railway, twenty-five miles
north of the city. This splendid
tract of valuable land was paid for
by voluntary subscriptions and presented to the National Government,

on condition that a permanent military post be established on it. The Government accepted this proposition, a provisional camp was erected within a few weeks, and two companies of the Sixth Infantry were stationed there. Since then a number of permanent buildings, officers' quarters, barracks, guard house, mess house, stables, etc., have been erected. Aside from the companies of regular soldiers, the band of the Fifteenth Regiment is located there. When the new buildings are completed, about 600 men will be permanently stationed at the fort. The work is now progressing very favorably. The immediate proximity of Lake Michigan, as well as the topographical features of the site, make it one of the most desirable forts in America. It will amply repay a visit.

Foundlings' Home is on Wood Street, south of Madison Street, and is a handsome and conveniently arranged structure. It is supported by voluntary contributions, and many of the little ones find permanent homes in respectable families.

Free Circulating Libraries. —The great Public Library is, of course, the main circulating library of Chicago, but there are several smaller institutions, in various parts of the city, which circulate many books, mostly religious. Among these, the most prominent are: The Union Catholic Library; the suburban public libraries at Pullman, Ravenswood, and South Chicago; the Athenæum Library, and the libraries of the Illinois Tract Society, the International Tract and Missionary Society, and the Lincoln Street Methodist Episcopal Free Library.

Free Masonry thrives and flourishes throughout the whole

jurisdiction of the Grand Lodge of the State of Illinois, which meets annually in Chicago during the first week of October. All ranks and degrees of Masonry have their representatives here. For years the different Masonic organizations have found homes wherever they could, but the day is close at hand when their temple shall be the landmark for the city (see Masonic Temple), and all the divisions of the great army camped in this city, will be so represented in the great center as to be easily communicated with. There is no city in the Union where the truths of Masonry have so much influence on the thoughts and actions of men as in Chicago, nor is there a city in the world where there are so many Masons striving to live up to the precepts of brotherhood, as inculcated in both the letter and spirit of the teachings and practices of this most ancient and honorable order. The various divisions of this grand army are eager and earnest workers, whether on the walls or in the vineyards.

Free Methodist Churches.— The following is a list of the names and locations of those in Chicago:
First Church, 49 North Morgan Street.
Second Church, Ogden Avenue, near West Polk Street.
South Side Church, 5251 Dearborn Street.
Milwaukee Avenue Church, Mozart Avenue, near Armitage Avenue.

Free Sons of Israel Cemetery.—Located at Waldheim, ten miles from the City Hall. Take train at the Grand Central Depot, via Chicago & Northern Pacific Railroad. (See *Waldheim Cemetery*.)

Fruit Market.—That Chicago is one of the largest fruit markets in the world is evidenced by the amount of fruit handled in a year by her commission men. For last year the figures were as follows: 1,800 car loads of bananas, 3,000,000 pounds of grapes, 80,000 barrels of cranberries, 300,000 barrels of apples, 200,-000 baskets of peaches, 300,000 cases of strawberries, 2,000 barrels of pears, 700 car loads of California oranges, 400,000 boxes of Florida oranges, 70,000 boxes of Jamaica oranges, 10,000 barrels of Malaga grapes, and about 1,500 cases of California peaches, plums, and pears.

Furniture.—Chicago, beyond doubt or question, is the leading city of the nation in the number and variety of her furniture manufactories, and also in the amount both used here and shipped abroad. A dozen or more large factories, employing a host of workmen, are kept busy in turning out every variety of furniture imaginable, while over five hundred stores, wholesale and retail, dispose of the product. The skill of the Chicago manufacturers is so well recognized that many neighboring cities and towns in the lumber districts send their raw material here to be finished and upholstered, and very probably to be shipped back again for sale. Chicagoans when furnishing a house are satisfied with nothing short of the best and latest styles, and the plain straight-backed chairs, bedsteads, and sofas of our ancestors have given place to a luxuriance in make and finish that would have startled ancient Rome. The furniture business in Chicago is in fact one of the most profitable of all branches of trades.

Garden City.—The popular or metaphorical name for Chicago, doubtless originating from the great number of shade-trees, plants, and flowers, which grow beside the streets in the residence districts.

Garibaldi Legion, meets at Uhlich's Hall.

Gas.—Chicago is still largely dependent upon gas for illumination. But, little by little, the electric lamps, with their brilliant white light, are replacing the old gas lanterns which barely made darkness visible. The gas companies, started in competition with the older ones, finally "pooled their issues" in a syndicate, which comprises among its officers some of the shrewdest men in that line in the city. The syndicate is supposed to furnish a gas which, when burned at the ordinary pressure in a burner consuming five feet an hour, will equal in its light the brilliancy of sixteen sperm candles. But very few among the tens of thousands of consumers know anything about whether the regulation is complied with or not, but they are satisfied that there are many methods of lighting superior to the illuminating quality of Chicago gas. It is furnished at an average price of $1.25 per 1,000 cubic feet. The syndicate calculates that the "World's Columbian Exposition," and the natural growth of the city during that time, will require an expenditure of $2,500,000 for construction and improvements. The companies forming the trust are the North Side Company, the West Side Company, the South Side Company, the Consumers' Company, and the People's Company. The bills for the month, if paid on or before the twelfth of the month, are discounted about 16⅔ per cent. This insures prompt payment, and is cheaper than collectors' wages would be. The offices are furnished with samples of gas-stoves, on the principle of increasing business by promoting consumption of gas.

Geographical Center of Chicago, etc.—The geographical cen-

GEO—GER   96

ter of the present City of Chicago is located at the intersection of Ashland Avenue and Thirty-ninth Street. The distance between North Seventy-first Street, being the northern city limits, and One Hundred and Thirty-ninth Street, being the southern city limits, is twenty-four miles. State Street has the greatest extension north and south, running from North Avenue to the southern city limits, a distance of eighteen miles. Running east and west, Eighty-seventh Street represents the greatest extension of the city limits, with ten and a half miles.

Geology of Chicago and Vicinity.—Chicago is built on a bog, the top of which, consisting of accumulated vegetable matter, rested on a sandy sub-stratum. Beneath this is a wet, blue clay, and underneath this a quicksand; about an average of thirty feet brings us down to oil-bearing limestone, which here and there has been by pressure pushed to the surface. There have been strong indications of both coal and oil at different points in and about the city, but no one has had interest enough to follow up these traces. Before the fire, Dr. Patton's Presbyterian Church stood on Michigan Avenue, near Madison Street. It was built of stone taken from a quarry beyond Western Avenue. It was oil-bearing, and in the summer the oil oozed out of the stone, discolored it, and smelt unto high heaven. In some parts of the city the clay makes good bricks. That taken out of the water and river tunnels is used for that purpose. On the West Side an artesian well raises the water from thirty to forty feet above the surface, showing that its source of supply is located many miles away from the city. The whole formation is of the later series, evidently more or less due to the action of the lake upon its adjacent shores.

It seems possible that sooner or later coal and oil will be added to the marketable products of this versatile city.

German Ladies' Society has for its object a home for old and needy Germans.

German Lutheran Cemetery, located on North Clark Street, southeast corner of Graceland Avenue. Take North Clark Street cable cars. This cemetery is the property of the St. Paul and Emanuel Lutheran churches.

German Methodist Episcopal Churches.—The following list gives the names and locations of those in Chicago:

Ashland Avenue Church, 485 North Ashland Avenue.

Centennial Mission, Lake View.

Center Street Church, Dayton Street, corner Center Street.

Ebenezer Church, Ullman Street, corner Thirty-first Street.

Emanuel Church, West Nineteenth Street, corner Laflin Street.

First German Church, 51 and 53 Clybourn Avenue.

Maxwell Street Church, 308 Maxwell Street.

Maxwell Street Mission, 553 West Thirteenth Street.

Portland Avenue Church, Portland Avenue, corner Twenty-eighth.

Wentworth Avenue Church, Wentworth Avenue, near Thirty-seventh Street.

Western Avenue Church, Fullerton Avenue, corner Western Avenue.

German Opera.—German opera companies have frequently played in Chicago, and met with great success, but previous to the erection of the Schiller Theater German drama had no recognized headquarters in Chicago. The Schiller, however, gives German opera the most magnificent home in America, if not in the world.

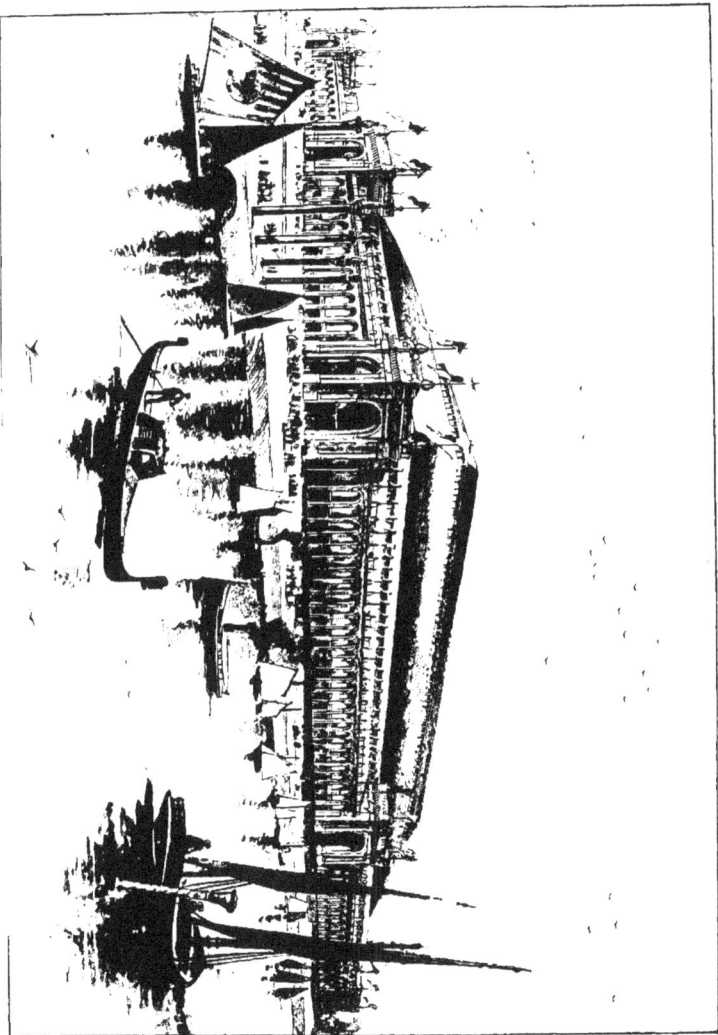

MANUFACTURES AND LIBERAL ARTS BUILDING.

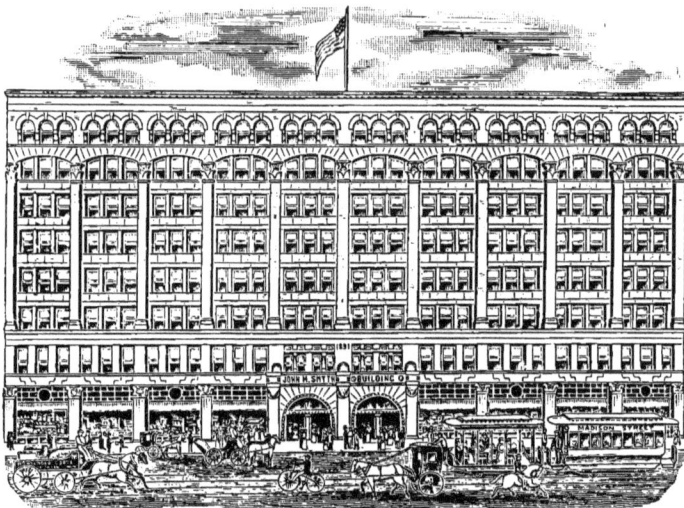

SMYTH'S TOWN MARKET

Is a household word in Chicago and the great scope of country tributary to this city. This Famous Furniture Institution is typical of Chicago in every sense of the word. From the smallest of beginnings it has reached the acme of commercial greatness. It has been completely destroyed by fire. but phœnix like it has risen from the ashes and now stands a monument to pluck and a credit to Chicago.

The above cut faintly outlines in miniature the substantial and ornate blue and buff stone front, with a frontage of 205 feet, depth 180 feet, with 8 stories giving the enormous aggregate of twelve acres of available floor space. It is justly entitled to the honor of being the largest furniture store in the world. The location of this house is on West Madison Street, near the river, running from No. 150 to 166.

It requires over 5,000 electric lights to illuminate this elegant palace, which is at all times completely stocked with bargains in everything that the furniture world can supply.

A visit to this great house is amply repaid by a view of the novelties exhibited if for nothing else.

German Society assists immigrants from the Fatherland in procuring employment and temporary support, and also German residents.

Gettysburg Cyclorama occupies a large circular building at the corner of Wabash Avenue and Panorama Place. This wonderful masterpiece, tne work of the French painter, Phillopoteaux, has been before the public since 1887, and still attracts thousands of visitors. It is a most accurate representation of the deciding battle of the Civil War, and may be ranked as one of the leading points of interest in the city.

Gold and Stock Telegraph.— Instruments of this company, usually termed "tickers," will be found in every broker's office, and in the principal hotels and restaurants. They print the reports of the New York Stock Exchange transactions during the day, automatically, upon a tape. Reports of the arrival of ocean steamers, and the result of sporting events of general interest, are also frequently sent over the wires of this line.

G r a c e l a n d Cemetery.—In addition to the natural beauties of the grounds of this cemetery there has been added a wealth of landscape gardening that displays the work of a master mind in that art. The three lakes in the broad expanse of exquisite scenery, are works of engineering skill; they are fed by living springs, besides which there is a mammoth system of water-works that will furnish a full supply throughout the entire 125 acres comprised in the grounds. The approach to Graceland is either by the Lake Shore Drive through Lincoln Park and North Clark Street, by the Clark Street cable, or State Street horse cars, or over the Chicago & Evanston Railroad, whose hand-some station (Swiss cottage architecture) is at the eastern approach to the grounds. Distance, five miles from City Hall. Pages could be written portraying the marvelous beauties of this noted place, and still other pages referring to the people, prominent in their time, who rest here, and of the rare pieces of monumental marble in the grounds, yet it is enough to say that Graceland is known to every Chicagoan, and to every visitor who appreciates the grand in nature and beautiful in art. Office, 115 Monroe Street.

Grand Boulevard.—This beautiful thoroughfare extends from Thirty-fifth Street south to Fifty-first Street Boulevard, and lies two blocks east of Prairie Avenue. It runs parallel with Drexel Boulevard, being three blocks west of it. The first improvement on the Grand Boulevard commenced at the north boundary in 1870. Kankakee Avenue was widened by the addition of 132 feet, taken from the east front in accordance with the Park Improvement Act. At Grand Boulevard it is 200 feet wide, including a pleasure drive through the center, sixty feet wide, and traffic roadways on each side. The pleasure drive can only be used for recreation. The improvement of the roadways is in three materials, viz.: asphalt, stone screenings, and Joliet gravel. The boulevard is completed as far south as Fifty-first Street, where it enters Washington Park. It is bordered on each side by large elm trees, and is the resort of hundreds each day. The expectations of the Commissioner have been much more than realized in the eagerness with which the carriage-riding public seeks the boulevards for recreation. This is especially true of Grand Boulevard, which is often crowded for a space of two miles with carriages averaging three abreast.

Grand Central Depot, Harrison Street and Fifth Avenue, was begun in October, 1888, and the building was opened for business December 8, 1890. It is one of the finest buildings of the kind in the world. It covers 3½ acres of ground, having a frontage of 680 feet on Fifth Avenue and 226 feet on Harrison Street. Part of the structure is seven stories high, and part four. The tower rises 212½ feet above the sidewalk, and contains the second largest bell in the country. Its hammer alone weighs 706 pounds. The dial of the tower clock is 13 feet 6 inches in diameter. The main waiting room is 71 feet wide, 207 feet long, and the ceiling, which is 25 feet from the floor, is supported by two rows of massive marble columns. Floors and wainscoting are of Champlain and Tennessee marbles. The station is provided with ladies' parlors, restaurants, bath-rooms, and all modern conveniences. The train shed is a great arch of corrugated iron and glass, 140 feet wide and 560 feet long. A carriage court, 146 feet wide and 117 feet deep, is one of the features of the depot. Three great stone arches, each having a span of thirty-seven feet, and a height of twenty-one feet, form the entrance to it. The track platforms are so arranged that incoming and outgoing passengers are kept apart from each other. The building is the property of the Chicago & Northern Railroad Company, and is used conjointly by that road and the Wisconsin Central, and the Chicago, St. Paul & Kansas City road. It is also the depot of the Northern Pacific Railroad. (See *Railroads*.) It cost in round numbers $1,000,000.

Grand Opera House.— Situated on Clark Street, between Randolph and Washington. This house,

one of the best and most prominent theatres in Chicago, has maintained its present high reputation for many years. Previous to 1880 it was, as now, under the management of the Hamlin Brothers, was known as "Hamlin's Theatre," and was conducted on a scale of popular prices. In September, 1880, the theatre was given the name of "Grand Opera House," and was dedicated by Emma Abbott, in her favorite drama, "The Child of the State."

The Grand, under its able managers, has become a recognized home both for the legitimate drama and for refined comedy. It is a strictly first-class house in every respect, equipped in the most modern style, and with all appointments and furnishings of the most rich and luxurious variety. The seating capacity is 1,820, and is generally taxed to the utmost. The proprietors, Messrs. Hamlin, rank among Chicago's most prominent business men.

Grant Monument.—The new colossal equestrian Grant Monument is in its place overlooking Lake Michigan from Lincoln Park. It will be visible for many miles on the water on clear days. It appears at the very entrance to the park along the shore boulevard to land folk approaching from the south. Foliage all but hides it from the interior of the park. From the north it does not appear until the observer is within a thousand feet. On clear mornings it is brilliant between the rising sun and the deep blue of the sky, against which it is so conspicuously silhouetted. The masonry foundation, which has been in place for some time, and which is more appropriate for a viaduct than for statuary, serves at least to give it eminence and security. It is the work of Rebisso, of Cincinnati; a gift to the park trustees by a number of citizens of

Chicago. This expensive work is open to serious criticism. The group of horse and man is stolid; it is a gigantic product of mechanics; it is a foundry marvel; it will attract attention; it will arouse curiosity; it would be indeed a pleasure were it possible to add that it will insure admiration and inspire delight. Its virtues and merits are alike set upon a hill; neither can be

Hack Fares.—Persons wishing to escape either imposition by, or a wrangle with, the driver at the end of a journey, will do well to have a distinct understanding with the latter, before entering the hack, about the amount to be paid, as the Chicago hack-driver is never content to accept the legal fare until convinced that he will get no more. If this precaution is not taken the next best thing to do

GRAND PACIFIC HOTEL, CLARK AND JACKSON STREETS.

concealed. One virtue it possesses. The rider sits squarely and with ease, and there is life in the modeling of the attitude above the saddle up to the head. That is the most that can be said of it. It might as well be any other cavalryman as Grant. The modeling in most details is crude and unscientific, and, in his efforts to create a Colossus, the modeler has failed of truth to nature.

is to consult the table of legal fares on page 100, a copy of which should be posted in the hack, together with the number of the license and the owner's name and address. Having done this, and figured out the sum which the driver is entitled to, tender it to him, and if he declines to take it, refuse to pay him any more, but call a policeman, who will effect a legal settlement. Carriages and cabs are found at the various railway depots on the arrival of trains, and at the principal hotels. Before your train reaches the city you will be approached by a number of uniformed agents, who will, if you desire it, take up your railroad baggage checks, giving you a receipt for the same, and undertake to deliver your trunk to any hotel or any part of the city within the old limits for 50 cents. Each additional trunk 25 cents. For 50 cents additional he will give you a ticket which will entitle you to transfer by omnibus to any other railroad depot, or to any hotel in the center of the city. There are several reputable transfer companies in Chicago, whose agents may be trusted fully.

Hack and Cab Rates.—The rates are established by city ordinance, and are as follows: For conveying one or two persons from one railroad depot to another railroad depot, $1. For conveying one or two passengers, not exceeding one mile, $1; for conveying one or two passengers any distance over one mile and less than two miles, $1.50. For each additional two passengers of the same party or family, 50 cents. For conveying one or two passengers any distance exceeding two miles, $2. For each additional passenger of the same party or family, 50 cents. For conveying children between five and fourteen years of age, half the above price may be charged for like distance, but for children under five years of age no charge shall be made providing that the distance from any railroad depot, steamboat landing, or hotel, to any other railroad depot, steamboat landing, or hotel shall, in all cases, be estimated as not exceeding one mile. For the use per day of any hackney coach or other vehicle, drawn by two horses, or other animals, with one or more pas-

sengers, $8. For the use of any such carriage or vehicle by the hour, with one or more passengers, with the privilege of going from place to place and stopping as often as may be required, as follows: For the first hour, $2; for each additional hour, or part of any hour, $1. Every passenger shall be allowed to have conveyed upon each vehicle, without charge, his ordinary traveling baggage, not exceeding, in any case, one trunk and twenty-five pounds of other baggage. For every additional package, where the whole weight of baggage is over 100 pounds, if conveyed to any place within the old city limits, the owner or driver shall be permitted to charge 15 cents.

HANSOM CABS, and other one-horse vehicles, are regulated by ordinance, as follows: One mile, or fraction thereof, for each passenger, for the first mile, 25 cents. One mile, or fraction thereof, for any distance after first mile, for one or more passengers, 25 cents. For the first hour, 75 cents. For each quarter hour additional after first hour, 20 cents. For service outside of city limits and in the parks, for the first hour, $1; for each quarter-hour additional after the first hour, 25 cents. The provisions regarding amount of baggage allowed free and rates of charge for excess, is the same as in the hack ordinance. When continuous stop of one-half hour or more is made, the charge per hour will be at the rate of 70 cents. When service is desired by the hour it must be so stated at the time of engaging the cab, otherwise the distance rate will be charged. Hour engagements, when the cab is discharged at a distance of over half a mile from the stand, the time necessary to return to the stand will be charged for. No time engagements will be made for less than the price for one hour.

Hahnemann Hospital, 2813 Cottage Grove Avenue, is the clinical annex to the Hahnemann Medical College.

Hahnemann Hospital and Dispensary, is at the college, 2813 Cottage Grove Avenue.

Halls.—Chicago is amply supplied in all parts of the city with commodious halls admirably adapted to the use to which they are put. The following is a complete list:

Auditorium, Michigan Avenue, Congress Street, and Wabash Avenue.

Accordia Hall, 112 and 114 Randolph Street.

Apollo Hall, 2726 to 2730 State Street.

Apollo Hall, fifth floor, 69 State Street.

Apollo Hall, Blue Island Avenue, corner West Twelfth Street.

Arbeiter Halle, 368 West Twelfth Street.

Arbeiter Halle, Sedgwick Street, corner Blackhawk Street.

Arlington Hall, 3032 Indiana Ave.

Atfield Hall, 465 State Street.

Athenæum Hall, 26 Van Buren St.

Aurora Turner Hall, West Huron Street, corner Milwaukee Avenue.

Battery D Armory, north of Exposition Building.

Benz's Hall, 787 West Lake Street.

Board of Trade, head of La Salle Street.

Bohemian Turner Hall, 74 and 76 West Taylor Street.

Bowman's Hall, 120 Chicago Avenue.

Brand's Hall, 160 to 170 North Clark Street.

Carpenters' Hall, 221 West Madison Street.

Castle's Hall, 615 to 625 West Lake Street.

Central Hall, 2139 Wabash Avenue.

Central Music Hall, State Street, southeast corner Randolph Street.

Chicago Opera House, Clark Street, southwest corner Washington Street.

City Hall, Washington Street, corner La Salle Street.

Columbia Theatre, 104 to 110 Monroe Street.

Concordia Hall, 235 and 237 Milwaukee Avenue.

Corinthian Hall, 187 Kinzie Street.

Covenant Hall, 86 La Salle Street.

Criterion Theatre, 274 Sedgwick Street.

Dearborn Hall, 40 Dearborn Street.

De Wald's Hall, 334 North Avenue.

Dooley's Hall, West Twenty-first Street, corner Paulina Street.

Douglas Hall, South Park Avenue, southeast corner Twenty-seventh Street.

Eisfeldt's Hall, 690 Clybourn Avenue.

Excelsior Hall, 13 South Halsted Street.

Excelsior Hall, 107 Clark Street.

Exposition Building, Michigan Avenue, foot of Adams Street.

Farwell Hall, 148 Madison Street.

Finucane's Hall, 2901 Archer Avenue.

First Cavalry Armory, north of Exposition Building.

Fitzgerald's Hall, South Halsted Street, corner West Adams Street.

Folz's Hall, 267 and 269 North Avenue.

Franchere's Hall, 188 Blue Island Avenue.

Freiberg's Music Hall, 180 Twenty-second Street.

Garfield Hall, Lincoln Avenue, corner Garfield Avenue.

Germania Hall, 62 North Clark Street.

Grand Army Hall, 210 Dearborn Street.

Grand Opera House, 87 Clark Street,

Greenebaum Hall, 72 to 82 Fifth Avenue.

Horan's Halls, 255 South Halsted Street.

Healey Hall, 2728 Archer Avenue.

Kastner's Hall, 3001 Archer Avenue.

Kawalinski Hall, 709 Milwaukee Avenue.

Klare's Hall, 72 North Clark Street.

CENTRAL MUSIC HALL, STATE AND RANDOLPH STREETS.

Hoefer's Hall, 227 North Avenue.

Hoeber's Hall, 220 to 224 West Twelfth Street.

Jefferson Hall, 48 and 50 Throop Street.

Landmark Hall, Cottage Grove Avenue, corner Thirty-seventh Street.

Lumber Exchange, 8 Water Street, northwest corner Franklin Street.

Lumberman's Exchange, 238 South Water Street.

Lyceum Theatre, 54 South Desplaines Street.

Madison Street Theatre, 83 Madison Street.

Martine's Hall, 55 South Ada Street, and Twenty-second Street, northwest corner Indiana Avenue.

Maskel Hall, 173 South Desplaines Street.

McVicker's Theatre, 78 to 84 Madison Street.

Meridian Hall, 97 and 99 West Randolph Street.

Methodist Church Block Auditorium and Hall, Clark Street, southeast corner Washington Street.

Mueller's Hall, 356 to 364 North Avenue.

National Hall, Centre Avenue, corner West Eighteenth Street.

Oakley Hall, West Polk Street, corner Oakley Avenue.

O'Callaghan's Hall, 628 and 630 West Indiana Street.

Odd Fellows' Hall, 406 and 408 Milwaukee Avenue.

Olympic Theatre, 49 Clark Street.

O'Neill Hall, 679 and 681 West Lake Street.

Open Board of Trade, Pacific Avenue, near Van Buren Street.

Oriental Hall, 122 La Salle Street.

Orpheus Hall, 239 and 241 Lake Street.

Owsley's Hall, 785 to 789 West Madison Street.

Phelan's Hall, 541 West Indiana Street.

Pleiades Hall, 220 South Halsted Street.

Rust's Hall, 368 West Twelfth Street, corner Waller Street.

St. George's Hall, 182 Madison Street.

St. Peter's Hall, 328 and 330 State Street.

Sack's Hall, West Twentieth Street, northwest corner Brown Street.

Schlotthauer's Hall, 328 Sedgwick Street.

Schnaitmann's Hall, 634 Larrabee Street.

Standard Hall, Michigan Avenue, southwest corner Thirteenth Street.

Turner Hall, 259 North Clark Street.

Turner Hall, 253 West Twelfth Street.

Union Hall, 181 Clark Street.

Union Hall, 3607 to 3611 South Halsted Street.

Union Park Hall, 517 West Madison Street.

Van Buren Hall, West Madison Street, corner California Avenue.

Weber Music Hall, 241 Wabash Avenue.

Walther's Hall, 3932 State Street.

Weiner's Hall, 3001 South Halsted Street.

Westphal's Hall, 691 and 693 South Halsted Street.

Wolff's Hall, 432 Milwaukee Avenue.

Workingmen's Halls, 368 West Twelfth Street; 54 West Lake Street, and 192 Washington Street.

Hand-Ball.—The game of hand-ball, as a winter diversion, is becoming extremely popular in the city, especially among base-ball players, who find it an unequaled exercise to keep the muscles in good condition. McGurn's Court, on the North Side, and Kennedy's, on the South Side, are the best hand-ball courts in the city.

Harbor.—The Government harbor, when completed, will include a sheltered area sixteen feet in depth, covering 270 acres, with communicating slips along the lake front covering 185 acres, making a total of 455 acres; this is in addition to the river, with which the outer harbor communicates. There is also an exterior breakwater one-third of a mile north of the end of the North Pier, so situated as to protect vessels entering the mouth of the river. The length of this outer breakwater will be 5,436 feet, of which 3,136 feet have been completed. The North Pier, measuring from the outer end of the Michigan Street Slip, is 1,600 feet long and extends 600 feet beyond the easterly breakwater, which latter, beginning at the outer end of the South Pier, extends directly south 4,060 feet, and is a distance of 3,300 feet from the present shore line south of Monroe Street. A channel 800 feet wide intervenes between this and the north end of the southerly breakwater. This latter breakwater continues for a short distance due south, then turns at an angle of 30° and extends in a southwesterly direction to within 1,550 feet of the present shore line, and 550 feet from the dock line. This breakwater is 3,950 feet in length. There is a lighthouse on the shore end, and a beacon light on the end of the easterly breakwater. The Life Saving Station is at the lake end of the northern-most railroad wharf, directly adjoining the South Pier. Boats run from the lake shore, opposite Van Buren Street, to these breakwaters during the summer months.

At present this is only a harbor in name so far as the shipping is concerned. Nearly every vessel that enters this port seeks the piers along the various branches of the river. These river branches have their ramification through the city, and in consequence the shipping is strung out for many miles, presenting an insignificant appearance, but in the aggregate it is greater than that of any port in America. The river is cramped and totally inadequate for the vast commerce that threads its way through the murky, filthy channel. The proper place for the shipping interests is within the harbor, and sooner or later it must come to this. When this revolution is effected, Chicago will present a harbor scene that can scarcely be rivaled in any part of the world. The irritating nuisance of swinging bridges would be abated and, while it would make the lake front portion of the city undèsirable for elegant hotels and aristocratic residences, the property would be enhanced in value for purposes of shipping and commerce. This one great mistake of using the insignificant river instead of the grand lake front for shipping purposes, must be rectified, or Chicago will suffer from a condition that is utterly ridiculous and constitutes the greatest nuisance possible for an enlightened people to tolerate.

The Haymarket Theatre— This modern temple of the drama is situated on the north side of West Madison Street, just east of the intersection of Halsted Street. It was built by a stock company in '87 for Mr. William J. Davis, its present lessee and proprietor. It is the largest and most comfortably arranged theatre in the city, and has greater exit space than any other. Its dimensions on the ground are 93 by 120, and this great width gives it the very best audience room possible for géneral theatrical purposes. It has a stage fifty feet deep, ninety feet wide and seventy-two feet high, and the best furnished and most comfortable dressing rooms of any theatre in Chicago, if not in the United States. Its audience room is divided into orchestra, orchestra circle, dress circle, balcony circle, family circle and boys' gallery, having one more tier than any other theatre in the city. Its prices are arranged on what is known as the popular scale and are scheduled from 15 cents in the boys' gallery to $1.50 in the Turkish chairs that are found in the orchestra proper. It has eight very large private boxes on the orchestra floor and six on the balcony floor, and this double capacity of sitting-room accommodates 2,456 persons. With the available standing room the Haymarket easily accommodates upward of 3,000 people, and on occasions when the theatre is crowded, the sight is something worth traveling many miles to see. But it is not alone in the admirable arrangement that it excels. Mr. Davis has presented, since the opening of the theatre, a round of the most popular attractions of the age. It has been his aim to present to his patrons every style of legitimate amusement, ranging all the way from vaudeville to grand opera, and what is most remarkable in connection with such a diversified bill of amusement, he has never changed the prices which he established on the original opening of the theatre. Another satisfactory feature of the Haymarket is its magnificent foyer and staircase, both of which are situated in the building in front of the theatre proper. The foyer is magnificently furnished, its marble floors being covered with heavy Oriental rugs and its walls decorated with photographs of the leading theatrical lights of the ·age. It is forty feet square and is surmounted by another foyer off the balcony, of the same dimensions, to which the grand staircase mentioned above leads. The vestibules leading from the street to this foyer are twenty-four feet wide, and are finished in marble with marble panels and handsomely frescoed ceilings. The color treatment of the Haymarket Theatre is unique and original. Commencing with old Indian red in the carpets, the same treatment is carried into the walls and ceilings. The ceilings are dotted with electric lights that are ingeniously worked into the design of decoration. The only relief to this color is the light blue silk plush curtains of the boxes, and the copper bronze that is used for the high lights in the decoration and around the columns which support the balcony and family circle. Mr. Will Davis is the lessee and proprietor. Mr. George A. Fair the business manager, and Mr. Sam W. Pickering the treasurer of the theatre. All Madison Street cable cars pass its doors.

Haymarket Massacre.—West Randolph Street passes directly through the former site of a West Side market now forming the celebrated Haymarket Square. At the intersection of Desplaines with Randolph Street stands a bronze figure of a policeman in full uniform, with the right hand upraised. On the polished granite pedestal is carved this legend: "In the name of the people of Illinois, I command peace." The grateful citizens of Chicago erected this monument in memory of the brave officers who, defending the law, sacrificed life and health, and whose cowardly assassination sounded the death-knell of anarchy in this city and country. The tragedy did not take place in the square itself, but outside of the northeast corner, where the anarchist speakers addressed the crowd from a wagon standing near Crane Bros.' steps, on the night of May 4, 1886. The city authorities, fearing the effect of the inflammatory speeches, and the unreasonable denunciations of those in authority, ordered six companies of policemen from the Desplaines Street police station to disperse the mob. The police came on at quick-step, in close order, by companies. When close to the wagon, they halted, and the commanding officer "read the riot act," in the now memorable words upon the monument. Hardly was the utterance finished when, in defiant answer, the dynamite bomb, hurtling through the air, fell between the second and third companies of policemen, killing, or wounding fatally, seven policemen, besides seriously injuring many others. The sneaking thrower showed his cruel cowardice by endangering the women in the crowd, as well as his own friends. It is not known how many of the mob the bomb slew, for, following the customs of the savages, whose bloodthirstiness they imitated, they carried away their dead and wounded, quietly burying all as soon as they were fit, lest evidence accumulate against themselves. The ring-leaders, Fielden, Spies, Engel, Lingg, Neebe, Schwab, and Fischer were arrested. The *Arbeiter Zeitung* office, on Fifth Avenue, was searched, and proved to be an arsenal of dynamite, arms, bombs, and infernal machines. Bombs were discovered in lumberyards, under sidewalks, and in the homes of anarchists. Parsons, like the coward he was, got away, and then tried to bulldoze the people of Illinois into an acquittal by a sensational surrender. These "apostles of unrest," and refugees from the laws of their native lands, were given ample opportunity to prove any extenuating circumstances. They could offer nothing but a demon-led desire for blood, and an insane craving for notoriety. The sentence voiced the sentiment of the whole American people, who really were the jury in this *cause celebre.* Nothing stayed the hand of justice, nor the coming of the 11th day of November, 1887, appointed for execution. The "tiger anarchist," Lingg, blew his head off with dynamite. Parsons, Spies, Engel, and Fischer died on the gallows. Fielden,

Schwab, and Neebe went to the penitentiary, the first two for life. The executed defile Waldheim Cemetery, where those who seek chaos, hating peace and harmony, make pilgrimages to air their obstinacy.

Health Department. — Headquarters, basement of City Hall.

Heath Club is composed almost entirely of Scotchmen, who meet for literary and social enjoyment at 153 Clark Street.

Hebrew Benevolent Society Cemetery, located a short distance south of Graceland Cemetery (which see). It may be reached in the same manner.

Hegewisch.—This is a manufacturing village of 3,000 inhabitants, situated in the forks of Calumet River, which offers the very best advantages for the location of other factories. The river furnishes abundance of water sufficiently deep to float the largest lake vessels.

Hermosa.—This neat suburb is just one mile beyond Humboldt Park, on the Chicago, Milwaukee & St. Paul Railway. It has rapidly filled up with residences and manufactories. It is within the city limits.

Heterodox Congregations.— If there is one thing more than another upon which Chicago people pride themselves, it is their liberty to think, untrammeled by all the lines of old, musty thought, and especially if crystallized into creeds. This feeling has led to the separation of two broad-minded clergymen from the sects to which they belonged and the establishment of independent congregations, who have hitherto well maintained themselves in the relations of pastor and people.

PROFESSOR SWING was, after due trial, adjudged a heretic by the Presbyterian Church authorities, and his relations therewith sundered. His friends, comprising nearly all his congregation, and many outsiders, at once organized and rented Central Music Hall, where for years he has preached Sundays to an ever-increasing membership of the Central Church, who believe in the broad philanthropy of universal brotherhood, unlimited by credal bounds.

REV. H. W. THOMAS occupies the same position toward the Methodist Episcopal Church as is held by Prof. Swing to the Presbyterian Church. He preaches every Sunday to the People's Church at the Chicago Opera House. Rev. Dr. Thomas is a magnetic speaker, of wonderful power, and also a thinker of advanced and liberal thought. He is beloved by all his people, and, with Professor Swing, marks a new era in the church organizations of the world.

High Schools.—The largest of the Chicago high schools is the West Division at the corner of Ogden Avenue and Congress Street. This school is attended by 1,200 pupils. Next in size is the South Division, State and Twenty-sixth streets, with 600 pupils; third, the North Division, Wells and Wendell streets, attended by 500 students. The other high schools of the city are Northwest Division, English High and Manual Training School, and the formerly suburban high schools at Lake View, Hyde Park, Englewood, South Chicago, and Lake.

Historical Society, The Chicago, located corner of Dearborn Avenue and Ontario Street. This most important society was organized April 24, 1856. It was in a flourishing condition at the time of the fire but all of its valuable possessions were consumed at that time. The entire collection, including over 100,000 books, manuscripts, etc., with many fine oil paintings, perished; also the original draft of Lincoln's Emancipation Proclamation. The institution, however, has partially recovered from this sad blow. It now has a library of 16,000 volumes, 40,000 pamphlets, and in addition a valuable collection of manuscripts and portraits. The society is about to erect a new building from a liberal fund provided for that purpose. Visitors courteously received.

Holidays.—Upon the six legal holidays, the banks, and the public and Government offices, are obliged by law to close, and business throughout the city is very generally suspended. The names and dates of these are: Christmas, December 25; New Year's Day, January 1; Washington's Birthday, February 22; Decoration Day, May 30; Independence Day, July 4, and Thanksgiving Day, appointed annually by special proclamation of the President of the United States, and usually fixed for the last Thursday in November. The festivities occurring upon these days are almost entirely of a family character. A very general interchange of presents among near relatives and friends, and the discussion of a good dinner, form the traditional programme for Christmas, religious services being held, as a rule, only in the Roman Catholic and Episcopal churches. On New Year's the quaint old Dutch custom for the men to pay visits to all their lady friends, while the ladies remain at home to receive them and proffer hospitalities, is observed among certain classes of society. Washington's Birthday passes quite without special observance, but Decoration Day now receives marked attention. It is set apart in memory of the men who have died in the active service of the United States, and was instituted after the Civil War. A procession, including the main military display of the year, and vans loaded with flowers, proceed to the adjacent cemeteries, and they decorate the graves of the soldiers buried there. The Fourth of July, as Independence Day is now generally called, was formerly marked by a grand military display and the free use of gunpowder and fireworks. The demoralizing effects of the heat upon the soldiers, and the number of fires resulting from the careless use of explosives, has led partially to the abandonment of the former and the prohibition of the latter. However, the Mayor's proclamation prohibiting the use of fireworks, usually proves a dead letter. As many persons as can do so usually leave the city on that day, which now differs little on the public streets from any Sunday. The observance of a day of thanksgiving is of Puritan origin, and religious services are generally held in the churches. Family reunions and the most bountiful feast of the year, are its other traditional observances.

Home for the Aged.— This institution is under the management of the Little Sisters of the Poor, and is located at the corner of Throop and Harrison streets. It provides a home for men and women over sixty years of age.

Home for the Friendless, Wabash Avenue and Twentieth Street, provides assistance for worthy women and children in indigent circumstances. The grounds and buildings are extensive.

Homeopathic Medical College owns and occupies a hand-some building which is located on South Wood Street, corner of York Street, within a stone's throw of the Cook County Hospital. The institution is one of the substantial educational establishments in Chicago, giving a practical and thorough course of training to its students. Its corps of instructors includes representative practitioners who stand high in their profession, not alone in Chicago, but who are known favorably throughout the medical world.

Hooley's Theatre.—In 1870, Mr. R. M. Hooley—familiarly known as "Uncle Dick"—became proprietor of Bryan's Hall, standing where the Grand Opera House now is. On January 2, 1871, he opened with Hooley's Minstrels, which had a successful run. The autumn attraction was Giocometti's tragedy, *Elizabeth*, but when October 9th arrived, the fire had left the city and Hooley's in ruins. By the middle of October, 1872, Hooley's new theatre was finished on the present site—Randolph Street, opposite the City Hall. It is 112x65 feet, and the auditorium is 67x65 feet, 65 feet high, and the stage 66x45 feet. The grand hallway leading to the foyer entrance is twenty feet wide, while the interior is both comfortable, cozy, and tastefully decorated, with twelve richly upholstered private boxes. Many prominent in dramatic and operatic art have appeared here, and many popular attractions, authors, and actors here received their introduction to fame; from here Robson and Crane started their brilliant combination; so, too, *Adonis*, with Dixey in the title rôle. It was through Mr. Hooley's efforts that the piece was first presented. He saw its worth; its phenomenal success proves it; Bartley Campbell, the brilliant author, also dates his success as a playwright, from Hooley's. This house is specially ventilated with patent ventilators and smoke-escapes, and as the proscenium is principally cast-iron, it is therefore practically fire-proof. Light opera and high-grade comedy hold reign at Hooley's, and Mr. Augustin Daly's combination occupies the boards every summer. ᛫

Horse Exchange.—The Chicago American Horse Exchange is to occupy a new building at the corner of Dearborn and Sixteenth streets. The structure is to be two stories high, and will surround an open space in which auction sales will take place. An exhibition track will be laid out in this open court, and 500 stalls will surround it.

Horse Show.— The Chicago Horse Show has for some years past been held in the Exposition Building, but after the condemnation of that structure, will probably find quarters near the Columbian Exposition. The Horse Show has become one of the most fashionable events of Chicago society, and the Exposition Building was, last year, crowded with the best people of the city gathered to see a splendid exhibit of horses and carriages of every description. Some very fine horses are brought forward at this show, and exciting contests in hurdle racing and high jumping furnish great delight to the sportively inclined among the spectators.

Hospitals and Dispensaries. —The hospital system of Chicago is one of the most admirable in the country. There are twenty hospitals, all open to the sick and injured, and twenty-five dispensaries where medicines may be obtained free of charge by those too poor to pay. The principal hospitals are :

Alexian Brothers, 539 North Market Street.
Hospital for Women and Children, West Adams and Paulina streets.
Cook County, Wood and Harrison streets.
Hahnemann (homeopathic), 2813 Groveland Avenue.
Mercy, Calumet Avenue and Twenty-sixth Street.   ᛫
Michael Reese, Twenty-ninth Street and Groveland Avenue.
Presbyterian, Congress and Wood streets.
St. Joseph's, Garfield Avenue and Burling Street.
United States Marine, Lake View.
Woman's, Thirty-second Street and Rhodes Avenue.
Emergency, 194 Superior Street.
Augustana, 151 Lincoln Avenue.
Bennett, Ada and Fulton streets.
Chicago Homeopathic, York and Wood streets.
Chicago Floating, North Pier, Lincoln Park.
German, 754 Larrabee Street.
Maurice Porter Free, 606 Fullerton Avenue.
National Temperance, 3411 Cottage Grove Avenue.
Railway Brotherhood, Ada and Fulton streets.
St. Vincent's Maternity, 191 La Salle Avenue.
Wesley, 355 East Ohio Street.
The Cook County Hospital is one of the largest in the world, employing 200 people, and having, on an average, 500 patients every day.
The principal dispensaries are :
Alexian Brothers, 539 North Market Street.
American College of Dental Surgery, 78 State Street.
Armour Mission, Thirty-third and Butterfield streets.
Bennett Free, Ada and Fulton streets.
Bethesda Medical Mission, 406 Clark Street.

Central Free, Wood and Harrison streets.
Central Homeopathic, Wood and York streets.
Clinic Association, 70 State Street.
Hospital for Women and Children, Adams and Paulina streets.
Policlinic, 176 Chicago Avenue.
Chicago Spectacle Clinic, 70 State Street:
German Hospital, 754 Larrabee Street.
Hahnemann College, 2813 Groveland Avenue.
Illinois Eye and Ear Infirmary, 121 South Peoria Street.
Lincoln Street Dispensary, 335 South Lincoln Street.
Michael Reese, Michael Reese Hospital.
National Temperance, National Temperance Hospital.
North Star, 192 Superior Street.
Northwestern College of Dental Surgery, 1203 Wabash Avenue.
Chicago College of Dental Surgery, 122 Wabash Avenue.
South Side Free, Twenty-sixth Street and Prairie Avenue.
West Side, Honore and Harrison streets.
St. Luke's, 1420 Indiana Avenue.
Woman's Hospital, Thirty-second Street and Rhodes Avenue.
Young Women's Christian Association, 39 Howland Block.

Hotel Metropole, on Twenty-third Street and Michigan Avenue, is owned by Messrs. George Miller and Francis Kennet. It contains 350 rooms and is seven stories high. The exterior is of pressed brick and the interior is finished in marbles, mosaics, and plaster-relief work. It is fire-proof and is valued at about $425,000.

Hotels.—No city in the world is supplied with more numerous or better hotels than Chicago. There are nearly 1,500 hotels of all kinds, and many more are in process of construction. Among the best known are:
THE AUDITORIUM.—One of the grandest in the country, and the most fashionable in the city. Occupies the eastern half of the Auditorium Building.
BRIGGS HOUSE.—Randolph Street and Fifth Avenue. A most popular hotel for commercial travelers and tourists.
GRAND PACIFIC HOTEL.—Clark and Jackson streets. A first-class hotel in every respect, and one of the largest and best known in Chicago.
LELAND HOTEL.—Michigan Boulevard and Jackson Street. Splendidly located, and a favorite family resort.
PALMER HOUSE.—State and Monroe streets. Conducted on the European plan, and one of the most popular hotels, having a daily average of 1,500 guests.
RICHELIEU HOTEL.—On Michigan Boulevard, near the Leland Hotel. An exclusive and extremely luxurious hotel, famous for its magnificence in every department.
SHERMAN HOUSE. — Corner of Clark and Randolph streets. A hotel which, under its present name, has been in existence for more than fifty years. A first-class hotel in every respect.
TREMONT HOUSE.—Southeast corner of Lake and Dearborn streets. One of the oldest hotels in the city, and much patronized by persons in search of repose and quiet.
VIRGINIA HOTEL, 78 Rush Street, is a new hotel, and one of the most elegant in the city.
COMMERCIAL HOTEL.—Corner of Lake and Dearborn streets. Much patronized by country visitors and the theatrical profession.
CLIFTON HOUSE.—Monroe Street and Wabash Avenue. A handsomely furnished and very respectable hotel.

GAULT HOUSE. — West Madison and Clinton streets. Leading hotel of the West Side.

HOTEL WELLINGTON. — Wabash Avenue and Jackson Street. An extremely fashionable house.

Other high-class houses well known to fame, are:

Burke's European Hotel, Madison Street, between La Salle and Clark streets.

Continental Hotel, Wabash Avenue and Madison Street.

Gore's Hotel, 266 South Clark Street.

Hotel Brevoort, Madison Street, between La Salle and Clark streets.

Hotel Grace, Clark and Jackson streets.

Hotel Drexel, 3956 Drexel Boulevard.

Hotel Woodruff, Wabash Avenue and Twenty-first Street.

Victoria Hotel, Michigan Avenue and Van Buren Street.

Hyde Park Hotel, Lake Avenue and Fifty-first Street.

McCoy's Hotel, Clark and Van Buren streets.

Saratoga Hotel, 155 Dearborn Street.

Southern Hotel, Wabash Avenue and Twenty-second Street.

Barnes House, 36 West Randolph Street.

Deming Hotel, 136 Madison Street. Grand Palace Hotel, 103 North Clark Street.

Hotel Brunswick, Michigan Avenue and Adams Street.

Windsor Hotel, 145 Dearborn Street.

Columbia Hotel, State and Thirty-first streets.

Hotels—Moderate Rates.—

Besides the great and high-priced hotels of Chicago, there are a large number of respectable houses, charging moderate prices, and furnishing excellent accommodations. Among these may be named the following South Side hotels:

Albemarle, 262 State Street.
Alma European, 109 State Street.
Arcade, 164 Clark Street.
Austrian, 117 Franklin Street.
Baldwin, 74 Van Buren Street.
Bartl, 355 State Street.
Belvidere, 47 State Street.
Bennett, 73 Monroe Street.
Brown's, 68 Van Buren Street.
Carleton, 78 Adams Street.
Central European, 13 South Water Street.
Central, 250 State Street.
Chicago European, 156 Clark Street.
Choate, 268 State Street.
City, State and Sixteenth streets.
Columbade, 256 Michigan Avenue.
Conroy's, 407 State Street.
Cosmopolitan, 307 Clark Street.
Court, 487 State Street.
Crescent, 347 Fifth Avenue.
Damon, 51 Clark Street.
Debus, 341 Clark Street.
Dorley, 45 Michigan Avenue.
Eureka, 75 Jackson Street.
Exeter, 146 Madison Street.
Flint's, 80 Van Buren Street.
Garden City, 46 Sherman Street.
Garden, 312 State Street.
Germania 180 Randolph Street.
Golden Star, 203 Plymouth Place.
Goldston's, 286 Wabash Avenue.
Grand, 230 State Street.
Hagemann's, 147 Randolph Street.
Hamburg, 86 Sherman Street.
Hamburg, 186 Randolph Street.
Harrison, 128 Harrison Street.
Hoffman, 170 Clark Street.
Bristol, 214 Thirty-first Street.
Adams, 4703 State Street.
Boyd, 2010–12 Wabash Avenue.
Brunswick, Adams Street and Michigan Avenue.
Cortland, 16 Adams Street.
Crystal, 34 Washington Street.
Dearborn, 398 State Street.
Dixon, 310 State Street.
Fargo, 248 State Street.

Glenarm, 167 Madison Street.
Henrici, 70 Randolph Street.
Irvine, 71 Van Buren Street.
Kirkwood, 69 Randolph Street.
Langham, 1840 Wabash Avenue.
Lincoln, 70 Jackson Street.
Midland, 135 Adams Street.
Nicollet, Randolph Street and Fifth Avenue.
Richland, 168 Clark Street.
Richmond, State and Van Buren streets.
Royal, 1714 Indiana Avenue.
International, 167 Harrison Street.
Kuhn's, 165 Clark Street.
Lakeside, 3619 Lake Avenue.
La Salle, 47 La Salle Street.
Mackinac, 326 State Street.
Allen, Union Stock Yards.
Massasoit, South Water Street and Central Avenue.
Mather, 362½ Wabash Avenue.
May's European, 421 Clark Street.
Merchants' Exchange, 12 South Water.
Michigan, 346 State Street.
Muskegon, 21 Michigan Avenue.
National, 230 State Street.
Northern Pacific, 62 Sherman Street.
Oakland, Oakwood and Drexel boulevards.
Ogden, 100 Franklin Street.
Old Metropolitan, 192 Randolph Street.
Panorama, 49 Hubbard Court.
Park View, 310 Michigan Avenue.
Paxton, 2458 State Street.
People's, 368 State Street.
Putnam's, 163 Adams Street.
Randolph, 102 Randolph Street.
Rausley, 499 State Street.
Rock Island, 50 Sherman Street.
Rose, 365 Wabash Avenue.
Royal European, 37 Adams Street.
South Side Madison, 164 Madison Street.
Stafford's European, 131 Van Buren Street.
St. Bernard, 10 Madison Street.
St. Charles, 15 Clark Street.

St. Nicholas, 200 Washington Street.
Van Ness, 224 Clark Street.
Waverly, 130 Lake Street.
Wayne, 97 Michigan Street.
Windsor European, 145 Dearborn Street.
Witbeck, 74 Adams Street.
Wyndham, 2934 Prairie Avenue.
Boyle's, Forty-fifth and State streets.
Burton, 4119 Halsted Street.
Butcher, Loomis and Forty-fifth streets.
Calumet, 9001 Ontario Street.
Central, Seventy-fifth Street and South Chicago Avenue.
Commercial, 243 Sixty-third Street.
Commercial, 9440 Commercial Avenue.
Davies, Cummings.
Delmonico, 9347 Commercial Avenue.
Douglas, 3500 Cottage Grove Avenue.
Empire, 4141 South Halsted Street.
Englewood, 315 Sixty-third Street.
Ewing, One Hundredth Street and Ewing Avenue.
Exchange, 7325 South Chicago Avenue.
Gladstone, 3035 Michigan Avenue.
Greenwood Avenue, Greenwood Avenue and Seventy-sixth Street.
Alger, Fifty-first Street and Trumbull Avenue.
Florence, Wall Avenue and One Hundred and Eleventh Street.
Mechanic's Hall, The Strand, Hegewisch.
Julian, Stewart Avenue and Sixty-third Street.
Kemp, Seventy-sixth Street and Woodlawn Avenue.
Riverdale, Riverdale.
Roy's, Hegewisch.
Sharpshooters' Park, Jefferson and One Hundred and Eighteenth streets.
South Chicago, Ninety-second Street and Commercial Avenue.

INTERIOR VIEW OF GRAND OPERA HOUSE,
87 Clark Street, Chicago.

QUEEN ᴬᴺᴰ CRESCENT ROUTE

SHORTEST AND QUICKEST LINE FROM

CINCINNATI TO POINTS SOUTH.

MAP OF THE
EAST TENN. VA.& GA. &
QUEEN & CRESCENT
RAILWAY SYSTEMS

(left margin, vertical) SOLID VESTIBULED TRAINS, CINCINNATI TO NEW ORLEANS.

(right margin, vertical) SOLID VESTIBULED TRAINS, CINCINNATI TO ST. AUGUSTINE, FLA.

The only line running Solid Vestibuled Trains south of the Ohio River. The Florida Limited leaves Cincinnati daily via Lexington. Chattanooga, Macon, Atlanta, Jacksonville to St. Augustine, Florida.

The Queen & Crescent Special leaves Cincinnati daily via Lexington, Lookout Mountain. Birmingham, Meridian to New Orleans.

Through cars from Cincinnati via Knoxville, Ashville, and Hot Springs to Charleston, S. C.

Shortest and Quickest Line, Cincinnati to Florida and Southeastern Points. Shortest and Quickest Line via New Orleans or Shreveport to Texas. Mexico, and California.

Personally conducted Excursions to Texas, Mexico, and California, leave Cincinnati Thursday, January 21st, and every other Thursday thereafter.

For further information, address

H. A. CHERRIER, Northwestern Passenger Agent,
193 Clark Street, CHICAGO.

D. MILLER, Traffic Manager, **D. G. EDWARDS,** General Passenger Agent,
CINCINNATI.

113 HOT—HOT

Sunnyside, Clark Street and Sunnyside Avenue.
Transit, Union Stock Yards.
Walhalla, One Hundred and Fifteenth Street.
Walters', Ninety-fourth Street and Anthony Avenue.

NORTH SIDE HOTELS.

American, 120 Kinzie Street.
Anna, 102 North Clark Street.
Clarendon, 152 North Clark Street.
Davenport, 180 North Clark Street.
Gaines, 180 North Clark Street.
Garden City, 101 Wells Street.
Grand Palace, 127 North Clark Street.
Columbia, 15 North State Street.
Denmark, 126 Kinzie Street.
Dayton, 74 North Clark Street.
Delavan, 143 North Clark Street.
Le Grand, 39 Wells Street.
St. Benedict, Chicago Avenue and Cass Street.
Svea, 131 Chicago Avenue.
Vendome, North Park and Centre avenues.
Wisconsin, 22 Wisconsin Street.
Metropolitan, 26 North Wells Street.
North City, 89 North Wells Street.
Scandinavian, 87 Townsend Street.
Schaefer's, 965 North Clark Street.
Shelburne, 306 Chicago Avenue.
Wells Street, 95 Wells Street.
Westminster, 462 North Clark Street.

WEST SIDE HOTELS.

American, 113 South Canal Street.
Arlington, 34 West Madison Street.
Barnes, 36 West Randolph Street.
Boulevard, 328 Washington Boulevard.
Brighton, Western and Archer avenues.
Burlington, 680 South Canal Street.
Colorado, 123 South Canal Street.
Cullen, 191 West Madison Street.
Dannevirke, 219 Milwaukee Avenue.

Depot, 119 South Canal Street.
Dowling, 137 South Canal Street.
Farwell, Jackson and South Halsted streets.
Giles', 995 West Madison Street.
Haymarket, 157 West Madison Street.
Edwards, 334 Washington Boulevard.
Harvard, 100 West Madison Street.
Milan, 153 South Halsted Street.
Orient, 693 South Halsted Street.
Humboldt Park, California and North avenues.
Jefferson's European, 145 South Canal Street.
Keller, 125 West Madison Street.
La Pierre, 181 Washington Boulevard.
Logan Square, 480 North Kedzie Avenue.
McEwan's Temperance, 91 West Madison.
Myers', 14 Bishop Court.
New England, 129 South Canal Street.
Norwood, 91 South Desplaines Street.
Oxford, 159 South Canal Street.
Park, Jefferson Park.
Phoenix, 77 South Canal Street.
Reaper, 1185 Blue Island Avenue.
Rodgers, 4209 West Lake Street.
St. Caroline's Court, 18 Elizabeth Street.
St. Cloud, 201 West Randolph Street.
St. James, 36 South Halsted Street.
Union Exchange, 115 South Canal Street.
Union Park, 521 West Madison Street.
Washington, 17 West Madison Street.
Waukegan, 183 West Lake Street.
Waverly, 63 West Lake Street.
West End, 503 West Madison.
West Side Commercial, 116 West Madison Street.
Wheeling, 82 West Lake Street.

8

House-Hunting.—If you want to hire a house or apartments your easiest way of proceeding is to go to the different real estate dealers, and get their lists of what they have for rent at about the price you want to pay, and then go to the houses themselves, and see which will suit you best. If you know nothing about the neighborhood, are a stranger, and have no reason to trust the dealers' word, you had better make inquiries of the police if there is anything at all suspicious. Having satisfied yourself that the quarters are what you want, don't forget to examine the water faucets, closets and traps. It is safe to sign a lease wherein the owner agrees to keep the premises in thorough repair. All taxes and assessments, including water tax, are paid by the owners of houses. The only thing you will have to look after in that direction is the gas. Gas companies exact a deposit for each meter furnished by them, which deposit they will refund when you surrender their receipt for the amount. Do not, under any pressure whatever, pay the gas bill of a former tenant. Almost any kind of a house or apartments may be had in any of the residence portions of the city. Rents vary considerably, owing to location. In some of the ultra-fashionable neighborhoods a tenant may pay $2,000 per year for a fine house. Many poor families occupy quarters in uninviting districts, for which they pay anywhere from $4 to $10 per month.

House of Providence, next to Mercy Hospital, furnishes a home for women and girls out of employment.

House of the Good Shepherd is an asylum for women and female children. It is a handsome five-story building, surrounded by fine grounds, at North Market and Hurlburt streets.

Humane Society.—The Illinois Humane Society, office No. 43 Auditorium Building, Wabash Avenue front, was incorporated the 25th day of March, 1869, under the Revised Statutes of Illinois. The officers and Board of Directors consist of thirty members, among whom will be found the most prominent ladies and gentlemen of Chicago. The society also has a list of honorary members, and a large number of life members, who are elected by the society, and they pay the sum of $100 per year. Active members pay $10 per year. The society employs a number of agents who investigate cases of cruelty, and prosecute the same. The manifold objects of this society are: To stop cruelty to children; to rescue them from vicious influences and remedy their condition; to stop the beating of animals, dog fights, over-loading horse cars, over-loading teams; the use of tight check reins; over-driving; clipping dogs' ears and tails; underfeeding and neglect of shelter for animals; bagging cows; cruelties on railroad stock trains; bleeding calves; plucking live fowls; the clipping of horses; driving galled and disabled animals; tying calves' and sheep's legs; to introduce better roads and pavements, better methods of slaughtering, better methods of horse-shoeing; improved cattle cars; drinking fountains, and to introduce humane literature in schools and homes. The society also aims to induce children to be humane, teachers to teach kindness to animals, clergymen to preach it, authors to write it, editors to keep it before the people; drivers and trainers of horses to try kindness; owners of animals to feed regularly; people to protect insectiverous birds; boys not to molest birds' nests; men to take better care of stock; everybody not to sell the old family horse to owners of tip-carts; people of all the States to form humane societies; men to give money to forward this good cause; women to interest themselves in the noble work; people to appreciate the intelligence and virtue of animals, and, generally, to make men, women, and children better because more humane.

This society is doing a noble work, as its annual report of cases investigated and children rescued and their condition remedied, testifies. The society has the hearty and practical support of the police and all officers of the law. The public and press give abundant moral support,and the ordinances of the city and the laws of the State are ample,and need only enforcement to improve the conditions of life generally. A man can not beat his child or animal in this city with impunity, for the law forbids cruelty, and punishes the ·offender. The public is notified to report all cases of cruelty to animals or children at once to the Humane Society or to the society's agents, whether requiring prosecution or not. Give name and residence of offender, when known, and the name or number upon the vehicle,if licensed. Get name of owner or receiver of animals driven or carried in a cruel manner; name of owner and driver of horses or other animals used in unfit condition, or otherwise abused. If prosecution is required, furnish names of two or more witnesses, and a full statement of facts. All communications are regarded as confidential by the society.

Hyde Park is situated on the Illinois Central Railroad. It has one of the finest systems of water-works, worth more than $500,000. It provides sterling advantages

for the education of the young, both religious, social, and educational. It contains the Rosalie Music Hall, in which all entertainments are held, and which has a seating capacity of 700. Hyde Park is the home of many business men of Chicago on account of its nearness to the city. It has several suburbs.

Idlewilds.—A social club of Evanston, noted for hospitality, and the prowess of its indoor ball team.

Illinois Charitable Eye and Ear Infirmary, is located corner of West Adams and Peoria streets. It is open to indigent residents of the State. This is an institution that Chicago and the State of Illinois can well be proud of, as the management is of a high order.

Illinois Club occupies the premises at 154 South Ashland Avenue, and the buildings and grounds are very attractive. The furnishings, decoration, and works of art of the interior, form a combination of beautiful surroundings that are very rare, even in so rich a club as the Illinois. Their musical and literary entertainments are highly enjoyed by those fortunate enough to be present. Ashland Avenue is the fashionable thoroughfare of the West Side.

Illinois National Guard.— The militia organizations of the city have always been a just source of pride to Chicagoans, for here alone has the National Guard system attained anything like the standard which was contemplated by the act which created it. The inalienable right to bear arms seems to be dear to the hearts of the people of the city. The report of the Adjutant-General of Illinois for the year 1890, shows the aggregate strength of the Illinois National Guard to be **3,790**

officers and men, and it is declared that the organization of the forces was never more effective. Two regiments of the Illinois National Guards, the First and Second, are stationed in Chicago.

FIRST BRIGADIER-GENERAL, AND STAFF.—Headquarters, Second Regiment Armory, 135 Michigan Avenue.

FIRST REGIMENT I. N. G.—Organized in August, 1874. Forty-eight men were enrolled at the first meeting. In January, 1875, having grown into seven companies, the regiment took quarters on Lake Street, adopted its uniform, and received its equipment of arms from Springfield. On May 13th it made its first public appearance with 520 men in line. From that day to this the First Regiment has enjoyed the utmost popularity. In 1877, during the railroad riots, the regiment twice dispersed mobs at the point of the bayonet, without firing a shot. In 1878 the First removed to its armory on Jackson Street. During the riots of 1886, at the Union Stock Yards and other points in the city, the regiment was called into service to quell disorder. The enrollment at present is 530 men. Armory, 22 to 26 Jackson Street.

NEW ARMORY of the First Regiment is located at the northeast corner of Sixteenth Street and Michigan Avenue, reached by Wabash Avenue cable road. It is perhaps the most massive structure in Chicago. Heavy stone work rises on each of the four sides to the height of thirty-five feet, and is unbroken save by the sally-port, through which an army might march company front. This great doorway is in perfect harmony with the whole. An arch in form, it spreads at the base forty feet, and supports a keystone thirty-five feet above the first floor. The massive oak and steel portcullis, suggesting memories of a mediæval fortress, rests back of the embrasures in the thickness of the walls, protected by firing slots on both sides. Above the stone work the walls are built into battlements, and four turrets at the corners. The windows are narrow, and strengthened by steel and iron, being but well-guarded posts for riflemen. An enfilading fire can be directed throughout the force of the structure, and a force entering the armory would have absolute protection against everything except heavy artillery. The space covered by the building, 174x164 feet, gave room for a very large drill hall on the first floor. It is surrounded by galleries for visitors. There is also a large banquet hall and a splendid gymnasium. This armory, which is said to be the best building of the kind in the United States, was built by subscription, and will be cared for by a board of trustees. A ninety-nine year lease of the valuable site was the contribution of Marshall Field. This gift is valued at $500,-000.

BATTERY D, FIRST ARTILLERY.—Armory located at present on Michigan Avenue, Lake Front, foot of Monroe Street. A well-equipped and valuable arm of the State military service.

SECOND REGIMENT I. N. G.—This regiment was organized in 1875. Armories located at Washington Boulevard and Curtis Street, and 35 Michigan Avenue. This regiment was originally composed of ten companies, and its first colonel was James Quirk. A few years later, owing to the reduction of the militia by the Legislature, the Second was consolidated with the Sixth battalion, commanded by Col. Thompson. In 1884 he resigned and Col. Harris A. Wheeler was elected to the command. From this important period in its history, the success of the regiment dates. The regiment is now commanded by Col. Louis S. Judd and is in a thoroughly prosperous condition, with a membership of 950. It is the largest command in the West and is in every sense of the word all that could be desired in the way of a military organization. The band of the Second Regiment numbers ninety pieces, including drum, fife, and bugle corps. It is certainly an organization of the highest efficiency.

CHICAGO HUSSARS, a recent military organization, but perhaps destined to become one of the most notable in the country. It is strictly private and partakes much of the nature of an elegant club. The new armory of the Hussars will be located on Thirty-fifth Street, near Cottage Grove Avenue, a lot 100x230 feet having been purchased for that purpose. This space will be entirely covered with buildings, which will include a club house, armory riding school, and stables. At present there are forty-one members of the company, each one of whom is the possessor of a handsome horse. In time each member of this company will be mounted on a coal-black horse.

ELLSWORTH CHICAGO ZOUAVES. —This one time famous organization no longer exists. Its history dates back to 1856. In that year the National Grand Cadets was dissolved, and Col. E. E. Ellsworth reorganized the disbanded company under the name of United States Zouave Cadets. Owing to the popularity of the commander, they soon became known all over the country as the Ellsworth Zouaves. They made a tour of the principal cities in 1860, giving their wonderful exhibitions. The members became scattered shortly after the outburst of the Rebellion. Ellsworth was killed on May 24, 1861, by J. W. Jackson, the proprietor of the Marshall House, at Alexandria, Va. He had heroically torn down a Confederate flag that was flying from the roof of that building, and was shot while descending the stairs.

EVANSTON ZOUAVES.—An independent, self-supporting military company, organized in 1886 as the "Evanston Cadets." The members are young boys of the best families. When they appear in public they never fail to elicit applause for their skill in correctly performing the drill and intricate maneuvering of the Zouave tactics.

VETERAN SOCIETIES—CHICAGO ASSOCIATION OF UNION EX-PRISONERS OF WAR, meets third Mondays at Grand Pacific Hotel.

CHICAGO BOARD OF TRADE BATTERY MEMORIAL ASSOCIATION meets at Armory First Cavalry Regiment.

CHICAGO MERCANTILE BATTERY VETERAN ASSOCIATION meets at 4 Lake Street.

CHICAGO UNION VETERAN CLUB meets second Mondays at Grand Pacific Hotel.

DANISH VETERAN SOCIETY meets second and fourth Fridays at 432 Milwaukee Avenue.

EIGHTY-SECOND ILLINOIS VETERAN SOCIETY meets first Saturdays at 122 La Salle Street.

MEXICAN WAR VETERANS meet fourth Sundays at 106 Randolph Street, second floor.

MCCLELLAN VETERAN CLUB.— Room 14, 40 Dearborn Street; open daily.

NINETEENTH ILLINOIS VETERAN CLUB meets second Sundays 2.30 P. M., at 104 Randolph Street, second floor.

TAYLOR'S BATTERY VETERAN ASSOCIATION meets at call of secretary, 206 Randolph Street.

TWENTY-FOURTH ILLINOIS VET-

ERAN SOCIETY meets first Sundays, 2 P. M., 171 North Clark Street.

VETERAN UNION LEAGUE. — 204 Dearborn Street ; rooms third floor ; open daily ; regular meetings, first Wednesdays.

OTHER MILITARY ORGANIZATIONS. —There are fully 50,000 drilled men in Chicago outside of the regular military organizations, who are qualified to take the field as trained soldiers. Many of these are found in the Masonic, Odd Fellows, Knights of Pythias, and other secret orders.

Immigrants.—Thousands of Europeans annually settle in Chicago, and hundreds of them arrive every week over the different railroads. They seem to fit quietly into the social structure; their fellow countrymen receive them with open arms, and ere long they become part and parcel of the population. As is shown by the census tables, the Germans are most numerous among the immigrants; the Irish are a good second, with the Scandinavians, Poles, and Bohemians next in order. There is now considerable immigration of Italians and Russian Jews, but this will probably be only temporary.

Independent Churches.—The following is a list of the names and locations of those in Chicago:

Chicago Avenue Church (Moody's), corner Chicago and La Salle avenues.

Central Church, Central Music Hall, State Street, corner Randolph Street.

People's Church, Hooley's Theatre.

Indians.—The Pottawatomie tribe were in possession of the country around Chicago in ancient times, although bands of Miamis and Mascoutins often roamed over the same territory. The Pottawatomies were mainly responsible for the Fort Dearborn massacre of 1812, and lingered in the vicinity of Lake Michigan until 1835 or '36, when they went West.

Quite a number of Chicagoans, mostly of French nomenclature, have a tinge of Pottawatomie blood, and some of these were, in 1889, claimants to a division of the tribal funds. Many Indians and half-breeds, employed by circuses and medicine troupes, make Chicago their home. A few years ago there were forty Caughnawaga Iroquois, and several Sioux half-breeds, living on Eagle Street, an obscure alley on the West Side.

Indoor Ball.—An amusement which is purely Chicagoan, invented by a Chicagoan, and little known outside the city limits, is "indoor base ball."

The game was invented in 1888 by George W. Hancock, of the Farragut Club, and has now become a recognized and leading feature among winter diversions. It is played in any hall large enough for the purpose, with a miniature diamond marked in chalk, a soft ball, and a light bat. All other features are those of the outdoor game. There are 100 organized indoor ball clubs in Chicago, and their games attract thousands of spectators of the best classes. In fact, indoor ball is particularly a sport of gentlemen, and especially of club members.

Institute of Building Arts is located at 63 and 65 Washington Street. The above institute is a free permanent exposition of building materials, devices, improvements, and inventions appertaining to architecture and its kindred arts, and a bureau of information for the benefit of the general building public. It gives courses of free lectures on architectural subjects, makes tests of building materials and devices, and supports a large library of architectural works. It is owned and conducted by the Illinois Chapter of the American Institute of Architects, and is under the immediate management of Mr. H. W. Perce, a gentleman of many years' experience in in matters appertaining to architecture and building. The welfare of the institute is under the direct supervision of a Board of Trustees and the Executive Committee of the Chapter.

Institution for the Blind.— Chicago has no place for the instruction of the blind, but depends upon the State institution at Jacksonville, which is maintained by an annual appropriation of $120,000.

Irish-American Club, 90 Washington Street, is the oldest club of the kind in this country; it is social and literary in purpose.

Irish Catholic Colonization of the United States is composed of Irish immigrants, and its purpose is their colonization in the western States and Territories.

Iroquois Club, originally the Chicago Democratic Club, is located at 110 Monroe Street, Columbia Theatre, and is furnished with all modern club house appointments. The Iroquois is a powerful organization, and makes itself felt in national politics. It numbers among its members men of high position, socially and politically.

Italians.—The Italian population of Chicago numbers about 10,000, largely made up of laborers, rag-pickers and fruit venders, who are industrious, economical, and dirty. Most of them will suffer many privations for the sake of sav-ing a little money, and though they have a miserable appearance, there are no beggars among them. As a rule they are found in the worst parts of the city. They rarely speak the English language and mingle little with people of other nationalities. They are commonly sober, but when they do become intoxicated, it is nearly certain that they will quarrel, and not rarely, with fatal results. It is a mistake to suppose that the majority of organ grinders and strolling players which roam the streets are Italians. These nuisances are mostly Germans. Another calling to which our Italians answer is that of waiters in restaurants, a business for which their natural politeness renders them peculiarly fit. Ascending their social ladder we find a host of Italian musicians, music and language teachers, some of whom stand very high in their profession, and others have devoted themselves to literary pursuits or to the higher branches of trade. On South Water Street, as a rule, the large fruit dealers are of this nationality.

Jackson Club, a new social organization of the West Side, which bids fair to rival in membership and importance any similar club in the city. The club house is at No. 709 West Adams Street, and is the resort of over 300 members.

Jackson Street Theatre.— Chicago is to have a new theatre, modeled on the English plan, with stalls similar to those in use in the more fashionable London theatres, and a concert garden, café, and promenade on the roof of the building. The lease for the ground has already been negotiated and turned over to the projectors of the enterprise, and the new place of amusement will be completed May 1, 1892. Chicago capitalists have secured for ninety-nine years a lease on the grounds now occupied by the old First Regiment Armory, on Jackson Street, just west of the Leland Hotel. The Armory Building will be removed, and the new theatre and office building will be constructed on the lot, the dimensions of which are 80x160 feet. The building is to be twelve stories high and constructed of iron, steel, terra cotta, and stone. Work on the new structure was commenced November 1, 1891. The plan of the theatre will be who·ly different from any other in the country. Its seating capacity will be 1,300, and that portion of the house known in American theatres as the balcony, will, in this theatre, be the circle *de rigueur*, especially arranged for patrons who desire to attend the performance in full‑evening dress. This circle will be composed of private boxes, such as are seen in the fashionable theatres of London. The arrangement for the parquet seats will be the same as in other theatres. Several perfectly appointed reception rooms for ladies and gentlemen, will be located on the main floor. The entrance to the theatre will be a marvel of beauty. The foyer will be circular in form. There will be no gallery, one balcony only being arranged above the main floor of the auditorium. The concert-garden and café upon the roof will be inclosed with plate glass in such a manner that the best effects may be had at once, and at the same time the plate glass frames will be so arranged that they may be swung so as to leave the roof free circulation of air. A fine view of Lake Michigan will be had from the roof-garden. Aside from the attractions of the promenade outside the garden, an electric fountain and tropical plants in profusion will ornament the roof-garden. A fine orchestra will be maintained in·the

garden, and visitors to the theatre will have the use of the elevators during the intermission, which will be arranged for thirty minutes. During the World's Fair, waiters of all nationalities will be employed in the café. The attractions for the new theatre will be furnished through a stock company composed of the best artists of Europe and America. The location of the new amusement enterprise could not have been better chosen. It will be within a few blocks of the leading hotels of the city, and within easy distance of the railway terminals of the South Side, including the South Side elevated road, when it is completed. The cost of the building will be no less than $600,000. , Another new feature of this theatre will be the arrangement of a box for the use of representatives of the press exclusively, and the apportionment of a room on the main floor of the building for the same purpose.

Jefferson Park.—On a beautiful tract of five and one-half acres, bounded on the north and south by Monroe and Adams streets, and on the east and west by Throop and Loomis streets, the city has, since its purchase of Judge Thomas in 1848 for $1,200, expended about $50,000 in ‑improvements. Although less pretentious than some of the larger parks, it is a perfect little gem, made so by the work of accomplished artisans. Ponds and fountains, rustic bowers and bridges, and stone cascades, pretty elevations and depressions, and the evergreens and‑shrubberies, all combine to make it one of the coziest and most delightful resorts in the city. Its beauty is heightened by the excellent class of mansions and cultivated grounds which surround it on every side, and of these the presence of the park has, in turn, greatly heightened the value. This park is reached by the Adams Street cars.

Jewish Synagogues.—The following is a list of the names and locations of those in Chicago:

Anshe Emes, 341 Sedgwick Street.

Anshe Kanesses Israel, southeast corner of Judd and Clinton streets.

Anshe Russia-Pola-Sedek, 519 South Canal Street.

Congregation Beth Hamedrash Hack Odosch, 439 Clark Street.

Congregation Beth Hamedrash, 134 Pacific Avenue.

Congregation B'nai Abraham, southeast corner of Wright Street and Newberry Avenue.

Congregation Emmanuel, 280 and 282 North Franklin Street.

Congregation Ohaveh Emunah, 386 Clark Street.

Congregation Ohaveh Sholom, 582 South Canal Street.

Congregation of the North Side, northeast corner of Rush Street and Walton Place.

Congregation Moses Montefiore, 130 Augusta Street.

Congregation Bethel, North May Street, near West Huron Street.

Kehilath Anshe Mauriv (Congregation of the Men of the West), Indiana Avenue and Twenty-sixth Street.

Kehilath B'nai Sholom (Sons of Peace), 1455 Michigan Avenue.

Sinai Congregation, Indiana Avenue and Twenty-first Street.

Zion Congregation, southeast corner of Washington Boulevard and Ogden Avenue.

Jews.—The Jewish population of Chicago is very large, and continually increasing. They number, probably, 15,000 or more, and are mainly German-Jews, with a sprinkling of Poles and Russians—the latter element now being greatly augmented by immigration.

The Jews of Chicago are very prosperous, thrifty, and mostly excellent members of society. Their children attend the public schools and mingle freely with the "Gentiles," on equal ground. As a natural result, Jew and Christian in Chicago are on terms of excellent friendship, and the Hebrew population is an element of recognized value.

John Crerar Library is not yet located. In 1890, John Crerar, a wealthy Chicagoan, bequeathed at his death about $2,000,000 to the creation and maintenance of a free public library, to be located on the South Side.

Judicial.—Chicago courts have never been accused of any dereliction from justice, and the enforcement of the law in equity, as interpreted by the keen intellect and comprehensive knowledge of her judges. Chicago has the honor of having one of her brightest lawyers appointed Chief Justice of the United States Supreme Court. Hon. Melville W. Fuller is an honor to the city, State, and county.

The United States Court of Claims, United States Circuit Court, and United States District Court can be reached in Chicago. The Register in Bankruptcy for the Northern District of Illinois resides in Chicago, as does also the United States Commissioner for the Northern District of Illinois. The courts belonging to the county and city are:

APPELLATE COURT OF THE FIRST DISTRICT OF ILLINOIS, meets at room 411, Chicago Opera House Building.

CIRCUIT COURT OF COOK COUNTY, meets in the County Building. Terms, third Monday of each month.

SUPERIOR COURT OF COOK COUNTY, meets in the County Building. Terms, first Monday of each month.

CRIMINAL COURT OF COOK COUNTY, meets in Criminal Court Building, Michigan Street, northwest corner Dearborn Avenue. Terms, first Monday in each month.

COUNTY COURT OF COOK COUNTY, meets in room 217, County Building. Terms, second Monday in each month.

PROBATE COURT, meets in room 121, County Building. Terms, third Monday in each month.

SOUTH DIVISION POLICE COURT, Harrison Street corner Pacific Avenue.

NORTH DIVISION POLICE COURT, 242 Chicago Avenue.

WEST DIVISION POLICE COURT, (2nd precinct) West Twelfth Street, corner Johnson Street.

WEST DIVISION POLICE COURT, (3d precinct) 19 South Desplaines Street.

WEST DIVISION POLICE COURT, (4th precinct) West Chicago Avenue corner May Street.

Kehilath Anshe Maariv, a new Jewish Synagogue, located at Thirty-first Street and Indiana Avenue. It cost $110,000, and is a beautiful structure of the orthodox type of architecture. This congregation was organized in 1837, with a membership of forty. It has grown and is now one of the prospered, and is now one of the wealthiest and most influential in the city. Dr. I. S. Moses is rabbi of the congregation.

Kensington, a railroad suburb, on the Illinois Central, fifteen miles south of the center of the city.

Kenwood, a portion of Hyde Park, on the Illinois Central Railroad, south of Forty-third Street. It is a beautiful suburb, and is the residence of many wealthy business men. Of all the smaller suburbs of Hyde Park proper, Kenwood is the most aristocratic. The residences are all first-class, many being of imposing appearance. Kenwood Club is the gathering place for wealthy residents, and to belong to it entitles one to a place in Kenwood's best society. The Kenwood Institute is here, and occupies a handsome building. To reach Kenwood take the Cottage Grove Avenue cable.

Kenwood Club. — The social center of the suburb of Kenwood, and a family club of high standing. Located at Forty-seventh Street and Lake Avenue.

Kinsley's Restaurant.—Kinsley is the Delmonico of Chicago. His establishment is a beautiful piece of architectural construction, and was erected in 1885. The style is Moresque, after the famous Alhambra at Grenada. Few, if indeed any, cities, boast so magnificent a building for such purposes. The bay windows, of which there are five, consist of copper *en repoussé* work, with graceful, gilded columns supporting terra cotta in unique designs, and are set with stained and plate glass. The interior, however, is where the proprietor's fastidious taste has been indulged most. The first floor, devoted to ladies' and gentlemen's dining, luncheon, and sample rooms, is decorated in Persian colorings and designs, with the floors laid in English tiling of costly patterns. The second floor is the restaurant and café, and is gorgeous in its furnishings and ornamentation. On the third floor are the select dining-rooms and banqueting - rooms, while the fourth is divided into two grand banqueting-rooms, 40x60 feet each. The flooring and wainscoting is done in marble, and the whole interior is on a scale of magnificence rarely equaled outside of Oriental domains. Such, briefly, is the building and furnishings, except that two handsome passenger elevators, which are inclosed in ornamental electro-plated bronze basket work, pass up and down at all hours. As to the reputation of the proprietor and his ability as a caterer, ask the fashionable world, the representative business men, the club men, etc., and you will be informed that "Kinsley's" is acknowledged the equal, if not superior, to anything of the kind in America.

Kitchen Garden.—The Chicago Kitchen Garden Association was formed in May, 1883. Ladies representing many churches organized the association, the work of which was confined to various city nurseries, but in 1886 a training school for servants was fitted up for a Kitchen Garden and Cooking School, under Central Church mission, on Clybourn Avenue. In 1889 a completely equipped school was established on Wentworth Avenue, and March, 1891, the association made an application to introduce cooking into one of the public schools and was granted the use of one room in the Huron Street School, after school hours. Cooking and all household duties are taught, and the managers realizing that they are doing good work, are much encouraged. The number of pupils is increasing, and the growing needs should induce every woman to aid in the noble and practical work. The cry for reform goes up from suffering housewives, and the reform should begin at the foundation, in the homes from which the servants are gathered.

Labor Organizations. — No city in the Union is so prolific of Labor Unions as Chicago, and for the most part they agree in arbitrating their differences, when any such arise, with their employers. We give a partial list;

BROTHERHOOD OF LOCOMOTIVE ENGINEERS.—Division No. 10, meets at Eighteenth Street, corner State Street; Division No. 96, at 241 Milwaukee Avenue; Division No. 111, at 4747 State Street; Division No. 253, at South Jefferson Street, corner State Street; Division No. 294, at Western Avenue, corner Indiana Street; Division No. 302, at 3934 State Street.

BROTHERHOOD OF LOCOMOTIVE FIREMEN.—Triumph Lodge No. 47, meets at Eighteenth Street, corner State Street; Garden City Lodge No. 50, at 5001 State Street; Chicago Lodge No. 95, at 237 Milwaukee Avenue; S. S. Merrill Lodge No. 188, Western Avenue corner Indiana Street; Central Park Lodge, at Tilton Hall; T. P. O'Rourke Lodge No. 244, at 5520 Wentworth Avenue; Central Labor Union, at 54 West Lake Street.

KNIGHTS OF LABOR.—District Assembly No. 57 meets at 3002 South Halsted Street; District Assembly No. 136, at 99 West Randolph Street.

ORDER OF RAILWAY CONDUCTORS. — Chicago Division No. 1 meets at 82 West Randolph Street; Stenchfield Division No. 41, at 4847 State Street.

SEAMAN'S UNION, meets at 99 West Randolph Street.

TYPOGRAPHICAL UNION No. 9 (German), meets at 45 Clark Street.

TYPOGRAPHICAL UNION, No. 16, meets at 86 La Salle Street.

TYPOGRAPHICAL UNION (Scandinavian), meets at 106 Randolph Street.

UNITED CARPENTERS' COUNCIL, meets at Room 14, 163 Washington Street.

INTERNATIONAL CIGAR-MAKERS' UNION No. 14 meets at 99 West Randolph Street.

IRON MOULDERS' UNION No. 239, meets at 82 West Madison Street,

WEST DIVISION STREET RAIL-
WAY EMPLOYES' BENEVOLENT AS-
SOCIATION, meets at 99 Randolph
Street.

STAIR BUILDERS' UNION meets at
71 West Lake Street.

PROGRESS LODGE, SWITCHMAN'S
MUTUAL AID ASSOCIATION OF M. A.,
meets at Michlies Hall, Western
Avenue, corner Indiana Street.

UNITED ORDER OF PLASTERERS
meets at 36 La Salle Street.

STONE MASONS' ASSOCIATION (German) meets at 62 North Clark
Street.

Labor Statistics of Chicago.
—The enumerators for the school
census reported a total population in
the city of 1,208,699 in May, 1890.
The number of persons over fourteen years was 859,247, representing
about 800,000 able-bodied individuals
at gainful work or household
duties. An estimate of 250,000 families and the great number of female
help for families and private boarding and lodging houses, would take
about 350,000 females out of the
categories of gainful trades, enumerated as employing 407,000 in
wholesale, retail, professional, personal, and transportation services.
This would leave 102,000 adults of
both sexes unaccounted for in the
enumeration of gainful trades. But
there are over 125,000 buildings and
several hundred thousand lots owned
by the resident population, and a
large number of persons hold shares
of corporations or earn an income on
various investments. This class of
bread-winners can not be counted
under the tax-law, and their numbers
can not be estimated because the
standard of expenditures varies
with the different nationalities which
compose the mixed population of
Chicago. Italians, Poles, Bohemians,
Scandinavians, Irish, English,
Germans, and native Americans

have different standards of comfort
and competence. They begin to
leave active business and to live on
incomes at different heights of individual prosperity. Frugal living
and habits of extreme penuriousness
and lack of enterprise tend to place
large numbers of these wage-working
nationalities on the retired lists, living in comfortable semi-idleness on a
small income from rents, mortgages,
etc., while the English, Germans,
and Americans would push forward
and risk their capital and exert their
working capacity in the attempt to
increase their possessions and to
speculate on futures. Old men
are not numerous in factories, workshops, stores, and at the desks of
commercial firms, which proves that
they earned fair wages during their
manhood and were able to save for
an old age of leisure. The mere
occupancy of town lots enriches the
owners in consequence of a great
immigration, which imparts a market value to the land and furnishes
customers for the middle-class
traders. The establishment of great
enterprises in Chicago and vicinity
furnishes employment to large numbers of working people, and the
capitalist should provide suitable
dwellings in the neighborhood of the
work places to prevent overcrowd-
ing, and to keep rents within reasonable limits. The housing of great
masses of working people should not
be left to the small lot owners, who
are not able to furnish the sanitary
arrangements for crowded habita-
tions. Chicago is one of the great
business centers of the globe, and its
public-spirited capitalists should aid
in improving the common standard
of living of the working people who
come here from all civilized countries. We must, in self-defense,
raise the economic and social standard of the various immigrant peoples,
to guard the integrity of the estab-

lished equality of our whole people. Chicago cannot tolerate any inferior classes, and therefore we protect children by means of compulsory education and by restriction of child labor, and manual training schools will soon be added to the public school system.

There were 8,250 manufacturing firms in the city in 1890, employing a total capital of $190.000,000, giving work to 177,000 persons. These manufacturers paid in wages during that year $96,200,000. The value of the product was $538,000,000. Manufacturing is increasing at the rate of 25 per cent. per annum.

Ladies' Clubs.—There are several women's societies in Chicago, mostly organized for philanthropic purposes. As yet, there is no purely social ladies' club of any prominence. Among the best known ladies' organizations are:

THE CHICAGO WOMEN'S CLUB, devoted to literary and philanthropic work. Many of the greatest local charities originated with this club, and many others have received valuable assistance from the organization.

THE FORTNIGHTLY CLUB, which meets at the Art Institute, more nearly approximates a social club than any other of the feminine organizations. Literary work and study, is, however, the chief aim of the society.

THE WOMEN'S SUFFRAGE CLUB meets at the Sherman House, and, as its name implies, is devoted to the advocacy of equal political rights.

Lake and River Frontage.— Chicago has a frontage on Lake Michigan of twenty-two miles and a river frontage of about fifty-eight miles (both sides), 22½ miles of which are navigable. There are three lakes within the city limits, covering an area of about 4,095.6 acres as follows;

Calumet Lake, 3,122 acres; Hyde Lake, 330.8 acres, and that portion of Wolf Lake lying within the city limits, 624.8 acres. Calumet and Wolf lakes are navigable. The other lakes have a depth of water varying from four to eight feet. Big and Little Calumet rivers penetrate the extreme southern part of the city.

Lake and River Shipping.— As a maritime center, Chicago is fast gaining in importance. The lake traffic is enormous, and the river may be justly described as "bristling with a thousand masts."

In 1890 there were 388 vessels owned in Chicago, 178 of which were schooners, and fifty-nine propellers. Five large side-wheel steamers were also included in the number.

The arrivals and clearances of vessels exceed those of New York by at least one-half; amount to three-fifths as many as the total arrivals and clearances of all the United States seaport towns, and reach one-fourth of the total lake clearances. There were, during 1890, 11,300 arrivals and 11,401 clearances; 8,173,-000 bushels of grain were shipped to Canada, and 73,349,000 bushels to other ports.

Lake Side Club occupies spacious and elaborately furnished buildings at Thirtieth Street and Wabash Avenue.

Lakeside Summer Sanitarium, foot of Twenty-fifth Street, provides nursing and care for infant children of the poor in hot weather.

Lake View.—This is a large township extending north from the old city limits. The village is beautifully laid out in grove lots, on which are handsome residences. It contains the Deering Works, which occupy forty acres, and the North Side Rolling Mills. Lake View contains St. Joseph's Hospital and the McCormick Seminary. It is now part of the city.

Lamps, Street.—The city's electric light system has been extended during the past year by erecting and putting in operation an additional plant on the pumping works grounds on Fourteenth Street and Indiana Avenue. At this station there is a capacity for 850 lights, but at present only 200 lamps are in operation in this district. The number of public electric lights last reported is 1,092, in all. The present four plants, with a moderate increase of steam power, have a combined capacity of 9,000 lights. The plants should be utilized by the establishment of additional lamps as soon as practicable, and the eight districts throughout the city should be supplied with light stations as rapidly as the funds for the purpose will admit. This modern and superior system of illuminating the public highways affords additional security to travel, and greatly enhances the attractiveness of the streets. It is also an efficient aid to the police service. The total expenditures of the city's electric lights to date are $526,-184.47. At the close of the year there were, including those on the bridges, viaducts, parks, and boulevards, 1,025 oil lamps, 8,080 gasoline lamps, and 26,236 gas lamps. The oil and gasoline lamps cost the city about $15 each per annum, and the gas lamps $20 per annum. However, by a recent contract with the gas company this price will be reduced in the near future to $15 per lamp per annum, and the payment annually into the city treasury of $150,000 by the gas company for the use of the streets.

La Salle Club.—A political and social organization of the West Side, located at 552 West Monroe Street. One of the most prominent and popular clubs in the city, with elegant quarters, recently enlarged and remodeled.

Law Institute.—The Chicago Law Institute is a most powerful legal society, including nearly every noted lawyer of the city in its membership. Its library is one of the finest of the kind in the world, and is located in the County Building. An insignificant annual fee entitles any lawyer to the privileges of this library, whose works have been selected with great judgment and due attention to every branch of the legal profession.

Lawn Tennis. — The level ground of Chicago and the large yards of the wealthy inhabitants offer ample space for hundreds of tennis courts, and nearly every available plat of land in the residence districts of the upper classes is utilized for the game. There are several tennis clubs, of which the most important are: The Chicago Tennis Club, 2901 Indiana Avenue; the Excello Tennis Club, and the North End Tennis Club, besides the tennis organizations flourishing under the wings of the Ashland, Jackson, and other social clubs.

Leiter Building.—The immense building which Mr. L. Z. Leiter has recently erected on State Street, between Van Buren and Congress streets, is certainly an imposing edifice. It was completed in the spring of 1892. The structure occupies just half a block, the frontage being 402 feet on State Street and 144 feet each on Van Buren and Congress streets. Its height is eight stories. Its cost was $1,500,000,

Leroy Payne's livery stables.
No. 167 to 174 Michigan Boulevard, are distinctively the fashionable stables of Chicago, and draw patronage from the local élite and from the leading hotels. The finest horses, the best equipages, skilled and careful drivers, and reasonable charges have given Leroy Payne a well-earned reputation throughout the land.

Leroy Payne's famous stables are will not attempt to overcharge or take advantage of strangers.

Leland Hotel.—Messrs. L. A. Kittredge and A. L. Skeels are the proprietors The situation of this house was well selected for a hotel. Fronting on Michigan Boulevard, the fashionable drive of the city, within full view of the lake and Lake Park, one could hardly find a more desirable place to be while in

LELAND HOTEL, CORNER MICHIGAN AVENUE AND JACKSON STREET.

considered the best, not only in Chicago, but west of New York.

Hacks, cabs, carriages, and vehicles of every kind are kept ever ready to a call, and the horses in the stalls are the most valuable animals of the kind in the country.

The drivers employed by the Payne company are trustworthy men, and, unlike the average cabman, the city. The management, however, and luxuriant interior, have much to do with establishing the popularity of the Leland. It is here the guest has every comfort and convenience possible to provide, hence the house receives the patronage of people who expect, and appreciate, being well taken care of. The rates are $3 to $5 per day.

Lexington Hotel.—This is a new hotel project, with site at the northeast corner of Twenty-second Street and Michigan Avenue. The plans contemplate a mammoth structure.

Libby Prison and War Museum.—The old Richmond Libby Prison has been removed from Richmond, Va., to Chicago, and is located between Fourteenth and Sixteenth streets. Take Wabash Avenue cable cars. The building has from both Northern and Southern standpoints. Strangers to the city will find that a visit to this institution will prove highly profitable and interesting.

Library of the Chicago Law Institute is located in the County Court House Building. It is one of the finest legal collections in the United States.

Lincoln Park is one of the oldest parks in the system, and when

LIBBY PRISON, WABASH AVENUE, BETWEEN FOURTEENTH AND SIXTEENTH STREETS.

been erected just as it stood in the capital of the Southern Confederacy. It has been converted into a great museum, illustrating the Civil War, and African slavery in America. It is filled with thousands of genuine relics of the war, such as scenes, views, portraits, arms, guns, original orders of all of the prominent officers, both North and South. No sectional animosity is intended—no North, no South—but a fair representation of the great Civil War first laid out was just beyond the North Side Cemetery. But after Rose Hill was purchased, the old cemetery was sold to the park authorities, and the dead were removed to their new home. The present area of Lincoln Park is 250 acres. It is bounded on the west by Clark Street, on the north by Diversey Street, on the east by Lake Michigan, and on the south by North Avenue. It has been under State supervision ever since 1869, when the

HORTICULTURE BUILDING.

South of the entrance to Jackson Park from the Midway Plaisance, and facing east on the lagoon. 1000 feet long, with an

DAIRY BUILDING.

first Board of Park Commissioners were appointed. No park, anywhere in the country, of equal size, contains as many attractions as this. Through the good taste of those in charge, art simply has supplemented nature by increasing her effects. The result has been that there is none more charming in our whole system of parks, than this, the eldest. The elements of its principal attractions are: The undulating character of the grounds, the beautiful lakes, the handsome bridges, the brilliant foliage, the graceful winding of the avenues, which curve in every direction, stretching away into dim, delightful vistas, the splendid statuary, the gorgeous beds, avenues, and banks of superb flowers, the wonderfully rare shrubbery, the quiet little nooks, dells and knolls, that peep out from a suggested concealment beneath the noble trees, and by no means least, the famous zoölogical collection for which Lincoln Park is especially noted. Here was unveiled, but a few months since, the Grant Monument, forever to face Lake Michigan on the Lake Shore Drive. This was Chicago's gift, and cost $100,000. St. Gauden's statue of Lincoln faces the main entrance. While considered one of the finest pieces of sculpture in the world, it has the better merit of being an accurate likeness of the famous president. This statue cost $50,000 and was presented, together with a drinking fountain, by the late Eli Bates. The late Martin Ryerson also presented an "Indian Group" in bronze, and the Hon. Lambert Tree a monument to the explorer La Salle. There is also a monument to Schiller, from the German residents of Chicago. Twice a week during the summer a fountain plays at night, illuminated with colored lights by some mechanical device. It is always sure of a good audience. A

new palm-house is the latest attraction. It is of steel and glass, picturesque, airy and light, resting upon a foundation of split granite. The entire length of the building is 238 feet, consisting of a main building 168x70 feet, and an extension in the rear of seventy feet. The lobby in front of the main building is to be 25x60 feet and this is approached by a lobby twenty feet square. The interior of the main building gives an unbroken stretch, save only for a few light, supporting iron columns for the glass roof. In the rear of the palm house is a conservotory thirty feet wide. A room 30x60 feet wide at the north end is exclusively devoted to the culture of orchids. An observatory tower of pressed brick and têrra cotta trimmings, ornaments this room. The building stands on two terraces, a little east of north of the canal vista, and the animals' summer quarters. The terraces occupy the space due north of the former green-houses, which were removed on the completion of the palm-house. The main approach to the palm-house is from the floral gardens. It is to cost $60,000.

Linne Monument.—The monument erected to the memory of Carl von Linné, the great naturalist, by the Swedish societies of Chicago, was unveiled with appropriate ceremonies, May 23, 1891. This monument stands at the foot of Fullerton Avenue in Lincoln Park, and is an exact reproduction of the famous Linné monument in Stockholm, Sweden. The figure is of bronze, the work of Dyreman, the Swedish sculptor, and was modeled by Gustav Mayer, of Stockholm. It is sixteen feet high, resting on a granite pedestal thirty-eight feet high. The famous botanist is presented in the national costume which he wore during his wanderings

9

LAKE SHORE DRIVE, LINCOLN PARK.

(130)

through the green fields and woods of his native country. In his left hand he holds a book and the *Linnæ Boralius*, the flower to which he gave his name.

Lodgings.—The constant ebb and flow of travel to and from Chicago, creates a demand for a great many furnished rooms. A large number of families in the respectable quarters of the city, whose incomes do not allow of the high rents, by renting out a furnished room or two, succeed in holding their position. This enables all concerned to combine reasonable price and stylish residence. For a few weeks' residence in the city, when one expects to be constantly on the "go," for either business or pleasure, this style of living offers the most liberty, with a lower rate of expense than any other method.

LODGING HOUSES.—But there are houses given up entirely to lodgers, here and there, in all the divisions of the city. The lowest class of lodging houses are in the business section of the South Side. Here the tired tramp, or "poor traveler," may sleep all night for a nickel. He who, stranded, friendless, and forlorn, at night is the possessor of 5 cents depreciated coin of the realm, can stumble down into a cellar, and by delivering up his wealth to the stony-hearted proprietor, will be allowed to climb into one of the bunks, ranged tier above tier, on either side of the yawning cavern. Here, with your unremoved clothing for mattress and coverlet, and your arm for a pillow, you can sleep the sleep of the honest poor. But it lays over "moving on" through the streets, from the falling of the night to the breaking of the day. There is at least protection from the weather, if luxurious comfort is not thrown in. In the winter, a red-hot stove in the middle of the cellar keeps all the guests warm, even if the temperature outside is hovering about zero. In the summer-time, the cellar is not over-heated by exposure to the blazing rays of the sun, and is always fairly cool. No robberies are ever committed in these cellars, and the reasons are very plain. Before a man chooses this style of lodging he has probably put his portable valuables where their care will never more worry him. There are grades even in lodging cellars. So a dime will pay for a bunk, with a straw mattress thrown in. The patrons of the 5-cent ground hotels regard the lodgers at the higher-priced places as "bloomin' judes." There are still other houses where a real bedstead, bedding, and covering, may be rented at the uniform price of fifteen cents, with a bowl of soup at night, and a hunk of bread and a bowl of coffee to begin the day with, and it only costs twenty-five cents in some houses for a single room. Generally there is more single than room about it, but the patrons don't kick, and the proprietor grows rich faster than mine hosts of the Grand Pacific and the Palmer House. But it is only aristocrats who squander twenty-five cents for a night's lodging in the "Levee" or "Cheyenne." To most of these patrons of cheap shelter, twenty-five cents includes within its milled edge, three straight drinks of barrel-house sour mash, a free lunch, a cigar, and a bed. But think what we may of the cheap lodging houses, they are very often as cleanly (if kept by an old sailor, as they often are) and as comfortable as the homes of their patrons.

Lumber District.—During the year 1890 Chicago received 1,941,-392,000 feet of lumber, and shipped 812,655,000 feet; of shingles, 515,-

575,000 were received, and 108,822,-000 were shipped. This enormous business is carried on in what is known as the "Lumber District." It lies south of Twenty-second Street, between Halsted Street and Ashland Avenue, its western limits being near the West Side water works. Take Canalport cars. Here is a city, the streets of which are lined with blocks of lumber, aggregating billions of feet, in all forms. Thousands of men are employed and the scene is at all times interesting and instructive. The facility with which vessels are loaded and discharged, also cars, is novel to those who are not familiar with this huge industry.

Lunch Counters.—Perhaps nowhere is the genuine Chicago spirit of hurry and rush more clearly revealed than at the many lunch counters of the city. There, at noontime, a crowd, which is characteristic as to numbers, rushes in, quiet and orderly, but fearfully in a hurry, and with more characteristic hurry dispatches lunches, the consumption of which averages less than ten minutes' duration. In no other city of the United States will institutions be found conducted on just the same principle as these same lunch counters. A hollow square of continuous counters; On the inside a hurrying, howling mob of white-robed waiters, and across the barrier an equally hurrying crowd of hungry business men. Every stool is occupied, and behind every occupant stands a prospective luncher, looking enviously at every morsel his predecessor disposes of.

The lunch counter waiters are a tribe unto themselves. There are no tips for them, and no chance for insolent indifference to orders. They must be very rapid, accurate, and work for their salaries only. With half a dozen small orders ringing in his ears, the lunch-counter waiter hurls sandwiches, pie, and temperance drinks at his customers with the ease of a mail-distributor at the post office. He never wastes words, and never loses a motion. Everything counts.

But if the waiters are interesting, the counters are doubly so. They represent all classes, from millionaires to messenger-boys, and no matter what their station in life may be, their all-consuming desire is to lunch and get away. Occasionally a deliberate man strays into such a lunch-house. He looks around him for a choice seat and deliberately sits down. A waiter charges at him, slams knife, fork, and spoon upon the counter, gasps for breath, and yells, "What you goin' to have, sah?" The deliberate man attempts to order, with becoming slowness, and by the time he has told the tale of his desire the waiter has disposed of six or eight customers and is back again. Usually the deliberate man goes away hungering.

The business done by some of the counters is enormous. One Clark Street house feeds 5,000 people every day. Another handles 2,500, and a third modestly attempts to lunch 1,700 hungry men, between sun and sun. The average length of a lunch is between seven and eight minutes, and the average price paid is 15 cents. Thus many of the business men of the city eat their noon repast at the rate of 2 cents per minute for less than ten minutes, and go away satisfied. In winter hot cakes, muffins, beans, and that sort of thing, are called for, while in summer, bread and milk, fruit, ice-cream, and lemonade are the most popular; pie and sandwiches are in demand the year around. Eating-houses of this character are to be found in the immediate vicinity of the Board of Trade, City Hall, and other busy localities. As a rule, they are orderly and well kept.

Lutheran Cemetery, situated at the corner of Graceland Avenue and North Clark Street. A very pretty cemetery shared in common by the Emanuel and St. Paul churches.

Lutheran Churches. — The Lutheran Church has a large membership in Chicago, and many churches. These are located as follows:

ENGLISH LUTHERAN. — Grace Church, Belden Avenue and Larrabee Street.

Holy Trinity Church, 398 La Salle Avenue.

Wicker Park Church, Wicker Park.

DANISH LUTHERAN.—St. Stephen's Church, Thirty-sixth and Dearborn streets.

Bethel Church, West Lake and West Forty-second streets.

Trinity Church, 440 West Superior Street.

GERMAN LUTHERAN.—Bethlehem Church, North Paulina and Mc-Reynolds streets.

Christ Church, Byron Avenue and Humboldt Street.

Holy Cross Church, James Avenue and Ullmann Street.

Emanuel Church, Ashland Avenue and Twelfth Street.

Gnaden Church, 169 Twenty-third Place.

Nazareth Church, Fullerton and Forest avenues.

St. John's Church, Superior and Bickerdike streets.

St. Mark's Church, Augusta Street and Ashland Avenue.

St. Jacobi Church, Garfield Avenue and Fremont Street.

St. Matthew's Church, Hoyne Avenue and Twentieth Street.

St. Paul's Church, Franklin and Superior streets.

St. Peter's Church, Dearborn Street near Thirty-ninth Street.

St. Simons Church, 1,339 West North Avenue.

St. Thomas' Church, Iowa Street and Washtenaw Avenue.

Trinity Church, Hanover Street and Twenty-fifth Place.

Trinity Church, 9 Snell Street.

Zion Church, Johnson and Nineteenth streets.

NORWEGIAN LUTHERAN.—Bethlehem Church, Centre Avenue and Huron Street.

Bethnia Church, Indiana and Carpenter streets.

Norwegian Church, Erie and Franklin streets.

Our Savior's Church, May and Erie streets.

St. Paul's Church, Park and North Lincoln streets.

St. Peter's Church, Seymour Avenue and Hirsch Street.

Trinity Church, Peoria and Indiana streets.

SWEDISH LUTHERAN.—Gethsemane Church, May and Huron streets.

Immanuel Church, Hobbie and Sedgwick streets.

Mission Church, Franklin and Whiting streets.

Salem Church, Thirty-fifth Street and Wentworth Avenue.

Tabernacle Church, La Salle and Thirtieth streets.

SEPARATIST LUTHERAN—Church of Peace, Wood and Iowa streets.

First Church, 270 Augusta Street.

Lyceum Theatre.—This theatre is on the West Side, the location being Desplaines Street north, half a block from Madison Street. This house is a perfect little gem, with its balcony, upper tier, orchestra chairs, private boxes, and beautiful frescoes. It presents variety performances of the better class, and seats about 1,200 persons very comfortably. T. L. Grenier, proprietor.

Manhattan Building, at 307 to 321 Dearborn Street, is an imposing structure of no less than sixteen stories. On Dearborn Street the frontage is 150 feet, and on Third Avenue the same, the depth being sixty-eight feet. Steel, brick, and terra cotta are the chief materials of construction. The first story is of ornamental iron, the second and third, carved, gray granite, and the remainder light-colored brick, and ornamental terra cotta. There are two large entrances, one on Dearborn Street, and one on Third Avenue, opening into a hallway twenty feet wide, leading to the half dozen or more passenger elevators. The interior is finished in metal work and marble mosaics. All the window openings are capacious. From the third story to the tenth, the Dearborn Street front is varied by three tiers of projecting windows, octagonal in shape, placed over the front entrance. Over the twelfth story a broad band of terra-cotta extends across the entire front, forming a division or base for the remaining stories. The roof cornice is 200 feet above the sidewalk. The building is designed for office purposes, is owned by Mr. C. C. Heisen, and cost $700,000.

Manual Training Schools.— THE CHICAGO MANUAL TRAINING SCHOOL, which has been in existence since 1883, is considered the banner school of the kind in the West, if not in the whole country. The course of education, both mental and manual, is very thorough; but the high tuition fees—$300 for the entire course—place instruction in this school beyond the reach of the poorer classes. The Chicago Manual Training School is located at Twelfth Street and Michigan Avenue.

THE CHICAGO ENGLISH HIGH AND MANUAL TRAINING SCHOOL is un-der the public school system, and, although formerly merely an auxiliary to the West Division High School, is now classed as an independent school, with a distinctive course of education. The Board of Education contemplates other free manual training schools, and there are several manual schools under the care of various charitable organizations.

Manufactures.—While Chicago has been expending on all lines, it has never neglected to cultivate its manufactures, and it is rapidly taking its place as a large manufacturing city, based upon its location, and many natural advantages. Well authenticated statistics show the present number of manufacturing establishments in Chicago to be about 2,000, employing between 60,000 and 70,000 men, using a capital of $100,000,000, and turning out annually products valued at $210,000,000. These consist of almost every conceivable variety of goods. They consume vast quantities of all kinds of materials, the products of which are distributed all over this country, and shipped to foreign lands. In this way, employment is furnished to a large proportion of the inhabitants of this section of the country. It pays a large share of the taxes, and constitutes the bulk of the traffic carried on by the various lines of transportation to and fro through the country. In general, it represents the most important part of the wealth, industry, enterprise, commercial activity, the exchange of benefits and services, not only to its own citizens, but to all mankind. Among the manufactured articles for which Chicago stands preëminent as a manufacturing center, are boots and shoes, beer and ale, block-paving, clothing, cotton goods, drugs, butterine, artificial limbs, carriage varnishes, dumb waiters, fancy goods, jewelry, hardware, wines and liquors, millinery, oleomargerine, pianos and organs, safety vaults, stoves, and toys. While there may not be every kind of manufactured article in Chicago, it is true that you can find every kind of artisan here, who is capable of doing, if necessary, skilled work in any line of manual labor. The mechanics are mostly foreigners, who have learned their trades in the old country. Competent judges assert that the day is not far distant when Chicago will rank first in the market of American manufacturing cities.

Markets.—Chicago is the great market where the northwest disposes of her products, and to do this she subdivides the different lines which have gradually centered themselves in different quarters of the city. If a dealer wants to buy fruits or vegetables, fresh, canned or imported, he goes to South Water Street. Here, in the morning, are poured in, during the fruit season, from steamer and car, from the east, the west, the north and the south and the Pacific coast, boxes, barrels, baskets, and crates of all sizes and description, and all full. They are stacked up all over the sidewalk, with just a narrow passage to squeeze through. The visitor says to himself: "Surely some of this perishable merchandise will spoil." But the commission men, who see this act repeated day after day for six months, only smile, and mentally count their gains. Two hours later the street is filled to overflowing with the express wagons of the retail dealers, and by 3 o'clock the whole mass of the daily supply of food for the city has been distributed to the groceries and meat markets all over the city. No city in the Union is better or longer supplied with early and late fruit and vegetables, and

nearly all the immense supply pours through a half dozen blocks on South Water Street.

GRAIN MARKET.—All the grains, wheat, corn, oats, rye, and buckwheat are handled by the Board of Trade operators, who buy, store, and ship whatever amount may be offered by the producers at any time, summer or winter.

MARKET WAGON STAND.—The Haymarket space is now occupied by farmers, who drive in from the immediate suburbs, and market their own truck from their wagons during the day, thus saving the expense of middlemen's profits. It is the only place in the city where trade is so made direct between the producer and the consumer. It is quite an interesting sight to see the amount and variety of stuff that is collected together here every day and disposed of by 2 o'clock.

Martha Washingtonian Home, Graceland Avenue, is under the same control as the Washingtonian, but its doors are open to women inebriates only.

Masonic Temple.—This structure, which is erected on the northeast corner of State and Randolph streets, is the highest and most magnificent building in the world. Alterations and important improvements are being constantly made in the original plans, which will mark the building as a marvelous one in the history of architecture. For instance, it is now intended that the main entrance will be 42 feet high and 28 feet wide, with a marble tesselated floor of special unique design. Sixteen elevators with a capacity for carrying 36,000 to 40,000 passengers are provided for, three of which will be used for carrying visitors and sightseers to the observatory on the roof, where a pavilion garden will present a scene of surpassing beauty and interest. In this sky parlor refreshments will be served and an orchestra will furnish excellent music. The floors of the building will not be numbered as in ordinary structures, but will be given suggestive and appropriate names. For instance, the elevator conductor will be asked to let off a passenger at "Gassette" Avenue, "Barnard" Street, or "Bliss" Arcade. A twelve-foot corridor will run on every street around the interior of the building, and as on the main floor, so on those streets stores, offices, etc., will be for rent. Many who desire to be on State Street, but can not because of the rent asked, can here obtain a store on State Street at a moderate rental, and they will be given a guarantee that the elevators will land 2,000 people before their doors every day. Altitude will therefore disappear. As there are no arbitrary partitions in the building, lessees can have room 10 x 14 to 60 x 100, large enough for a cigar stand or for a wholesale store. This order of affairs continues until the seventeenth story is reached. This and the eighteenth will be occupied by the Masonic rooms, drill rooms, etc., large enough to seat 1,500 people viewing the drilling of a battalion. Counting from bottom to top this unsurpassed temple is twenty stories, or, in other words, 265 feet. The gigantic façades suggest the. Romanesque style of architecture, but in many respects it is original. The first three stories are faced with dressed red Montello granite from Wisconsin, with carvings. The other stories are faced with gray brick, made in size and tint to resemble blocks of granite. Streets and alleys surround the entire site, for which the Masonic Fraternity Association paid $1,100,000. The estimated cost of the building

alone is $2,000,000. The interior structure is of steel, iron, and terra cotta. The interior finish is composed of mosaic floors, marble and onyx walls and old oak woodwork. This building in height and style will be without a parallel in America, or any other country, for that matter.

Maurice Porter Hospital is located at Belden Avenue and North Halsted Street.

McCoy's New European Hotel.—This hotel is a most magnificent architectural triumph. Its location, corner Clark and Van Buren streets, is in the immediate vicinity of the grandest business structures that have ever been erected in this or any country. The Board of Trade, United States Custom House, Union League Club-house, Rock Island Railroad depot, and the terminus of La Salle Street, where the great trade of Chicago centers, are only a block and a half from its doors. The hotel has 250 superbly furnished rooms, east, south and west front, with fire alarm call in each room, though the building is perfectly fire-proof. It is provided with hydraulic passenger elevator and a first-class restaurant in the building. The rates are from one dollar a day and upward, as guests desire. Mr. William McCoy is the owner.

McVicker's Theatre. — This theatre is now in its thirtieth year of continued success. There is not, in all the country, another play house more perfect in its entirety than McVicker's, of Chicago. This magnificent theatre stands unique. It combines the good qualities of other famous theatres in Europe and America with the original ideas of the veteran actor and manager, J. H. McVicker, practically expressed in foyer, auditorium and stage, showing the acme of excellence which the science of theatre construction and equipment has attained. McVicker's is luxurious, and in decoration equals, if not surpasses, the parlor and drawing-room appointments of the most costly residences. The chairs are built for ease and comfort, while the boxes are perfect gems. The cooling apparatus for hot weather works like a charm, and the he iting and ventilating is so perfect that the house is filled with fresh air continually. Behind the scenes in a theatre is, to the average patron, a tantalizing, curiosity-inciting sort of place, that is as mysterious as the interior of the Dark Continent. If a patron of this theatre desires to becom ; acquainted with a realm of novelties, write to the management for a copy of " McVicker's Observanda Accueil," a well-written and clearly illustrated book of fifty pages, showing McVicker's as it is. This theatre is located on Madison Street, near State Street. Only first-class attractions presented.

Meat Markets. — There are 1,550 retail meat markets in the city, employing 3,510 males, and 550 females; there are 33 wholesale meat markets, with 302 male employés. Total meat markets, 1,583, employing 4,332 persons. This does not include the meat packing-houses (which see).

Medical Associations. — The physicians of Chicago have several well-known societies, of which the most prominent are:

Chicago Academy of Homeopathic Physicians and Surgeons.

Chicago Dental Society.

Chicago Eclectic Medical Society.

Chicago Medical Society.

Chicago Gynecological Society.

Chicago Medical Press Association.

Hahnemann Hospital Clinical Society.

Chicago Pathological Society.

Post-graduate Policlinic of Eclectic Medicine and Surgery.

Woman's Homeopathic Medical Society.

Woman's Physiological Institute.

STATE SOCIETIES.

Illinois State Board of Dental Examiners.

Illinois State Dental Society.

Illinois State Board of Health.

Illinois State Board of Pharmacy.

Illinois State Medical Society.

Illinois State Eclectic Medical Society.

Medical Colleges. —There are enough medical colleges in Chicago, and enough students in attendance, to supply doctors for the whole civilized world. These colleges are situated as follows:

Bennett Medical College, Ada and Fulton streets.

Chicago Homeopathic Medical College, York and Wood streets.

Chicago Medical College, Prairie Avenue and Twenty-sixth Street.

Hahnemann Medical College, 2811 Cottage Grove Avenue.

Rush Medical College, Wood and Harrison streets.

Woman's Medical College, 335 South Lincoln Street.

Chicago College of Pharmacy, 465 State Street.

Chicago Veterinary College, 2537 State Street.

College of Physicians and Surgeons, Honore and Harrison streets.

Illinois College of Pharmacy, 40 Dearborn Street.

Illinois Training School for Nurses, Honore and Harrison streets.

St. Luke's Hospital, 1420 Wabash Avenue.

Woman's Hospital, Thirty-second Street and Prairie Avenue.

American College of Dental Surgery, 78 State Street.

Chicago College of Dental Surgery, 122 Wabash Avenue.

German-American College of Dental Surgery, 167 North Clark Street.

Northwestern College of Dental Surgery, 1203 Wabash Avenue.

Mercantile Club is a business man's social organization,with rooms at 136 Madison Street.

Mercy .Hospital is located at the corner of Calumet Avenue and Twenty-sixth Street. It is conducted by the Sisters of Mercy and has for its main object the care of the sick poor, after which as many of those who are able to pay as can be accommodated. This institution, the oldest hospital in Chicago, now occupies an elegant new building, constructed on the best sanitary principles and arranged to accommodate 300 patients. Its location near the lake shore is in one of the healthiest and pleasantest parts of the city. The patients are assigned to particular departments, according to the nature of their disease. which receives the attention of prominent physicians and surgeons.

Messenger Service.—There are now several companies who, for a fixed charge per month, will place an instrument in your house contained in a miniature iron box, having a small crank on the outside. By means of this you can summon at will a policeman, a fireman with an extinguisher, and notify the Fire Department, or a boy messenger in uniform, who will execute any commission you desire. These instruments are to be found at the disposal of any person in the offices of all first-class hotels and restaurants and are very convenient for the delivery

of notes, invitations, circulars, the carrying of parcels or hand luggage, etc. The charge for messenger service is based upon the standard of 30 cents per hour, but a tariff book is furnished by the company, with each instrument, which gives the exact price of service from that point to all others in the city. The oldest of these is the American District Telegraph Company, which is a part of the Western Union Telegraph system. The main offices of the American District Telegraph are located in the Pullman Building, on Michigan Avenue. There are also companies which deliver letters or circulars in quantities. (See *City Directory.*)

Methodist Episcopal Churches.—The following list gives the names and location of those in Chicago :

Ada Street Church, Ada Street, between West Lake and Fulton streets.

Asbury Church, Thirty-first Street, corner Fifth Avenue.

Brighton Church, Brighton Park.

Centenary Church, West Monroe Street, near Morgan Street.

Deering Church, corner Dunning and Ward streets.

Dickson Street Church, Dickson Street, near North Avenue.

First Church, corner Clark and Washington streets, Methodist Church block.

Fulton Street Church, corner of Fulton Street and Artesian Avenue.

Grace Church, corner La Salle Avenue and White Street.

Halsted Street Church, 778 to 784 South Halsted Street.

Jackson Street Church, West Jackson Street, corner Francisco Street.

Lincoln Street Church, South Lincoln Street, corner Ambrose Street.

Marie Chapel, Wentworth Avenue, corner Twenty-third Place.

Marshfield Avenue Church, Marshfield Avenue, near West Van Buren Street.

Michigan Avenue Church, Michigan Avenue, south of Thirty-second Street.

North West Church, Milwaukee Avenue, corner Western Avenue.

Oakland Church, Oakwood Boulevard, corner Langley Avenue.

Park Avenue Church, corner Park Avenue and Robey Street.

Paulina Street Church, 3342 South Paulina Street.

State Street Church, corner Forty-seventh and State streets.

St. Paul's Church, corner Newberry and Maxwell streets.

Trinity Church, Indiana Avenue, near Twenty-fourth Street.

Wabash Avenue Church, corner Fourteenth Street and Wabash Avenue.

Wesley Church, 1028 North Halsted Street.

Western Avenue Church, corner West Monroe Street and Western Avenue.

Winter Street Church, Dashiel Street, corner Forty-first Street.

Michael Reese Hospital, Twenty-ninth Street and Groveland Avenue, is under the management of the Hebrew Relief Association, and receives both male and female patients.

Military Department of the Missouri.—Headquarters of the Major-General Commanding, Pullman Building, southwest corner of Michigan Avenue and Adams Street, Lake Front. The Missouri Division embraces the entire Western country, from the Alleghany Mountains to the Rocky Mountains. Many of the hostile Indian tribes are located within this district, and the principal

Indian campaigns have been for years past, and are now, conducted from Chicago headquarters. The engineer's office is room No. 411, Exchange Building, corner Pacific Avenue and Van Buren Street. This officer has charge of the river and harbor improvements. Depot and Purchasing Commissary of Subsistence, office 3, East Washington Street. Recruiting offices, 10 South Clark Street, and 82 to 88 West Madison Street. Signal officer, Auditorium building, seventeenth floor. The entire number of men stationed in the vicinity of Chicago is about 600. Barracks, Fort Sheridan (which see).

Military Schools.—The Illinois Military Academy is situated at Morgan Park, on the Rock Island Railroad. The school is conducted after the pattern of West Point, and highly praised for the efficiency of its drills and exercises.

Milk.—Eighty thousand gallons of milk are required every morning for Chicago consumption, and 800 milk depots are maintained as mediums between the consumer and the farmer. A tract of country 150 miles long, and eighty wide, is taxed to furnish this vast supply, and from 40,000 to 50,000 cows are necessary for dairy service.

The milk supply of Chicago is much superior to that of many large cities, owing partly to the vigilance of the milk inspectors, and partly to the close vicinity of the dairy farms and the speed of transportation.

Miscellaneous Churches.—The following is a list of the names and locations of those in Chicago:

Central Meeting of Friends, room 4, Athenæum building; services every first day at 10.45 A. M.

Disciples of Christ meet every first day at 10.30 A. M., and 7.00 P. M.

Disciples of Jesus, the Christ, meet at 156 Evergreen Avenue.

First Society of Spiritualists meet at 55 South Ada Street, at 10.45 A. M., and 7.45 P. M., Sundays.

South Side Mediums' Society, meet Sundays at 15 Twenty-second Street.

Radical Progressive Spiritualist Association meets Sundays at 517 West Madison Street.

Young People's Progressive Association meets Sundays at Twenty-fifth Street and Indiana Avenue.

Friends'(Orthodox) Meeting-house, Twenty-sixth Street, between Indiana and Prairie avenues. Services at 10.30 A. M. and 7.30 P. M.

German Advent, 272 and 274 Augusta Street; services 10.30 A. M. and 7.30 P. M.

Scandinavian Chapel, 269 West Erie Street. Services, Saturday, at '0 A. M.

Miscellaneous Data, 1892.—
Chicago covers an area of 181.5 square miles, or 116,160 acres.

Population of city as per school census of 1892, 1,428,318.

Total city bonded indebtedness, $13,554,400.

Total value of real estate buildings, etc., owned by the city, $50,000,000.

Assessed valuation of real and personal property, $219,359,368.

Number of public-school buildings owned by the city, 221.

Number of rented buildings used for school purposes, 65.

Average number of children attending public-schools, 119,602.

Average number of children attending private schools, 65,016.

Number of teachers in public-schools, 2,920.

Number of teachers in private schools, 1,854.

Number of churches, 397.

Number of railroads entering the city, 35.

Miles of railroad centering in Chicago, 76,865.

Arrivals and departures by railroad each day, 175,000.

Through express and mail trains each day, 262.

Local suburban and accommodation trains each day, 660.

Freight, grain, stock, and lumber trains each day, 164.

Number of street-car companies, 8.

Number of miles of street railroad track laid, 395.8.

Number of police-station buildings, 35.

Number of men employed on the force, 2,306.

Number of horses in use, 179.

Number of patrol wagons, 39.

Number of ambulance wagons, 2.

Number of fire-engines and hook-and-ladder houses, 89.

Number of fire-engines, 72.

Number of fire-boats, 3.

Number of hook-and-ladder trucks, 28.

Number of chemical fire-engines, 22.

Number of firemen employed, 970.

Number of horses in use in the department, 421.

Number of police and fire-alarm boxes, 1,830.

Number of miles of electric wire used by the city, 1,200.

Number of electric lights for street lighting purposes, 1,092.

Number of acres in public parks, 8,123.

Number of miles in drives in parks and boulevards, 75.

Number of miles of walk in parks, 51.

Number of miles of streets in city, 2,335.

Miles of paved streets, 670.

Miles of sidewalks, 2,537.

Miles of main sewers, 888.

Miles of water mains, 1,346.

Miles of water tunnels in use 9.5.

Miles of water tunnels in process of construction, 8.

Number of river-traffic tunnels, 3.

Number of bridges over the Chicago River, 53.

Number of bridges over the Calumet River, 5.

Number of bridges over the canal, 3.

Number of viaducts over railroad, tracks, 29.

Number of street lamps in city, 37,000.

Number of miles river frontage, both sides, 58.

Number of vessels owned in Chicago, 339.

Value of vessels owned in Chicago, $3,088,350.

Number of vessels arriving during the year, 10,507.

Number of vessels departing during the year, 10,547 representing a tonnage of 5,150,645.

Duties collected on foreign imports, 1891, $5,182,476.

Number of feet of lumber received in 1890, 1,964,000,000.

Number of bushels of grain received, 203,708,776.

Number of barrels of flour received, 4,358,958.

Number of heads of hogs, cattle, and sheep received, 13,354,202.

Number of pounds of cured and dressed beef received, 400,903,075.

Bank clearings for the year 1890, $4,093,145,904.48.

Post Office receipts from stamps, cards, and money orders during the year 1890, $13,248,956.48.

Number of pieces of mail matter handled, 326,273,617.

Number of clerks employed, 842.

Number of carriers employed, 769.

Number of horses in use, 57.

Monadnock and Kearsarge Building, now completed and located at the corner of Dearborn and Jackson streets, is the property of the Brookes estate of Boston. Its height is sixteen stories, or 204 feet. The building has a large interior corridor, 68 by 102 feet in size, and is provided with six passenger and two freight elevators.

Monuments in Lincoln Park. —Lincoln Park is not gaining in art as it gains in monuments. The La Salle bronze statue is monstrous in drawing and ridiculous in detail. Instead of a *preux chevalier*, who would have dressed consistently for his mission—that of an explorer in a country of rude climatic conditions —who would have been courtier at court and soldier in the field, we have a mongrel combination of half-breed iu human type, dressed up in lace at the wrists, cavalry-boots on his supposed legs, a sword in his belt, and no covering on his head. The Schiller bronze statue, a rather better effigy in art, is ideally unfair to the subject; prosaic and austere, it is more pedagogue than poet. As for the Linnæus piece, the sculptor carried incongruity to madness. A squat figure in art proportions, too broad for its height, is made broader by a huge cloak which exaggerates its false dimensions. If the naturalist needed the cloak, why was he sent forth uncovered? Sculptors do as absurd things as other men, but greater absurdity than the drapery of the Linnæus can not be found in art.

Fortunately, Lincoln Park possesses two monuments worthy of public place, the glorious Lincoln of St. Gaudens, and the refined but vivid Indian group by Boyle. The Grant Monument is also in this park (which see).

Morgan Park is a suburb of great beauty, both as to location and improvements. At the station on the Chicago, Rock Island & Pacific, is a charming little park, gradually rising to a ridge, on which is situated some handsome residences. Here are located the Baptist Union Theological Seminary, Morgan Park Military Academy, and the Chicago Female College, all large and handsome buildings.

Morgue.—Located in the rear of the County Hospital. There are always a number of bodies on view, either picked from the streets, victims of accident or sudden decease, or taken from the waters of the lake or river. Besides the county morgue, many bodies—especially of the victims of murders—are taken to private morgues, of which Klaner's, on Monroe Street, is the most prominent. A new morgue on the hospital premises is now ready for occupancy.

Moses Montefiore Cemetery, is located at Waldheim (which see), and may be reached in a similar manner.

Mount Greenwood Cemetery.—This beautiful home of the dead is very appropriately named, as the ground on which it is laid out reaches an altitude of seventy feet above Lake Michigan, and is perhaps the highest piece of natural ground within a like distance from Chicago.

Nature has also provided one other feature necessary to the adornment of a park or large burying ground, and that is forest trees; here they are abundant, some of them monsters of the primæval forest. Mount Greenwood lies along One Hundred and Eleventh Street, California Avenue, and Western Avenue, and is reached by the Chicago & Grand Trunk Railway, from Dearborn station, Polk Street, and by carriages, over well-kept roads, via

Western Avenue, Halsted, and State streets, or the old Vincennes road through South Englewood. The grounds contain eighty acres, and have greenhouses, water-works, and, it is said, the largest receiving vault in the State. It has been chosen as the resting place for the remains of many of Chicago's prominent and wealthy citizens, and it contains a large number of costly and appropriate monuments, among which is that of the Elks. The management of Mount Greenwood Cemetery Association is in able hands, as will be seen by the following officers: James W. Brockway, president; Leslie P. Voorhees, vice-president; Norman B. Rexford, treasurer; Willis N. Rudd, secretary. This cemetery may also be reached via Chicago, Rock Island & Pacific Railway; depot, Van Buren Street.

Mount Hope Cemetery, a recent burying ground, located at Washington Heights, south of the city.

Mount Olive Cemetery, located at Dunning, nine miles northwest of the City Hall. This beautiful cemetery is the burying place of the Scandinavian dead. While scarcely five years old, it contains over 5,000 graves. The secretary and treasurer is Paul O. Stensland. Office, corner of Carpenter Street and Milwaukee Avenue. Take train at Union depot, via Chicago, Milwaukee & St. Paul Railway.

Mount Olivet Cemetery, located one-half mile west of the suburb of Morgan Park. Take train at Dearborn station, via Chicago & Grand Trunk Railway.

Moving.—To transfer one's household goods from one place to another, without seriously damaging, or entirely ruining, at least a portion of them, is not so difficult a task nowadays as it was formerly, owing mainly to the fact that a number of responsible firms are now making this and the furnishing of storage-room for furniture their sole business. If one wants to move, however, on Chicago's great annual moving day, the 1st of May, he will find many obstacles that he would escape at other times of the year. In the first place, it will be difficult to get drays and men unless ordered some time before they are needed; and, in the second place, there being so many customers requiring to be attended to, hurry and, consequently, carelessness are the result. Most of the storage firms who do the moving will take the risk of breakage on payment of an extra rate. Moving of trunks is done by the local express companies at low rates. (See *Expresses*.)

Museums.—Several museums flourish in Chicago, and appear to receive large incomes. Previous to the Great Fire of 1871, Wood's Museum, at the corner of Clark and Randolph streets, was one of the best in the country. After the fire it was re opened, but a subsequent conflagration put an end to its existence. Several years ago, Messrs. Kohl & Middleton conceived the idea of the "dime museum," and started two such places, one on Clark Street, and one on West Madison Street. The venture proved a great success, and the profits justified the partners in erecting a new museum and theatre, which will be located on West Madison Street, near the site of the first dime museum, which was destroyed by fire in 1891.

There are now in Chicago, three dime museums: Kohl & Middleton's South Side dime museum, at 146 South Clark Street; Kohl & Middleton's Globe museum, on State Street, near Harrison, and Epstean's New dime museum, on Randolph Street, near Clark.

In the way of high-class museums may be mentioned the Eden Musee, on Wabash Avenue, and the Libby Prison war museum, on Wabash Avenue and Fourteenth Street.

Musical Societies.—There are several musical societies in Chicago, some of which have earned no little fame and prominence.

Among these may be mentioned The Apollo Club, whose concerts are noticeable events in the musical world, and whose headquarters are in Central Music Hall, and the Germania Maennerchor, which possesses one of the finest club-houses in Chicago, and is in every way a famous musical and social organization.

Newberry Library.—To Walter Loomis Newberry Chicago is indebted for this institution, which, when completed, will easily rank as the first library in America. The sum bequeathed to the library is $2,149,201. The ground occupied by the old Newberry homestead before the fire, a complete square, bounded by Dearborn Avenue, Clark, Oak, and Walton Place, will in time be covered by the Library Building which is now being erected. In addition to the enormous amount of money stated, this exceptional and valuable property was also donated. W. F. Poole, LL. D., late of the Chicago Public Library, is the chosen librarian. Temporary quarters have been erected at 328 Ontario Street, where the books already collected are accessible for reference. Take North Clark Street or North State Street cars.

Newsboys' Home, 1418 Wabash Avenue, was founded for the purpose of supplying indigent boys with a home, provided they were disposed to earn a living.

Newspapers of Chicago.

DAILIES.

Abend Post, 181 Washington Street, evening, independent, $3.

Afton Bladet, Skandia, 192 and 194 Washington Street, evening, independent, $3.

Argus, 6221 Wentworth Avenue, morning, independent.

Business, 170 East Van Buren Street, evening, financial, $5.

Chicagoer Arbeiter-Zeitung, 274 West Twelfth Street, evening, socialist, $7.50.

Chicago Dispatch, 113–115 Fifth Avenue, evening, independent, $3.50.

Chicago Freie Presse, 94 Fifth Avenue, morning and evening, independent republican, $8.

Dagbladet, 79 Dearborn Street, evening, independent, $4.

Drovers' Journal, Union Stock Yards, evening, live-stock interests, $4.

Dziemik Chicagoski, 141 and 143 West Division Street, morning, independent, $3.

Evening Journal, 161 Dearborn Street, republican, $6.

Evening Post, 164 Washington Street, independent, $6.00.

Globe, 118 Fifth Avenue, morning, democratic, $3.

Herald, 152 Washington Street, morning, democratic, $6.

Illinois Staats-Zeitung, East Washington Street, corner of Fifth Avenue, morning, independent, $8.

Inter Ocean, 85 Madison Street, morning, republican, $8.

Mail, 120 Fifth Avenue, evening, independent, $3.50.

Market Review, 176 Fifth Avenue, evening, live stock, $4.

National Hotel Reporter, 61 La Salle Street, morning, hotel affairs, $8.

News, 123 Fifth Avenue, morning and evening, independent, $3.

Skandinaver, 187 North Peoria Street, morning, republican, $3.

South Chicago Calumet, Commercial and South Chicago avenues, evening, $6.

Sun, Union Stock Yards, evening, republican, $3.

Svornost, 150 West Twelfth Street, evening, independent, $7.50.

Times, Washington Street, corner of Fifth Avenue, morning, democratic, $6.

Tribune, Madison Street, corner of Dearborn Street, morning, republican, $6.

WEEKLIES.

Advance, 236 and 238 La Salle Street, congregational. $2.50.

America, 180 Monroe Street, literary, $3.50.

American Artisan, Tinner and House Furnisher, 69 Dearborn Street, commercial, $2.

American Bee Journal, 246 East Madison Street, bee culture, $1.

American Contractor, 53 State Street, architectural and commercial, $5.

American Engineer, 230 La Salle Street, engineering, $2.

American Field, 243 State Street, sporting, $5.

American Florist, 54 La Salle Street, floriculture, $1.

Amerika, 284 West Indiana Street, independent, $2.50.

Amerikan, 150 West Twelfth Street, independent, $2.50.

Anchor and Shield, 87 Washington Street, Ancient Order of United Workmen, $1.25.

Apparel Gazette, 184 and 186 Monroe Street, commercial, $2.

Appeal, 325 Dearborn Street, republican, $2.

ADMINISTRATION BUILDING.

At the west end of the great court, in the southern part of the Park, looking eastward. Pavilions, 82½ feet square. Dome, 277½ feet in height. Cost, $650,000. Architect, Richard M. Hunt, New York.

MINES AND MINING BUILDING.

At the southern extremity of the western lagoon or lake.   350 x 700 feet.   Architect, S. S. Beman, Chicago.

145 NEW—NEW

Appleton's In the Swim, Pullman building, literary, $2.

Argus, 76 Fifth Avenue,——,$1.50.

Arkansaw Traveler, 182 Monroe Street, humor, $2.

Bearings, 328 and 334 Dearborn Street, cycling, $1.

Bladet, 346 Wells Street, indedendent, $1.50.

Breeders' Gazette, 226 La Salle Street, live stock, $2.

Call, 3907 Cottage Grove Avenue, advertising, $1.

Canadian American, Van Buren Street, corner Pacific Avenue, independent, $2.

Catholic Home, 405 and 425 Dearborn Street, Catholic Order of Foresters, $2.

Cechos Covan, 566 Centre Avenue, Bohemian, $2.25.

Champion of Freedom and Right, 45 La Salle Street, anti-prohibition, $2.50.

Christian Cynosure, 221 West Madison Street, anti-secret societies, $2.

Christian Oracle, 415 Dearborn Street, disciples, $1.50.

Christian Worker, 415 Dearborn Street, friends, $1.50.

Chronicle, 763 West Madison Street, republican, $1.

Citizen, 79 Dearborn Street, republican, $2.50.

Columbia, Delmar Publishing Co., literary, $2.50.

Commercial Gazette, 8 Lake Street, commercial, $2.

Commercial Union, Tacoma Building, commercial, $3.

Congregational News, 167 Adams Street, religious, 50 cents.

Conservator, 180 South Clark Street, negro organ, $2.

Courier de L'Illinois, 156 Blue Island Avenue, independent, $2.

Democrat, 53 Dearborn Street, democratic, $1.

Den Chrestelige Talsmand, 157 West Indiana Street, methodist episcopal, $1.60.

10

De Nederlander, 545 Blue Island Avenue, Hollandish, $1.50.

Der Beobachter, 156 West Randolph Street, republican, $2.

Der Postillion, Lake View, independent, $3

Der Weltburger, 220 Hudson Avenue, catholic, $2.50.

Deutsche Allgemeine Zeitung, 151 Washington Street, German evangelical, $1.50.

Die Buehne, 327 Sedgwick Street, literary, $1.50.

Die Rundschau, 370 Dearborn Street, independent, $1.50.

Dry Goods Bulletin and General Storekeeper, 170 Madison Street, commercial, $2.

Dry Goods Reporter and Wholesale Price List, 167 Adams Street, commercial, $2.

Duch Casu, 150 West Twelfth Street, humorous, $2.

Eagle, 120 Fifth Avenue, independent, $2.00, H. F. Donovan, proprietor.

Economist, 97 Washington Street, financial, commercial, and real estate, $5.

Élite News, Pullman Building, society, $1.50.

Emerald, 162 East Washington Street, catholic, $2.

Epworth Herald, 57 Washington Street, methodist episcopal, $1.50.

Equity, 149 and 150 Michigan Avenue, independent, $2.

Evangelisten, 75 Warren Avenue, independent, $2.

Express, 192 Madison Street, independent, $1.

Eye, 134 Van Buren Street, photography, $2.50.

Farmers' Review, 215 Dearborn Street, agricultural, $1.25.

Farmers' Voice, 323 Dearborn Street, alliance, $1.

Farm, Field, and Stockman, Times Building, agriculture, $1.

Figaro, 170 Madison Street, society and drama, $4.

Flaming Sword, 3619 Cottage Grove Avenue, social reform, $1.50.

Folke-Vennen, 332 West Indiana Street, evangelical, $1.50.

Framat, 141 East Chicago Avenue, illustrated, $1.

Free Methodist, 104 Franklin Street, free methodist, $2.

Gamla Och Nya Hemlandet, 175 East Chicago Avenue, republican, $2.

Gazeta Katolicka, 635 Noble Street, catholic, $2.

Gazeta Polska, 532 Noble Street, independent republican, $2.

Graphic, 69 and 71 Dearborn Street, republican, $3.

Grocer, 19 Wabash Avenue, commercial, $2.

Grocer's Criterion, 34 Wabash Avenue, commercial, $2.

Hegewisch Journal, Hegewisch, independent, $1.50.

Hero, 192 Mather Street, democratic, $3.

Hide and Leather, 334 Dearborn Street, commercial, $2.

Home Light, 79 and 81 Randolph Street, literary, $2.

Horseman, 182 State Street, sporting. $4.

Hotel World, Van Buren Street, corner Pacific Avenue, commercial, $2.50.

Humoristen, 63 East Kinzie Street, humorous, $2.50.

Index, 325 Dearborn Street, fiction, $2.50.

Indicator, 225 Dearborn Street, musical, $3.

Industrial Record, 229 Honore Street, labor. $1.

Industrial World and Iron Worker, 51 La Salle Street, commercial, $3.

Interior, 45 and 46 McCormick Block, presbyterian, $2.50.

Investigator, 177 La Salle Street, insurance, $3.

Israelite, 320 Dearborn Street, Jewish, $4.

Journal of Commerce, Clark, corner Adams Street, commercial, $3.

Journal of American Medical Association, 68 Wabash Avenue, $5.

Juvenile, 44 State Street, philanthropic, $2.

Katholisches Wochenblatt, 648 Sedgwick Street, catholic, $2.50.

Lake View Democrat, 791 Lincoln Avenue, independent, $1.50.

Lake View Independent, 509 Lincoln Avenue, independent, $1.50.

Lake View Tribune, 1460 Noble Avenue, independent, $1.50.

Le Combat, 441 Centre Avenue, independent, $1.50.

Ledger, 116 and 118 Dearborn Street, literary, $1.50.

Legal Adviser, 78 Fifth Avenue, legal, $2.

Legal News, 87 Clark Street, legal, $2.25.

Lever, 134 Van Buren Street, prohibition, $1.

Life, 206 Inter Ocean building, pictorial, $2.25.

L'Italia, 404 South Clark Street, independent, $2.

Living Church, 162 Washington Street, protestant episcopal, $1.

Loyal American,'635 The Rookery, political and religious reform, $1.50.

Markets, Times building, commercial, $1.

Merchant Traveler, 229 and 231 State Street, commercial, $2.

Missions—Wanneu, 103 East Chicago Avenue, evangelical, $1.50.

Mixed Drinks, 205 La Salle Street, anti-prohibition, $2.

National Corporation Reporter, 122 La Salle Street, commercial, $5.

National Weekly, 359 Dearborn Street, humorous, $2.

Norden, 369 Milwaukee Avenue, independent, $2.

Northwestern Christian Advocate, 57 Washington Street, methodist episcopal, $2.

Northwestern Lumberman, 325 Dearborn Street, commercial, $4.

Nowezycie, 823 Thirty-first Street, independent, $1.

Nya Wecko Posten, 115 Sedgwick Street, baptist, $1.50.

Occident, 152 East Lake Street, independent, $3.

Odd Fellow, 40 Dearborn Street, odd fellowship, $1.

Open Court, 175 La Salle Street, scientific, $2.

Opinion, 417 Dearborn Street, independent, $1.50.

Orange Judd Farmer, 226 La Salle Street, agricultural, $1.

Ordensblatt der Hermanns-sœhne, 910 Milwaukee Avenue, organ of Grand Lodge Sons of Hermann, $1.

Paint, Oil and Drug Review, 166 Randolph Street, commercial, $2.

Personal Rights Advocate, 84 and 86 Fifth Avenue, organ of Personal Rights League, $2.

Pilot, 79 Randolph Street, catholic, $2.

Plattdeutsche Zeitung, 113 West Randolph Street, independent, $2.

Prairie Farmer, 166-168 Adams Street, agricultural, $1.

Pritel Diteck, 702 Allport Avenue, independent, $1.50.

Produce Trade Reporter and Shippers' Gazette, Produce Exchange, commercial, $2.

Railway Age, 205 La Salle Street, commercial, $4.

Railway Review, The Rookery, technical, $4.

Real Estate and Building Journal, 164 Washington Street, commercial, $5.

Record, 415 Dearborn Street, democratic, $1.

Record, Grand Crossing, republican, $1.50.

Record, LakeView, independent, $1.

Referee, 328 and 334 Dearborn Street, sporting, $2.

Religio-Philosophical Journal, 92 La Salle Street, spiritualist, $2.50.

Rights of Labor, 163 Washington Street, labor, $1.50.

Sanderbudet, 126 Oak Street, methodist episcopal, $1.50.

Sanitary News, 88 and 90 La Salle Street, commercial, $2.

Saturday Blade, 116 and 118 Dearborn Street, fiction, $2.

Saturday Evening Herald, 89 Clark Street, society, $2.

Saturday Evening Post, 37 North Clark Street, society, $1.

Sentinel, 544 Ogden Avenue, independent, $1.

Shoe and Leather Review, 180 and 182 Monroe Street, commercial, $3.

Society News, 1268 West Madison Street, independent, $1.

South Side Advocate, 39 Thirty-first Street, independent, $1.

Sportsman, 12 Sherman Street, sports, $1.50.

Standard, 69 Dearborn Street, baptist, $2.50.

Stationary Engineer, 9 Lakeside Building, engineering, $2.

Suburban Times, 112 and 114 Fifth Avenue, independent, $1.50.

Svenska Amerikanaren, 35 South Clark Street, independent, $2.25.

Svenska Kuriren, 26 North Clark Street, independent, $2.25.

Thrift, 55 Dearborn Street, agricultural, $1.

Timberman, 161 and 163 Randolph Street, commercial, $2.

Trade and Mining Review, 162 Washington Street, commercial, $2.

Union Signal, 161 La Salle Street, temperance, $1.50.

Unity, 175 Dearborn Street, unitarian, $1.

Universalist, 69 Dearborn Street, universalist, $2.50.

Verdens Gang, 187 North Peoria Street, independent, 50 cents.

Vim, 3805 Cottage Grove Avenue, independent, 50 cents.

Vort Blad, 1862 Shober Street, lutheran, $1.

West End Advocate, 59 West Randolph Street, commercial, $1.

Western British American, 253 and 255 Dearborn Street, $2.

Western Catholic News, 134 Van Buren Street, catholic, $1.50.

Western Electrician, 6 Lakeside building, mechanical, $3.

Western Fireman, 177 La Salle Street, firemen's interests, $2.

Western Good Templar, 167 Adams Street, temperance, $1.

Western Jeweler, 51 and 53 Dearborn Street, commercial, $2.

Western Rural and American Stockman, 158 Clark Street, agricultural, $1.50.

West Side Vindicator, Dearborn Street, corner of Harrison Street, citizens' party, $1.

Wiara I Ojczyzna, 141 and 143 West Division Street, catholic, $2.

Young Men's Era, 10 Arcade Court, evangelical, $1.50.

Young People's Weekly, 25 Washington Street, evangelical, $1.25.

Zgoda, 112 West Division Street, independent, $2.

BI-WEEKLIES.

Journal of Work, 681 West Lake Street, mercantile pursuits, 25 cents.

Katholischer Jugenfreund, 3 North Clark Street, catholic, $1.

Sons of Veterans National Reveille, 78 Fifth Avenue, patriotic, $1.

Western Paper Trade, 155 Washington Street, commercial, $1.50.

Western Stationer, 155 Washington Street, commercial, $1.50.

SEMI-MONTHLY.

Amerikanisshe Jagd und Schuetzen Zeitung, 161 La Salle Street, sporting, $2.

Argus, 161 La Salle Street, insurance, $3.

Black Diamond, Home Insurance building, commercial, $2.

Clark's Horse Review, 61 Washington Street, horse-breeding, $2.

Der Wahrheits Zeuge, 860 Milwaukee Avenue, evangelical, $1.

Lumber Trade Journal, 92 and 94 La Salle Street, commercial, $2.

Lutherischer Hausfreund, 225 Dearborn Street, lutheran, $1.

National Laundry Journal, 195 Washington Street, commercial, $1.

Presto, 113 Adams Street, musical and dramatic, $1.50.

Railway Red Book, 88 and 90 Washington Street, railroad timetable, $2.

R. M. S. Bugle, Clark Street, corner of Van Buren Street, postal service, $1.

Sabbath Visitor, 182 Monroe Street, Jewish, juvenile, $1.50.

School Herald, 185 Wabash Avenue, educational, 75 cents.

Social World, 78 Fifth Avenue, social, $1.

Stationer and Printer, 164 Dearborn Street, commercial, $2.

Telegrapher, 13 North Curtis Street, telegraphy, $1.

Vor Talsmand, 504 Fulton Street, independent, 60 cents.

Western Broker, 196 La Salle Street, commercial, $1.

Young Crusader, 161 La Salle Street, temperance, 50 cents.

MONTHLIES.

Alliance Herald, 161 La Salle Street, methodist episcopal, 50 cents.

American Advertiser, 557 and 559 The Rookery, advertising and window dressing, $2.

American Building Association News, 155 Washington Street, building associations, $1.

American Checker Review, 182 Monroe Street, checkers, $1.50.

American Elevator and Grain Trade, 184 Dearborn Street, commercial, $1.

American Farmer, Live Stock, and Poultry Raiser, 125 Clark Street, animals, 50 cents.

American Furniture Gazette, 150 Dearborn Street, commercial, 50 cents.

American Harness and Horse

Journal, 182 Monroe Street, commercial, $1.

American Jeweler, 341 to 351 Dearborn Street, commercial, $1.

American Liveryman and Horse Owner, 415 Dearborn Street, commercial, $1.

American Miller, 184 Dearborn Street, commercial, $1.

American Poultry Journal, 113 Adams Street, poultry-raising, $1.

American Sheep-breeder and Wool-grower, 170 Madison Street, live stock, $1.

American Soap Journal, 28 and 30 Market Street, commercial, $2.

American Storekeeper, 557 and 559 The Rookery, commercial, $1.

American Swineherd, 113 Adams Street, agricultural, 50 cents.

Baker's Helper, 136 West Washington Street, commercial, $1.

Beacon. Tribune building, photography, $1.

Black and White, 196 and 198 Clark Street, insurance, $2.

Blazes, 58 La Salle Street, firemen's association, $1.

Brainard's Musical World, 145 and 147 Wabash Avenue, musical, $1.50.

Brickmaker, 180 and 182 Monroe Street, commercial, $3.

Building Budget, 90 La Salle Street, commercial, $3.

Business Record, 132 West Van Buren Street, commercial, $1.

Carriage and Wagon Maker, 99 Washington Street.

Carriage Journal, 61 La Salle Street, commercial, $1.

Christian Science, 87 Washington Street, mental healing, $1.

Climax, fiction $1.

Clinique, 1823 Michigan Avenue, medical, $2.

Confectioner and Baker, 96 Fifth Avenue, commercial, $1.

Cork, Traders' building, anti-prohibition, $2.

Credit Review, Times building, financial, $2.

Dairy World, 85 Washington Street, dairying $1.

Dental Review, 66 Madison Street, dental, $2.50.

Der Brauer und Maelzer Brewer and Maltster, Lake Street, corner Clark Street, commercial, $5.

Der Glaubensbote, 161 La Salle Street, evangelical, $1.

Dial, 117 Wabash Avenue, literary, $1.50.

Die Gegenwart, 336 North Ashland·Avenue, literary, $1.

Domestic Engineering, 557 and 559 The Rookery, engineering, $1.

Druggists' Gazette, 108 Franklin Street, pharmaceutical, $1.

Easter's Implement World, 115 Dearborn Street, commercial, $1.

Electrical Industries, 351 The Rookery, industrial, $3.

Evangelical Standard, 189 La Salle Street, evangelical, 25 cents.

Evangelists' Sendebud, 28 College Place, evangelical, 75 cents.

Farm Implement News, 325 Dearborn Street, commercial, $1.

Freedom, Avondale Station, anarchist, 75 cents.

Furniture, 222 Franklin Street, commercial, $1.

General Manager, 94 and 95 Traders' building, commercial, $1.

German-American Miller, Clark Street, corner Lake Street, commercial, $1.

Good Stories, 23 Ashland Block, fiction, $1.

Gospel Sword, 269 West Kinzie, holiness, 50 cents.

Guardsman, 315 Wabash Avenue, Grand Army of the Republic, $2.

Health and Home, 2301 Wabash Avenue, hygienic, $1.

Heart and Hand, 69 Dearborn Street, matrimonial, 50 cents.

Hemmet,—household, $1.

Hermetist, 619 Jackson Boulevard, theosophical, $1.

Holzarbeiter (woodworker), Clark Street, corner Lake Street, $1.

Home and Society, 96, 123 Randolph Street, society, $1.
Home Art, 415 Dearborn building, art, $1.
Homeless Boy, 47 Jackson Street, charitable. $1.
Home, School, and Nation, 204 Dearborn Street, educational, $1.50.
Home Visitor, 1926 Wabash Avenue, Home for the Friendless, 60 cents.
Humane Journal, 242 Wabash Avenue, prevention of cruelty to.animals, $1.
Humboldt Hustler, 167 Adams Street, methodist episcopal, 50 cents.
Illustrated Home Journal, 246 East Madison Street, literary, $1.
Illustrator, 148 and 150 Madison Street, evangelical, 60 cents.
Independent, 334 Dearborn Street, insurance, $1.
Independent Forester, Rooms 6 and 7, 53 Dearborn Street, Independent Order of Foresters, $1.
Ink Fiend, 59 Dearborn Street, mechanics, $1.
Inland Architect and News Record, 19 Tribune Building, architectural, $3.
Inland Printer, 183 Monroe Street, commercial, $2.
Ironmonger, 150 Dearborn Street, commercial, $1.
Jeweler, 557 and 559 The Rookery, commercial, $1.50.
Jewelers' Journal, 107 Madison Street, commercial, $1.50.
Journal of Industrial Education, 243 State Street, educational, $1.
Journal of the World's Statistics, 184 Dearborn Street, statistical, $3.
Kindergarten, 161 La Salle Street, educational, $2.
Knight Errant, 337 and 339 Dearborn Street, Knights of Pythias, $1.
Ladies' Fashion Journal and Shopping Magazine, Auditorium building, fashion, $1.
Ladies' Standard Magazine, 159 State Street, 50 cents.

Law Journal, 103 Washington Street, legal, $3.
Lincoln Park Church Monthly, 141 Lincoln Avenue, congregational, 20 cents.
Literary Transcript, 254 and 256 Franklin Street, literary, $1.
Manford's Magazine, 774 West Van Buren Street, universalist, $1.50.
Master Steam Fitter and Heating Engineer, 9 Lakeside building, commercial, $1.
Medical Current, 182 Clark Street, medical, $2.
Medical Era, 190 Thirty-first Street, medical, $2.
Medical Standard, 69 and 71 Dearborn Street, medical, $1.25.
Medical Times, 291 Dearborn Street, medical, $2.
Medical Visitor, 1833 Indiana Avenue, medical, $1.
Medicinal Zeitung, medical, $1.
Metal und Eisen Zeitung (Metal and Iron Journal) Lake Street, corner Clark Street, commercial, $1.
Misk-wi-nen-ne, 182 Clark Street, Improved Order of Red Men, $1.
Mission Studies, 59 Dearborn Street, congregational, 25 cents.
Mixed Stocks, 918 The Rookery, commercial, $1.
Modern Reporter, 1302 West Madison Street, shorthand and typewriting, $1.
Monumental News, 243 State Street, commercial, $1.
National Builder, 115 Adams Express building, commercial, $3.
National Harness Review, 415 Dearborn Street, commercial, $2.
National Journalist, 21 and 25 Third Avenue, journalism, $1.
National Magazine, Madison Street, corner Fifth Avenue, literary, $1.
National Steamship and Railway Gazette, 75 West North Avenue, commercial, $1.
New Church Independent and Review, 144 Thirty-seventh Street, swedenborgian, $2.

151 NEW—NEW

Nordens Vaktare, evangelical, 50 cents.

Oak and Ivy Leaf, 161 La Salle Street, temperance, 25 cents.

Orkney and Shetland American, 2929 Shields Avenue, nationality, $1.

Paint and Varnish Journal, 170 East Van Buren Street, commercial, $1.

Parish Messenger, 456 Englewood Avenue, protestant episcopal, $1.

People's Health Journal, 441 Dearborn Avenue, hygienic, $1.

Picture and Art Trade, 164 Dearborn Street, commercial, $1.50.

Picture Gallery for Young Folks, 308 Dearborn Street, juvenile, 75 cents.

Printers' Album and Electrotyper, 303 Dearborn Street, typographical, $1.

Pythian Record, Clark Street, corner Van Buren Street, Knights of Pythias, $1.

Railway Master Mechanics, 816 The Rookery, mechanical, $1.

Rand-McNally Bankers' Monthly, 168 Adams Street, financial, $4.

Rand-McNally Official Railway Guide and Handbook, 168 Adams Street, railway statistics, $3.

Record of Christian Work, 148 Madison Street, undenominational, 50 cents.

Registered Pharmacist, 175 Dearborn Street, commercial, $1.

Reporter, 204 Washington Boulevard, mechanical, $2.

Roadmaster and Foreman, 271 Franklin Street, trade union, $1.

Schuh und Leder Anzeiger, 108 and 110 Franklin Street, commercial, $1.

Sewing Machine Advance, 158 South Clark Street, commercial, $1.

Sokol Americky, 126 West Taylor Street, commercial, $1.

Soldier and Citizen, 700 Rialto Building, Grand Army of the Republic, $1.

Song Friend, 243 State Street, musical, $1.

Sporting Goods Dealer, 116 and 118 Dearborn Street, commercial, $1.

Sporting Review, 116 and 118 Dearborn Avenue, sporting, $1.

Statesman, 167 Adams Street, political economy, $2.

Street Railway Gazette, 8 Lakeside Building, commercial, $2.

Switchmen's Journal, 14 and 16 Pacific Avenue, trade union, $1.

True Protestant, 122 North Carpenter Street, evangelical, 50 cents.

Trumpet-Call of the Loyal Sunday School Army, 148 Madison Street, evangelical.

Truth, ————, evangelical, $1.

Voice of Masonry and Family Magazine, 182 South Clark Street, Masonic, $3.

Washingtonian, 566 West Madison Street, temperance, 65 cents.

Western Banker, and Bank Clerks' Journal, 170 Madison Street, banking, $2.

Western Bottler, 229 East Randolph Street, commercial, $1.

Western Manufacturer, 99 Washington Street, commercial, $3.

Western Druggist, 69 Dearborn Street, commercial, $1.

Western Medical Reporter, 163 State Street, medical, $1.

Western Undertaker, 226 South Lincoln Street, undertaking, $1.

Woman's News, McVicker's Theatre Building, woman's suffrage, $1.

World Wide Missions, 334 Dearborn Street, methodist episcopal, 25 cents.

Young Ladies' Bazar, 230 and 232 La Salle Street, fashions, $1.

Zion's Vatakre, 28 College Place, evangelical, 75 cents.

BI-MONTHLIES.

American Review, 17 and 18 Lakeside Building, reform, $2.

Deutsch-Amerikanische Homopathische Zeitscriff, 330 La Salle Avenue, medical, 50 cents.

Farmers' **Advance**, agricultural, free.

Friends' Bible School, 415 Dearborn Street, friends, 20 cents.

Monist, 175 La Salle Street, scientific, $2.

Great Northern Hotel.—

Among the immense number of hotels erected to meet the present and prospective 1ush of travel attracted to Chicago by the Columbian Exposition, the "Great Northern" is a splendid sample of what Chicago can offer as a first-class hotel. Its whole equipment represents an investment of about $3,000,000. Every dollar has been put where "it will do the most good" to its patrons, in comfort and convenience. It occupies the square bounded by Quincy, Dearborn, and Jackson streets, fronting on Dearborn Street, opposite the Post Office, with the ladies' entrance on Quincy Street. It is built after the Chicago construction style of pressed brick, terra cotta, and steel. Fourteen stories carry its roof into the upper air 185 feet from the pavement. Notwithstanding its immense height for a hotel, it has no inaccessible sky parlors, for all the floors are brought clo:ely together by the constant service of six rapid elevators.

The main office is on the first floor, also the guests' "café," wash room, barber shop, lavatory, etc. Not a single detail of the most elaborate furnishing known to modern travelers has been omitted, including a Western Union telegraph office and Leroy Payne's livery telephone service, which is the best in the city. The well-known proprietors, Messrs. Alvin Hulbert and W. S. Eden, who have superintended the building from the cement foundation, determined that it should be fire-

proof enough to withstand a repetition of the great conflagration of 1871. There are 450 bedrooms, 5,000 electric lights, and 400 employes. Every floor has its own bell station, supplied with stationery, ice-water, etc., and is connected with the main office.

The Leroy Payne livery telephone service, which is the best in the city, has a branch office in the "Great Northern," and prompt attention is given to all orders received here for carriages, cabs, etc. Mr. Leroy Payne is one of Chicago's most prominent business men. He has branch offices of his livery telephone service at most all the principal hotels in Chicago.

Northwestern University is located in Evanston, which is the most beautiful suburb of Chicago, and is one of the best and most healthy summer-resorts on the great lakes, having all the advantages of city, and all the enjoyments of rural life It is a model university village, and unusually free from immoral influences. By the laws of the State the sale of intoxicating liquor is forbidden within four miles of the university. The university campus contains thirty acres on the shore of Lake Michigan. The buildings are shaded by native oaks, through which one catches glimpses of the blue waters of the great lake. There are connected with the university 111 professors and instructors, and more than 1,900 students.

In all the departments the highest advantages of education are given at a moderate cost.

The university includes the following departments:

The College of Liberal Arts, which has four regular courses of study, and opportunity for a select course.

The College of Medicine.

The College of Law.

The College of Pharmacy.
The College of Oral and Dental Surgery.
The Preparatory School.
The School of Elocution.
The Conservatory of Music.
Department of Art.
Garret Biblical Institute.
Swedish Theological Seminary.
Norwegian and Danish Theological Seminary

The Woman's College is a large and elegant building that gives to young women the advantages of a well-regulated home.

There is also a college cottage, which offers special advantages to young women of limited means.

The three theological schools are on the grounds of the university, but are under distinct corporations.

The colleges of medicine, of law, of pharmacy, and of dental and oral surgery, are in Chicago, and the other departments are in Evanston.

In the college of liberal art, the college of law, and in the departments of elocution, of music, and art, young women are admitted to the same privileges, the same courses of study, and receive the same degrees as young men.

In the preparatory school, the special work of which is to prepare students for college so as to meet the most advanced requirements of the highest and best colleges of the country, there is also provision for a general and academic education for students who wish to prepare themselves for the study of medicine, law, teaching in public schools, or for business. There has recently been erected on the college campus a large and well-furnished hall of science, which affords unusually good accommodations for the departments of chemistry and physics.

Practical instruction is given in the laboratories, in this building, in the department of chemistry and physics, and also in the biological laboratory in University Hall.

The university museum contains large and valuable collections for illustrating the departments of natural history. The specimens are properly labeled and are well adapted to aid the student. The museum contains·

1. An herbarium, consisting of nine large and valuable collections of plants from various parts of the country.

2. A zoölogical collection of 5,000 specimens.

3. A collection of specimens in mineralogy, lithology, and geology. In ethnology, it contains a number of well-selected specimens, illustrating various stages of civilization.

The university library contains about 26,000 volumes, besides 8,000 unbound pamphlets. It contains a large number of books for general reading and reference, and for use in the several departments of study. It is unusually complete in the department of Greek and Latin literature. Every author is represented by the best editions, from the earliest date. In the related subjects, also, of archæology, criticism, and history, the library is correspondingly full, so that in the special field of classical philology it ranks with the best in America. In modern literature, it is well supplied with standard works in German, French, Spanish, and Italian. There is also a valuable selection of books illustrating the history and best productions of the fine arts.

There is a reading-room in connection with the library, open morning and afternoon, supplied with a good collection of reviews and other periodicals. Every student is entitled to its privileges.

Gentlemen of liberality and large means have also promised a library building, which will be one of the finest and best in the country. The endowment of the university is large, and rapidly increasing by the sale and lease of property which has been unproductive. In a very few years its income will be largely increased, and then there will be a corresponding increase in its resources and facilities for instruction.

The famous Dearborn Observatory is also located on the grounds of the university. This telescope, whose object-glass is eighteen inches in diameter, is one of the best, as lately it was the largest telescope in the world. Numerous and valuable discoveries have been made with it.

Nurses.—There are enough trained and skilled professional nurses in Chicago to supply all demands. There are, exclusive of those employed in hospitals, over 200 nurses, and the number is continually increasing by the accession of graduates of the training-school.

THE ILLINOIS TRAINING SCHOOL FOR NURSES is located at No. 304 Honore Street, and is in prosperous circumstances. The nurses of this school—about 100 in number—have charge of all the nursing in the Presbyterian Hospital, and of most of the same kind of work in the great County Hospital.

Oakland.—This attractive little suburb is situated on the Illinois Central Railroad. The growth of Oakland has been rapid, and the settlement quite extensive. It is a little over four miles from the City Hall.

Oakwoods Cemetery.—This is another of the beautiful park-like places of this city's enterprise, in which the departed have final sepulchre. The grounds, containing 200 acres, are on the east side of Cottage Grove Avenue from Sixty-seventh Street. They contain four charming lakes, each one of which covers from three to four acres in extent. Eight large greenhouses, in which almost every variety of plant is grown, are also a part of the possessions of this noted cemetery, besides a very handsome cottage for the use of the superintendent, a commodious receiving vault and a chapel tend to further the completion of the improvements. The design used for laying out the grounds is after the lawn system, which is divided into sections, each with mounds of different sizes and shapes, while through the whole there is an abundance of shrubbery. The monument to the soldiers who have died at the Home for Old Soldiers, is a mammoth figure of a soldier on guard, and is of white marble. In the south part of the grounds, over 6,000 dead lie buried. These were Confederates—men who were prisoners at Camp Douglas. This cemetery contains the graves of some of Chicago's earliest settlers, also many of her former influential citizens. James H. Woodworth, a two-term mayor of the city and also member of congress: Col. W. J. Foster, geologist and author; Mr. Wm. Jones, an old settler; Dr. C. E. Dyer; Mr. Chas. Hitchcock, and others equally well known, are buried here. The Cemetery Association has offices on Dearborn Street, room 102, No. 85, and Mr. Marcus A. Farwell is the presiding officer. This is one of the three great prominent native Protestant cemeteries of the city. A charming drive to this place is via Michigan Avenue and Grand Boulevard and Washington Park.

Ohavey Emunah Cemetery, located at Waldheim, ten miles from the City Hall. Take train at

Grand Central depot via Chicago & Northern Pacific Railroad. Trains leave at 12:01 P. M. daily, including Sundays (see *Waldheim Cemetery*).

Ohavey Scholom Cemetery, located at Oakwoods, Sixty-seventh Street and Cottage Grove Avenue. Take Cottage Grove Avenue cable cars or Illinois Central train, foot of Randolph Street. (See *Oakwoods Cemetery.*)

Old People's Home, Indiana Avenue near Thirty-ninth Street. It is open to those residents in Chicago for two years, who are sixty years of age. An admission fee of $300 is charged, and inmates furnish their own rooms.

Olympic Theatre.—This is one of the oldest of the theatres, and is on Clark Street, north of Randolph Street. It has a handsome auditorium running parallel with the street. This is a variety house, where the very best combinations, representing a varied line of novel specialties, appear. The management conducts the theater on the popular plan of moderate prices, consequently there is always a full house. Kohl & Middleton and Cassel, proprietors.

Opium Dens.—The vice of opium smoking, which always comes with the Chinese, has established itself in Chicago along with the 1,200 Chinese who live in the western metropolis. South Clark Street is noted for opium " joints," and the nightly raids of the police usually result in quite a haul of victims of the habit, both white and yellow. As yet the majority of these opium-smokers are Mongolians, but the number of white devotees of the pipe is continually increasing.

Orphan Asylum of the Guardian Angel is under the management of the Guardian Angel German Catholic Society, and is located at Rose Hill (which see).

Packing-House Odors. — In 1874 the sanitary board passed a regulation that all packing and rendering houses within the city limits should put in an apparatus to consume the gases from the rendering tanks. In compliance with this regulation a majority of the packers employed the system in use at the agricultural works at Deptford, England. That is, to condense all the aqueous vapors, and discharge them into the sewers, and to pass the dry gases over the fire under the boilers; where, coming ;in contact with the live coals, all the animal matter carried by the gas is consumed. The other establishments where this plan was not used, adopted the plan of first carbonizing the gases and then burning them. Both systems were successful and resulted in much good, both to the city and the packing-houses.

Packingtown is the name often given to the Union Stock Yards proper and their immediate environment. If they were situated by themselves, in any other part of the country, they would make a large city that would be considered of remarkable interest by the chroniclers, and the amount of business done there of immense importance. But it is so overshadowed by the greatness of Chicago, of which it is only a part, that its individuality is in danger of being unnoticed. There is but one Packingtown in the world and that is in Chicago. Whoever visits the city and fails to visit this center of industry, misses an opportunity. The Stock Yards proper, located on the corner of Esom Avenue and

Halsted Street, were commenced in June, 1865, and on the following Christmas were thrown open for business. To Col. R. M. Hough, one of the original settlers of this city, belongs the credit of this display of energetic push. The company owns 345 acres; of this, 146 acres are occupied by the yard and pens. The present capacity of these yards is 25,000 head of cattle, 150,000 head of hogs, 20,000 sheep, and stabling for 1,000 horses. Forty miles of railroad track, 50 miles of switch-tracks, all laid with steel rails, belong to the company. All the railroad lines in the United States converge to this point, and it is the pronounced opinion of experts, both in Europe and the United States, that it is the most perfect in plan, appointments, arrangements, and detail, of any similar institution in the world; $3,000,-000 has already been put into the construction account by the company, to say nothing of the capital invested in the business by private enterprise. A few years ago the publisher of a live-stock paper introduced the custom of having a tent erected at the yards for the display of improved breeds of stock, etc. This has now become a permanent feature. A pavilion ha٠ been erected, capable of seating 600 persons, with plenty of room for the display and sale of stock. Cattle from noted herds in all parts of the United States and Canada are sold here, and a regular horse-market for the sale of imported and American bred horses has been established. Within the company's grounds is The Transit, a first-class hotel costing a quarter of a million dollars, where stockmen can get the best, for $2 per day. The Exchange Building, a two-and-a-half story brick structure 60x380 feet, standing in the middle of the yards, has a Board of Trade Room, the main offices of the company, post office, telegraph office, restaurant, and numerous private offices of commission firms. Two large artesian wells, one 1,100 and the other 1,200 feet in depth, help out the enormous water supply needed. Here buyers and sellers meet from all over the Union. There is no sixty or ninety days, but it is a cash market. Just outside the limits of the company's grounds is a fringe of packing-houses, where the vast herds constantly pouring into the yards from the prairies of the West, are made into commercial material. Over one-seventh of all the hogs marketed in the United States come to Chicago. Neither money nor enterprise has been spared to complete and perfect all details, so as to reach as nearly as possible the utmost dispatch, cleanliness and economy in the manufacture of hog products. It has been said that the only two things about the animal they have failed to save and utilize, are the squeal and curl of the tail. The packing-houses turn out about 18,-000,000 carcasses per annum. Another peculiar industry is the shipment of dressed beef to the Eastern and Middle States. Against all the bitter opposition at first manifested, it is constantly increasing. Perhaps a reason for this lies in the fact that a car will carry but eighteen live animals, but holds thirty carcasses, and the cost of slaughtering here is much less than anything that could be done East. The men who stand at the head of the packing business, are the wealthiest and 'most public spirited of all Chicago's enterprising citizens. The hundreds of employés who find employment here, reside close by. So, a large city, with its schools, churches, and places of amusement, has grown up about the manufacturing nucleus. It is not to be wondered at that the inhabitants are peculiar in some things, for their business is peculiar. But after all there is nothing very perceptible, only that the workmen are largely made up of men of foreign birth.

Palmer House.—The external appearance of this remarkable building is such that it is a wonder to strangers and a "joy forever" to the citizens. Its construction was commenced in July, 1871. The plan of

time were the Grand, at Paris, and the Beau Rivage d'Angleterre at Geneva. Mr. Palmer's determination was to eclipse them all, and the unanimous opinion of travelers is that he has done it. The substantial points characteristic of this hotel are the massiveness and solidity with which it is built. The edifice contains 17,000,000 bricks, of which over 1,000,000 go into partition walls. There are about 90,000

PALMER HOUSE, STATE AND MONROE STREETS.

the Palmer House was only evolved after several plans had been submitted to the proprietor, Mr. Potter Palmer, by the best Chicago architects, and after he had, with the architect selected for the purpose, traveled over Europe and availed himself, not only of the hints of the architects there, but of the ideas to be gathered from the finest hotels in that center of civilization and luxury. The best hotels in Europe at that

square feet of marble tiling in the floors of the building, and all the flooring is laid upon massive beds of cement, supported by I beams brought from Belgium, with intervening arches of corrugated iron. The precautions against fire are, in all respects, very complete. There are also about this hotel many novel and exceptionally thorough arrangements for admitting light liberally everywhere, avoiding unpleasant kitchen and closet odors etc., which can not be particularized here. The dimensions of the building are, on State Street, 254 feet; on Monroe Street, 250 feet, and on Wabash Avenue, 131 feet. Total area covered, 72,500 square feet. This is necessarily divided up by courts, and of these, the carriage court, entered by *portes cocheres* from three streets, is 90x120 feet in dimensions. The facings of the several fronts are of gray sandstone, with the first story and *entresol* of massive iron castings which alone cost $100,000. Of the facing stone 160,000 cubic feet were used. The peculiarity which, after all, most impresses the visitor, is the more than palatial richness of the interior finish. The immense office of the hotel, 64x106 feet and 24 feet in height, is wainscoted everywhere with Italian marble, studded with panels of remarkably rich rose brocatello marble, many of the natural mosaics exhibited in these panels being of rare and curious beauty. The wainscoting of the counter is the same. The next feature on which the wealth of the builder has been most conspicuously lavished, is the grand staircase of Carrara marble, springing from the ground to the uppermost floor, and constructed upon that wonderful self-supporting plan, whereby each step has only to be fixed at one end—the whole stretching outward from the wall, with apparently no support at all. The principle is a variation of the keystone, and is applied in only one other instance in America—Girard College. Some idea of the startling weight thus suspended in mid-air may be conjectured from the fact that at each landing (of which there are several to each story) there is a square block weighing 5,200 pounds. The intermediate stairs are of solid blocks, and weigh perhaps 1,200 pounds each. The total cost of the edifice is $2,000,000. The style of the furnishings is correspondingly elegant, and the bill for that item was not less than $500,000. All the front rooms, up to the fourth or fifth floor, are furnished with satin or velvet upholstery, Wilton or moquette carpets, and have elegantly carved mantels on which stand clocks of bronze, gilt, or ormolu, with other ornaments to match. The dining-room, and other *salles à manger*, five in number, are located contiguously to each other, and have a total area of 12,033 square feet. The principal dining-room, 64x76 feet in size, is arranged so as to suggest an open Italian court, the sweep of the eye being relieved by massive fluted columns extending around the room as if supporting piazzas. There are 708 rooms in the Palmer House, and the electric apparatus by which the occupants of each communicate with the office, includes nearly 100 miles of wire. From 1,000 to 2,400 guests are usually accommodated in this, one of the largest and costliest hotels in the world. The new Palmer House was opened in the year 1873 by Mr. Potter Palmer, who was then, and is now, the sole proprietor and manager. The traveler can have his choice of plans while stopping at the Palmer—either the American or European. In connection with the Palmer House are the famous bathhouse and barber shop, said to surpass anything of the kind in the United States, if not the world. They merit a visit of inspection by strangers who desire to see the highest style of art bestowed on such places of convenience.

Leroy Payne's well-known livery stables have telephone connection with this hotel, and a carriage or other conveyance can be summoned at any time. The rates of the Payne company are very reasonable and its stables the finest in Chicago.

Park System.—The fathers builded better than they knew in their bestowment upon Chicago of its splendid system of parks and boulevards. Many of these so-called fathers are still in the active enjoyment of life, and are able to witness the rare fact that "their works do praise them." The second city in the United States, the fifth in the world, has outgrown all the boundaries hitherto designed for it, and now finds within its enlarged limits a park and boulevard system such as no other city can show.

The three acts providing for a park system in Chicago was passed by the same Legislature in February, 1869. The first commissioners were: Lincoln Park—E. C. McCagg, J. B. Turner, Joseph Stockton, Jacob Rehm, and Andrew Nelson. South Park—John M. Wilson, George W. Gage, Chauncey F. Bowen, L. B. Sidway, and Paul Cornell. West Side—Charles C. P. Holden, Henry Greenebaum, George W. Stanford, E. E. Runyan, Isaac R. Hitt, Clark Lipe, and P. W. Gates. Others among the living and dead who should have honorable mention here are George M. Kimbark, W. H. Crosby, George S. Bowen, and James H. Bowen, who were most prominent, and by their personal efforts at Springfield made it possible for Chicago to secure the necessary legislation. The South Park bill was drawn by the late Corydon Beckwith, and was a masterly document, creating a Park Commission independent of the city or State authorities. To pass such a bill, opposed by a lobby of able croakers, required hard and earnest work. After many weeks of such effort, news at length came that the bill could be passed, provided the

park lands could be located and described by metes and bounds in the proposed park bill. A committee was appointed to locate the parks, consisting of Chauncey Bowen, James H. Rees, and Seneca D. Kimbark. These gentlemen were requested to do their part of the work the day following their appointment, so that they did not have much time for the examination and consideration of the sites. But they took a carriage early next morning, taking with them a map of Cook County, returning in the evening with pencil lines drawn around what are now Washington and Jackson parks, and Midway Plaisance connecting them, having located about 1,200 acres of what then appeared worthless land, for the future grand parks of Chicago. Many of the old citizens were amazed at the boldness of the scheme, declaring that it would ruin the city. But time has told the story, and there is no one to-day but is proud of the Chicago park system —the finest in the world. The parks and public squares of Chicago are accurately described as covering 1,974.61 acres, the largest area being that of Jackson Park, recently brought into prominence—586 acres, the larger part being as yet unimproved. Washington Park, also made prominent as the site of the World's Fair, has 371 acres, and is handsomely improved. The total expenditure for land purchase and improvements are to date about $12,000,000. Midway Plaisance, also part of the World's Fair site, is a broad strip connecting Washington and Jackson parks, and covers eighty acres. These parks, the Plaisance, and the grand boulevard system (see *Boulevards*) are under the jurisdiction of the South Park Commissioners, appointed by the judges of the Circuit Court of Cook County for terms of five years, one term expiring each year. The jurisdiction of these Commissioners covers 1,057 acres of parks and 16.37 miles of boulevards. It should be stated that the much-controverted Lake Front of forty-one acres is not under the jurisdiction of the South Park Commissioners, although their boulevard system begins at Jackson Street.

The principal West Side parks are Garfield (originally called Central) Park, 185 acres; Douglas, 179 acres, and Humboldt, 200 acres. The lesser parks under the jurisdiction of the West Chicago Park Commissioners, are Union, Jefferson, Vernon, Wicker, and Campbell, in all thirty acres, and the aggregate acreage of parks and boulevards controlled by the Board is 940 acres, of which 422 acres are improved, leaving 518 unimproved. The Commissioners first appointed, in 1869, found their territory a broad expanse of level prairie, with scarcely a tree upon it. The expenditures on the West Side system in nineteen years have been about $3,000,000; the annual revenue from taxation is now about $200,000. The result has been that over 400 acres have been beautified with trees, artificial lakes, walks, and drives, and the Commissioners are energetic of purpose to push park improvements to completion. Lincoln Park was the old city cemetery, whose sleeping inmates were tenderly removed to other places of repose. As enlarged by the extension to the northward, Lincoln Park has a lake frontage of 2½ miles, along which is a beautiful lake-drive (which see), adorned with a splendid equestrian statue of General Grant. At the southern entrance to the park is the memorial statue to Lincoln. Elsewhere are statues of Schiller and Goethe, contributed by the German citizens of the North Side; the Linné Monument, erected by the Scandinavian citizens of Chicago;

also the magnificent Yerkes electric fountain. The artistic features of the park are most notable and it is also becoming famous as a zoölogical garden. More than $3,000,000 have been expended on its improvement, and lands which were a barren waste of sand have been converted into a delightful pleasure resort for the people. The annual revenue available to the Commissioners now amounts to $275,000.

The following parks and public squares are situated within the city:

	ACRES.
Lake Front Park	41
Ellis Park	3.38
Washington Square	2.25
Dearborn Park	1.43
Congress Park	.07
Union Square	.05
Campbell Park	.05
Aldine Square	1.44
Oak Park	.25
Green Bay Park	.25
Lincoln Park	250
Wicker Park	4
Union Park	14.03
Jefferson Park (old city)	5.05
Jefferson Park (former town of Jefferson)	5
Vernon Park	4
Humboldt Park	200.62
Garfield Park	185.87
Douglas Park	179.79
Jackson Park	586
Washington Park	371
Gage Park	20
Midway Plaisance	80
Shedd's Park	1
Logan Square	4.25
Holstein Park	2.03
Woodlawn Park	3.86
Groveland Park	3.04
Douglas Monument Square	2.02
Total	1,974.61

In order to reach Lincoln Park from the center of the city take North Side cable cars. To reach

Garfield Park take Madison Street cable cars or Lake Street cars. An elevated road is now being built on Lake Street which will also pass Garfield Park. Take Milwaukee Avenue cable cars for Humboldt Park. Washington Park, Jackson Park, Douglas Monument Square, and Midway Plaisance are reached by two lines of cable cars, the State Street and Wabash Avenue lines also the Illinois Central railroad and by the Alley Elevated road when completed. Douglas Park is reached by Madison Street cable and Ogden Avenue cars

Park View Hotel.—Plans have been made for a magnificent structure, a combination of an hotel and a tower, to be erected on Stony Island Avenue, near Jackson Park, for the Park View Hotel & Tower Company. It will have a frontage of 160 feet, and a depth of 125 feet. The hotel will be seven stories high, built of pressed brick and stone for the exterior, with interior of steel construction, covered with gable roofs, finished in hardwood throughout, have marble and mosaic work, steam heat, electric light, probably six elevators, and all the latest improvements. The tower of steel construction will rise to a height of 533 feet, and be divided into four sections. Just above the roof of the hotel will be two balconies inclosed in glass, and above these will be an open balcony at each section. It is to be surmounted with a globe that will be provided with reflectors and electric light, enabling it to illuminate the surroundings for miles. The cost of this structure will approximate $800,000. E. W. Allen is the originator of the project.

Patrol System.—The attention of strangers is frequently called to a wagon, drawn by a spirited team

11

of horses, dashing through the streets after the manner of a vehicle of the Fire Department. These wagons are painted blue; the occupants, from two to eight, are fine specimens of manhood, and they are uniformed in blue, with helmets and badges. When the clanging gong of the patrol wagon is heard, other vehicles and pedestrians clear the track. These wagons, with the armed patrol, when seen under these circumstances, are going somewhere in the least possible time, perhaps to a fire, perhaps to the scene of a riot, or murder, or it may be to pick up a common "drunk." It is possible they have been summoned to the scene of an accident, someone has been injured, stricken with paralysis, or taken suddenly ill. Again, you may see these wagons moving slowly along the street. If you can look within you will see a person or persons who are not uniformed; they may be prisoners in manacles, or injured persons on stretchers, being conveyed as carefully as possible to a convenient hospital, or again it may be the body of an unknown on the way to the morgue. The patrol wagon system is a valuable auxiliary to the Police Department. The system had its origin in Chicago, and it is worked to perfection. The number of patrol wagons is thirty-five. From the patrol boxes, located at convenient corners, or by telephone from any point or place of business or residence, a patrol wagon, containing from four to eight police officers, may be summoned at any hour of the day or night. The response is quick. The telephone and telegraph are constantly employed in connection with the police system, and many arrests are made in this way that could not have been accomplished by the old methods. The patrol system is also an ambulance corps, and renders valuable assistance in rescuing the injured in accidents, or in carrying to hospitals those who are suddenly stricken with illness. Besides the patrol wagons there are two regular ambulances connected with the department, and others will be added.

Pawnbrokers.—These most useful gentry are known in Chicago by various slangy and semi-facetious appellations. "My Uncle's" is, perhaps, the commonest; but pawning articles is variously referred to by the class who patronize the pawnshops, as "spouting" and "hocking." The latter verb, "to hoc," is supposed to be derived from the Latin motto, *in hoc signo*, etc., its application lying in the fact that the pawnbroker's sign invariably consists of three golden balls suspended in a triangle above the doorway. Pawn-broking is a business almost entirely affected by the Jews. The volumes of unwritten history which are embalmed on the shelves of the pawn-shops of a great city, are not only a marvel, but a pity; and the student of human nature and the man who would calculate the sum of human misery, would do well to make them prominent among his text-books. Should anyone desire to study the trials of the improvident and the unthrifty, let him simply go to a pawn-shop and offer some article of value, and in a day or two redeem it. In many of the better class of these places private stalls are provided as a concession to the feelings of their patrons, but among the lower classes this is dispensed with. Along both sides of Clark Street and Halsted Street pawn-shops are most common; but one has not to seek far afield for one in any of the poorer quarters of Chicago. On State and Dearborn streets your high-class pawnbroker flourishes as a "loan agent" or "diamond broker," and he advertises his office in the financial columns of the daily papers. These, as a rule, lend money only on jewels, and have handsomely decorated offices. The pawnbroker is allowed by law to charge 10 per cent. per month on his loan, and to dispose of the goods at the expiration of one year, if the interest is not paid and the goods redeemed. They rarely advance over one-fourth to one-third of the actual value of the goods, and, as many of their pledges are never called for, their profits are large. Pawnbrokers' sales of unredeemed clothing are made at auction, but articles of value find their way into stores when unredeemed pledges are sold at private sale. The pawnbrokers' shops are licensed, and officers of the police force are assigned to investigate the goods pawned. Into these places many stolen articles find their way and are recovered. It not infrequently happens that pawn-shops are used as "fences" by thieves where they unload their plunder and receive a small amount on the value of the goods. It is a dangerous business to receive stolen goods, and some of these alleged pawnbrokers have found their way to the prison at Joliet.

People's Theatre.—This is a variety theatre, presenting also drama. The location is on State Street, south, at 339, and its seating capacity is about 2,000 persons. This house is exceedingly popular with lovers of first-class vaudeville performances. Jo Baylies, lessee and manager.

Pharmacy, Colleges of.—The Illinois College of Pharmacy, a department of Northwestern University, is located at 40 Dearborn Street, and is attended by nearly 300 students.

The Chicago College of Pharmacy is located at 465 State Street, and has about the same number of students as the Illinois College.

Picnic Grounds.—Picnics are a great feature of summer life in Chicago. Every Saturday large parties go forth to seek the woods and streams, while on Sundays the number of picnics is almost countless. Every social organization of the middle classes gives at least one picnic annually. Every nationality represented in the city must enjoy its Sunday picnic. There are a number of excellent and well-patronized picnic grounds in and about Chicago. Ogden's Grove, in the southwestern part of the city, is a great resort for labor and political merrymakers. Schuetzen (or Sharpshooters') Park, in Lake View, is the favorite picnic ground for the German Turner societies. The parks are the Mecca of Saturday picnics, while the Sunday gayeties find ample space at Downer's Grove, Willow Springs, Altenheim, Cedar Lake, and many other pleasant spots within easy reach of the city.

Police Department. — The peace and good order which prevails in Chicago is perhaps a fair criterion of the efficiency of the police force. Its members in the main have been attentive to their duties, thus the good name of the city for order and protection to person and property has, as a rule, been maintained. The duties of a police officer in this great city are varied and exacting. It is not strange that among so large a number some should err. The promotions, changes, and transfers that have occurred from time to time, have been made with the sole object of rewarding merit and improving the efficiency of the force; the results thus far are satisfactory. The Police

Department of Chicago is under the official control of the Mayor, and is conducted by a general superintendent, salary $5,000; five inspectors, $2,800 each; secretary, $2,000; two clerks, secretary's office, $1,100 each; stenographer, $1,000; custodian, $1,323; clerk detective office, $1,500; two assistant clerks, detective office, $1,200 each; night clerk, $900; thirteen captains, $2,250 each; two lieutenants, detective office, $1,700; sergeant, detective office, $1,600; forty-eight lieutenants, $1,500 each; forty-eight patrol sergeants, $1,200 each; twenty matrons, $630 each; photographer, $1,200; fifty detective patrolmen, $1,212.75 each; six police court bailiffs, $1,000 each; five pound keepers, $771.75 each; seventy four desk sergants, $1,102.50 each; patrolman, Mayor's office, $1,009; patrolman, comptroller's office, $500; sixteen lock-up keepers, $1,000 each; four inspectors of pawn-shops, $1,000 each; two inspectors of vehicles, $1,200 each; 180 patrolmen on duty at bridges, crossings, depots, etc., $1,000 each; 140 patrolmen, first-class for duty on patrol wagons, $1,000 each; 1,168 patrolmen, first-class for regular duty, $1,000 each; 100 patrolmen, second class, for patrol duty nine months, $60 per month; four engineers for police station, nine months, $83.33⅓ per month; four assistant engineers for police stations; eight months, $550 each; sixteen janitors, $530 each; veterinary, including medicine, $1,500; eight hostlers, $630 each; three watchmen, $750 each; five drivers of supply wagons, $750 each; seventy drivers of patrol wagons, $720 each. Total force, including officers and men, 1,870; total salaries of the department, $2,002,447.25. The number of stations, including the Central Detail Station, at the City Hall, is thirty-five. The number of arrests made in 1890 was 62,230. For patrol service the city is divided into five divisions and thirty-six precincts. The divisions are commanded by inspectors and the various precincts by captains and lieutenants. Each of the thirty-six precincts has its own building, generally called a station, containing quarters for the men, cells for the prisoners, and lodging for homeless persons. The division headquarters and precincts are located as follows:

HEADQUARTERS OF SUPERINTENDENT and Staff, first floor City Hall.

CENTRAL DETAIL, basement of City Hall. The officers of this department do patrol duty during the day time at street crossings, bridges, railroad depots, etc. These are picked men and will average six feet in height. This is in reality a sub-station of the first precinct, but nevertheless it is highly important.

DETECTIVE FORCE.—Headquarters, basement of City Hall. Detectives rank as patrolmen but receive more pay. They are not uniformed. The force usually numbers fifty, and it is impossible for a suspicious character to escape being observed. These men, as a rule, are expert, and have been selected on account of their ability to detect crime and hunt out criminals.

FIRST DIVISION.—Headquarters, Harrison Street and Pacific Avenue. First precinct, same building; second precinct, 318 Twenty-second Street; third precinct, 2523 Cottage Grove Avenue; fourth precinct, 142 Thirty-fifth Street; fifth precinct, Thirty-fifth Street, near South Halsted Street; sixth precinct, 2913 Deering Street.

SECOND DIVISION.—Headquarters, Fifty-third Street and Lake Avenue. Seventh precinct, Halsted and Root streets; eighth precinct, Fiftieth and State streets; ninth precinct, Fifty-third Street and Lake Avenue; tenth precinct, Sixty-fourth Street and Wentworth Avenue; eleventh precinct, Grand Crossing; twelfth precinct, South Chicago; thirteenth precinct, Hegewisch; fourteenth precinct, Kensington; fifteenth precinct, Brighton Park.

THIRD DIVISION.—Headquarters, Morgan and Maxwell streets; Sixteenth precinct, same building. Seventeenth precinct, 187 Canalport Avenue, near Halsted Street; eighteenth precinct, 691 Hinman Street, corner South Paulina Street; nineteenth precinct, 587 West Thirteenth Street, near Oakley Avenue; twentieth precinct, Lawndale.

FOURTH DIVISION. — Headquarters, 19 South Desplaines Street. Twenty-first precinct, West Lake and West Forty-third streets; twenty-second precinct, 19 South Desplaines Street; twenty-third precinct, 609 West Lake Street; twenty-fourth precinct, 256 Warren Avenue; twenty-fifth precinct, 231 West Chicago Avenue, near Milwaukee Avenue; twenty-sixth precinct, 34 Rawson Street, near Elston Avenue; twenty-seventh precinct, 478 West North Avenue, near Milwaukee Avenue; twenty-eighth precinct, Milwaukee Avenue and Attrill Street; twenty-ninth precinct, Irving Park.

FIFTH DIVISION.—Headquarters, 242 Chicago Avenue; thirtieth precinct, same building. Thirty-first precinct, Larrabee Street and North Avenue; thirty-second precinct, 958 North Halsted Street; thirty-third precinct, Diversey Street and Sheffield Avenue; thirty-fourth precinct, North Halsted Street and Addison Avenue; thirty-fifth precinct, Thirty-fifth Street, near South Halsted Street; thirty-sixth precinct, 2913 Deering Street, near Archer Avenue.

Police Pension Fund. — The policemen of Chicago are retired on half pay after twenty years of service. They have also a benevolent organization, assisted by the municipality, called, "The Policemen's Benevolent Association," w h i c h cares for its members if they become disabled, and for the wives and orphans of deceased officers. The pension fund receives 2 per cent. of all moneys received from licenses for saloons or dramshops, three-fourths of dog tax, one-fourth of all moneys received for licenses granted pawn-shops, one-fourth of all moneys received for licenses granted second-hand dealers, one-fourth of all moneys for licenses granted junk dealers; all moneys c llected for fines for carrying concealed weapons; one-half of all costs collected for violation of city ordinances, according to an act of the General Assembly approved April 29, 1887. The resources are at all times ample for the purpose indicated.

Political Parties.—The two great political parties are almost equally represented in Chicago, and every election is closely and bitterly contested. Careful attention has to be paid' to the wishes and requests of every nationality, and any blunder, which may transfer the vote of any particular nation to an opposing candidate, usually means a disastrous defeat. The prohibition party is too insignificant to be considered; the labor party, however, is slowly gaining strength at each election. In the old city proper, the democracy has now a large majority, but the farmers of the outlying districts and the country towns are almost solidly republican.

Pontiac Building is a magnificent fourteen-story office building, on Harrison Street, between Dearborn Street and Fourth Avenue. The material is brown pressed brick and steel. Upon both Dearborn Street and Fourth Avenue from the third story, to the eleventh, inclusive, there are three tiers of windows, and a single tier in the same stories on the Harrison street front. The first floor is so arranged that it can be divided into five stories. On Harrison Street the frontage is sixty-seven feet, and on Dearborn Street and Fourth Avenue, 100 each. It cost $350,000. It is owned by ·Mr. P. C. Brooks, of Boston.

Population of Chicago, by Years.—A glance over the following figures will show the stride Chicago is maintaining in order to reach the first place in the list of American cities. If the rate of increase is not diminished it will require less than two decades to accomplish the marvelous feat:

1830	70.
1840	4,853.
1845	12,088.
1850	29,963.
1855	60,627.
1860	112,172.
1865	178,900.
1870	298,977.
1871	334,270.
1872	364,377.
1880	503,185.
1890	1,208,669.
1891	1,250,000.
1892	1,500,000.

The population is divided among the nationalities as follows:

American	292,463.
German	384,958.
Irish	215,534.
Bohemian	54,209.
Polish	52,756.
Swedish	45,867.
Norwegian	44,615.
English	33,785.
French	12,963.
Scotch	11,927.
Welsh	2,966.

Russian	9,977.
Danes	9,891.
Italians	9,921.
Hollanders	4,912.
Hungarians	4,827.
Swiss	2,735.
Roumanians	4,350.
Canadians	6,989.
Belgians	682.
Greeks	698.
Spanish	297.
Portuguese	34.
East Indians	28.
West Indians	37.
Sandwich Islanders	31.
Mongolians	1,217.

Post Office.—Located in the square bounded by Adams Street on the north, Dearborn Street on the east, Jackson Street on the south, and Clark Street on the west, is, properly speaking, in the very heart of the South Side business district. The site is all that could be desired, and cost the Government $1,100,000, at the time the building was commenced, immediately after the Great Fire in 1871. This site, like other real estate in that vicinity, has at least doubled in value since that time. For the building the Government appropriated $4,000,000. The dimensions of the structure are 243 by 211 feet, and its utmost height 197 feet. The building is in the Florentine-Romanesque style of architecture, and of the Buena Vista, Ohio, sandstone—a very fine-grained stone, of rich, but gray-brown color. This building, notwithstanding its enormous cost, is an utter failure. It is dwarfed into insignificance by the handsome and lofty structures that surround it on all sides. The sinking of the foundation has shaken the huge pile almost to pieces, and were it not for continued repairs it would have tumbled down long since. It is regarded as unsafe, and aside from being an eyesore, it is entirely too small for the present demands of the city. It was supposed that it would furnish sufficient facilities for at least fifty years. As a matter of fact the business outgrew the structure in ten years. A new post-office building, to cost about $6,000,-000, will soon be erected on the same site. The upper floors of the old building are occupied by the Government officers, also the United States courts and custom house. The first floor and basement are occupied as the post office. About 1,600 men are employed in the collection, sorting and delivery of the 522,512,667 letters, newspapers, etc., handled during the year 1890. The receipts for the same time (exclusive of the fifty-three outlying post offices in the city) amounted to $3,126,840-68, and the expenses, $1,131,474.24, showing a net income of $1,995,-366.44, or a profit of nearly $2,000,-000. The money order transactions reached $1,879,292, aggregating a sum of $19,288,947.54. The amount of mail in transit through the city of Chicago, and transferred from incoming to out-going trains, is estimated to have reached the enormous bulk of 27,375 tons for the year. The annual increase of business done by the Chicago post office is 12$\frac{1}{4}$ per cent. During the year of the World's Fair (1893) it is estimated that the receipts of this office will exceed $6,-000,000. In view of this, the urgency for a new office is very great.

Besides the general post office there are eleven carrier stations and twenty-two sub-postal stations. The limits or jurisdiction of the postmaster of the Chicago post office covers less than one-third of the area of the city proper; the outlying post offices (which see) number fifty-three. In time, no doubt, these offices in the new annexations will be abolished, and all this vast business will be under one head.

POST OFFICE AND CUSTOM HOUSE, CLARK AND JACKSON STREETS.

(167)

Mails are received and dispatched at the general post office at all hours during week days, and several times during the night. There is scarcely a point of any importance in the United States for which a mail is not made up at least twice a day, and in some instances more frequently. Foreign mails are dispatched in time to catch the outgoing steamers from New York and San Francisco. The time of closing these mails is posted at the general office and stations. Letters are delivered in all parts of the city by carriers at almost hourly intervals, from 8 A. M. to 7 P. M. during week-days. On Sundays there are no deliveries, but two collections are made from the lamp-post boxes. The general post office is open at all hours during the day and night on week days. Certain departments, however, are closed after 9 P. M. It is also open from 9 to 11 A. M. on Sundays. Stamps may be bought at the general office or sub-stations. The sub-stations, or branch offices, are numbered, and their location is as follows:

North Division station, 355 to 359 North Clark Street; Northwest station, 517 Milwaukee Avenue; West Division station, corner Washington and Halsted streets; West Madison Street station, 981 West Madison Street; Southwest station, 543 Blue Island Avenue; South Division, 3217 State Street; Cottage Grove Avenue station, 3704 Cottage Grove Avenue; Stock Yards station, corner South Halsted and Forty-second streets; Lake View station, 1353 Diversey Street; Humboldt Park station, 1576 Milwaukee Avenue; Hyde Park station, 142 Fifty-third Street.

SUB-POSTAL STATIONS:—Twenty-second Street station, 86 Twenty-second Street; Ogden Avenue station, 324 Ogden Avenue; Indiana Street station, corner Indiana and Paulina streets.

FREE DELIVERY OF LETTERS by carriers will be secured by having your mail addressed to the street and number of your residence or place of business.

THE INSPECTOR'S DEPARTMENT is located on the top floor of the Post Office Building; the Chicago division comprises the States of Illinois, Iowa, Michigan, Wisconsin, Minnesota, and Dakota. All cases of irregularities, depredations or violations of postal laws should be reported to the Inspector. There are over 10,000 postmasters in this division, and fifteen inspectors to look after them.

MAIL TRAIN SERVICE.—There are 220 mail trains arriving and departing from the city daily, excepting Sunday; of these trains 118 have railway post offices attached, in which 300 clerks are employed in the distribution of the mails while in transit. In addition to this number of railway clerks a force of thirty-three clerks employed by the Chicago post office is sent out on the night trains to the meeting point of incoming railway post-office trains, on which they return to distribute and make up the mail for the main office and stations, for immediate delivery by carriers upon arrival. This system of quick delivery is a recent innovation, and of Chicago origin. By this method about 70 per cent. of the mails received during the twenty-four hours are delivered before 9 A. M. There are 110 separate mails closed daily for dispatch, the first close being made at 3:30 A. M., and the last at 10:30 P. M. A corresponding number of mails are received daily. The headquarters of the Sixth Division Railway Mail Service, comprising the States of Illinois, Iowa, Nebraska, and Wyoming, are located in Chicago. In this division 856 railway clerks are employed in the distribution of the mails on the cars. These clerks, during the year 1890, traveled 33,330,704 miles.

RATES OF POSTAGE.—The letter rate of postage is 2 cents for each ounce or fraction thereof, throughout the United States and Dominion of Canada. The postage on letters dropped in the office for delivery in the city is 2 cents per ounce. All letters must be fully prepaid by stamps. The following class of letters are not advertised : Drop letters, box letters, letters directed and sent to hotels and thence returned to the post office unclaimed, letters returned from the dead-letter office to writers, and card request letters, circulars, free packets containing documents, speeches, and other printed matter. A request for the return of a letter to the writer within thirty days or less, written or printed with the writer's name, post office and State, across the left-hand side of the envelope, on the face side, will be complied with. Such letters will be returned to the writer free of postage. Mail matter of the second class embraces newspapers and other periodical publications issued no less than four times a year from a known office of publication and bearing the date of issue, and which have no cloth, leather, or other substantial binding. Such publications must have a legitimate list of subscribers and must not be designed primarily for advertising purposes or for free circulation. The rate of postage on second-class matter when sent from the office of publication (including sample copies), or when sent from a news agent to actual subscribers, or to other news agents, is 1 cent per pound or fraction thereof; but if sent by any other than the publisher or

a news agent is 1 cent for each four ounces or fraction thereof. Mail matter of the third class embraces transient newspapers and periodicals, books (printed), photographs, circulars, proof-sheets, and corrected proof-sheets, with manuscript copy accompanying the same, and all matter of the same general character as above enumerated. The rate of postage is 1 cent for each two ounces or fractional part thereof except on transient newspapers and periodicals of the second class, which will be 1 cent for each four ounces or fraction thereof. Mail matter of the fourth class embraces labels, patterns, playing cards, addressed toys, paper sacks, wrapping paper and blotting pads with or without printed advertisements thereon, billheads, letter-heads, envelopes, ornamented paper, and all other matter of the same general character. This class also includes merchandise and samples of merchandise, models, samples of ores, metals, minerals, seeds, etc., and any other matter not included in the first, second, or third classes, and which is not in its form or nature liable to damage the contents of the mail bag or harm the person. Postage rates thereon, 1 cent for each ounce or fraction thereof.

MONEY ORDERS.—The fees for money orders are: On orders not exceeding $5, 5 cents; over $5 and not exceeding $10, 8 cents; over $10 and not exceeding $15, 10 cents; over $15 and not exceeding $30, 15 cents; over $30 and not exceeding $40, 20 cents; over $40 and not exceeding $50, 25 cents; over $50 and not exceeding $60, 30 cents; over $60 and not exceeding $70, 35 cents; over $70 and not exceeding $80, 40 cents; over $80 and not exceeding $100, 45 cents, no fraction of cents to be introduced in the order. No single order issued for more than $100. Persons desiring to remit larger sums must obtain additional money orders. No applicant, however, can obtain, in one day, more than three orders payable at the same office and to the same payee.

INTERNATIONAL MONEY ORDER SYSTEM.—Orders can be obtained upon any money order office in Great Britain and Ireland, Germany, Austria, Belgium, Holland, Denmark, Sweden, Norway, Switzerland, Italy, Canada, France, Algeria, Japan, Portugal, the Hiwaiian Kingdom, Jamaica, New Zealand, New South Wales, Hungary, Eygpt and Hong Kong, India and Tasmania, Queensland, Cape Colony, the Windward Islands, and the Leeward Islands, for any sum not exceeding $50 in United States currency. No single order issued for more than $50. Parties desiring to remit larger sums must obtain additional money orders. There is no limit to the number of orders in the International Money Order System. The fees for international money orders are: On orders not exceeding $10, 10 cents; over $10 and not exceeding $20, 20 cents; $20 and not exceeding $30, 30 cents; $30 and not exceeding $40, 40 cents; $40 not exceeding $50, 50 cents.

POSTAL NOTES.—Postal notes for sums not exceeding $4.99 will be issued on payment of a fee of 3 cents each. These notes are made payable to bearer at any money order office in the United States which the purchaser may designate.

REGISTERED LETTERS. — Letters can be registered to all parts of the United States, upon payment of a fee of 10 cents, in addition to the regular postage.

OUTLYING CHICAGO POST OFFICES.—There are, aside from the general post office and its branches in the different divisions of the old

city, fifty-three separate and distinct post offices within the corporate limits of Chicago, as follows: Argyle Park, corner Winthrop Avenue and Argyle Street; Auburn Park, corner Seventy-ninth and Wright streets; Avondale, corner Kedzie and Belmont avenues; Bowmanville, Lincoln Avenue, near Fifty-ninth Street; Buena Park, opposite railroad-station of that name; Burnside Crossing, corner Cottage Grove and Lyon avenues; Calumet, Clinton, near Fifty-ninth Street; Central Park, 4131 West Lake Street; Cheltenham, 159 Cheltenham Place; Chicago Lawn, corner Sixty-third Street and Central Park Avenue; Colehour, 10301 Avenue K; Cragin, opposite railroad-station of that name; Crawford, Butler Avenue, near Twenty-fourth Street; Cummings, Torrence Avenue, near One-hundred-and-seventh Street; Dunning, corner Cherry Street and Irving Park Boulevard; Edgewater, on Chicago & Evanston Railroad; Elsdon, Fifty-first Street, near Trumbull Avenue; Englewood, 6211 Wentworth Avenue; Englewood Heights, corner Eighty-ninth and Page streets; Forest Glen, corner Elston and Forest Glen avenues; Forest Hill, corner Seventy-ninth and Robey streets; Gano, One hundred-and-sixteenth and Dearborn streets; Grand Crossing, corner Seventy-fifth Street and Wilson Avenue; Havelock, corner Front Street and Cemetery Avenue; Hegewisch, 13303 South Chicago Avenue; Hermosa, Armitage Street, near Keeney; High Ridge, corner Weber Avenue, Chicago & North-Western Railway; Irving Park, Charles Avenue, near Irving Park Boulevard; Jefferson, Milwaukee Avenue, near Manard Street; Judd, corner Ninety-third Street and Washington Avenue; Kensington, Kensington Avenue, near Front Street; Linden Park, corner of Robinson

Avenue and Kinzie Street; Mandell, corner West Forty-eighth and Harrison streets; Maplewood, corner of Evergreen and Maplewood Avenues; Mayfair, St. James Street, near Franklin; Mont Clare, at railroad station of that name; Moreland, corner West Forty-eighth and Kinzie streets; Pacific, at railroad station of that name; Park Manor, 6760 South Chicago Avenue; Parkside, Stony Island, and near Sixty-ninth Street; Pullman, corner Morse Avenue and One hundred-and-twelfth Street; Ravenswood, east of Ravenswood Park, near Wilson Avenue; Riverdale, corner Indiana Avenue and One-hundred-and-thirty-sixth Street; Roseland, corner Michigan Avenue and Union Street; Simons, Kimball Avenue, near Bloomingdale Road; South Chicago, 9150 Commercial Avenue; South Englewood, corner Vincennes Avenue and Halsted Street; South Lynne, Sixty-fifth Street and Chicago, St. Louis & Pittsburgh Railroad; Summerdale, near Fifty-ninth Street and Ravenswood Park; Washington Heights, Wildwood, Indiana Avenue, near One-hundred-and-thirty-third Street; Woodlawn Park, corner Sixty-third Street and Illinois Central Railroad.

Presbyterian Churches. — The following list gives the names and locations of all those in the city:

Belden Avenue Church, Belden Avenue, corner Seminary Avenue.

Campbell Park Church, Leavitt Street, corner Campbell Park.

Church of the Covenant, North Halsted Street, corner Belden Avenue.

Eighth Church, Washington Boulevard, corner Robey Street.

Fifth Church, Indiana Avenue, corner Thirtieth Street.

First Church, Indiana Avenue, corner Twenty-first Street.

First German Church, Howe Street, corner Center Street.

First Scotch Church, South Sangamon Street, corner West Adams Street.

First United Church, West Monroe Street, corner Paulina Street.

Forty-first Street Church, Prairie Avenue, corner Forty-first Street.

Fourth Church, Rush Street, corner Superior Street. .

Fullerton Avenue Church, Fullerton Avenue, near North Clark Street.

Holland Church, Noble Street, corner West Erie Street.

Jefferson Park Church, West Adams Street, corner Throop Street.

Lake Church, Dashiel Street, corner Forty-second Street.

Railroad Chapel, 1419 State Street.

Reunion Church, South Ashland Avenue, corner Hastings Street.

Second Church, Michigan Avenue, corner Twentieth Street.

Sixth Church, Vincennes Avenue, corner Oak Avenue.

Third Church, South Ashland Avenue, corner Ogden Avenue.

Twelfth Ward Church, West Madison Street, corner California Avenue.

Westminster Church, corner West Jackson and Peoria streets.

Welsh Church, West Monroe Street, corner Sangamon Street.

MISSIONS.

Burr, Third Avenue, near Fourteenth Street.

Fifth Avenue Mission, Archer Avenue and Thirty-first Street.

Hope Mission, Augusta Street, near Western Avenue.

Howe Street Mission, 75 Howe Street.

Moseley Mission, 2539 Calumet Avenue.

Onward Mission, West Indiana Street, corner Hoyne Avenue.

Presbyterian Hospital, adjoining the Rush Medical College, provides medical and surgical aid to sick or disabled persons of any nationality or creed.

Press Club is a social organization composed of gentlemen connected with the newspapers of the city in a literary way. They have handsome rooms, 133 Clark Street.

Prisons.—Prisoners arrested for petty offenses are kept over night in the cells of the police stations, and, if unable to pay their fines, are transferred to the House of Correction, popularly known as the Bridewell. This prison is located on California Avenue near Twenty-sixth Street, and receives, on an average, 10,000 prisoners annually. Prisoners charged with graver crimes are, if not released on bail, kept in the County Jail on the North Side, and if convicted, sent to the State's prison at Joliet.

The Joliet Penitentiary, which houses about 1,500 convicts, is a model institution of its kind, and is conducted upon the most modern ideas.

Produce Exchange.—The Chicago Produce Exchange is located at 144 South Water Street, and transacts a flourishing business.

Professional Societies.—The most noted professional societies of Chicago are: The Forty Club, composed of lawyers and journalists; the Sunset Club, a model society of business and professional gentlemen, who assemble for banquet and discussion; the famous Press Club of Chicago; the Whitechapel Club, a very unique and remarkable organization, and the Papyrus Club, composed of literary workers.

Proposed Elevated Road.— There was filed with the Secretary of State, August 20, 1891, articles of incorporation of the Chicago, Evanston & Southern Elevated Railroad Company, which proposes to build a street railway, beginning at a point in Evanston and running south between the west shore of Lake Michigan and the east line of the North-Western Railway to Wedgewood Avenue, to Franklin Street, thence south on or near Franklin Street to Kinzie Street; thence west across the North Branch of the Chicago River, on or near Kinzie Street, to Clinton Street; thence south on or near Clinton Street to Sixty-fourth Street, Englewood; thence east on or near Sixty-fourth Street to Jackson Park; thence southeast to Blue Island Avenue. The principal office is located at Chicago, and the capital stock is $20,000,000.

This elevated road is designed especially to pick up through travel across the city. There will be but one fare, and that a low one, between Evanston and Jackson Park.

Provident Hospital and Training School.—This may be regarded as a colored charity, as it originated in the African Methodist Church. This admirably equipped hospital is located at Twenty-ninth and Dearborn streets. Physicians, nurses, matron, and clerks, are all colored, and the patients as a rule are colored people, although no race distinctions are made.

Public Library.—Fourth floor of City Hall. This institution, after an existence of eighteen years, has become the third among the great libraries of the United States, having on its shelves at the close of 1890 a total of 156,243 volumes. This number is being increased at the rate of 10,000 volumes per year. The total circulation of the past year numbers 1,220,479. 843,971 volumes of which were taken for home reading. The number of visitors to the reading room was 436,412, and those to the several reference departments, not including the reading room, was 113,531, being a large increase over the corresponding figures of last year. The eighteen branch, or delivery stations, located in distant parts of the city, have had an aggregate issue during the year of 201,257 volumes. The library quarters are frequently visited by as high as 7,000 persons in one day. The great need of this valuable institution is a suitable building of adequate proportions to meet its growing wants, and better adapted to public access and convenience than the fourth floor of the City Hall. However, this want will soon cease to exist, as the City Council, by ordinance, has granted the right to use Dearborn Park for a site for a Public Library building. This has been supplemented by an act of the General Assembly of Illinois authorizing the proper authorities to erect and maintain a public library on Dearborn Park. By its provisions the Soldiers' Home is also authorized to transfer to the city of Chicago its interest in the northeast quarter of the park, on condition that a memorial hall be built in the library building, for the use of non-partisan soldier organizations of Cook County, for fifty years. The site of the new library building, which will be in every respect an ornament to the city, generally known as Dearborn Park, is bounded on the north by Randolph Street, on the east by Michigan Avenue, on the south by Washington Street, and on the west by an alley known as Dearborn Place.

Public Libraries. — Chicago possesses three of the greatest libraries in the world, besides numerous minor literary collections. The chief city libraries are: The Chicago Public Library, now in the City Hall, but soon to occupy a building on the Lake Front; the Newberry Library, Clark and Oak streets; and the John Crerar Library, for which a magnificent collection of books has been made, and which is to be located on the South Side.

Public Schools.—The public school system of Chicago, while one of the best in the country, is inadequate for the education of the entire scholastic population. The parochial schools assume part of the burden, but nevertheless the public schools are badly overcrowded, and the construction of new schools can hardly keep pace with the increase in population.

There are over 400 public schools in Cook County, with a scholastic population of about 300,000. Of this multitude, nearly 70,000 are enrolled in private and parochial schools, and about 150,000 in the public schools. The public schools employ 3,300 teachers and cost nearly $5,000,000 per year.

Pullman is located on the Calumet Lake, and is the most beautiful little city on the face of the earth. Its great manufacturing plants are surrounded by broad and sinuous drives, walks, lawns, miniature lakes, fountains, etc., that give it the appearance of a park rather than the seat of a great manufactory. The Arcade, an immense building, in which are all the shops or stores, a bank, a library, a theatre, etc.; the Market House, in which all meats and vegetables are sold; the hotel and all the residences, are built principally of pressed brick, showing Gothic, Swiss, and other styles of architecture. Pages could be written about Pullman, and yet not present half its attractiveness. Everyone visiting Chicago should take the Illinois Central and see Pullman.

This is the home of the famous Pullman palace and sleeping cars, and the place of their origin and manufacture.

Race-tracks.—The race-courses of Chicago are considered among the finest in the country. There are three of them: Washington Park, West Side Driving Park, and Corrigan's Track.

WASHINGTON PARK course was planned and built after the most improved designs. Neither money nor labor has been spared to make the club-house, the grand stand, the grounds, buildings, and track unsurpassed anywhere in the United States. The regular running meet commences the last of June, lasting four weeks, closing the last of July. There is also a spring meeting. At both of these there are always events of the greatest interest to all the breeders and sporting men throughout the country. It is also true that the Derby Day of the mid-summer series is becoming more and more a holiday for Chicago's citizens. The park is easily reached by the Illinois Central Railroad or by the South Side cable car lines.

THE WEST SIDE DRIVING PARK has always held a prominent place in popular esteem. Many spirited events, both trotting and running, have taken place within i s inclosure. Until Washington Park was built it was the best trotting course Chicago had ever had. Visitors can reach this locality by the Wisconsin Central Railroad or the Madison Street cable line.

CORRIGAN'S TRACK.—This is the newest driving park in the city, and, as its name indicates, is at present in private hands. It is certainly one of the most elegant tracks ever laid out in the country. It is located in the town of Cicero, just beyond the city limits. No better ground can be found near Chicago, as it runs along a ridge that permits thorough drainage. The soil is a sandy, black loam, that even a heavy rain can not pack. It lies seven and a half miles from the Court House. It is within easy distance of the Freeport branch of the Illinois Central Railroad, the Burlington & Quincy, and Atchison & Santa Fé. It is only half a mile from the Belt Line Railroad, which connects with all the railroads running into the city.

Rag-pickers.—The rag-pickers of the city are mostly Italians and Germans. The homes of the Italians are found in the South Clark Street district, and of the Germans on the North Side, in the vicinity of the river. The rag-picker starts from home between 4 and 6 o'clock every morning, and returns from his first expedition in time for breakfast at eight. But before satisfying his appetite he proceeds to the cellar underneath the house, and there empties the yield of his journey upon the ground, that he may separate the fat from the glass, and the iron from the rags, making a separate pile of each, and afterward disposing of the fat to the offal-dealer, the rags to the paper-maker, and the iron to the junkman. After breakfast he makes a second expedition, and he continues his rounds throughout the day. Although the business does not seem profitable to one who merely sees the rag-picker with his bag and hook, their places of abode are usually remarkably clean and well furnished, and some of these people, while still pursuing their humble occupation, have considerable bank accounts.

Railroad Depots.—The railroads centering in Chicago found out some time ago that there was much advantage in coöperation, so they have united both in the building and use of the various railroad stations scattered over the city, of which one is located in the West Division, and one in the North Division, and the other four in the South Division. Those going to the depots on the North and West sides are likely to meet the delays from the swinging of the bridges, which do not discommode those on the South Side.

THE POLK STREET DEPOT is used by the Atchison, Topeka & Santa Fé; the Chicago & Erie; the Chicago & Eastern Illinois; the Chicago & Grand Trunk; The Louisville, New Albany & Chicago; Monon Route, and the Wabash railroads. This depot on the South Side is located on Polk Street, facing Dearborn Street. It can be reached by street cars on State Street and Clark Street, going south, and by a special line running from the Northwestern depot to Polk on Dearborn Street. It is a magnificent building, comparatively new, of brick, with the most ample accommodations in the way of waiting rooms, offices, and conveniences of every description for the traveling public, which the management evidently believe it to be both a duty, and to their interest, to cater to. Passengers from the extreme Northeast can go to the extreme Southwest of the United States, without going from under cover, and by a little care in choosing their trains can make such close connections as to seem to be on a continuous train. The officials about the station are particularly courteous.

GRAND CENTRAL DEPOT.—See description page 98.

EXPOSITION BUILDING. — T h i s building, at the foot of Monroe Street, offers meagre facilities to the Baltimore & Ohio Railroad, during the times when nothing stirring is taking place in the building itself. Since the Baltimore & Ohio obtained right of way into the city, there has been some obstruction to its entrance into the Illinois Central depot. Outsiders have no knowledge, whatever, of the reason why. When it reached the Exposition Building, several years ago, it took what was then supposed to be temporary quarters in the Exposition Building, by running up a partition or two, and to the surprise of the public, has made no improvement since. Whether they are waiting for some man to die, or not, does not appear. But it is evidently a matter of legal status, from the slowness with which arrangements are made for more convenient surroundings. It is, however, only a short distance from the business center, and thus, in a manner, offers compensation for anything disagreeable. Once on board the trains, however, all this annoyance vanishes, and the pleasant things take in place.

UNION DEPOT.—To and from this station are almost constantly moving trains belonging to the Chicago & Alton; Chicago, Burlington & Quincy; Chicago, Milwaukee & St. Paul; Chicago, St. Louis & Pitts-burg; Pittsburg, Ft. Wayne & Chicago railroads. It is an immense building on the West Side. Its grounds stretch along the bank of the river for some half-dozen blocks, and about a block in width. These are covered with tracks and switches. The switch-house is elevated after the most improved method, and uses a system of interlocking switches, under the charge of two men. These are constantly on duty day and night, with suitable reliefs. The station is of brick, fronting on Canal Street. A long, stationary awning covers the sidewalk along the front. The stories above the street, devoted to waiting rooms and offices,

Best Line to and from

CHICAGO

ST. PAUL and

MINNEAPOLIS

CHICAGO GREAT WESTERN RAILWAY

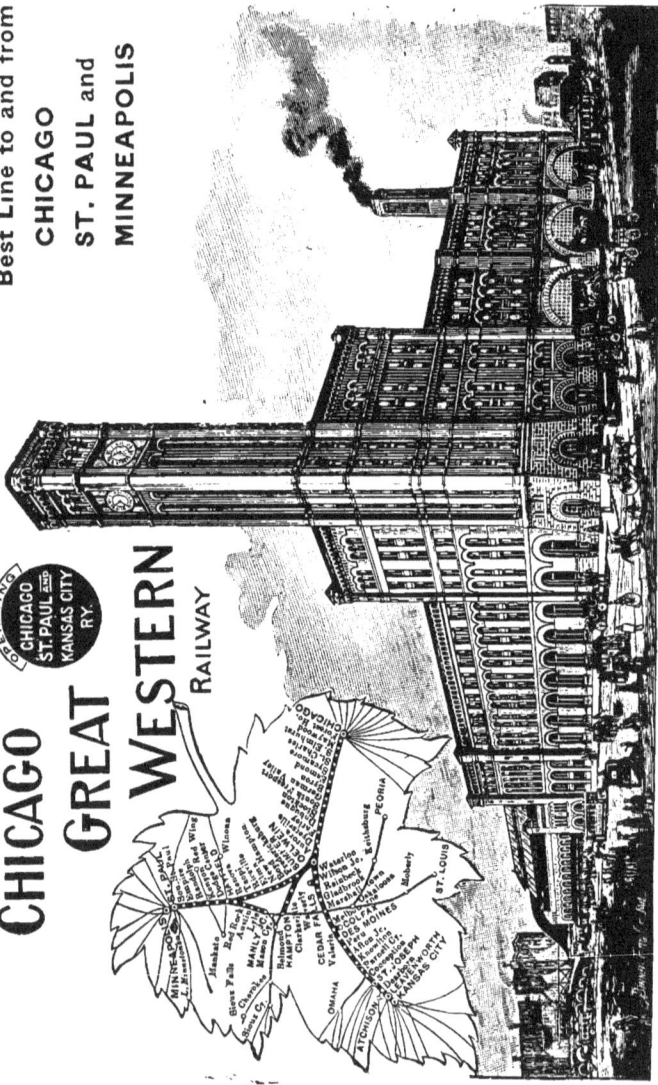

OPERATING
CHICAGO ST. PAUL AND KANSAS CITY RY

GRAND CENTRAL PASSENGER STATION, HARRISON STREET AND FIFTH AVENUE.
Occupied jointly by Chicago Great Western and Baltimore & Ohio Railroads

are ample for all needed purposes.
Broad and easy stairways lead down,
nearly one story, to the level of the
tracks, where the trains wait for
their occupants.   A   substantial
stone wall holds the "filling in" of
the street, for the whole length of
the yards,from encroachment. Trains
from the East, West and South here
transfer their burdens by close con-
direction, and the Wells Street depot
close at hand. The North-Western
Railway Company spared no pains
in making this a commodious, convenient structure, resembling, in general plan, the Union depot, inasmuch
as the street is elevated a story above
the tracks, to which access is had by
stairways both outer and inner. As
the three divisions of the North-

UNION DEPOT, CANAL AND ADAMS STREETS.

nection.   It is in every sense a
Union Depot.
  WELLS STREET DEPOT. — Before
the Great Fire there was a North
and South Wells Street. For good
reasons the city fathers,when rebuild-
ing commenced, changed the name of
South Wells Street to Fifth Avenue.
But the portion beyond the river re-
tained the old name, so the traveler,
leaving any of the South Side hotels
or depots, passes along Fifth Avenue
north, and, crossing the bridge over
the main river, finds himself on Wells
Street without having changed his
12
Western Railway tap some of the
most desirable residence country in
the State of Illinois, its suburban
traffic is simply enormous, and when
the rush is on, of incoming business
men in the morning, one wonders
where the immense crowds will be-
stow themselves during the day ; but
when one stops to think that this is
but one of six, his wonder may well
grow apace at Chicago's size.
  CHICAGO, ROCK ISLAND & PACIFIC
DEPOT. — This structure, built of
stone, and standing at the head of
La Salle Street, accommodates the

Chicago, Rock Island & Pacific, and the Lake Shore & Michigan Southern railroads. At first La Salle Street extended to the front door ; but when the Chicago Board of Trade was seeking a new and larger home, the block between Van Buren and Jackson streets, by some legal technicality, was reclaimed by its owner, the street finally exchanged for two streets east and west, and the new Chamber of Commerce and Rialto Building built in front. The depot was burnt at the Great Fire of 1871, and immediately rebuilt on the same plan. It is the oldest depot standing in the city.

ILLINOIS CENTRAL DEPOT.—This, occupying a position on the Lake Front, has been quite a bone of contention between the company and some of the citizens, in regard to the right of the corporation to use a part of the Lake Front, at present included in its grounds. It is occupied by the Illinois Central, the Michigan Central, and the Cleveland, Cincinnati, Chicago & St. Louis railroads. It was burnt at the Great Fire of 1871, and promptly rebuilt, But it was soon after again burnt, and since has been allowed to stand a ruin, as an instance of corporative economy and thrift. When their litigation is settled, the depot will be rebuilt, perhaps in time for the World's Columbian Exposition. It is to be hoped so, for the Illinois Central expects to have the bulk of transit of visitors to and from the grounds at Jackson Park.

Railroads.—Chicago is the child of railroads, and this stupendous agent of prosperity, with its capacity for infinite harm or good, may be said to have originated since 1851, up to which date, when the New York & Erie Railroad opened, the method was practically on trial. It then became a system, and as such has expanded. The ocean built Tyre and Carthage; Aleppo was the child of a route for the camel and the pilgrim; St. Louis was predestined when the Mississippi opened its way, but Chicago is peculiarly the child of this new and mighty system. So distinct and inseparable is the inter dependence between that system at large and the city which has spontaneously shot up at the point indicating its focus, that no comprehensive view of the one can logically exclude the other. If a railroad be compassed for the Lake Winnipeg region, or up the Valley of the Saskatchawan, in a country more habitable than Sweden, a thousand miles north of the source of the Mississippi, it is impossible to dissociate the thought from Chicago; if it be suggested that without the West, Boston, or even New York, would languish, the idea of a qualified dependence on Chicago is immediately raised. The surveys of the Yellowstone Valley, conducted in the interest and at the expense of the nation, were but the exploiting of Chicago engineers, the moment it is recollected that the Northern Pacific railroad was to connect that region with the most accessible of the great commercial marts. The time has already come when the arrest of developing manufactures in California, by the opening of the Pacific railroads, which exposed them to the competing wares of lower-paid labor in the East, engaged the pecuniary sagacity of Chicago in preparing and making her the great shop for supplying the infinite demand of the Far West. Alaska itself is not extolled as a fur trader without · implying Chicago as the future purchaser. The like remark may be made of Texas and of Mexico. The unaccountable but indisputable tendency of the Southwest toward a lake market shown at an early day, in derogation of the most eligible water connections southward, is evidently ineradicable.

Such considerations really warrant the question, What railways in North America are not in some degree tributary to Chicago? It is an expressive fact that the corporate names of over fifty railroads embrace that of Chicago. However, it is not easy to demonstrate, even of a single road, in what its "tributary" element consists. Anxious to avoid even the appearance of exaggeration, we shall ignore the majority of these fifty courtiers for the favor of the country represented by Chicago, and shall, in placing before our readers the most comprehensive list of the Chicago railroads with their mileage, confine ourselves for the present to the twenty and more great corporations having their terminus and principal offices in Chicago. This city is practically the terminal point of all the great trunk lines of railway, North, South, East, and West in the United States, the Dominion of Canada, and the Republic of Mexico. Over 85,000 miles of railway center in Chicago at the present time, and this city is conceded to be the greatest railway depot in the world; more passengers arrive and depart, more merchandise is received and shipped here daily than in any other city on the globe. On the 30th of June, 1891, the total line mileage of railroads in the United States was 157,759, of which Chicago justly claimed 85,000 as directly tributary. The roads that radiate from this center are:

ATCHISON, TOPEKA & SANTA FE RAILROAD. — Mr. W. F. White, passenger traffic manager; Geo. T. Nicholson, general passenger and ticket agent, Topeka, Kansas; city ticket office, 212 Clark Street; passenger depot, Polk Street and

Third Avenue; freight depot 12th and State streets. Total mileage, 9,300.96. The equipment is thoroughly first-class. This system extends to and has its ramifications in the following States and Territories: Illinois, Iowa, Missouri, Arkansas; Kansas, Nebraska, Oklahoma, Indian Territory, Texas, Colorado, New Mexico, Arizona, California, as well as points in the Republic of Mexico. For arrival and departure of trains see daily papers. For general information consult time table and folders which are to be found at all hotels, depots, and public places. This is a favorite route for tourists West and South.

BALTIMORE & OHIO RAILROAD.— Mr. Charles O. Scull, general passenger agent, Baltimore, Md.; L. S. Allen, assistant general passenger agent, Rookery Building, Chicago; city ticket office, 193 Clark Street; freight depot, foot of South Water Street; passenger depot, Grand Central, Fifth Avenue and Harrison Street. The Baltimore & Ohio is the oldest trunk line of the United States. Total mileage, 1,950.9; entrance to Chicago is made over a line from Chicago Junction, a distance of 271 miles. This road is equipped in a magnificent manner, and its through trains to Washington, Baltimore, and other eastern cities, are models of elegance and comfort. The speed made over this steel-railed road is phenomenal. For particulars, regarding the arrival and departure of trains see daily papers, folders, etc.

CHICAGO, BURLINGTON & QUINCY RAILROAD.—Mr. P. S. Eustis, general passenger and ticket agent at general offices Franklin and Adams streets; city ticket office, 211 Clark Street; freight depot, Harrison and Canal streets; passenger depot, Canal and Adams streets. This is one of the greatest railway systems in the world. The total mileage

RAI—RAI

operated by this road is 7,000. The traveler will take this road for the principal points in the States of Illinois, Wisconsin, Iowa, Missouri, Minnesota, Nebraska, Kansas, Colorado, and Wyoming. The trains are elegant and the time made is fast. For particulars regarding the arrival and departure of trains see daily papers, folders, etc.

CHICAGO, MILWAUKEE & ST. PAUL RAILWAY.—Mr. George H. Heafford, general passenger and ticket agent at general offices, Rand-McNally Building on Adams Street, between La Salle Street and Fifth Avenue, Chicago; F. A. Miller, assistant general passenger agent, 207 Clark Street; city ticket office, 207 Clark Street; freight depot, 70 North Union Street; passenger depot, Canal and Adams streets. This is also one of the greatest railway systems in America with a total mileage of 6,901.19. Its lines gridiron the States of Illinois, Missouri, Wisconsin, Iowa, Minnesota, North Dakota, and South Dakota, while it makes connections at Kansas City, Omaha, and St. Paul with the three great trans-continental routes. The road-bed, track, and equipment is at all times as near perfect as possible, and the time made is fast. For particulars regarding the arrival and departure of trains see daily papers, time tables, folders, etc.

CHICAGO, ROCK ISLAND & PACIFIC RAILWAY.—Mr. John Sebastian, general passenger and ticket agent at the general offices on Van Buren and Sherman streets, Chicago; city ticket office, 104 Clark Street; freight depot, Taylor and Sherman streets; passenger depot, Van Buren and Sherman streets. This is one of the great systems of the world, with 4,084 miles of track, penetrating the States of Illinois, Iowa, Missouri, Kansas, Indian Territory, Nebraska, and Colorado, with direct connection

with lines operating in all the States and Territories, from the Mississippi River to the Pacific Ocean. The equipment is superb, and the time made is fast. For particulars regarding the arrival and departure of trains see daily papers, time cards, folders, etc.

CHICAGO, ST. PAUL & KANSAS CITY RAILWAY.—Mr. F. H. Lord, general passenger and ticket agent, Phœnix Building, Jackson Street and Pacific Avenue, Chicago; city ticket office, 188 Clark Street; freight depot, Polk Street and Fifth Avenue; passenger depot, Harrison Street and Fifth Avenue. This road is a direct line between Chicago, St. Paul, Minneapolis, St. Joseph, Leavenworth, and Kansas City, passing through the States of Illinois, Iowa, Minnesota, Missouri, and Kansas. For particulars regarding the arrival and departure of trains see daily papers, folders, etc.

CHICAGO & ALTON RAILROAD.—Mr. James Charlton, general passenger agent, Monadnock Block; city ticket office, 195 Clark Street; freight depot, 2 West Van Buren Street; passenger depot, Canal and Adams streets. The general direction of this great and favorite road is south and southwest, with terminals at Chicago, St. Louis, and Kansas City. It is the most direct line to these cities and intermediate points. The road is exceedingly popular, and its business enormous. The road-bed, track, and equipment is thoroughly abreast of the times. For full particulars regarding the arrival and departure of trains see daily papers, time tables, folders, etc.

CHICAGO & EASTERN ILLINOIS.—Mr. C. L. Stone, general passenger and ticket agent, First National Bank Building, Chicago; ticket office, 204 Clark Street; freight depot, Fourteenth and Dearborn streets; pas-

DEPOT OF C., R. I. & P. AND L. S. & M. S. RYS., VAN BUREN AND SHERMAN STREETS.

senger depot, Polk Street and Third Avenue. This road has 472 miles of steel-railed track, and runs a solid vestibule train, with dining car between Chicago and Nashville, Tenn., via Evansville, and the Louisville & Nashville railroad. For particulars regarding the arrival and departure of trains, see daily papers, time cards, folders, etc.

CHICAGO & GRAND TRUNK RAILWAY.—Mr. W. E. Davis, general pas-

nects this country with the Dominion of Canada, which it traverses in all directions. The traveler is advised to take this grand route for all points in Central and Northeastern Michigan ; for all points in the Dominion of Canada, and for all points in the upper Atlantic Coast States. It is a direct and favorite route to Niagara Falls, Buffalo, Toronto, Montreal, Portland, New York, and Boston. For full particulars regarding the

DEARBORN STATION, CORNER FOURTH AVENUE AND POLK STREET.

senger and ticket agent, Rialto Building, Chicago ; city ticket office, 103 Clark Street ; freight depot, Twelfth Street and Third Avenue ; passenger depot, Polk Street and Third Avenue. This is that portion of the line connecting the Grand Trunk Railway system of Canada with its system of railway in the United States, centering in Chicago. This road is thoroughly efficient, and highly important, for it is the link that con-

arrival and departure of trains see daily papers, time cards, folders, etc.

CHICAGO & NORTHERN PACIFIC RAILROAD. — This is a belt road around Chicago for suburban traffic and to furnish an entry to the city, and terminal facilities here for such roads as require such service. It has a complete belt around the city, crossing the tracks of every road that enters Chicago. It is used largely for transfer purposes. It runs thirty-five trains daily between Chicago and Conway Park. The general offices are located in the Grand Central depot, Harrison Street and Fifth Avenue.

CHICAGO & NORTH-WESTERN RAILWAY.—Mr. W. A. Thrall, general passenger and ticket agent at general offices, 22 Fifth Avenue, Chicago; city ticket office, 206 Clark Street; freight depot, 2 North State Street; passenger depot, Wells and Kinzie streets. This prosperous and remarkable system has 7,200 miles of Al railway, traversing the States

fertile country which it traverses. It employs over 1,000 conductors and requires 1,200 locomotives to haul its many trains. For full particulars regarding the arrival and departure of trains, points reached, etc., see daily papers, time cards, folders, etc., which are generously distributed in all hotels and public places. Its depot is one of the finest in this city.

CLEVELAND, CINCINNATI, CHICAGO & ST. LOUIS RAILWAY.—Mr. D. B. Martin, general passenger and ticket agent, Cincinnati, Ohio;

C. & N.-W. RY. DEPOT, CORNER WELLS AND KINZIE STREETS.

of Illinois, Wisconsin, Minnesota, North and South Dakota, Nebraska, Michigan, and Wyoming. The important points reached direct, are, Council Bluffs, Omaha, Sioux City, St. Paul, Minneapolis, Milwaukee, Marquette, Ashland, Duluth, Des Moines, Lincoln, Pierre, and all intermediate points. There are three principal divisions of lines of the Chicago & North-Western Railway, viz.: The Galena Division, the Milwaukee Division, and the Wisconsin Division, all tributary to Chicago. The tracks are steel, and the equipment is superb. It is not alone a Chicago favorite, but popular throughout the thousands of miles of

J. C. Tucker, northwestern passenger agent, 234 Clark Street, Chicago; city ticket office, 234 Clark Street; freight depot, foot of South Water Street, passenger depot, foot of Lake Street. This line is popularly known as the "Big Four Route," which signifies the quartette of cities which comprise its four terminals. It is part of the Vanderbilt system of railways, and as such is maintained in the best possible manner. It is the favorite and direct route to the cities mentioned in its title, and all intermediate points. For full particulars regarding the arrival and departure of trains, see daily papers, time cards, and folders which can be had at all depots and hotels.

ILLINOIS CENTRAL RAILROAD.— Mr. A. H. Hanson, general passenger agent, 60 Wabash Avenue, Chicago; city ticket office, 194 Clark Street; freight depot, foot of South Water Street; passenger depot, foot of Lake Street. This old and popular system operates 2,875 miles of first-class road, and is the direct artery connecting Lake Michigan with the Gulf of Mexico. The road enters Chicago from the south, winding along the lake shore with six tracks, every one of which is in constant use with its enormous through passenger, freight, and suburban traffic. It is safe to say that its suburban traffic is greater than that of any other road entering the city. It is the direct route to Cairo, Memphis, New Orleans, St. Louis, and all intermediate points, which may be numbered by the thousands. This railway traverses the States of Illinois, Kentucky, Tennessee, Mississippi, and Louisiana. For full particulars regarding the arrival and departure of trains, see daily papers, time cards, folders, etc., which will be found in all hotels, depots, and public places.

LAKE SHORE & MICHIGAN SOUTHERN RAILWAY.—Mr. A. J. Smith, general passenger and ticket agent, Cleveland, Ohio; C. K. Wilbur, western passenger agent, Van Buren Street depot, Chicago; city ticket-office, 66 Clark Street; freight depot, Polk Street and Pacific Avenue; passenger depot, Van Buren and Sherman streets. This road is part of and one of the most important lines in the Vanderbilt system. It is the famous trunk line between Chicago and New York. In the main line and branches there are 2,319 miles of steel track. The passenger trains on this road are superb. The time made is exceedingly fast. It is the

direct route to all points of interest and importance in Michigan, Northern Ohio, Pennsylvania, New York, and the New England States, as well as New Jersey, Rhode Island, and Maryland. The Lake Shore connects directly with the New York Central and Hudson River Railroad, and passengers over this line have an opportunity of viewing the magnificent scenery of the Hudson River. It also connects with the Boston & Albany Railroad, passing through the famous Berkshire Hills. For full particulars regarding the arrival and departure of trains see daily papers, also time cards and folders.

LOUISVILLE, NEW ALBANY & CHICAGO RAILWAY.—Mr. James Barker, general passenger agent, 320 Dearborn Street, Chicago; city ticket office, 73 Clark Street; freight depot, Fourth Avenue and Taylor Street; passenger depot, Polk Street and Third Avenue. This road is popularly known as the "Monon Route." It is the direct route between Chicago and Cincinnati, and Chicago and Louisville, and Chicago and Indianapolis, and the South. This is a high class road in every respect, and a favorite road with Florida tourists. For full particulars regarding arrival and departure of trains see daily papers, also time cards and folders.

MICHIGAN CENTRAL RAILROAD.— Mr. O. W. Ruggles, general passenger and ticket agent, Adams Express Building, 185 to 189 Dearborn Street, Chicago; city ticket office, 67 Clark Street; freight depot, foot of South Water Street; passenger depot, foot of Lake Street. This may be regarded as the "Niagara Falls Route." It is the direct road for points in Michigan and Canada, and for Buffalo, N. Y. The time consumed in traveling over the Michigan Central between Chicago and principal Eastern points, is the fastest on record. The tracks are of steel, and the equipment superb. For full particulars regarding the arrival and departure of trains, see daily papers, time cards, folders, etc., which will be found in all hotels, depots, and public places.

NEW YORK, LAKE ERIE & WESTERN RAILROAD.—Mr. D. I. Roberts, general passenger agent, New York; Mr. F. W. Buskirk, assistant general passenger agent, Phœnix Building, Chicago; city ticket office, 242 Clark Street; freight depot, Fourteenth and Clark streets; passenger depot, Polk Street and Third Avenue. This is the main stem of the Erie Railway system, and one of the important lines between New York and Chicago. The total length of road operated by this system is 2,057 miles. The Chicago connection of the Erie system is the Chicago & Erie Railroad, at one time known as the Chicago & Atlantic Railroad. Practically it is one road, for trains from Chicago to the principal points covered by the Erie system are run through without change of cars. It is in every respect a magnificent road, with a train service that is not surpassed. Take this road for points in Northern Indiana, and many of the principal cities in Ohio, Pennsylvania, New York, and the Atlantic seaboard. For full particulars regarding the arrival and depart ure of trains see daily papers, time cards, folders, etc.

PITTSBURG, CINCINNATI, CHICAGO & ST. LOUIS RAILROAD.—J. H. Luce, assistant general passenger agent, 248 Clark Street, Chicago; city ticket office, 248 Clark Street; freight depot, 199 North Halsted Street; passenger depot, Canal and Adams streets. This road is familiarly known as the Pan Handle Route, and is one of the most important roads in the Pennsylvania Company's immense system. The road-bed is in splendid condition at all times and the train equipment is faultless. The Chicago & Louisville line, which is a direct route to Louisville, Kentucky, and all intermediate points, and the Chicago & Cincinnati line, which is a direct route to Cincinnati, Ohio, and all intermediate points, are also links in the famous "Pan Handle" system. It is also a direct route to many of the principal cities in Indiana, Ohio, Pennsylvania, the Eastern and Middle States. For full particulars regarding the arrival and departure of trains, see daily papers, etc., also time cards, folders, etc., which may be found with other railroad literature, in all hotels, depots, and other public places.

MILWAUKEE, LAKE SHORE & WESTERN RAILROAD.—Mr. C. L. Ryder, general agent, 197 Clark Street, Chicago; city ticket office, 197 Clark Street; passenger depot, Wells and Kinzie streets, North Side. This splendid road is generally known as the "Ashland Route." It is the direct and popular route from Chicago and Milwaukee, with fast trains to Sheboygan, Manitowoc, Appleton, New London, Wausau, and all Fox River manufacturing cities and the lumbering districts of Northern Wisconsin and Michigan. Also direct line to Gogebic, Penokee, and Montreal iron ranges, Gogebic, Wakefield, Bessemer, Ironwood, Hurley, and Ashland. For full particulars see daily papers, time cards, folders, etc.

NEW YORK, CHICAGO & ST. LOUIS RAILROAD. — Mr. C. H. Walker, western passenger agent, 79 Clark Street, Chicago; city ticket office, 79 Clark Street; freight depot, Taylor and Clark streets; passenger depot, Van Buren and Sherman streets. This road is popularly known as the "Nickle Plate" Route. It is a splendid road, elegantly equipped with fast trains from Chicago to Valparaiso and Fort Wayne, Ind.; Fostoria, Bellevue, and Cleveland, in Ohio; Erie, Penn.; Dunkirk, Buffalo and New York. For full particulars regarding the arrival and departure of trains see daily papers, time cards, folders, etc.

PITTSBURG, FT. WAYNE & CHICAGO RAILROAD.—Mr. J. H. Luce, assistant general passenger agent, 248 Clark Street, Chicago; city ticket office, 248 Clark Street; freight depot, 2 West Madison Street; passenger depot, Canal and Adams streets.

This is one of the oldest and most popular roads running into this city. It is generally known as the Fort Wayne & Pennsylvania Route, and is owned by the Pennsylvania Company. It is absolutely perfect as a railroad, running the most elegant and fastest trains between Chicago and Eastern cities, via Pittsburg. It is a direct line to Fort Wayne, Ind.; Crestline, Ohio; Pittsburg, Altoona, Harrisburg, and Philadelphia in Pennsylvania; Baltimore, Washington, Jersey City, New York, Brooklyn, and Boston. For full particulars regarding the arrival and departure of trains see daily papers, time cards, folders, etc., which may be found at all hotels, depots, and public places.

UNION PACIFIC RAILROAD.—Mr. E. L. Lomax, general passenger and ticket agent, Omaha, Neb.; city ticket office, 191 Clark Street; passenger depot, corner of Wells and Kinzie streets, North Side.

Chicago is now practically the Eastern terminal of this great transcontinental system, for by a contract arrangement with the Chicago & North-Western Railway, through trains, freight and passenger, both ways, are now run daily by the Union Pacific Railroad between Chicago and its principal Western terminal points. The number of miles of track operated by this im- mense system is over 8,000. The road is ably managed and the track and equipment is all that could be desired. The Union Pacific extends to all points of importance in the States and Territories of Nebraska, Kansas, Colorado, Wyoming, Utah, Idaho, Montana, Nevada, California, Oregon, and the Republic of Mexico. For full particulars, see daily papers, time cards, folders, etc., or call at the city ticket office and be supplied with printed matter, descriptive of all the country traversed by this great artery.

NORTHERN PACIFIC RAILROAD.— Mr. Charles S. Fee, general passenger and ticket agent, St. Paul, Minn.; city ticket office, 210 Clark Street; passenger depot—Grand Central— Harrison Street and Fifth Avenue, Chicago.

On April 1, 1890, the Northern Pacific Railroad Company entered into a contract with the Wisconsin Central Company, whereby the former obtained a lease of all the lines of railroad owned, controlled, and operated by the latter. Therefore, Chicago is practically the eastern terminus of the Northern Pacific, with its mighty trans-continental system. Through sleeping-cars, however, are run from Chicago to Northern Pacific points in connection with both the Wisconsin Central and Chicago, Milwaukee & St. Paul lines.

The road and equipment is maintained at the point of highest excellence, and the country traversed is unexcelled in interesting and picturesque scenery.

The Northern Pacific was the first trans-continental line to introduce dining-cars, and the general excellence of this service has largely earned for the road its present enviable reputation.

By this route the grand Yellowstone National Park, with all its wonders; the picturesque region of Puget Sound; California, and Alaska, the land of great glaciers and huge mountain peaks, are reached.

WABASH RAILROAD.—Mr. F. A. Palmer, assistant general passenger agent, 201 Clark Street, Chicago; city ticket office, 201 Clark Street; freight depot, Third Avenue and Twelfth Street; passenger depot, Polk Street and Third Avenue. The Wabash is a favorite route from Chicago to St. Louis; distance, 290 miles. It passes through many of the large and prosperous towns and cities of Illinois, among which may be mentioned Reddick, Forrest, Gibson, Mansfield, Decatur, Taylorsville, Litchfield, Edwardsville, and others. It crosses the Mississippi at St. Louis on the famous steel bridge. For full particulars regarding the arrival and departure of trains see daily papers, time cards, folders, etc.

WISCONSIN CENTRAL RAILWAY.— Mr. James C. Pond, general passenger agent, Chicago; Mr. G. K. Thompson, city passenger agent, 205 Clark Street; city ticket office, 205 Clark Street; freight depot, Fifth Avenue and Polk Street; passenger depot, Grand Central, Harrison Street and Fifth Avenue.

As this road is the Chicago link of the Northern Pacific Railroad, the traveler will, of course, take it for all points reached by that great system. The Wisconsin Central is unexcelled in road-bed, track, and equipment. It is essentially a Wisconsin road, and there is scarcely a point of interest and importance in that State which it does not reach, either direct or by its connections. For full particulars regarding the arrival and departure of trains, see daily papers, time cards, folders, etc., or call at the city ticket office, 205 Clark Street.

Railway Cable and Horse Cars—Night Time Table.—

SOUTH SIDE.

COTTAGE GROVE AVENUE.—Last cable car going south leaves Madison Street at 12.30 A. M.; going north, leaves Thirty-ninth Street at 11.50 P. M. Horse car then leaves Thirty-ninth Street at 12.24 A. M., and one leaves each and every thirty-four minutes thereafter during the night.

STATE STREET.—Last cable car going south leaves at 12.26 A. M.; going north, at 11. 30 P. M. Horse cars then leave each and every twenty-two minutes thereafter during the night. Connection made at Thirty-ninth Street for Sixty-third Street until 12.30 A. M.; for Stock Yards, 12.10 A. M. Last car leaves Stock Yards, going north via State Street, at 12.40 A. M.

ARCHER AVENUE. — Car leaves Madison Street, going south, at 12.26 A. M.; Nineteenth Street at 12.54 A. M.; going north, leaves the river at 12.30 A. M., and each end every sixty-six minutes thereafter during the night.

INDIANA AVENUE. — Last car leaves Madison Street, going south, at 12.00 midnight. Last car leaves Thirty-ninth Street, going north, at 11.16 P. M.

WENTWORTH AVENUE.—Last car leaves Washington Street, going south, at 11.32 P. M.; going north, leaves Thirty-ninth Street at 10.52 P. M.

HANOVER AND BUTLER STREETS. —Last car leaves Madison and State streets, going south, at 11.38 P. M. Leaves Thirty-first Street at 10.59 P. M.

HALSTED STREET.—Last car leaves Archer Avenue, going south, at 12.30 A. M. Last car via Halsted Street, leaves Stock Yards, going north, at 12.58 A. M.

THIRTY-FIRST STREET (crosstown). —Last car leaves the lake, going west, at 11.10 P. M.; last car leaves the river, going east, at 10.36 P. M.

WEST SIDE.

MADISON AND FORTIETH STREETS. —Last car leaves Fortieth Street at 11.36 P. M.; last cable car leaves La Salle Street at 12.00 midnight.

HALSTED STREET.—All night cars. —From O'Neil Street, every forty-five minutes after 11.30 P. M.; from State Street, every forty-five minutes after 12.15 A. M.

TWELFTH STREET.—All night cars via Randolph Street to State Street. From Western Avenue, every forty-five minutes after 11.45 P. M.: from State Street, every forty-five minutes after 12.40 A. M.

INDIANA STREET.—All night cars. From Western Avenue, every eighty minutes after 11.40 P. M.; from State and Randolph streets, every eighty minutes after 12.20 A.M.

OGDEN AVENUE.—Via Randolph to State Street.— Last car leaves Western Avenue at 7.45 P. M.; State and Randolph streets at 8.21 P. M.

MADISON STREET.—Night cars.— Running every twenty minutes, from California Avenue, after 12.00 midnight; from State and Washington streets every twenty minutes after 12.40 A. M.

ADAMS STREET.—Last cars leave Michigan Avenue at 11.58 P. M.; 12.04 A. M., and 12.10 A. M.

Rand-McNally Building. — This elegant building was completed about July 1, 1890. It is a ten-story, steel-constructed, fire-proof building, extending 149 feet on Adams Street, and 166 feet back to Quincy. Its height is 142 feet. The interior court is 60x60 feet. One of the main features of the building is its cantilever construction, carrying the party walls, thereby avoiding all danger of settling to the adjoining property-owners. The interior court is faced entirely with white, glazed brick, and terra cotta. The exterior is entirely of terra cotta, of a dark, brown shade. The structure is provided with four passenger and three freight elevators. Among the tenants are the Chicago, Milwaukee & St. Paul road, World's Fair management, and the enormous printing house of Rand, McNally & Co. It has been estimated that this house contains a total of 3,700 tons of steel. There are fifteen miles of steel railway sixty-five-pound rails in the foundation, twelve miles of steam pipes, twelve miles of fifteen-inch steel beams, and 350,000 rivets and bolts. It cost $1,000,000.

Reform Clubs.—Several "reform societies" flourish in Chicago, and seem to find plenty of occupation. Of these, the most prominent are: The Citizens' League of Chicago, the Citizens' Association of Chicago, the Civil Service Reform League, the Illinois Tariff Reform League, the international Law and Order League, the Revenue Reform League of Cook County, and the Western Society for the Suppression of Vice. The Citizens' League, whose object is the enforcement of the laws regulating the sale of intoxicating liquors, is the most active and successful of these societies.

Reformed Episcopal Churches. — The Episcopal Reformed churches of Chicago are :

St. John's, Langley Avenue and Thirty-seventh Street.

St. Mary's, Maplewood.

St. Matthew's, Larrabee Street and Fullerton Avenue.

St. Ansgarius', Chicago Avenue and Sedgwick Street.

St. Barnabas', Forty-fourth Street and Park Avenue.

St. Bartholomew's, Sixty - fifth Street and Stewart Avenue.
St. George's, Grand Crossing.
St. James', Cass and Huron streets.
St. Luke's, 388 South Western Avenue.
St. Mark's, Thirty-ninth Street and Cottage Grove Avenue.
St. Paul's, 4928 Lake Avenue.

many of the finest eating-houses in the country. Of these, perhaps the best known are : Rector's Oyster House, Monroe and Clark streets ; the Lakeside Oyster House, Adams and Clark streets ; H. M. Kinsley's great catering establishment, on Adams Street, opposite the Post Office ; Weber's, on Washington

RAND-MCNALLY BUILDING, ADAMS AND QUINCY STREETS, NEAR LASALLE.

Christ Church, Twenty - fourth Street and Michigan Avenue.
Emanuel, Twenty-eighth and Hanover streets.
Trinity, Englewood.
Tyng Mission, Twenty-first Street and Archer Avenue.
Episcopal Reformed (missionary), St. Paul's Church, West Adams Street and Winchester Avenue.

Restaurants.—There are nearly 700 restaurants in Chicago, including

Street, near Wabash Avenue; Thomson's Oyster House, on Dearborn Street, near Monroe ; Kohlsaat's numerous down - town branches ; the Chicago Oyster House, on Madison Street, near Clark Street : Lansing & McGarigle's, on Clark Street, and the Boston Oyster House, Madison and Clark streets.

Riding Schools.—Riding, as an exercise, is becoming more popular in Chicago every year, and the boulevards are the chief resort of the equestrians. There are several riding schools, where first-class instruction can be obtained from well-known horsemen. On North Clark Street, near Lincoln Park, is an excellent school, and there is another on Sixteenth Street, near Michigan Avenue.

Rogues' Gallery, or Bureau of Identification, as it is called, is a collection of photographs of persistent and notorious criminals who have, at one time or another, fallen into the hands of the police. That in Chicago is in the hands of the detective office at police headquarters, basement of the City Hall, and consists of over a thousand cartes-de-visite of all sorts of faces, from that of the coarse, sensual felon to the sleek, sanctimonious confidence operator. An official photographer is employed by the Police Department, at a salary of $1,200, to take the photographs of criminals. Once a picture is placed in this gallery it is only removed when its subject dies or disappears from the criminal world, or when he has given ample proof of his intention to reform in the community, by leading an honest life for at least five years. Many daring burglaries, forgeries, etc., have been traced home to their perpetrators by the clews furnished by a comparison of these pictures with such descriptions of suspicious characters as were seen about the locality when the crime was committed.

Roman Catholic Churches.—
Archbishop of Chicago, Most Reverend Patrick A. Feehan, D. D.; Vicar-General, Very Reverend D. M. J. Dowling; Chancellor and Secretary, Rev. P. J. Muldoon, 311 Superior Street. The Roman Catholic churches of the city are located as follows:

Cathedral of the Holy Name, Superior and North State streets.

All Saints Church, southwest corner of Twenty-fifth Place and Wallace Street.

Chapel of our Lady of Mercy, St. Paul's Home.

Church of Notre Dame de Chicago (French), Vernon Park Place and Sibley Street.

Church of Our Lady of Good Counsel (Bohemian), Western Avenue and Cornelia Street.

Church of Our Lady of Mount Carmel, Wellington and Beecher streets.

Church of Our Lady of Sorrows, 1406 West Jackson Street.

Church of the Annunciation, southwest corner of Wabansia Avenue and North Paulina Street.

Church of the Assumption (Italian), Illinois Street, near North Market Street.

Church of the Holy Angels, 282 Oakwood Boulevard.

Church of the Holy Angels, Hoyne Avenue.

Church of the Holy Family, May and West Twelfth streets.

Church of the Holy Rosary, southwest corner of South Park Avenue and One Hundred and Thirteenth Street, Roseland.

Church of the Immaculate Conception, North Franklin Street, north of Schiller Street.

Church of the Nativity, Thirty-seventh and Dashiel streets.

Church of the Sacred Heart, southeast corner of West Nineteenth and Johnson streets.

Church of the Visitation, Fifty-first and Morgan streets.

Holy Trinity (German), South Lincoln and Taylor streets.

Holy Trinity (Polish), Noble and Ingraham streets.

Immaculate Conception B. V. M. (German), 2944 Bonfield Street near Archer Avenue.

Immaculate Conception B. V. M. (Polish), northwest corner Eighty-first Street and Commercial Avenue.

St. Albert's Church (Polish), West Seventeenth and Paulina streets.

St. Agnes, South Washtenaw Avenue near Thirty-eighth Street.

St. Aloysius (German), Thompson and Davis streets.

St. Alphonsius (German), Lincoln and Southport avenues.

St. Ann's, Fifty-fifth Street and Wentworth Avenue.

St. Anthony of Padua (German), southeast corner Twenty-fourth Place and Hanover Street.

St. Augustine (German), Fifty-first and Laflin streets.

St. Augustine (colored), 2251 Indiana Avenue.

St. Bernard, Sixty-sixth Street and Stewart Avenue.

St. Bernard's Church (French), Brighton Park.

St. Boniface (German), Cornell and Noble streets.

St. Bridget's, Archer Avenue and Church Place.

St. Cecilia, Bristol Street near Wentworth Avenue.

St. Charles Borromeo's, 87 to 91 Cypress Street.

St. Columbkill's, North Paulina and West Indiana streets.

St. Elizabeth's, northeast corner State and Forty-first streets.

St. Francis of Assisium (German), West Twelfth Street and Newberry Avenue.

St. Frances de Sales, Ewing Avenue and One Hundred and Second St.

St. Francis Xavier (German), Avondale.

St. Gabriel's, southeast corner Wallace and Forty-fifth streets.

St. George's (German), 3915 Fifth Avenue.

St. Hedwig's (Polish), North Side, Kosciusco, between North Hoyne Avenue and St. Hedwig's Street.

St. James', Wabash Avenue and Thirtieth Street.

St. Jarlath's, Hermitage Avenue and West Jackson Street.

St. John's, Eighteenth and Clark streets.

St. John Nepomucene's (Bohemian), Twenty-fifth Street and Portland Avenue.

St. John the Baptist (French), Thirty-third Street near South Wood Street.

St. Joseph's (German), North Market and Hill streets.

St. Joseph's (Polish), Forty-eighth and Paulina streets.

St. Josephat's (Polish), northwest corner Ward Street and Belden Avenue.

St. Laurence's, Seventy-fifth Street near Brooks Avenue.

St. Leo's, Wright Street and Schorling Avenue, Auburn Park.

St. Louis', Pullman.

St. Malachy's, Walnut Street and Western Avenue.

St. Martin's (German), Forty-ninth and School streets.

St. Mary's, Wabash Avenue and Eldridge Court.

St. Mary's of Perpetual Help (Polish), 9J1 Thirty-second Street near Ullman Street.

St. Mathias', Bowmanville.

St. Michael's (German), Eugenie Street and Cleveland Avenue.

St. Patrick's, Commercial Avenue near Ninety-fifth Street, South Chicago.

St. Patrick's, South Desplaines and West Adams streets.

St. Paul's (German), South Hoyne Avenue and Ambrose Street.

St. Peter's (German), Clark and Polk streets.

SS. Peter and Paul, Ninety-first Street and Exchange Avenue, South Chicago.

St. Philip's, Park Avenue and West Forty-third Street.

St. Pius, southeast corner West Nineteenth Street and South Ashland Avenue.

St. Procopius (Bohemian), Allport and West Eighteenth streets.

St. Rose of Lima, Ashland Avenue near Forty-eighth Street.

St. Stanislaus Kostka's (Polish), Noble and Ingraham streets.

St. Stephen's, North Sangamon and West Ohio streets.

St. Slyvester's, California and Shakespeare avenues.

St. Teresa's (German), Center and Clyde streets.

St. Thomas', Fifty-fifth Street, Hyde Park.

St. Viateur's, Belmont and Crawford avenues.

St. Vincent de Paul, Webster Avenue and Osgood Street.

St. Vitus, Paulina and Van Horn streets.

St. Wencelaus (Bohemian), 173 De Koven Street.

Rose Hill Cemetery contains five hundred acres of high ground and is situated on the Chicago & North-Western Railway, about six and a half miles from the city. The view had of this cemetery from passing trains, or from almost any point surrounding, with its winding carriage and footways, its beautiful lakes and its green and sloping lawns, reveals a picture of grand landscape work that is hardly excelled. The massive stone entrance, built in the old castle style of architecture, affords both office and chapel room, and the greenhouses, which are very large, contain almost every variety of plant and flower. The Rose Hill Cemetery Company was chartered February 11, 1859. Rose Hill contains many handsome and costly tombs and monuments, the most prominent of the latter being the Soldier's Monument at the head of the main avenue. This is one of the three prominent Protestant cemeteries, and may be reached, aside from the railroad, by a splendid drive via Lincoln Park,

Graceland, and the beautiful northern suburbs. It is seven miles north of the City Hall.

Rowing. — Rowing is confined almost entirely to the parks. Each of the larger parks contains a lake of considerable size, and a large number of boats are continually in use during pleasant weather. The various boat-clubs, located along the lake shore, enjoy themselves upon that body of water, but do not dare to venture outside of a very narrow strip of the inland sea, whose surface is decidedly treacherous.

Rush Medical College.—The history of this institution is known to the medical profession throughout the country. It is the oldest medical college in Chicago, and was organized in 1843, but began its work in 1837. The buildings are located at Wood and Harrison streets, West Side, and, with the buildings of the Presbyterian Hospital, which form part of the plant, constitute a mammoth medical educational group. The faculty is composed of some of the most prominent members of the professsion, and the classes are always large.

Safe Deposit Vaults.—It often happens, in a large city like Chicago, that a person, by thrift and economy, has come into possession of money or other valuables, for which they have no place for safe-keeping at home or elsewhere, and it may not be convenient for them to have a ponderous safe. For these the great coöperative safes of the city have been built and are managed. There are fifteen of them, nearly all built in connection with some banking institution, and offering almost perfect safety for the funds or valuables therein deposited. A description of one will cover all, in the main features. The vaults and other rooms connected therewith are all on the ground floor of the building. The space occupied is divided into a manager's office, a safe-vault, or "strong-room," a storage vault, an apartment for ladies, and also one for gentlemen, in which private examination of boxes can be is a large room, and not a simple passage-way between a row of safes on either hand. The space is usually not "cribbed, cabined, and confined," but is ample for light, air, and future developments. Great care is taken in their construction to make them proof against any fire that might occur in the building or

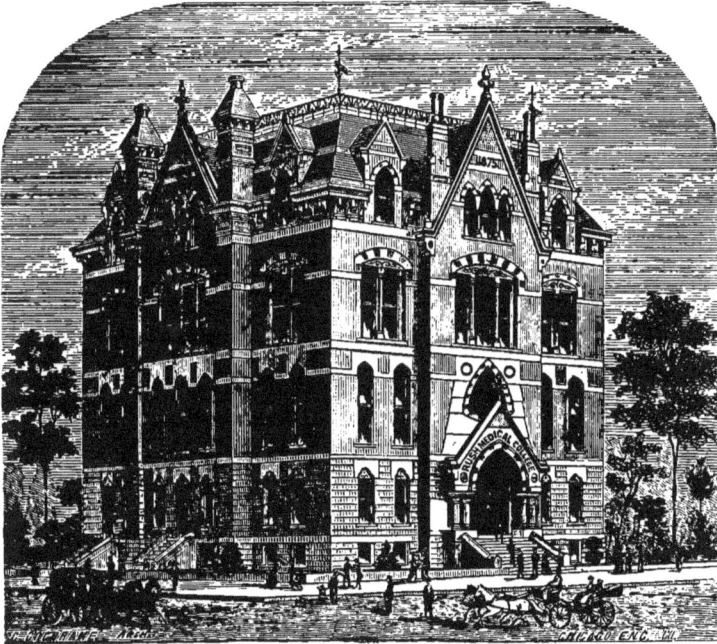

RUSH MEDICAL COLLEGE, HARRISON AND WOOD STREETS.

made. "Strong room" is the standard English name for what, in this country, is termed a large vault for the storage of valuables, such as cash, bonds, etc. This name of "strong-room" is peculiarly applicable to the vaults of the safety deposit companies, from the fact that it neighborhood, as also against the depredations of skilled burglars. The foundation is a solid mass of stone and concrete eight feet in thickness, commencing below the water-level. On this bed of concrete rests the walls of the vaults, which are thirty-six inches thick, built of hard brick, cements, and steel railroad rails, in such form and design as to make them proof against any attack of man or the elements. The top of the vaults are constructed in like manner as the sides, the center supports being heavy iron girders, resting on iron columns, the bases supported by piers, surrounded by the solid stone and concrete before mentioned. They are as absolutely fire and burglar proof as the ingenuity of man can devise. The entrances are guarded by double doors of most massive strength, the outer ones weighing in the neighborhood of half a ton. They are opened and closed by delicate and complicated machinery; without this they could not easily be handled. All the double-doors are locked with double combination locks, so arranged as to work separately, as may be desired. To make everything all the more secure, the entrances are supplied with chronometer locks, which, acting automatically, set the bolts when the doors are closed, releasing them at any time within two or three days. But whatever the fixed date may be, the machine holds its charge firmly until it comes, against all attack, except actual destruction. The "strong-room" will accommodate from 4,000 to 6,000 individual safes for the use of renters. These are provided, according to the fancy of the renter, with a key or combination lock. Every key is different from every other, and the lock is always changed before re renting. Each safe is provided with one or more tin cases to hold the contents. It is always under the entire and absolute control of the renter, and subject to his personal access only, or his duly accredited deputy. The "strong-room" is always brilliantly lighted with electric lights, and thus is anything but a noisome "vault." A writer, speaking of the English

"strong-room" says: "No one will ever know how many millions' worth of valuables are stored up in one of these great safe deposit companies, for each customer has his own special lock-up, and keeps his own key and counsel." There are a series of private retiring rooms, whose bolted doors secure privacy when examining the contents of the box for any purpose. Separate rooms are provided for ladies and gentlemen. Thoroughly reliable watchmen are always on guard at all hours, by day or night. The rooms opening from the street are lighted at all hours, thus giving a full view of the massive vault doors and interior arrangements to passers-by, who are thus involuntarily made a patrol and an additional safeguard. Electric apparatus communicates instantly with the police and fire departments. Included in these safe deposits are arrangements for the storage of trunks and boxes for a longer or shorter time. And all this security can be had at a nominal cost. Among these deserving of especial mention is the old and popular Commercial Safety Deposit Company, located at 88 Monroe Street, between Dearborn and State streets. Many of the most prominent people of the city place their valuables within its ample, reliable, and thoroughly safe vaults. "Keep your key and council," is the copyright trade-mark of this institution, and the advice it carries is thoroughly appreciated and invariably heeded.

St. Boniface Cemetery, located on North Clark Street, corner of Lawrence Avenue. Take North Clark Street cable line. This is the German Roman Catholic Cemetery.

St. George's Benevolent Association gives advice to English immigrants and grants relief to persons of English parentage not members of the association who are of good moral character. It assists the sick, buries the dead, and cares for the widows and orphans of deceased members.

St. Ignatius College, located at 413 West Twelfth Street. This splendid institution, for the higher education of the Catholic youth of Chicago and vicinity, was erected in 1869. It is conducted by the Fathers of the Society of Jesus. A charter was granted to the college by the Legislature of the State of Illinois, June 30, 1870, with power to confer the usual degrees of the various faculties of a university. The studies pursued in the college comprise the doctrines and evidences of the Catholic religion, logic, metaphysics, ethics, astronomy, natural philosophy, chemistry, mathematics, rhetoric, composition, elocution, history, geography, book-keeping, arithmetic, the Latin, Greek, English, German, and French languages, and literature. The college is intended for day scholars only. The collegiate year is divided into two terms, the first beginning on the first Monday of September, the second on the first Monday of February, but students are received at any time during the year. On completing the studies of the collegiate department, those who prove deserving of distinction receive the degree of Bachelor of Arts. Subsequently, by devoting one year more to the study of philosophy or two years to any of the learned professions, they may obtain the degree of Master of Arts.

St. Jarlath's Church.—This beautiful church is of thirteenth-century Gothic style, with the lofty, pointed gables, bold, deep buttresses, alternating lancet and trancined

windows, deeply recessed and molded doorways. It is built with massive stone from base to apex and every detail executed in the highest and purest type of the Gothic builders' art, while a splendid and graceful tower, surmounted by an appropriate spire, flanks the main front and adds grace and dignity to the chaste exterior. The interior is, however, the feature of this edifice, for while in strict harmony with the external design, it is a revelation of the real dimensions and proportions of the structure, the auditorium or church apartment being fifty-eight feet in clear width, 130 feet in length, and fifty feet in clear height from floor to ceiling. This extensive chamber is spanned by bold and sweeping arched roof-trusses which spring from the floor-level, and by their peculiar and ingenious construction enable the architect to bridge over and secure a graceful outline for the ceiling, which, in conformity with the lines of such construction, assumes a polygonal form and is subdivided into numerous rich panelings, which are defined by the main constructive features of the roof. A deeply-recessed chancel at the end of this auditorium gives an added length to the interior effect. This chancel, or sanctuary portion, is richly embellished by a molded arch and ornate ceiling, and is lighted by five richly-stained windows, representing the crucifixion and the four evangelists, while all around are other windows embellished with figures and emblems of the saints and martyrs of the church. Ample vestries are placed at either side of the chancel and are connected by an ambulatory, which extends behind the apside end of the sanctuary. The internal finishing is mainly of polished red oak and mahogany, and the colored decorations of the walls and ceilings blend harmoniously with the architectural features. The building was designed and its construction superintended by Mr. James J. Egan, who was also the architect of the City Hall and Court House. This beautiful Catholic church was dedicated October 24, 1886. The Rev. Thomas F. Cashman is in charge. Located Hermitage Avenue, corner of West Jackson Street.

St. Joseph's Home for the Friendless is a refuge for respectable young girls out of employment, situated at 409 and 411 South May Street.

St. Joseph's Hospital is located at 360 Garfield Avenue and is conducted by the Sisters of Charity. Patients who can are expected to pay for treatment.

St. Joseph's Orphan Asylum is at 3 and 5 Douglas Place under the management of the Sisters of St. Joseph. Boys and girls are received from four to eight years of age and educated.

St. Luke's Hospital is one of the largest in the city, and is located at Michigan Avenue and Thirty-seventh Street. The medical staff are men of the highest standing in the profession. The hospital is under Episcopalian management, yet no distinction is made to admission.

St. Mary's Training School is conducted by the Christian Brothers. It is located at Feehanville, Cook County. Boys, principally waifs, are cared for and given instructions in agriculture and mechanics.

St. Vincent's Infant Asylum admits children under six years of age. Children are boarded here by their parents, and others are brought in by the police. The Sisters of Charity, by whom it is conducted, have recently moved into their new and handsome building, located at 191 La Salle Avenue.

Saint Xavier's Academy.— This is certainly a handsome structure. The institution was first opened in 1846, since which time it has occupied a position in the educational history of Chicago worthy of note. It is conducted by the Sisters of Mercy, who devote their time and abilities to the moral, as well as practical education of their young lady pupils. The building is admirably located on Wabash Avenue, corner of Twenty-ninth Street. It is commodious, substantially built, and its interior is provided with all the comforts and conveniences that go to make a healthful, pleasant home. The course of study includes the various branches of education that fit a young lady to occupy her proper position in the walks of life.

Saloons.—January 1, 1891, there were 5,650 saloons in Chicago, employing 17,050 males, and 3,900 females; total, 20,950 persons. Thus it will be observed that it requires quite an army of people to serve the people of Chicago who are not adverse to looking upon the wine when it is red, or the beer when it foams in the glass. The saloons pay a license to the city of $500 each per year, and a revenue tax to the Government of $25 per year for the privilege of selling cigars and tobacco. This is a revenue to the city of $2,825,000, and to the Government of $141,250.

Sanitarium, The Lincoln Park, is situated on the lake shore at the foot of Fullerton Avenue, in Lincoln Park. The building was especially designed for the purpose and is directly over the water, being erected on a great platform, 90 feet wide, projecting into the lake over 200 feet. The broad roof, with its over-hanging eaves, covers a floor space of nearly 18,000 square feet, over which swing hundreds of infants' hammocks. The wide verandas and an open-air court at the lake extremity furnish accommodations for the mothers and older children. At the shore end are grouped the necessary offices. On the right of the entrance is a commodious reception-room from which the guests pass to the doctor's office for examination and for medical attention when required. Thence the guests are registered in the office and the matron gives them in charge of trained nurses—who assign them to suitable quarters, provide hammocks, chairs, etc. The matron's room, connecting both with the office and the physician's room, is a large dormitory for the care of critical cases which it may be necessary to keep over night. There are also kitchen, pantries, store-rooms, bath-rooms, closets, etc. The west front of the Sanitarium is connected with the park by a broad bridge, with a gentle ascent for baby carriages. Being in close proximity to the zoölogical department and other features of interest in the park, the other children, who in many cases must be brought with the baby, find enjoyment and pastime without encroaching upon the Sanitarium proper. The total cost of the building and equipment of the Sanitarium to date is $12,375; of this sum the Daily News contributed $1,000 and advanced $10,049.25 as a loan, which is gradually being paid by public contributions. The Sanitarium is free to all, but it is especially designed for the children of those compelled to live in crowded tenement houses, or in the dirty, dingy back streets, where the sun beats down pitilessly,

and the air in the stuffy little rooms is fairly stifling. Babies of this class get a new hold on life by spending a few days every week at the Sanitarium. The cost of entertaining each little guest is about ten cents a day, a sum which can be spared by almost every one. This is a noble charity and should be encouraged. Thousands of the babies are cared for in this place every day throughout the summer months.

Sanitary Police.—At present the roster of the sanitary police force of the Health Department numbers 34 men, one from each ward in the city. Chicago may well be proud of her sanitary squad. There are few cities in the Union that can show a squad of men possessed of as much intelligence and certainly none containing as many faithful workers. The salary of a sanitary policeman is the same as a member of the police force ($1,000) per annum. The total number of notices to abate nuisances served during the past year by the sanitary police was 29,386.

Scandinavian Methodist Episcopal Churches.—The following list gives the names and locations of those in Chicago:

First Norwegian Church, corner West Indiana and Sangamon streets.

First Swedish Church, northwest corner Market and Oak streets.

Immanual Norwegian Church, West Ohio Street, corner Noble Street.

Maplewood Avenue Norwegian Church, corner Thompson and Maplewood avenues.

Second Swedish Church, North May Street, between West Ohio and West Erie streets.

Third Swedish Church, Fifth Avenue, corner Thirty-third Street.

Schools, Public.—There is nothing within the range of political economy that more enriches the world, and no more potent factor in the development and advancement of an enlightened civilization, than a comprehensive system of public education. The methods and achievements of past generations have been recognized and improved by the people of the present period, and it is gratifying that the record indicates Chicago to be in the front rank in her facilities, and methods for training the minds and molding the character of the youth of to-day, and preparing for the coming generation. It is also gratifying that the public school system of this city receives that generous support and attention from our citizens, that its magnitude and importance is entitled to. In 1887 the amount appropriated and otherwise available for educational purposes was nearly $2,250,000, in 1888, nearly $2,500,000, in 1889, about the same amount, in 1890, nearly $4,750,000, and the present year over $5,500,000. Thus it will be seen, that over $17,250,000 have been appropriated during the past five years for the construction and maintenance of our schools. About 86 per cent. of this amount is from taxation, the balance, the revenue from school property. There are 218 school buildings with a seating capacity of 125,000. There were 186 school rooms added during the past year; over $500,000 were expended during the same period for additional land and buildings. The total enrollment of pupils reaches 139,000. There are nearly 7,000 pupils in 65 buildings rented at an expense of nearly $32,000, which, capitalized at 4 per cent., equals $800,000, or representing the interest on the estimated cost of ten sixteen-room buildings. Comment is unnecessary. There has been expended for school purposes in the annexed districts about $1,250,000, to meet this the same territory provides a trifle over $750,000. Night schools cost the city nearly $77,000 during the year; the compulsory feature about $15 000; deaf and dumb tuition $5,000; manual training $10,001; music nearly $13,000; drawing over $17,500; and physical culture about $15,500; foreign languages $115,000. It is estimated that the average pupil leaves the public school about the age of 12 to 14 years; and hence to avail him or herself of the advantages of the various branches taught in the public schools and also to acquire a fair knowledge of those essential branches that will best fit them for the battle of life, they should be studious and industrious during their limited period of attendance.

The present cost value of the school property of Chicago is $11,000,000. By far the greater part of this has been accumulated since the fire of 1871 which destroyed many buildings. The school-houses are all that could be desired being thoroughly modern, artistic, convenient, and comfortable.

The public schools of Chicago are conducted under the supervision of a Board of Education which consists of 15 members (some of whom are females) appointed by the Mayor. They serve without compensation and are about equally divided politically. The executive department is in charge of a superintendent, salary $5,000; two assistant superintendents, salary, $4,000; three assistant superintendents, salary, $3,500; clerk, attorney, school agent, building and supply agent, book-keeper, assistant clerk, assistant clerk and messenger, assistant to building and supply agent, stenographer and type-writer, messenger and assistant to supply department, and chief engineer. The salaries of the above are from $300 to $3,500 per year. Including the principals of the various schools there are 2 920 teachers employed. The salaries paid teachers range from $400 to $2,400 per annum. These salaries are graded by the position and length of service. The schools are graded from primary to high schools, and the student who leaves the high schools with a diploma is far enough advanced to enter any of the famous institutions of learning in the land.

Scientific and Learned Societies.—Eastern cavilers to the contrary notwithstanding, Chicago has a large number of educated scientists, who have formed several societies, among which may be mentioned:

THE CHICAGO ACADEMY OF SCIENCES, founded in 1857, and at present located in the Exposition Building. A new structure will be erected, or new quarters will be found in th? Art Institute, or on the World's Fair grounds.

CHICAGO ASTRONOMICAL SOCIETY. founded in 1863. Owns the telescope in use at Northwestern University.

HORTICULTURAL SOCIETY, incorporated 1890, for the purpose of annual horticultural exhibitions.

RIDGWAY ORNITHOLOGICAL CLUB, 131 Wabash Avenue.

STATE MICROSCOPICAL SOCIETY, 184 Wabash Avenue.

Seating Capacity of Theatres.—Chicago, with twenty theatres all told, and a population of 1,500,000, has a seating capacity for theatrical patrons of 24,000, while New York, with thirty-three theatres, has a seating capacity of double this number. It will be seen from this statement that Chicago would support more places of amusement in the shape of first-class play houses.

Seminary of the Sacred Heart.—Blind, indeed, would be any sight-seer in Chicago, who could ride on the West Twelfth Street cars, from Halsted Street to Ashland Avenue, and fail to notice the substantial buildings and spacious grounds of the Seminary of the Sacred Heart at 485 West Taylor Street. The structures are built of a gray brick, in the gothic form of a cross, and show the massive solidity peculiar to the establishments of the Catholic Church. They cover but a small part of the ten acres of grounds, included in the block bounded by Taylor and Sibley streets, Gilpin Place and Throop Street. These grounds are kept in nice order and tell of the unwearied care in all minor details necessary for successful management. This institution was founded in 1860 and incorporated in 1870. It is maintained as a boarding school for young ladies, with ample accommodations for about 200 students. The whole interior is conveniently arranged and tastefully fitted, so far as color and decoration are concerned, for the purpose for which it is designed. The school is in charge of the Religieuse of the Sacred Heart, who also maintain here a parochial school of about 1,000 girls, where all branches are taught that are taught in the public schools. The Order, in addition, carry on a branch school on the North Side (see Academy of the Sacred Heart). It is conceded by all who have means for judging, that there is no finer school in the country for the education of young ladies than this, And though but a third of a century old, its graduates rank most favorably with those of any other institution, whether State or private. The Lady Superior, Miss Spalding, is a sister of Bishop Spalding of Peoria. She is well known throughout the country for her eminent fitness for the place she so admirably fills.

Servite Sisters' Industrial Home for Girls is at 1396 West Van Buren Street.

Servants are human. This is a fact which most of the persons who are unable to keep a servant in their houses for any length of time are apt to forget. On the other hand, the atmosphere of republican institutions is fatal to good service. You may take your choice in Chicago of Irish, Negro, Swedish, French, or German "help," as it is called, and it is largely a matter of taste. There are good servants to be found among those of each race. If you want a servant the best way is to advertise in one of the daily papers. Having selected from among the applicants one who appears to answer your requirements, personally investigate his or her character, as written characters are as a rule untrustworthy and not worth the trouble of reading. Intelligence offices have around them ordinarily only the worthless and refractory servants who never stay long in any one place, and whose faces constantly recur at these haunts. It is a useless waste of time, energy, and money to call upon those servants who advertise in the daily papers, as it only encourages them in this practice to run after them. Added to this is the, by no means small, danger to a lady of being molested in the tenement houses and vile neighborhoods from which many of these impudent advertisements are put forth. The wages demanded by servants average at present about as follows: Females to do chamber work, $10 to $14 per month; to do general housework, $14 to $16 per month; to cook, $12 to $20 per month; for plain cooking and for fine cooking, from $20 upward; coachmen who board themselves, $40 to $60 per month; male waiters from $20 to $25 per month, with board. These figures of course vary with the size of the family and the nature of the work. Servants are not entitled to any perquisites whatever, and if you allow them to do your purchasing of groceries, meat, vegetables, it is not unlikely that you will find that they receive a percentage upon your bills from tradesmen. It is useless to forbid female servants to have "followers," as their love, like that of their betters, laughs at locksmiths. The best way is to allow them to receive their visitors under certain regulations that you may make, and after acquainting yourself with the character of the visitor.

Sewerage of Chicago.—On February 16, 1847, a legislative act supplementary to the city charter granted power to the common council to build and repair sewers by special assessments upon the property benefited thereby. In the year 1849 Madison Street east and west and State Street north and south were decided upon as the summit in the South Division of the city; the grade of that portion lying north of Madison Street and west of State Street to slope to the north and drain into the main river. The portion east of State Street to slope east and drain into the lake. The portion south of Madison Street and west of State Street to slope west and discharge into the South Branch of the river. Nothing was done in the way of drainage, except open ditches, until the year 1850, when triangular shaped wooden box sewers were built in Clark, La Salle, and Wells streets from the main river to the alleys south of Randolph Street; the cost of these sewers was $2,871.90, which amount was wholly paid for by the property benefited.

By act of Legislature, dated June 23, 1852, a commission consisting of seven members was appointed and empowered to locate, construct, and maintain ditches, culverts, and embankments, bridges, and roads in any lands lying in Townships 37, 38, 39, and 40 north, Ranges 12, 13, and 14 east of the third principal meridian (Cook County), and to take the land and material necessary for these improvements and assess the costs of such work upon the land they deemed to be benefited thereby.

An examination showed the commissioner that nearly 100,000 acres of swamp land was contained within the limits of their commission, much of which was considered to be nearly worthless owing to the lack of drainage, and the service of which was from five to twelve feet above the lake level, and need only properly constructed ditches to reclaim and make a large portion of it available for agricultural purposes and occupation. In two years the Commission expended about $100,000 in legal improvements, and large tracts of land were reclaimed from swamps and made suitable for cultivation and occupation, which had been considered uninhabitable. The land drained extended about four miles north, eight miles west, and ten miles south from the then city limits, nearly all of which has since been annexed to the city. From 1856 to 1860 there were 53.70 miles of sewer built by the Sewerage Commissioners. By act of the Legislature, 1861, the Board of Sewerage Commissioners was abolished, and a Board of Public Works was created. The Board of Public Works was continued in power until September 19, 1876. Total number of miles of sewers in place December 31, 1876, 265.80. Nearly 72 miles of sewers have been added to the system during the year 1890, making the total in the city 785 miles. Dur-

ing the same year, 800 miles of sewers and 1,200 catch-basins have been cleaned; 6,000 of the latter were raised to grade, and 47 miles of house drains were laid. An area lying between Sixtieth and Ninety-fifth streets, and Vincennes Avenue and the lake, comprising about 9,300 acres, is too low to drain by gravity, therefore the storm water and sewage must be taken care of by machinery and other special means, which are now under consideration. The Bureau of Sewers is under the Department of Public Works. During the year 1890 this bureau expended $1,111,399.21. The sewers are of brick and pipe, and are from 9 inches to 7½ feet in diameter. In lineal feet they measure in the aggregate 4,149,317 feet. The total catch-basins are 26,489, number of man-holes 30,016, total number of house drains put in 127,570, total cost of cleaning sewers and catch-basins $971,338.88. Street intersections and repairs of sewers $759,489.01. Total cost of construction $10,965,669.98. These figures represent the total cost for the construction of sewers and catch-basins, and maintaining same since the establishment of the sewerage system, in 1855, to January 1, 1891. Through the medium of the drainage canal (which see), in time the entire sewerage of Chicago will find its way into the Mississippi River, leaving Lake Michigan, the great reservoir from which the city obtains its water supply, pure and free from the contamination of sewerage.

Sewer-Gas.—There is no more prolific source of such deadly diseases as typhoid fever, diphtheria, and malarial affections generally, than the presence, often undetected, of sewer-gas in dwelling houses. The first care of persons into apartments or dwellings should be to examine the waste pipes to see that they are properly trapped with automatic or elbow trap. This simple trap, which acts by always retaining a certain quantity of water in the bend, which the gas can not penetrate, is the only one which never gets out of order. There should not only be a large trap, where the main waste pipe joins the sewer, but there must be a trap to every opening, whether wash-hand basin, wash-tub sink, water closet, or bath tub. If they are missing, the landlord or agent of the place should be notified at once, and if he fails to supply the deficiencies, by notifying the Board of Health, City Hall, either personally or by letter, a sanitary inspector will be detailed to examine the premises and compel the owner to make the proper alterations.

Sheridan's Statue. — Union Park is to have a statue of the late Gen. P. H. Sheridan, and it is to be the gift of Charles T. Yerkes. Two years ago, while attending the Paris Exposition, Mr. Yerkes arranged for the electric fountain at Lincoln Park, and last year, on his annual visit, he contracted with a prominent sculptor for the Sheridan statue. The statue will be life size, cast in bronze, and will represent the hero on horseback, as nearly as possible as he appeared in his famous ride from Winchester. The statue will be placed in position during the coming year.

Sheriff's Offices.—The offices of the Sheriff of Cook County are in the county wing of the City Hall, in the northeast corner, on the ground floor, fronting on Clark and Randolph streets. Business hours correspond with the usual hours of the city; but communication can always be had with the authority resting there, through deputies.

Sherman House. —There is hardly a traveler who has ever passed

through Chicago that has not heard of, visited, or been a guest of, the Sherman. In the first place, the location is directly in the midst of the heart of the town—all the theatres, all of the railroad offices, the court house, and many of the banks are in its immediate vicinity—hence the desirability of being at this house; secondly, it is one of the best equipped and well managed of hotels. Its rates are always reasonable while the service, the appointments, the cuisine, etc., are in every respect just what one would desire. Mr. J. I. Pierce is proprietor. Located northwest corner of Clark and Randolph streets.

Sight-Seeing.—People do not come to Chicago to gather moss off venerable walls, or pluck grass out of the streets, but to see the symbol of American pluck and energy in its purest intensity. You will not find here time-eaten cathedrals, spacious art galleries, in which the choicest treasures have been collecting for centuries. When our civilization is as old as the Eastern, it will be just as interesting, and will not be baptized with blood either. We have no antique museums, nor historic structures which reek with crime or the wrongs of mankind against his fellow. Still, for a city over whose known site a hundred years have not yet passed, we think visitors may find many items of interest in the stirring records with which the present generation are familiar, and indeed were a part of. We have the Libby Prison Museum, full of the relics of the late "unpleasantness," the Historical Society, the Public Library, the Newberry Library, the Crerar Library, whose dimensions and scope are but just outlined. In the art galleries and trade museums, the shops and warehouses, are stored the collections made from every part of the globe, fully exemplifying, by their artistic beauty, the art-skill of the hands that fashioned, and the brains that conceived, them. A tour of the shops would be a very satisfying trip to the lover of the beautiful. In their proper places will be found a description of the great Roman Catholic Cathedrals and other endowments, also of other. churches of note. Then there are benevolent and reformatory institutions. While we can not furnish as full a dose of prison as New York city, we can do as well on the institutions designed to make a man better, and keep him so. We have the custom house and post office, the breakwater belonging to the United States Government, the City Hall, the Auditorium Tower and the weather clerk, the Chamber of Commerce and its tower, from which, with a fair glass, on a clear day, one can see the west shores of Michigan. Then the Masonic Temple, with its twenty stories, will tempt a climb to "see how the weather is up there." Then there is South Water Street, from which the city supplies its table; the stock yards, from whence comes its meats; the great grain elevators; the magnificent depots; the tunnels under the river: the water works; the park and boulevard system; the press rooms of the great daily papers; and the largest map manufactory in the world, Rand, McNally & Co. Then there are the cycloramas, and the theatres, and the coming World's Columbian Exposition to take up weeks of a visitor's stay. It is all new, and young men manage it all. It can hardly be said that Chicago is the paradise of old men. Those who desire to see the old and musty must not turn their faces toward the young and virile West.

Signal Service.—The United States Army Signal Service has its

Chicago station in the Auditorium tower. The office is in charge of a sergeant and his assistant. Reports are received by telegraph from 150 other stations distributed over the country; observations are taken and forwarded to these stations; and cautionary signals are displayed whenever a storm is threatened.

Sinai Congregational Cemetery.—Located at Rosehill. (See *Rosehill Cemetery*.)

Sinai Temple, in Moorish style of architecture, is located on Indiana Avenue corner Twenty-first Street. The Sinai congregation includes many of the leading Jewish families of the city. The auditorium is in amphitheatre style, and the interior finishing and furnishing are very fine. Rev. E. G. Hirsch is minister.

Site of Fort Dearborn.—The original Fort Dearborn was erected in 1803, the exact site of which was at the junction of River Street and Michigan Avenue, against the South end of Rush Street bridge. The large and beautiful building of the W. M. Hoyt Company, grocers, now occupies this valuable and historical spot of ground. This building bears on its north side a marble tablet on which is engraved the following: "This building occupies the site of old Fort Dearborn, which extended a little across Michigan Avenue and somewhat into the river as it now is. The fort was built in 1803-4 forming our outmost defense. By order of General Hull it was evacuated August 15, 1812, after the stores and provisions had been distributed among the Indians. Very soon after the Indians attacked and massacred about fifty of the troops and a number of citizens, including women and children, and next day burned the fort. In 1816 it was rebuilt, but after the Black Hawk war it went into gradual disuse, and in May, 1837, was abandoned by the Army, but was occupied by various Government offices till 1857, when it was torn down, excepting a single building which stood upon the site till the great fire of October 9, 1871."

"At the suggestion of the Chicago Historical Society, this tablet was erected Nov., 1880, by W. M. Hoyt."

Size of Cities.—The existing Paris covers 19,275 acres, or about thirty square miles, while London with 4,000,000 population contains 118 square miles, and Chicago as recently enlarged provides an area of 181 square miles for 1,250,000. The average distance from the center of Paris to the circumference is only three miles. Minneapolis with only 165,000 people has a municipal area more than twice as large as Paris. Almost the entire population of Paris is housed in the flats of tenement structures averaging from four to five stories in height. There are about 75,000 houses in Paris with an average of thirty people in a house. In the old arrondissements of the inner Paris there are about 30,000 houses accommodating about 1,000,-000 people. London will average about eight persons to a house for the whole metropolis, but the people of Paris are better housed, all things considered, than those of London. A population of 2,500,000 within a circle whose radius is only three miles is certainly very dense, but it must be remembered that Paris is a many-storied city.

Skating.—Skating in Chicago was formerly a popular winter amusement, but the semi-tropical nature of the winters since 1888 has almost destroyed the pastime. The parks, especially Lincoln, furnish excellent facilities for skating, and a

short spell of cold weather brings out thousands of skillful skaters. A small strip of the lake close to the shore can also be utilized for this enjoyment.

"Slot" Machines.—In many public places such as railway stations, museums, etc., are to be found numerous automatic machines for various purposes. By dropping a cent or a five-cent piece, as the case may be, into a slot, the machine is set in motion. Some tell the patron his exact weight, some perfume his handkerchief with cologne water, some provide him with candy, chewing gum, or a paper-bound novel; some serve you with cigars, others with mineral waters; some give electric shocks; some set in motion an exquisitely constructed miniature locomotive, steamboat, or fire-engine while a music box plays an air, and at least one gives the patron a tin-type portrait of himself. Many of the Edison phonographs are operated in the same way. Occasionally these machines are out of order, and the customer loses the money deposited in the slot. At many of the theatres, boxes are placed at the backs of the seats, each containing an excellent opera-glass, which may be taken from the box and used during the performance by the simple act of dropping a ten-cent piece into a slot.

Smoke.—"After 100 years of commercialism we have learned to breathe dirt as well as to eat it" says a foreign writer. The same assertion is true in a modified degree as to the denizens of Chicago. Long familiarity with smoke and soot has bred indifference to them, if not proverbial contempt. The effects, however, are visible on every hand in pallid faces, faltering steps, and decrepit forms. A lack of vitality is seen on every hand. Lassitude has usurped the place of energy, and in many instances enterprise starting forth with vigor and enthusiasm of a fresh revelation has relaxed its hold and degenerated into a simple remin- iscence. The City Council has fre- quently legislated against this evil, the smoke-inspector has done won- ders in abating the nuisance, yet the fact remains, that the city is still afflicted in a very large degree with the dusky incubus. The pure air of heaven wafted over the broad ex- panse of Lake Michigan from the east, or carried over the broad prai- ries from the south and west becomes contaminated, and when inhaled in- to the lungs produces physical re- sults prejudicial to the public health and well-being. But the evil effects of a system that tolerates the smoke nuisance are not confined to physical conditions; they affect the moral and intellectual standing of the commu- nity. Sidney Smith once said that a filthy man can never be a moral man. Neither can a city or a community, enveloped in smoke and dirt be a prosperous place. A few may reap rich harvests from the toil of the many, but squalor will perch upon every gate post and poverty keep watch and ward at every window and door of the mass of the people.

The evils which flow directly and indirectly from our present system, or want of system, are too numerous to mention. They are beyond mone- tary calculation. They affect the adult population, but more especially the rising generation. They shadow the lives of the young with a blight that can never be removed. They render the closing days of the aged less endurable by accumulating upon their heads ills from which they should be exempt. The all-pervad- ing smoke permeates every home and saturates the air we breathe, the water we drink, and the food we eat.

The most sacred precincts of every home are defiled: the very founts from which infancy draws its suste- nance are polluted. The smoke is- sue is a present and a pressing one in Chicago. Much has already been done to mitigate the nuisance; much more needs to be done. By radical measures the city may be rid of an evil that can find no excuse for ex- istence, and thus conduce largely to the physical beauty and general wel- fare of Chicago. During the past year this branch of the health de- partment has demonstrated beyond any doubt—and a very decided change in our atmosphere bears wit- ness—that the smoke nuisance can be abated by rigidly enforcing the existing ordinances. There are sev- eral smoke-consuming devices on the market that are reasonably effective, and they should be on every furnace that consumes large quantities of bituminous coal. The railroads as a rule are conforming with the ordi- nance, and every factory should be compelled to do so.

Societa Operaia Italian helps needy Italians and uses its influence to prevent the organ-grind- ing and street-begging class from making a living that way. It was organized by Italian mechanics and laborers.

Societies. — Saracen, meets at residences of its members.

Chicago Liberal League, Madison and Halsted streets.

Society of Ethical Culture, Secre- tary can be found at 170 State Street.

Moral Educational Society, meets at Grand Pacific, Secretary, 383 Washington Boulevard.

Margaret Fuller Society, meets at Grand Pacific Hotel.

Illinois Association of Sons of Vermont, meets semi-annually, room 70, Government building.

Deak Verein, is a Hungarian benevolent society and assists needy Hungarians.

Scandinavian Emigrant Relief Society, looks after the interests of Scandinavian immigrants.

Svea Society, devoted to literary and benevolent purposes, is a Swedish organization.

Western Seamen's Friend Society, dates back to 1830, and is the oldest charitable organization in the city. Its object is to promote the welfare of boatmen and their families, who depend on the western lakes and rivers for support.

Society for Home Teaching of the Blind, has a free lending library of several hundred volumes of choice books printed in raised letters. The society employs a teacher to give instructions to the blind at their own homes.

South Chicago is the seat of the great rolling mills of two large companies, besides iron works of various other kinds, also tin-plate ware, sash and blind factories, and a number of large lumber concerns. It lies on the lake in full view from Lake Park and with its towering chimneys, smokestacks, furnace-flues, etc., presents a busy scene of manufacturing habitation.

Sons of Maine, hold social re-unions at the Palmer House.

South Side Free Dispensary is at Twenty-sixth Street and Prairie Avenue. Physicians from this dispensary visit the poor who are unable to call at the hospital, for which no charge is made.

Special Assessments, Bureau of.—The streets of Chicago are improved; that is to say, graded, paved, sewered, etc., by special assessments made on the abutting prop-

erty. These assessments are paid in five yearly installments, with interest at 6 per cent. per year, or the entire amount may be paid at one time, at the option of the person assessed. The assessments are made by the Bureau of Special Assessments, which is composed of three commissioners. This is, however, a bureau in the department of public works. The aggregate special assessments for the past thirty years reaches the enormous amount of $47,694,099.70. The average amount for each year being $1,589,803.32. During the year 1890 the amount levied on abutting and adjoining property for all descriptions of street improvements, was $6,987,155.48, or about $6.50 per capita of population. As compared with the previous year, it shows an increase of $2,766,285.55, or 63 3-10 per cent. The willingness with which the property-owners impose upon themselves this enormous amount of special taxation is the best evidence of their material prosperity, and their unbounded faith in the commercial destiny of this city.

Spiritualists.—There are several societies of these which hold meetings more or less regularly every Sunday, but they have no fixed quarters. Besides these meetings, "seances" are given at private houses, to which admission is generally procurable by the payment of an entrance fee of $1 or less. Both meetings and "seances" are advertised in the religious columns of the daily papers. There are also many so-called mediums who give private seances, and profess to divine one's future.

Standard Theatre.—This theatre is on the West Side, at Halsted and Jackson streets. Its interior is very fine, both in decoration and arrangement, and there is a double balcony, parquette circle, and ten private boxes. The heating and ventilation is perfect, and it is a first-class house in all respects, presenting standard attractions during the season.

Standard Club—is composed principally of Jewish gentlemen, and has rooms at 1302 Michigan Avenue.

State Banks.—The Auditor of public accounts issued a statement August 28, 1891, of the condition of the State banks located at Chicago, in which the following figures were given: Number of State banks in Chicago, twenty-three, with a total capital stock of $12,197,000; total deposits, $51,359,724; loans and discounts, $47,000,000, with resources and liabilities of $69,187.011. It will thus be observed that the State banks of Chic·go compare favorably with national banks in popularity.

State Street.—This splendid thoroughfare is one of the longest, the broadest, the most important in a business way, and the one on which the fine retail business of the city finds its maximum development. It extends from North Avenue and Lincoln Park in the North Dvision, to a point far down toward the south end of the county, where the surveying chain of man runneth not to the contrary—in all, at least nineteen miles in a straight line from north to south. Of this stretch the northernmost mile is occupied chiefly by residences of the better class, though the State Street of the North Side is by no means the aristocratic avenue that Dearborn Street is. It is well paved, however, and before the fire was well lined with stately elms and honored with a number of large churches. The glory of State Street begins at Lake Street, where the solid wholesale warehouses of the district near the river give way to the more showy stores which abound further south. These can not be even mentioned, they are so numerous; let it suffice that from Lake Street to Twelfth Street, a distance of over a mile, there stands as good an exhibition of ornate, graceful, varied, and costly business architecture as can be found in any equal space of a single street on this continent. Among the especially notable structures are the Masonic Temple, Central Music Hall, Palmer House, Marshall Field's retail store, The Fair, the Leiter building, and further south the Alhambra Theatre. The crowds on this street are at all times equal to those on Broadway, New York. The street railroads from all directions empty their passengers here, and a jostling, elbowing, hurrying through is the result. The stranger needs no direction; he will find himself on this floating stream of life, and then it will require all his energy and skill to navigate his own little craft.

Steamboats and Water Transportation.—Chicago not only lays her hand upon the traffic of the United States through her enormous mileage of tributary railroads, but during the summer time, when the straits are open, she is really a maritime city, just as easy of access as any of the ocean seaports, because of her situation on Lake Michigan, and through the chain of lakes, canals, and the St. Lawrence River, to the ocean. It is only when winter closes the straits of Sault Ste. Marie, that the owners of land transportation routes give freights a little upward boost. But the cost of transportation has always been held down by the carrying capacity of the great water-route. There are several lines of steamers running to Milwaukee daily, and to the upper lakes; also to the east shore. These latter bring to the city, during the season, enormous amounts of berries, fruit, and vegetables, and transport return freight on the out-trip. Most of the steamers are propeller-built, but there are some side-wheelers.

Steam Heat and Power.—The improvements that have been made from year to year, in the transmission of heat and power from a central point, a great many of them having been invented by residents of Chicago, have rendered it possible to heat our big office buildings already finished, and those of eighteen and twenty stories, still climbing heavenward, at the minimum cost of labor and material. Let us imagine the old-fashioned method of heating by individual stoves in each office, in a building containing from 1,000 to 2,000 or 3,000 tenants; coal to carry up, ashes to carry down; beside the sundry other odd jobs, a stove is constantly demanding of its owner or manager. It would take the strength of a Samson, and the wisdom of a Solomon, to accomplish the work. But before the plastering hides the rough studding, iron pipes radiate through the whole building from a central point in the basement, running in pairs. When the building is finished a huge plant of boilers, managed by a couple of men, become the heart of the whole system, the steam is forced to the farthest room, and a return exhaust disposes of the water and dust. The engineer burns the soft coal, the cheapest fuel, which a stove could not utilize. The ashes are on the ground floor, when dropped from the furnace bars. A turn of the wrist sends the steam, on call, through the whole building. The tenant gives a turn or two to a little wheel in his office, and the unseen force throbs and pulsates through the radiator and supplies an equal temperature all day long without any attention on his part. Not only is this true, but there are large buildings rented out, in like manner, to manufacturers of small wares, requiring a lathe or two, or a stamping press, whose whole plant only occupies a room or two. Instead of each running a separate boiler and engine, they are all supplied with power from a common point in the building, to the mutual advantage of all. Chicago has introduced coöperation on many lines, and will, undoubtedly, on many more.

Stock Exchange.—For many years, traders in stocks resident in Chicago, were obliged to place their deals on the New York Stock Exchange. Finally as the invested interests grew larger, those most interested, concluded to found a Chicago Stock Exchange. To say was to do. This institution is located in the Stock Exchange building, Monroe Street corner of Dearborn Street. It has two calls daily, one at 10.30 A. M., the other at 2.15 P. M. It deals in all the stocks and bonds listed on the New York Stock Exchange, and quite a number that are peculiar to Chicago. It was not until 1890, however, that the Chicago Stock Exchange manifested any particular potency as a factor in the financial situation of the West. A deep interest was taken in the market, and trading was very active. The gain over the preceding year, was 912,349 shares, and the decrease of $760,900 worth of bonds. Chicago maintained her position as the second city in the United States, by thus being only surpassed in her stock operations, by Wall Street. Investors prefer this Exchange, in which to sell our local stocks, for they command a better price here, where they are known, than in New York, where they are crowded, more or less, by other bet-

FORESTRY BUILDING.

ter-known securities. The Exchange building was re-modeled and fitted up with especial regard to the needs of brokers and bankers, all the offices are arranged with an eye to the quick despatch of all business. Bankers, who make a specialty of handling securities and the documentary wealth of great corporations, occupy all the ground floor, which is not used for the purposes of the Exchange itself. During business hours, the main hall is full of brokers, who are trading on the prices of the last call. It is hardly necessary to say, that they are in touch with all the rest of the financial world by telegraph or telephone, and are ready to compete with Wall Street itself, if the chances are anywhere near even. Its present President, Charles Henrotin, did business here, as a prominent broker, long before the Exchange was organized.

Storage. — Large warehouses where one can hire rooms, small enough to put in two or three trunks, or large enough to receive the furniture of an entire building, have of late been established in every part of the city. Besides renting the space for storing articles, the managers of these places will insure them against both fire and robbery, while some will advance money thereon. Ordinarily the person hiring a room is furnished with a key, which gives him access at all reasonable hours. At these places, also, wagons, trucks and porters may be ordered for moving furniture from one part of the city to the other. (See *Moving.*)

Street and Avenue Guide.— The Chicago river and its north and south branches, divide the city into three divisions—north, south, and west. Streets that cross the main river are north and south streets; if they run in the same direction on the West Side, Randolph Street is the

14

dividing line as far as Union Park, and beyond that, Lake Street marks the center.

A (N. D.), 125 Southport Ave. west to Dominick.

Abbott Ct. (L. V.), 1722 Diversey north one block.

Aberdeen (W. D.), 328 Madison south to 87th.

Aberdeen (L. V.), Southport Ave. east to Sheffield Ave.

Ada N. (W. D.), 435 Randolph north to Erie.

Ada S. (W. D.), 434 Randolph south to Madison.

Ada (L.), 47th to 87th.

Adams (S. D.), 157 Michigan Ave. west to river.

Adams (W. D.), river west to 48th.

Adams Ave. (H. P.), 75th south to 77th.

Addison Ave. (L. V.), N. Western Ave. east to the lake.

Addison Ave. (H. P.), 69th south to 71st.

Adelaide (L. V.), 124 School north to Cornelia.

Alaska (W. D.), 385 Larrabee west to Town.

Albany Ave. N. (W. D.), 1452 Lake north to Grand Ave.

Albany Ave. S. (W. D.), 1451 Lake south to Archer Ave.

Albert (W. D.), 583 18th south one-half block.

Aldine (L. V.), 340 Evanston Ave. east to the lake.

Aldine (S. D.), Aldine Square south to Egan Ave.

Aldine Square (S. D.), 3726 Vincennes Ave. west one-half block.

Alexander (S. D.), 2246 Wentworth Ave. west to Stewart Ave.

Alice Pl. (W. D.), 1263 N. Western Ave. west to Perry Ave.

Alexander Ave. (L. V.), Byron north to Sulzer.

Allport (W. D.), 433 16th south to 22d.

Almond (W. D.), 952 Taylor south to 85 Ashland Ave.

Ambrose (W. D.), 1001 S. Wood west to S. California Ave.

Ann N. (W. D.), 361 Randolph north to Kinzie.

Ann S. (W. D.), 362 Randolph south to Madison.

Anna (W. D.), 1405 S. Western Ave. south to Washtenaw Ave.

Anna Ave. (L. V.), 35 School north to Cornelia.

Arbor Pl. (W. D.), 122 N. Ada west to N. Ashland Ave.

Arch (S. D.), 2943 Archer Ave. southeast to 31st.

Archer Ave. (S. D.), 1906 State southwest to city limits.

Archibald (W. D.), 1178 Francisco east three-fourths block.

Ardmore Ave. (L. V.), Evanston Ave. east to Sheffield Ave.

Argyle (L. V.), 3462 N. Clark east to the lake.

Armitage Ave. (W. D.), Mendell west to city limits.

Armitage Ct. (W. D.), 85 Clarkson Ave. west to Kedzie Ave.

Armour (W. D.), 505 Kinzie north to Chicago Ave.

Arnold (S. D.), now S. La Salle.

Artesian Ave. (W. D.), 1040 Lake north to Ohio.

Arthington (W. D.), 285 Centre Ave. west to Loomis.

Arthur (W. D.), 35 16th south to 18th.

Arthur (H. P.), 134 79th south to 83d Pl.

Ash (W. D.), 1803 31st south to Ill. & Mich. Canal.

Ashkum Ave. (H. P.), 567 87th south to 95th.

Ashland (W. D.), 505 S. Robey west to Olive.

Ashland Ave. N. (W. D.), 578 Lake north to Clybourn Pl.

Ashland Ave. S. (W. D.), 578 Lake south to 87th.

Ashland Ave. (N.D. and L. V.), 820 Clybourn Ave. north to city limits.

Ashland Ct. (W. D.), 180 N. Ashland Ave. east one-half block.

Ashley (W. D.), now Emerson Ave.

Astor (N. D.), 583 Division north to North Ave.

Atlantic (L.), continuation of Fifth Ave.

Attica (S. D.), 65 Auburn west to Laurel.

Attrill (W. D.), 119 Stave northeast to Milwaukee Ave.

Auburn (S. D.), 799 31st south to 35th.

Augusta (W. D.), Elston Ave. west to Crawford Ave.

Austin Ave. (W. D.), 152 N. Jefferson west to Seymour Ave.

Avenue A (H. P.), 116th south to Wolf Lake.

Avenue B (H. P.), Indiana Boul. south to Wolf Lake.

Avenue C (H. P.), 105th south to Wolf Lake.

Avenue D (H. P.), 99th south to 119th.

Avenue E (H. P.), 98th south to Wolf Lake.

Avenue F (H. P.), 102d south to 120th.

Avenue G (H. P.), 102d south to 118th.

Avenue H (H. P.), 102d south to Hyde Lake.

Avenue I (H. P.), 102d south to 110th.

Avenue J (H. P.), 102d south to Hyde Lake.

Avenue K (H. P.), 102d south to Hyde Lake.

Avenue L (H. P.), 102d south to Hyde Lake.

Avenue M (H. P.), 102d south to Hyde Lake.

Avers Ave. N. (W. D.), Kinzie north to North Ave.

Avers Ave. S. (W. D.), 1706 Ogden Ave. south to 31st.

Avon Ave. (L.), 60th south to 67th.

Avon Pl. (W. D.), 267 S. Robey west to Hoyne Ave.

Avondale Ave. (W. D.), N. California Ave. northwest to Belmont Ave.

Ayres Ct. (W. D.), 279 Chicago Ave. south to Huron.

B (N. D.), 93 Southport Ave. west to Dominick.

Baker (L.), Stewart Ave. west to Wallace.

Baldwin (W. D.),721 Kinzie north to Austin Ave.

Ballou Ave. (W. D.), 1283 North Ave. north to Fullerton Ave.

Balmoral Ave. (L. V.), Robey east to Sheffield Ave.

Baltimore Ave. (H. P.), 410 83d south to 87th.

Banks (N. D.), 473 State east to Lake Shore Drive.

Barber (W. D.), 101 Stewart Ave. west to S. Halsted.

Barclay (W. D.), 559 Linwood Pl. north to Division.

Barry Ave. (L. V.), 184 Evanston Ave. east to the lake.

Bartlett Ave. (W. D.), 687 N. Kedzie Ave. west to Homan Ave.

Basil Ave. (W. D.), 1035 North Ave. north to Bloomingdale Road.

Bates (W. D.), Lumber west to Stewart Ave.

Bauwans (W. D.), 587 N. Ashland Ave. northwest to Blackhawk.

Baxter (L. V.), 1326 Wellington Ave. north to Roscoe.

Beach (W. D.), 38 Harrison south to 12th.

Beach Ave. (W. D.), 753 N. Kedzie Ave. west to Sheridan.

Beethoven Pl. (N. D.), 281 Sedgwick east to Wells.

Belden Ave. (N. D.), 24 Perry east to Lincoln Park.

Belden Ave. (W. D.), 1275 Homan Ave. west to Central Park Ave.

Belden Pl. (N. D.), 458 Belden Ave. north one-half block.

Belknap (W. D.), 419 S. Morgan west one-half blk.

Belle Plaine Ave. (L. V.), N. Western Ave. east to N. Ashland Ave.

Bellevue Pl. (N. D.), 313 State east to the lake.

Belmont Ave. (L. V.), Western Ave. east to the lake.

Belmont Ave. (W. D.), the river west to Crawford Ave.

Benson (S. D.), 1081 31st south to 32d.

Benton Pl. (S. D.), 415 State east one and one-half blocks.

Berg Pl. (W. D.), 41 Brand Pl. west to N. Robey.

Berkeley Ave. (H. P.), 70 Bowen Ave. southeast to 45th.

Berlin (W. D.), 1285 N. Leavitt west to Western Ave.

Berteau Ave. (L. V.), Western Ave. east to Ashland Ave.

Berwyn Ave. (L. V.), 2338 Evanston Ave. east to Sheffield Ave.

Best Ave. (L. V.), 1436 Wrightwood Ave. north to Diversey.

Bethuel (W. D.), 1975 16th south to 19th.

Better (W. D.), 81 Sholto west to S. May.

Bickerdike (W. D.), 411 Indiana north to Chicago Ave.

Bickerdike Sq. (W. D.), Bickerdike west to Armour.

Bingham (W. D.), 585 Armitage Ave. north to Cornelia.

Binzo (W. D.), railroad northeast to Elston Ave.

Birch (W. D.), 425 S. Robey west to Kendall.

Bishop Ct. (W. D.), 478 Washington Boul. south to Madison.

Bismarck (W. D.), 693 N. Rockwell west to Humboldt Park.

Bismarck Ct. (W. D.), 111 Huron west to Noble.

Bissell (W. D.), 137 Dayton north-west to Belden Ave.

Bissell Ave. (H. P.), 41st south to 43d.

Bixby Pl. (W. D.), 459 Kinzie north to Austin Ave.

Blackhawk (N. D.), the river northeast and east to Sedgwick.

Blackhawk (W. D.), the river west to N. Paulina.

Blackwell (S. D.), 231 18th south to 20th.

Blaine (W. D.), 1219 Rockwell west to Washtenaw Ave.

Blair (W. D.), 31 Canalport Ave. south to 20th.

Blake (S. D.), 3623 Archer Ave. southwest one-half block.

Blanchard Ave. (L.), continuation of S. Rockwell.

Blanchard Pl. (S. D.), 189 24th south to 25th.

Blanche (W. D.), the river west to 718 N. Ashland Ave.

Bliss (N. D.), 224 North Branch northeast to North Branch Canal.

Block (N. D.), 301 North Ave. north to Eugenie.

Bloom (S. D.), 1395 34th south to 38th.

Bloomingdale Road (W. D.), 661 Elston Ave. to city limits.

Blucher (L. V.), 35 Lull Pl. west to Wood.

Blue Island Ave. (W. D.), Halsted and Harrison southwest to Western Ave.

Boardman (S. D.), 36th southeast to Archer Ave.

Boardman Pl. (L. V.), Southport Ave. west one-half block.

Bonaparte (S. D.), 2924 Arch southwest to Lock.

Bond (L.), C. & G. T. R. R. west to Reese Ave.

Bond Ave. (H. P.), 78 71st south to Illinois Ave.

Bonfield (S. D.), 2721 Hickory southeast to 31st.

Bonney Ave. (W. D.), 394 Colorado Ave. south to 53d.

Boomer (L.), 443 39th south to 40th.

Boone (W. D.), 121 De Kalb west to S. Leavitt.

Boston Ave. (W. D.), 197 S. Desplaines west to Halsted.

Bosworth Ave. (L. V.), Roscoe north to Grace Ave.

Boulevard (N. D.), 427 Ohio north to Ontario.

Bowen Ave. (S. D.), 4110 Lake Ave. west to Grand Boul.

Bowery The (W. D.), 294 Van Buren south to Congress.

Bowmanville Road (L. V.), Western Ave. northeast to C. & N.-W. R. R.

Bradley (W. D.), 303 Elston Ave. west to Holt.

Brand Pl. (W. D.), 33 Fullerton Ave. north and northwest to N. Robey.

Breckenridge Ave. (W. D.), 903 N. Hamlin Ave. west to Crawford Ave.

Bremen (W. D.), 69 Myrtle Ave. west to Cromwell.

Bremen Pl. (W. D.),1229 N. Leavitt west to Western Ave.

Breslau (W. D.), 163 Hamburg north to Elms.

Brigham (W. D.), 673 N. Ashland Ave. west to N. Wood.

Bristol (L.), 4518 State west to Stewart Ave.

Broad (S.D.), C. & A. R. R. southeast to 31st.

Brompton Ave. (L. V.), 1856 Halsted east to Evanston Ave.

Bronson (L.), Center Ave. west to Laflin.

Brooks Ave. (H. P.), 73d south to 86th.

Broom (W. D.), 561 Indiana north to Ohio.

Bross Ave. (S. D.), 3118 Robey southwest to Rockwell.

Brown (W. D.), 316 Taylor south to the river.

Bryan Pl. (W. D.), 485 Randolph northwest to Lake.

Bryant Ave.(S. D.),3540 Vincennes Ave. west to Stanton Ave.

Bryn Mawr (L. V.), 3860 Clark east to Sheffield Ave.

Buchanan (W. D.), continuation of Washtenaw Ave.

Buckingham Pl. (L. V.), Evanston Ave. one-half block west.

Buena Ave. (L. V.), C. E. & L. S. R. R. east to Halsted.

Buena Vista Pl. (S. D.), 2521

Emerald Ave. northeast one-half block.

Buffalo Ave. (H. P.), 831 south to 92d.

Bunker (W. D.), 159 Beach west to S. Halsted.

Burchell Ave. (W. D.), 599 Fullerton Ave. north to Diversey.

Burling (N. D.), 183 North Ave. north to Davey Ct.

Burlington (W. D.). 95 16 h south to 18th.

Burnett (W. D.), 445 N. Robey west to N. Leavitt.

Burnside Ave. (H. P.), Cottage Grove Ave. northwest to St. Lawrence Ave.

Burtis (L.), 48th south to 67th.

Burton Pl. (N. D.), 608 Clark east to the lake.

Butler (S. D.), 2361 Archer Ave. southeast to 53d.

Butterfield (S. D.), 201 16th south to Garfield Boul.

Byford Ave. (W. D.), Douglas Park Boul. south to 16th.

Byron Ave. (W. D.), 1101 N. California Ave. west to Humbo'dt Park.

Byron Ave. (L. V.), Robey east to the lake.

C (N. D.), 61 Southport Ave. west to Dominick.

Calhoun Pl. (S. D.), 118 State west to Market.

California Ave., N. (W. D.), 1272 Lake north to Belmont Ave.

California Ave., S. (W. D), 1272 Lake south to 83d.

Calumet Ave. (S. D.), 1 18th south to city limits.

Campbell (S. D.), 31st southeast two blocks.

Campbell Ave., N. (W. D.), 1072 Lake north to Kinzie.

Campbell Ave., S. (W. D.), 1072 Lake south to Illinois & Michigan Canal.

Campbell Park (W. D.), 357 S. Leavitt west to S. Oakley Ave.

Canal, N. (W. D.), 29 Randolph north to Kinzie.

Canal, S. (W. D.), 29 Randolph south to Lumber.

Canal Pl. (W. D.), north branch river west to Elston Ave.

Canalport Ave. (W. D.), 735 S. Canal southwest to 22d.

Carl (N. D.), 548 Wells east to LaSalle Ave.

Carlin Ave. (H. P.), 76th south to 79th.

Carpenter, N. (W. D.), 301 Randolph north to the river.

Carpenter, S. (W. D.), 301 Randolph south to Madison.

Carpenter (L.), 48th south to 87th.

Carroll Ave. (W. D.), 98 N. Canal west to 48th.

Cass (N. D.), 263 Kinzie north to Rush.

Castello Ave. (W. D.), Springfield Ave. west to Crawford Ave.

Catherine (W. D.), 432 N. Homan Ave. east one block.

Cedar (N. D.), 347 Rush east to the lake.

Cedar (L.), 347 Rush east to the lake.

Central Ave. (S. D.), 9 Water south to Randolph.

Central Park Ave., N. (W. D.), 1766 Lake north to Fullerton Ave.

Central Park Ave., S. (W. D.), 1736 Madison south to 71st.

Central Park Boul. (W. D.), 165 N. Central Ave. west to Central Park Ave.

Centre (N. D.), 28 Racine Ave. east to Clark.

Centre (L. V.), C. & N.-W. R. R. east to Evanston Ave.

Centre Ave. (W. D.), 382 Madison south to Lumber.

Centre Ave. (L.), 47th south to 87th.

Centre Ave., N. (W. D.), 374 Kinzie north to Augusta.

Centre Ave. (W. D.), 1801 Elston Ave. southwest to Kedzie Ave.

Chalmers Pl. (N. D.), Halsted west to Sheffield Ave.

Champlain (S. D.), Bross Ave. south to 37th.

Champlain Ave. (H. P.), 352 42d south to 67th.
Channay (W. D.), 87 Point north-east one-half block.
Chapin (W. D.), 543 Noble east to Currier.
Charles Pl. (S. D.), 324 Fifth Ave. west to Franklin.
Charles (W. D.), 6 Van Buren south to Harrison.
Charlotte (W. D.), 545 S. Central Park Ave. west to Lawndale Ave.
Charlton (S. D.), 33d south to 35th.
Charlton (L. V.), 1140 Ridge Ave. north of Francis.
Chase (W. D.), 312 Chicago Ave. north to Cornell.
Chase Ave. (W. D.), 1589 North Ave. north to Bloomingdale Road.
Chase Ct. (W. D.), 230 Coulter south to Blue Island Ave.
Chatham Ct. (N. D.), Hobbie north to Division.
Chauncey Ave. (H. P.), 76th south to 85th.
Cheltenham Ave. (H. P.), 2 83d south to 85th.
Cheltenham Pl. (H. P.), 7838 Lake Ave. southwest to 79th.
Cherry (L.), C. & G. T. R. R. west to Reese Ave.
Cherry Ave. (N. D.), 224 North Branch northwest to North Ave.
Cherry Pl. (W. D.), 93 Powell Ave. west to Perry Ave.
Chester (N. D.), 833 Clybourn Ave. southwest, west, and north to Fullerton Ave.
Chestnut (N. D.), 240 Market east to the lake.
Chestnut (L.), 6126 Wentworth Ave. west to Halsted.
Chestnut Pl. (N. D.), 417 Chestnut northwest to Walton Pl.
Chicago Ave. (N. D.), the river east to the lake.
Chicago Ave. (W. D.), the river west to city limits.
Chicago Terrace (W. D.), 273 Harding Ave. west to Crawford Ave.

Christiana Ave. (W. D), 621 Grand Ave. north to Division.
Church Ct. (W. D.), 83 S. Morgan west to Centre Ave.
Church Pl. (S. D.), 59 Fuller southeast to Archer Ave.
Church Road (L. V.), Western Ave. east to Clark.
Churchill (W. D.), 889 N. Robey west to Leavitt.
Cicero Ct. (W. D.), 1078 Jackson south to Harrison.
Clara Pl. (W. D.), 1291 N. Western Ave. west to Perry Ave.
Claremont Ave. (W. D.), 944 Van Buren south to Grenshaw.
Clarence (L. V.), 1326 Nellie Ave. north to Byron.
Clarinda (W. D.), 34 Holt west to Wood.
Clark, S. (S. D.), the river south to city limits,
Clark, N. (N. D.), the river north to North Ave. and northwest to city limits.
Clarkson Ave. (W. D.),1083 Bloomingdale Road north to Palmer Pl.
Clarkson Ct. (W. D.), 1299 Lake south to Washington Boul.
Clay (N. D.), 156 Sheffield Ave. east to Halsted.
Clay Ave. (L. V.), Huck Ave. east to Robey.
Clayton (W. D.), 395 Johnson west to May.
Cleaver (W. D.), 761 Milwaukee Ave. north to Blanche.
Clement Ave. (L.), 43d south to 45th.
Cleveland (L.), Wallace west to Wright.
Cleveland Ave. (N. D.), 48 Clybourn Ave. north to Fullerton Ave.
Cleveland Ave. (L. V.), 980 Racine Ave. east to Sheffield Ave.
Clifton Ave. (W. D.), 567 Fullerton Ave. north to Diversey.
Clifton Ave. (L. V.), 1226 Wellington Ave. north to Roscoe.
Clifton Park Ave. (W. D.), 16th south to Swift.

Clinton, N. (W. D.), 61 Randolph north to Kinzie.

Clinton, S. (W. D.), 61 Randolph south to Maxwell.

Cloud Ct. (L.), State west to Wentworth Ave.

Clybourn Ave. (N. D. and L. V.), 305 Division northwest to Belmont Ave.

Clybourn Pl. (N. D.), 549 Clybourn Ave. west to the river.

Clybourn Pl. (W. D.), the river west to N. Robey.

Clyde (N. D.), 484 Clybourn Ave. northeast to Center.

Coblentz (W. D.), 1013 N. Robey west to Western Ave.

Coles Ave. (H. P.), 128 71st south to 79th.

Colfax Ave. (H. P.), 65th south to 67th.

College Pl. (S. D.), 3326 Cottage Grove Ave. west to Rhodes Ave.

Collins (W. D.), 721 S. Albany Ave. west to Kedzie Ave.

Collins Ct. (W. D.), 92 Laughlin south to Coulter.

Cologne (S. D.), 2500 Quarry southwest to Fuller.

Colorado Ave. (W. D.), 1250 Madi son southwest to city limits.

Commercial (W. D.), 320 North Ave. north to Armitage Ave.

Commercial (L. V.), 1259 N. Paulina north and northwest to Webster Ave.

Commercial Ave. (H. P.), 242 79th south to 99th.

Concord (L.), Stewart Ave. west to Morgan.

Concord Pl. (N. D.), 341 Clybourn Ave. west to Sheffield Ave.

Congress (S. D.), Michigan Ave. west to State; and 5th Ave. west to the river.

Congress (W. D.), 225 S. Clinton west to 46th.

Congress Pk. (W. D.), 1112 Van Buren south to Harrison.

Connor (N. D.), 62 Cleveland Ave. east to Sedgwick.

Conrad (W. D.), 93 Ruble west to S. Union.

Cook (W. D.), the river southwest to N. Jefferson.

Cook (L.), 1323 47th south to 61st.

Cook (L. V.), Hamilton Ave. east to Ashland Ave.

Cooper (N. D.), 802 Clybourn Ave. north to Fullerton Ave.

Cooper (L.), 63d south to 67th.

Cork (W. D.), 215 N. Ashland Ave. west to Paulina.

Cornelia (W. D.), 606 Milwaukee Ave. west to Seymour Ave.

Cornelia (W. D.), 53 Point northeast to Milwaukee Ave.

Cornelia (L. V.), N. Western Ave. east to the lake.

Cornell (W. D.), 536 Milwaukee Ave. west to Ashland Ave.

Cornell Ave. (H. P.), 48 51st south to 56th.

Cortez (W. D.), N. California Ave. west to Humboldt Pk.

Cortland (W. D.), 941 N. Robey west to city limits.

Cortland Ave. (L.), continuation of S. May.

Cortland Ct. (W. D.), 33 Clarkson Ave. west to Kedzie Ave.

Corwin (W. D.), 792 15th south to 16th.

Corwin Pl. (W. D.), 74 Moore south one-half block.

Cosgrove Ave. (L. V.), Lincoln Ave. east to N. Ashland Ave.

Cottage Grove Ave. (S. D.), 89 22d southeast to Calumet River.

Cottage Pl. (W. D.), 83 Throop west one block.

Couch Pl. (S. D.), State west to Market.

Coulter (W. D.), 1083 S. Robey southwest to California Ave.

Court Pl. (S. D.), State west to Market.

Court Pl. (L), Western Ave. west to railroad.

Coventry (W. D.), 145 North Ave. northwest to Clybourn Pl.

Crawford (S. D.), 465 22d south to Archer Ave.

Crawford Ave., N. (W. D.), 1984 Lake north to city limits.

Crawford Ave., S. (W. D.), 1984 Lake south to city limits.

Crawford Ct. (S. D.), 2218 McGlashen west to Crawford.

Crilly Pl. (N. D.), 137 Eugenie north to Florimond.

Crittenden (W. D.), 519 Noble east to Currier.

Cromwell (W. D.), 1847 Milwaukee Ave. north to Fullerton Ave.

Crooked (N. D.), 20 Southport Ave. southeast one-half block.

Crosby (N. D.), 81 Larrabee northwest to Division.

Cross (W. D.), 456 Colorado Ave. south to Harrison.

Crossing (W. D.), 83 Mendell we t to S. Paulina.

Crown Pl. (W. D.), 26th south to the river.

Crystal (W. D.), 556 N. Robey west to Leavitt.

Currier (W. D.), 70 Augusta north to Chapin.

Curtis, N. (W. D.), 321 Randolph north to Huron, northwest to May.

Curtis, S. (.W. D.), 321 Randolph south to Madison.

Custar Ave. (L.), see Spencer Ave.

Custom House Pl. (S. D.), 102 Jackson south to 14th.

Cynthia Ct. (W. D.), 1504 Ogden Ave. south to 22d.

Cypress (W. D.), 56 Kendall south to 12th.

Dakin (L. V.), 1478 Sheffield Ave. east to Evanston Ave.

Dale Pl. (W. D.), 724 22d south one-half block.

Daly (S. D.), 35th south to 37th.

Damen (W. D.), 91 Sholto west to S. May.

Dania Ave. (W. D.), 686 Division north to Bloomingdale Road.

Dashiel (S. D.), 539 26th south to 39th.

Dauphin (H. P.), 87th southwest to 92d.

Davis (W. D.), 622 Division north to Wabansia Ave.

Davis (L.), 57th south to 67th.

Davlin (W. D.), 1894 Lake north to Kinzie.

Dayton (N. D.), 140 Rees north to Belden Ave.

Dean (W. D.), 649 N. Paulina northwest to Brigham.

Dearborn (S. D.), the river south to Polk; 14th south to 59th.

Dearborn Ave. (N. D.), the river north to North Ave.

Dearborn Pl. (S. D.), 20 Randolph south to Madison.

Deering (S. D.), the river southeast to 31st.

DeKalb (W. D.), 26 Flournoy southwest to S. Leavitt.

DeKoven (W. D.), 151 Beach west to S. Halsted.

Delamater Pl. (W. D.), 1383 Bloomingdale Road north to Armitage Ave.

Delaware Pl. (N. D.), 277 Dearborn Ave. east to the lake.

Deming Ct. (L. V.), 588 Orchard east to Lake View Ave.

Dempster Pl. (L. V.), Clark east to Evanston Ave.

Depot (W. D.), 157 Stewart Ave. west to S. Halsted.

Depuyster (W. D.), 255 S. Desplaines west to S. Halsted.

Desplaines, N. (W. D.), 123 Randolph north to Erie.

Desplaines, S. (W. D.), 123 Randolph south to 12th.

Devon Ave. (L. V.), the lake west to Evanston Ave.

Dewey Ct. (L. V.), 1318 Halsted east to Clark.

Dexter Ave. (W. D.), S. Ashland Ave. southwest to 31st.

Dexter Ave. (L.), Stewart Ave. east to Wallace.

Dickens Ave. (W. D.), 1131 N. California Ave. west to Crawford Ave.

Dickey (L.), 63d south to 79th.

Dickey Ave. (W. D.), N. Kedzie Ave. west to N. Homan Ave.

Dickson (W. D.), 174 Division north to Bloomingdale Road.

Dieden (W. D.), 217 Elston Ave. southwest to Currier.

Diller (W. D.), 898 Fulton north to Ohio.

Diversey (L. V.), N. Western Ave. east to the lake.

Diversey (W. D.), the river west to city limits.

Division (N. D.), the river east to the lake.

Division (W. D.), the river west to city limits.

Dix (W. D.), 102 Chicago Ave. northwest to Sangamon.

Dock (S. D.), 46 River northwest to the river.

Dodge (W. D.), Lumber south to 14th.

Dominick (N. D.), 51 Southport Ave. northwest to Webster Ave.

Dor Pl. (W. D.), 665 N. Springfield Ave. west to Crawford Ave.

Douglas Ave. (H. P.), 107th south to 114th.

Douglas Pk. Boul. (W. D.), 687 S. Albany Ave. west to Hamlin Ave.

Douglas Pk. Pl. (W. D.), 707 S. Fairchild Ave. west to California Ave.

Drake Ave. (W. D.), Kinzie north to Chicago Ave.

Drexel Ave. (H. P.), 52d south to 87th.

Drexel Boul. (H. P.), 39th south to 51st.

Dreyer (L.), 47th south to 53d.

Drummond Ave. (W. D.), 991 Augusta north to Division.

Dudley (W. D.), 652 Chicago Ave. north to Webster Ave.

Duncan Ave. (H. P.), 7648 Railroad Ave. south to 82d.

Duncan Pk. (L.), Stewart Ave. west to Wallace.

Dunn (W. D.), 45 Kinzie northwest one block.

Dunning (L. V.), 1260 N. Paulina east to Halsted.

Dussold (W. D.), 483 S. Jefferson west to Halsted.

Eagle (W. D.), 20 N. Desplaines west to Halsted.

Earl (S. D.), 2920 Shields Ave. west to Stewart Ave.

Early Avenue (L. V.), Southport Ave. southeast to Evanston Ave.

East Ct. (L. V.), 1929 Belmont Ave. south one-half block.

East End Ave. (H. P.), 10 51st south to 56th.

Eastman (N. D.), North Branch northeast to Halsted.

Eberhart (W. D.), 633 N. Kedzie Ave. west to Homan Ave.

Eda (S. D.), 3610 Indiana Ave. west to State.

Edbrooke Pl. (W. D.), 1201 N. Western Ave. west to Perry Ave.

Eddy (L. V.), 1034 Racine Ave. east to Clark.

Edgar (W. D.), 265 North Ave. north to Clybourn Pl.

Edgerton Ave. (H. P.), 60th south to 61st.

Edgecomb Ct. (L. V.), 869 Evanston Ave. east to Sheffield Ave.

Edith (W. D.), 398 N. Homan Ave. east one block.

Edson Ave. (L. V.), 574 Lincoln Ave. north to Webster Ave.

Edwards Ave. (H. P.), 7812 Railroad Ave. south to 83d.

Eighth Ave. (H. P.), 47 97th south to 102d.

Eighteenth (S. D.), the lake west to the river.

Eighteenth (W. D.), the river west to the city limits.

Eighteenth Pl. (W. D.), 327 Johnson west to 56th.

Eightieth (H. P. and L.), Bond Ave. west to city limits.

Eighty-first (H. P. and L.), Ontario Ave. west to limits.

Eighty-second (H. P. and L.), Ontario Ave. west to Halsted.

Eighty-third (H. P. and L.), Cheltenham Ave. west to limits.

Eighty-third Pl. (H. P.), 8336 Ontario Ave. west to railroad.

Eighty-fourth (H. P. and L.), Cheltenham Ave. west to Ashland Ave.

Eighty-fifth (H. P. and L.), Cheltenham Ave. west to Ashland Ave.

Eighty-sixth (H. P. and L.), the lake west to Loomis.

Eighty-seventh (H. P. and L.), the lake west to limits.

Eighty-seventh Pl. (H. P.), Dauphin Ave. west to St. Lawrence Ave.

Eighty eighth (H. P.), the strand west to city limits.

Eighty eighth Pl. (H. P.), Dauphin Ave. west to St. Lawrence Ave.

Eighty-ninth (H. P.), the strand west to city limits.

Eighty-ninth Pl. (H. P.), Dauphin Ave. west to Langley Ave.

Elaine (L. V.), 1146 Roscoe northwest to Cornelia.

Eldredge Ct. (S. D.), 293 Michigan Ave. west to State.

Eleanor Ave. (H. P.), 83d south to 126th.

Eleventh (W. D.), 403 S. Morgan west to May.

Eleventh, W. (W. D.), 329 Throop west to Ashland Ave.

Elgin (S. D.), 2114 Purple west to Stewart Ave.

Elias (S. D.), 2881 Archer Ave. southeast to Lyman Ave.

Elizabeth, N. (W. D.), 403 Randolph north to Erie.

Elizabeth, S. (W. D.), 403 Randolph south to Madison.

Elizabeth (L.), Blanche to 87th.

Elizabeth (L.), Stewart Ave. west to Wright.

Elk (W. D.), Bauwans west to N. Paulina.

Elk Grove Ave. (W. D.), 733 N. Wood west and north to Webster Ave.

Ellen (W. D.), 984 Milwaukee Ave. southwest to Lincoln.

Ellery Ave. (L.), 79th south to Pierce.

Ellis Ave. (S. D. and L.), 35 35th southeast and south to 87th.

Ellis Park (S. D.), Prospect Place south to 37th.

Ellsworth (W. D.), 8 Harrison south to Polk.

Elm (N. D.), North Branch Canal northeast and east to the lake.

Elmwood Pl. (S. D.), 133 37th south to 39th.

Elston Av. (W. D.), 499 Milwaukee Ave. north and northwest to limits.

Emerald Ave. (S. D. and L.), 2473 Archer Ave. south to 83d.

Emerson Ave. (W. D.), 177 N. Wood west to Oakley Ave.

Emery (W. D.), 545 N. Kedzie Ave. west to Springfield Ave.

Emily (W. D.), 469 N. Ashland Ave. west to Wood.

Emma (W. D.), 704 Milwaukee Ave. west to Ashland Ave.

Emmet (L.), 47th south to 55th.

Ems (W. D.), 1201 N. Leavitt west to Western Ave.

Englewood Ave. (L.), 6228 Wentworth Ave. west to Halsted.

Erie (N. D.), the river east to the lake.

Erie (W. D.), the river west to Western Ave.

Erie Ave. (H. P.), 274 87th south to 98th.

Escanaba Ave. (H. P.), 370 84th south to 103d.

Essex Ave. (H. P.), 83d south to 103d.

Euclid Ave. (W. D.), 39 California Ave. west to Central Park Ave.

Eugenie (N. D.), 456 Larrabee east to Clark.

Evans Ave. (H. P.), 284 42d south to 87th.

Evans Ct. (W. D.), 629 S. Union west to Halsted.

Evanston Ave. (L. V.), Clark and Diversey northwest to Devon Ave.

Everett Ave. (H. P.), 55th south one block.

Evergreen Ave. (W. D.),1088 Milwaukee Ave. southwest to N. Leavitt.

Evergreen Ave. (W. D.), 1511 N.

Western Ave. west to Humboldt Ave.

Everts Ave. (L.), 47th south to 71st.

Ewing (W. D.), Beach west to Blue Island Ave.

Ewing Ave. (H. P.), 94th southeast and south to 106th.

Ewing Place (W. D.), 719 N. Robey west to N. Leavitt.

Exchange Ave. (H. P.), 84th south to 102d.

Exchange Pl. (S. D.), 128 Washington south to Madison.

Fairfield Ave., N. (W. D.), 1238 Lake north to Armitage Ave.

Fairfield Ave., S. (W. D.), 1344 Harvard south to 22d.

Fairview Ave. (W. D.), 345 Fullerton Ave. west to Diversey.

Fake (S. D.), 2971 Bonaparte southeast to Lyman.

Fall (W. D.), 1161 Lake south to Warren Ave.

Farrell (S. D.), Hickory southeast to 31st.

Fay (W. D.), 89 Erie north to Pratt.

Fayette Ct. (W. D.), 504 Harrison south to Vernon Park Pl.

Ferdinand (W. D.), 188 Noble west to Oakley Ave.

Fifteenth (S. D.), 1500 State west to Clark.

Fifteenth (W. D.), 131 Stewart Ave. west to Hamlin Ave.

Fifth Ave. (S. D.), the river south to Taylor; 311 26th south to 39th.

Fiftieth (H. P. and L.), 5000 Lake Ave. west to limits.

Fiftieth Ct. (H. P. and L.), 5034 Cottage Grove Ave. west to Oakley Ave.

Fifty-first (H. P. and L.), the lake west to limits.

Fifty-first Ct. (L.), Halsted west to Morgan.

Fifty-second (H. P. and L.), 5200 Lake Ave. west to limits.

Fifty-third (H. P. and L.), the lake west to limits.

Fifty-fourth (H. P. and L.), the lake west to limits.

Fifty-fourth Ct. (L.), Halsted west to Morgan.

Fifty-fourth Pl. (H. P.), Lake Ave. west to Drexel Ave.

Fifty-fifth (H. P. and L.), the lake west to Cottage Grove Ave.

Fifty-sixth (H. P. and L.), the lake west to Ashland Ave.

Fifty-seventh (H. P. and L.), 5700 Stony Island Ave. west to Ashland Ave.

Fifty-eighth (H. P. and L.), 5800 Washington Ave. west to Ashland Ave.

Fifty-eighth Ct. (L.), Stewart Ave. west to Wallace.

Fifty-ninth (H. P. and L.), Stony Island Ave. west to Crawford Ave.

Fifty-ninth Ct. (L. V.), Western Ave. east to the lake.

Fifty-ninth Ct. (L.), Wentworth Ave. west to Stewart Ave.

Fillmore (W. D.), 507 S. Western Ave. west to Crawford Ave.

First Ave. (H. P.), 209 95th south one-half block.

First Ave. (W. D.), 33 Schuyler Ave. northwest to Kedzie Ave.

Fisher Ave. (L. V.), 3728 Robey east to Clark.

Fisk (W. D.), 351 16th south to Lumber.

Fleetwood (W. D.), Elston Ave. north to Rawson.

Fletcher (L. V.), 1646 Oakley Ave. east to Evanston Ave.

Florence Ave. (L. V.), 156 Wrightwood Ave. north to Diversey.

Florence Ave. (L.), 42d to 43d.

Florimond (N. D.), 651 Franklin east to Wells.

Flournoy (W. D.), Ogden Ave. west to Albany Ave.

Follansbee (W. D.), 1946 Milwaukee Ave. west to Kedzie Ave.

Fontenoy Ct. (W. D.), 1146 Milwaukee Ave. southwest one block.

Ford Ave. (H. P.), 75th south to 79th.

Forest Ave. (S. D.), 175 31st south to limits.

Forest Ave. (W. D.), 377 Fullerton Ave, north to Elston Ave.

Forest Ave. (L. V.), Grand Ave. north to limits.

Forquer (W. D.), Beach west to Crawford Ave.

Forrestville Ave. (H. P.), 48th south one block.

Fortieth (H. P. and L.), the lake west to Halsted.

Fortieth Ct. (S. D.), 4024 Butler west to Wallace.

Forty-first (H. P. and L.), I. C. R. R. west to Wallace.

Forty-first W. (W. D.), Kinzie south to 12th.

Forty-second (H. P. and L.), I. C. R. R. west to Johnson Ave.

Forty-second W. (W. D.), Kinzie south to 12th.

Forty-second Ct. (L.), School west to Wallace.

Forty-second Pl. (H. P.), Drexel Boul. west to Grand Boul.

Forty-third, (H. P. and L.), I. C. R. R. west to Crawford Ave.

Forty-third W. (W. D.), Kinzie south to 12th.

Forty-fourth (H. P. and L.), 44 Greenwood Ave. west to Crawford Ave.

Forty-fourth W. (W. D.), Kinzie south to 12th.

Forty-fifth (H. P. and L.), Wood-lawn Ave. west to Crawford Ave.

Forty-fifth W. (W. D.), Kinzie south to 12th.

Forty-fifth Ct. (L.), State west to Wentworth Ave.

Forty-sixth (H. P. and L.), Lake Ave. west to Crawford Ave.

Forty-sixth W. (W. D.), Kinzie north and south to limits.

Forty-sixth Ct. (L.), C. & R. I. west to Stewart Ave.

Forty-seventh (H. P. and L.), I. C. R. R. west to limits.

Forty-seventh W. (W. D.), Kinzie north and south to North Ave. and 12th.

Forty-eighth (H. P. and L.), Madi-son Ave. west to Western Ave. Boul.

Forty-eighth W. (W. D.), Kinzie north and south to North Ave. and 12th.

Forty-ninth (H. and L.), Lake Ave. west to city limits.

Fourteenth (S. D.), Indiana Ave. west to Clark.

Fourteenth W. (W. D.), the river west to Ogden Ave.

Fourth Ave. (S. D.), see Custom House Pl.

Fourth Ave. (H. P.), 110 95th south to 102d.

Fowler (W. D.), 51 Evergreen Ave. west to N. Leavitt.

Fox (S. D.), 1025 31st south to 33d.

Fox Pl. (W. D.), 415 Elston Ave. west to Noble.

Francis (L. V.), Clark east to Ridge Ave.

Francis Pl. (W. D.), 64 Point southwest to California Ave.

Francisco N. (W. D.), 1332 Lake north to Elston Ave.

Francisco S. (W. D.), 1332 Lake south to 83d.

Frank (W. D.), 75 Waller west to Blue Island Ave.

Frankfort (W. D.), 1065 N. Robey west to Western Ave.

Franklin (S. D.), the river south to Harrison.

Franklin N. (N. D.), 77 Kinzie north to Menomonee.

Franklin Ave. (W. D.), N. West-ern Ave. west to Kedzie Ave.

Frazier (L.), 47th south to 49th.

Frederick (L. V.), 546 Orchard east to Clark.

Frederick Ave. (W. D.), 719 Cen-tral Park Ave. west to Harding Ave.

Freeman (S. D.), Western Ave. west to Bross Ave.

Fremont (N. D.), 36 Bissell north to Fullerton Ave.

French Ave. (H. P.), 205, 75th south to 81st.

Front (W. D.), 344 N. Halsted west to Elston Ave.

Front (L. V.), Bryn Mawr north to Peterson Ave.

Front (L. V.), Kensington Ave. southwest one block.

Fry (W. D.), 218 N. Center Ave. west to Ashland Ave.

Fuller (S. D.), the river east to Archer Ave.

Fullerton Ave. (N. D.), the river east to Lincoln Park.

Fullerton Ave., W. (W. D.), the river west to Crawford Ave.

Fulton (W. D.), the river west to city limits.

Fulton (L. V.), 3652 Robey east to C. & N.-W. R. R.

Furlong (W. D.), 481 Kedzie Ave. west to Grand Ave.

Gage (S. D.), 941 35th south to 39th.

Galt (L. V.), Sheffield Ave. east to Halsted.

Gano (S. D.), see 30th.

Garden (W. D.), 175 S. Morgan west to Aberdeen.

Garden Ave. (W. D.), 1683 N. California Ave. west to Kedzie Ave.

Gardner (N. D.), 49 Vine west to Halsted.

Garfield Ave. (N. D.), 40 Herndon east to Lincoln Park.

Garfield Ave. W. (W. D.), 1207 Kimball west to Central Park Ave.

Garfield Boul. (H. P. and L.), 5500 South Park Ave. west to Western Ave. Boul.

Garland Pl. (S. D.), 20 Randolph south to Madison.

Garrett (S. D.), 31st northeast to Ashland Ave.

Garvin Ave. (H. P.), 87th to 95th.

Gault Pl. (N. D.), 69 Oak north to Division.

Geary (N. D.), 437 Chestnut northwest to Walton Pl. -

Genesee Ave. (W. D.), 1901 Harrison northwest to Colorado Ave.

Geneva (W. D.), S. Rockwell west to California Ave.

George (W. D.), 350 N. Sangamon west to Elston Ave.

George (L. V.), Hoyne Ave. east to Halsted.

George Ave. (L. V.), 222 Evanston Ave. east to Lake View Ave.

George Pl. (W. D.), 749 Kinzie north one-half block.

Giddings (L. V.), Leavitt east to Robey.

Gilbert Pl. (L.), Vincennes Ave. northwest one block.

Gilpin Pl. (W. D.), 259 Center Ave. west to Loomis.

Girard (W. D.), 1139 Milwaukee Ave. northeast to Webster Ave.

Glenlake Ave. (L. V.), Evanston Ave. east to the lake.

Glenview Ave. (W. D.), 423 North Central Park Ave. west to Crawford Ave.

Gloy Pl. (W. D.), 20 Lister Ave. northeast to Elston Ave.

Goethe (N. D.), 301 Sedgwick east to the lake.

Gold (W. D.), 302 Harrison south to Gurley.

Goldsmith Ave. (L.), 75th to 79th.

Good (W. D.), 71 Sholto west to May.

Goodspeed (L.), 43d south to 71st.

Goodwin (W. D.), 603 S. Homan Ave. west two blocks.

Gordon (L.), 4230 State west to Halsted.

Goshen (L.), 4626 Wentworth Ave. west to Stewart Ave.

Grace (N. D.), 157 Division north to Vedder.

Grace (L. V.), Ravenswood Park east to the lake.

Grace Ave. (H. P.), 62d south to Jackson Park Terrace.

Graceland Ave. (L. V.), Western Ave. east to the lake.

Grand Ave. (W. D.), 177 N. Western Ave. northwest to North Ave.

Grand Ave. (L. V.), 3650 Robey east to the lake.

Grand Boul. (S. D.), 185 35th south to 51st.

Grant (N. D.), 605 La Salle Ave. east to Clark.

Grant Pl. (N. D.), 995 Clark west to Larrabee.

Grant Pl. (L. V.), Huck Ave. east to Robey.

Grant Pl. (L.), 69th south to 70th.

Graves Pl. (S. D.), 3212 Cottage Grove Ave. south to 33d.

Graylock Ave. (L.), Wentworth Ave. west to Stewart Ave.

Greeley Pl. (W. D.), George south one-half block.

Green N. (W. D.), 217 Randolph north to Front.

Green S. (W. D.), 217 Randolph south to Harrison.

Green S. (L.), Garfield Boul. south to 86th.

Green Bay Ave. (H. P.), 26 83d south to Harbor Ave.

Greenwich (W. D.), 915 N. Robey west to Leavitt.

Greenwood Ave. (H. P.), 4212 Lake Ave. south to 80th.

Greenwood Ave. (W. D.), 1359 N. Oakley Ave. west to Thomas Ave.

Grenshaw (W. D.), 55 Olive west to Central Park Ave.

Gross Ave. (W. D.), 825 North Ave. north to Cortlandt.

Gross Ave. (L.), 45th southwest to 47th.

Gross Ave. (H. P.), 91st to 95th.

Gross Park (L. V.), C. & N.-W. Ry. east to Paulina.

Gross Park Ave. (L. V.). 548 Belmont Ave. to Addison.

Gross Terrace (W. D.), 1386 Madison south to Colorado Ave.

Grove (S. D.), 281 16th southwest to Archer Ave.

Grove Ct. (N. D.), 719 Larrabee west to Orchard.

Grove Pl. (L.), 64th south one block.

Groveland Ave. (S. D.), 28th south to 33d.

Groveland Ct. (L.), Vincennes Ave. northwest to C., R. I. & P. R. R.

Groveland Park (S. D.), 3325 Cottage Grove Ave. east one block.

Gurley (W. D.), 41 Blue Island Ave. west to Centre Ave.

Guttenburg Ave. (W. D.), 1513 Bloomingdale Road north to Armitage Ave.

Haddock Pl. (S. D), Wabash Ave. west to Franklin.

Haines (N. D.), 32 Hickory Ave. northeast to North Branch Canal.

Hall (L. V.), 1702 Diversey north one block.

Halsted N. (W. D. and N. D.), 197 Randolph north to Belmont Ave.

Halsted S. (W. D. and S. D.), 198 Randolph south to limits.

Hamburg (W. D.), 1091 N. Robey west to Western Ave.

Hamilton Ave. (L. V.), Cemetery Drive north to Peterson Ave.

Hamilton Ave. (W. D.), 834 Monroe south to Pratt Pl.

Hamlin Ave. N. (W. D.), 1854 Lake north to Diversey.

Hamilton Ave. S. (W. D. & L.), 1854 Lake south to 61st.

Hammond (N. D.), 99 Eugenie north to Wisconsin.

Hammond Ave. (W. D.), 599 Diversey north to Avondale Ave.

Hampden Ct. (L. V.), Wrightwood Ave. northwest one-half block.

Hancock Ave. (W. D.), 1327 North Ave. north to Fullerton Ave.

Hanover (S. D.), 2301 Archer Ave. south to 60th.

Harbor Ave. (H. P.), 9060 The Strand southwest to S. Chicago Ave.

Harding Ave. N. (W. D.), Kinzie north to Chicago Ave.

Harding Ave. S. (W. D.), R. R. crossing south to 31st.

Harmon Ct. (S. D.), 314 Michigan Ave. west to State.

Harrison (S. D.), 233 Michigan Ave. west to the river.

Harrison W. (W. D.), the river west to limits.

Hart (W. D.), 701 Kinzie north to Austin Ave.

Hart Ave. (S. D.), Bross Ave. south to Egan Ave.

Hartwell Ave. (H. P.), 66th south to 67th.

Harvard (W. D.), 441 S. Western Ave. west to Crawford Ave.

Harvard (L.), 63d south to 83d.

Hastings (W. D.), 335 Blue Island Ave. west to Leavitt.

Haven (S. D.), 3020 Shields Ave. west to Stewart Ave.

Hawthorne Ave. (N. D.), 29 Larrabee northwest to Southport Ave.

Hawthorne Ave. (L.), Stewart Ave. southwest to Goldsmith.

Hawthorne Pl. (L. V.), 412 Evanston Ave. east to the lake.

Haynes Ct. (S. D.), 2923 Archer Ave. southeast to Lyman.

Hazel (L. V.), Buena Ave. north to Galt Ave.

Heald (L.), 59th south one block.

Hein (N. D.), 12 Cleveland Ave. east to Sedgwick.

Heine (W. D.), 955 North Ave. north to Armitage Ave.

Henry (W. D.), Margaret west to S. Robey.

Henry Ct. (W. D.), Point northeast to Stave.

Hermitage Ave. (W. D.), Jackson south to 12th.

Herndon (N. D.), Hawthorne Ave. northeast to Fullerton Ave.

Hervey (W. D.), 1083 N. Wood west to Robey.

Herves Ave. (H. P.), 99th south to 114th.

Hibbard Ave. (H. P.), 51st south to 53d.

Hickling Ave. (L.), Halsted west to Morgan.

Hickory (S. D.), Cologne southwest to the river.

Hickory Ave. (N. D.), 140 Branch northwest to North Ave.

High (N. D.), 68 Webster Ave. north to Fullerton Ave.

High Ave. (H. P.), 103d south to 106th.

Hill (N. D.), 209 Sedgwick east to Wells.

Hinman (W. D.), 753 Throop west to Boulevard.

Hinsche (N. D.), 192 Clybourn Ave. northeast to Blackhawk.

Hirsch (W. D.), 717 N. Leavitt west to California Ave.

Hobbie (N. D.), 138 Hawthorne Ave. east to Sedgwick.

Hoey (S. D.), 2708 Mary southwest one-quarter block.

Holden (W. D.), 44 12th south to 14th.

Holden Pl. (S. D.), Randolph to 21st.

Holland Settlement Road (L.), Vincennes Ave. southeast to 87th.

Hollywood Ave. (L. V.), Evanston Ave. east to Sheffield Ave.

Holt (W. D.), 418 Chicago Ave. north to Wabansia Ave.

Homan Ave. N. (W. D.), 1638 Lake north to Diversey.

Homan Ave. S. (W. D.), 1638 Lake south to limits.

Homer (W. D.), 967 N. Robey west to Washtenaw Ave.

Honore (W. D.), 718 Madison south to 87th.

Hood Ave. (L. V.), 3606 Robey east to Ridge Ave.

Hooker (N. D.),396 Halsted northwest to Cherry Ave.

Hope (W. D.), 65 Blue Island Ave. west to Morgan.

Hough Pl. (S. D.), 2560 Archer Ave. northwest one block.

Houston Ave. (H. P.), 230 81st south to 98th.

Howard Ct. (W. D.), Central Park Boul. west to Kedzie Ave.

Howe (N. D.), 22 Willow north to Garfield Ave.

Hoxie (H. P.), 95th south to 120th.

Hoyne Ave. N. (W. D. and L. V.), 832 Lake north to Grace Ave.

Hoyne Ave. S. (W. D.), 832 Lake south to 67th.

Hoyt (L.), 815 63d south to 67th.

Hubbard Ct. (S. D.), 252 Michigan Ave. west to State.

Huber (N. D.), 186 Herndon east to Racine Ave.

Hick Ave. (L. V.), Lawrence north two blocks.

Hudson (S. D.), Western Ave. west to Rockwell.

Hudson Ave. (N. D.), 47 Sigel north to Center.

Hull (N. D.), 51 Eugenie north to Menomonee.

Humboldt (W. D.),979 North Ave. north to Palmer Ave.

Humboldt Ave. (W. D.), 507 Western Ave. west to Crawford Ave.

Humboldt Ave. (W. D.), 421 Humboldt Boul. north to Belmont Ave.

Humboldt Park Boul. (W. D.), 1099 North Ave. north to Palmer Pl.

Huron (N. D.), Roberts east to the lake.

Huron W. (W. D.), 364 Milwaukee Ave. west to limits.

Hydraulic Pl. (S. D.), 184 State west to Clark.

Iglehart Pl. (S. D)., 27th south to 28th.

Illinois (N. D.), Kingsbury east to the lake.

Illinois Ave. (S. D.), 761 32d south to 33d.

Illinois Ave. (H. P.), 266 83d Pl. south to Ontario Ave.

Indiana (N. D.), the river east to the lake.

Indiana W. (W. D.), the river west to 48th.

Indiana Ave. (S. D.), 12th south to city limits.

Indiana Boul. (H. P.), 101st southeast to 106th.

Ingraham (W. D.), 333 Elston Ave. west to Noble.

Inkerman (L.), 345 45th south to Goshen.

Iowa (W. D.), 357 N. Wood west to California Ave.

Iron (S. D.), 33d southeast to 35th.

Irving Ave. (W. D.), 894 Monroe south to 14th.

Irving Pl. (W. D.), 848 Fulton north to Kinzie.

Isabella (W. D.), 466 N. Homan Ave. east one block.

Jackson (S. D.), Michigan Ave. west to the river.

Jackson W. (W. D.), the river west to 48th.

Jackson Ave. (H. P.), 608 54th south to 59th.

Jackson Park Terrace (H. P.), 6500 Stony Island Ave. west to Ill. Cent. R. R.

James (L. V.), Front to Ashland Ave.

James Ave. (S. D.), Laurel west to Pitney Ct.

Jamot (L. V.), Leavitt east to Robey.

Jane (W. D.), 812 Milwaukee Ave. west to California Ave.

Janssen (L. V.), 924 Roscoe north to Nellie.

Jasper (S. D.), 34th south to 35th.

Jay (N. D.), 60 Center north to Fullerton Ave.

Jefferson N. (W. D.), 93 Randolph north to the river.

Jefferson S. (W. D.), 93 Randolph south to 22d.

Jefferson Ave. (H. P.), 50th south to 57th.

Jefferson Ave. (L.), 69th to 71st.

Jefferson Ct. (W. D.), 69 Powell Ave west to Perry Ave.

Jeffery Ave. (H. P.), 67th south to 95th.

Jessie Pl. (W. D.), 769 Kinzie north one-half block.

John Pl. (W. D.), 879 S. Halsted west one block.

Johnson (W. D.), 292 Taylor south to 22d.

Johnson Ave. (S. D.), 27th south to 28th.

Johnston Ave. (W. D.), 1211 N. California Ave. west to Humboldt Park.

Joseph (S. D.), 2535 Hickory southeast to Archer Ave.

Joseph (L.), Washtenaw Ave. to California Ave. -

Judd (W. D.), Stewart Ave. west to S. Jefferson.

Judson (N. D.), Eastman northwest to Blackhawk.

Julia Ct. (W. D.), Stave southwest one half block.

Julian (W. D.), 699 N. Ashland Ave. west to Wood.

Julius (W. D.), 103 11th south one block.

Justine (L.), 45th south to 67th.

Kedzie Ave. N. (W. D.), 1512 Lake north to limits.

Kedzie Ave. S. (W. D.), 1512 Lake south to limits.

Keeley (S. D.), 2823 Archer Ave. southeast to 31st.

Keenon (W. D.), 749 N. Ashland Ave. west to Wood.

Keith (W. D.), 303 Chicago Ave. south to Huron.

Kemper Pl. (N. D.), 462 Orchard east to Larrabee.

Kendall (W. D.), 840 Polk southwest to Taylor.

Kensington Ave. (H. P.), Lake Calumet west to Thornton Ave.

Kenwood Ave. (H. P.), 66 47th south to 49th.

Kimbark Ave. (H. P.), 106 47th south to 59th.

Kingsbury (N. D.), 27 Kinzie north to Chicago Ave.

Kingston Ave. (H. P.), 83d south to 87th.

Kinzie (N. D.), the river east to N. Water.

Kinzie W. (W. D.), the river west to limits.

Koenig (W. D.), 375 Warsaw Ave. northeast to Lee Ave.

Kosciusko (W. D.), 1151 N. Robey west to Leavitt.

Kramer (W. D.), 511 S. Jefferson west to Halsted.

Kroll (W. D.), 122 Moore south two-thirds block.

Kruse Ave. (L.), C. & G. T. Ry. south two blocks.

Kuehl Pl. (W. D.), 110 Lister Ave. northeast to Elston Ave.

Kuhn's Ct. (W. D.), 1101 N. Western Ave. north one-half block.

Lafayette Ave. (H. P.), 1026 56th south to 57th.

Laflin (W. D.), 536 Madison south to limits.

Lake (S. D.), Central Ave. west to the river.

Lake W. (W. D.), the river west to limits.

Lake Ave. (S. D.), 15 35th south to limits.

Lake Park Ave. (S. D.), 23d southeast to 33d.

Lake Park Place (S. D.), railroad tracks west to 336 Michigan Ave.

Lake Shore Drive (N. D.), foot of Oak north to Lincoln Park.

Lake View Ave. (L. V.), Fullerton Ave. north to Belmont Ave.

Lane Pl. (N. D.), 412 Center north to Garfield Ave.

Langdon (N. D.), 183 Clybourn Ave. southwest one-half block.

Langley Ave. (S. D.), 115 37th south to 95th.

Larrabee (N. D.), 19 Chicago Ave. north to Deming Ct.

La Salle (S. D.), the river south to Van Buren; 237 16th south to Garfield Boul.

La Salle Ave. (N. D.), the river north to Clark.

Laughton (W. D.), 1151 S. Hoyne Ave. west to California Ave.

Laurel Ave. (W. D.), Fullerton Ave. north to Diversey.

15

Law Ave. (W. D.), Harrison south to Polk.

Lawndale Ave. N. (W. D.), Kinzie north to North Ave.

Lawndale Ave. S. (W. D.), 1936 Harrison south to 31st.

Lawrence (N. D.), North Branch east to Southport Ave.

Lawrence Ave. (L. V.), N. Western Ave. east to the lake.

Lay (W. D.), 1457 S. Western Ave. west to California Ave.

Layton (L.), 4430 Wentworth Ave. west to Halsted.

Leavitt N. (W. D.), 892 Lake north to limits.

Leavitt S. (W. D. and S. D.), 892 Lake south to 39th.

Leddy (W. D.), 189 McGovern north to Fullerton Ave.

Lee Ave. (W. D.), 1779 N. California Ave. west to Avondale Ave.

Lee Pl. (W. D.), 273 N. Robey west to N. Hoyne Ave.

Legcate Ave. (S. D.), see Francisco Ave.

Leipzig (W. D.), Hamburg north to Ems.

Leland Ave. (L. V.), Leavitt east to Clark.

Le Moyne (W. D.), 695 N. Robey west to N. Leavitt.

Leo (S. D.), 2547 Archer Ave. south to 27th.

Lessing (W. D.), 124 Chicago Ave. north to Dix.

Levant Ave. (H. P.), 75th south to 87th.

Levee (W. D.), the river southwest three blocks.

Lewis (N. D.), 796 Hawthorn Ave. north to Diversey.

Lexington Ave. (W. D.), 35 De Kalb west to Crawford Ave.

Lexington Ave. (H. P.), 370 51st south to 67th.

Liberty (W. D.), 73 Stewart Ave. west to Halsted.

Lill (W. D.), 44 Station west to N. Western Ave.

Lill Ave. (N. D.), 184 Perry east to Halsted.

Lime (S. D.), the river south to 27th.

Lincoln N. (W. D.), 722 Lake north to Milwaukee Ave.

Lincoln S. (W. D.), 722 Lake south to limits.

Lincoln Ave. (N. D.), 739 Wells northwest to Belmont Ave.

Lincoln Pl. (N. D.), 500 Garfield Ave. north to Webster Ave.

Linden (L. V.), Lawrence Ave. north to Argyle.

Linden Ave. (W. D.), Fullerton Ave. north to Diversey.

Linwood Pl. (W. D.), 443 N. California Ave. west to Humboldt Park.

Lisle (W. D.), 755 S. Union west to Halsted.

Lister Ave. (W. D.), 143 Webster Ave. northwest to Robey.

Lock (S. D.), Fuller southeast to 31st.

Lockport (S. D.), railroad southeast to Archer Ave.

Locust (N. D.), Townsend east to Clark.

Logan (S. D.), 2651 Hickory southeast to railroad.

Logan (L.), Stewart Ave. west to Halsted.

Logan Square (W. D.), Kedzie Ave. and Humboldt Boul.

Lonergan (N. D.), 44 Wisconsin north to Lincoln Ave.

Loomis (W. D.), 486 Madison south to limits.

Lowe Ave. (S. D.), 515 26th south to 39th.

Lubeck (W. D.), 1039 N. Robey west to Western Ave.

Luce (W. D.), 61 Blackhawk northwest one-half block.

Luella Ave. (H. P.), 83d south to 95th.

Lull Pl. (W. D.), Ellen southwest to N. Wood.

Lumber (W. D.), 18 12th southwest to Halsted.

Lundy's Lane (S. D.), 1489 32d south to 37th.

Lunn Ct. (W. D.), 605 S. Western Ave. west one block.

Luther (W. D.), 1171 S. Rockwell west to Washtenaw.

Lutz (N. D.), 254 North Ave. west one-third block.

Lydia (W. D.), 54 N. Desplaines west to Halsted.

Lyman (L. V.), Sulzer north to Lawrence.

Lyman (S. D.), 2878 Main southwest to 31st.

Lynch Pl. (S. D.), 32d south to 33d.

Lyons Ave. (H. P.), Cottage Grove Ave. northwest to 93d.

Lytle (W. D.), 474 Harrison south to 12th.

MacAllister Pl. (W. D.), 229 Center Ave. west to Loomis.

Macedonia (W. D.), 316 Division north to Ellen.

Mackinaw Ave (H. P.), 59 83d south to 136th.

Madison (S. D.), Michigan Ave. west to the river.

Madison W. (W. D.), the river west to city limits.

Madison Ave. (H. P.), 47th south to 87th.

Madison Ct. (H. P.), 66th to 67th.

Madison Park (H. P.), 5080 Madison Ave. west to Woodlawn Ave.

Main (S. D.), the river southeast to 31st.

Manistee Ave. (H. P.), 452 87th south to 99th.

Maple (N. D.), 366 La Salle Ave. east to State.

Maple (L.), C. & G. T. R. R. west to Reese Ave.

Maple Pl. (W. D.), 1137 N. Western Ave. west to Powell Ave.

Maplewood Ave. (W. D.), 1104 Lake north to Elston Ave.

Maplewood S. (W. D.), 1855 W. 31st south to Illinois and Michigan Canal.

Maplewood Pl. (W. D.), 860 Ogden Ave. south to 15th.

Mara Ave. (L. V.), 224 School north to Addison Ave.

Marble Pl. (S. D.), State west to 5th Ave.

Marble Pl. (W. D.), 125 S. Desplaines west to Halsted.

Marcy (N. D.), 53 Sheffield Ave. northwest to Clybourn Pl.

Margaret (W. D.), 402 14th south to 15th.

Margaret Pl. (W. D.), 2001 16th south to 19th.

Marianna (L. V.), 474 Southport Ave. east to Florence Ave.

Marion Pl. (W. D.), 328 Division north to Ellen.

Mark (W. D.), 689 S. Union west to S. Halsted.

Market (S. D.), 253 Lake south to Congress.

Market N. (N. D.), the river north to North Ave.

Market Square (S. D.), 31st southeast to Ashland Ave.

Marquette Ave. (H. P.), 490 87th south to 105th.

Marshfield Ave. (W. D.), 600 Jackson south to 12th; 34th south to 71st.

Martin (W. D.), 1151 S. Rockwell west to Washtenaw Ave.

Marvin (W. D.), 1159 S. Oakley Ave. west to California Ave.

Mary (S. D.), 2509 Hickory southeast to Hoey.

Maryland Ave. (H. P.), 65th south to 67th.

Mather (W. D.), Ellsworth west to Halsted.

Mathew (W. D.), 215 Ogden Ave. west to Wood.

Matteson (L.), Stewart Ave. west to Halsted.

Mattison Ave. (H. P.), 200 74th south one block.

Maud Ave. (N. D.), 125 Sheffield Ave. northwest to Racine Ave.

Mautene Ct. (W. D.), 912 Milwaukee Ave. southwest one-half block.

Maxwell (W. D.), the river west to 330 Blue Island Ave.

May (L. V.), 1500 Wrightwood Ave. north to George.

May, N. (W. D.), 341 Randolph north to George.

May, S. (W. D. and L.), 341 Randolph south to limits.

McAlpine (S. D.), Bross Ave. south to Douglas Ave.

McChesney Ave. (H. P.), 63d south to 67th.

McDermott (S. D.), C. & A. R. R. southeast to Archer Ave.

McDowell (W. D.), 1235 S. Washtenaw Ave. west one-half block.

McGlashen (S. D.), 1449 22d south to Archer Ave.

McGovern (W. D.), 1926 Milwaukee Ave. west to Kedzie Ave.

McHenry (W. D.), Blanche to the river.

McIlroy (W. D.), 517 N. Kedzie Ave. west one block.

McKibben Ave. (L.), 44th south to 46th.

McLean Ave. (W. D.), 1147 Homan Ave. west to Crawford Ave.

McMullen Ct. (W. D.), 103 Fisk west to Centre Ave.

McReynolds (W. D.), 727 N. Ashland Ave. west to Wood.

Mead (W. D.), Kènzie north to Fullerton Ave.

Meadow Lane (L. V.), Grand Ave. north to limits.

Meaghan (W. D.), 1610 S. Ashland Ave. east one-half block.

Meagher (W. D.), 143 Stewart Ave. west to Halsted.

Mechanic (W. D.), 41 18th south to Lumber.

Medill Ave. (W. D.), 1389 Kimball west to Central Park Ave.

Melrose (L. V.), Western Ave. east to the lake.

Mendell (W. D.), 141 Clybourn Pl. northwest to Canal Pl.

Menomonee (N. D.), 769 Clark west to Larrabee.

Mentmore Ave. (W. D.), 1259 Kedzie Ave. west to Crawford Ave.

Merian (W. D.),C., B. & Q. R. R. south to 22d.

Meridian (W. D.), 51 S. Desplaines west to Halsted.

Metropolitan Pl. (W. D.), 251 N. Harding Ave. west to Crawford Ave.

Michigan (N. D.), King-bury east to Water.

Michigan Ave. (S. D.), the river south to 99th.

Mill (S. D.), 3223 Ashland Ave. west to Paulina.

Millard Ave. (W. D.), 1292 12th south to Whitehouse.

Miller (W. D.), 346 Harrison south to Taylor.

Milton Ave. (N. D.), 57 Chicago Ave. north to Division.

Milwaukee Ave. (W. D.), 28 Lake northwest to limits.

Minnehaha Ave. (H. P.), 91st south to 94th.

Mitchell Ave. (W. D.), 1059 North Ave. north to Bloomingdale Road.

Moffat (W. D.), 977 Western Ave. west to Rockwell.

Mohawk (N. D.), 78 Clybourn Ave. north to Garfield Ave.

Monroe (S. D.), Michigan Ave. west to the river.

Monroe (W. D.), 111 S. Canal west to Central Park Ave.

Monroe Ave. (H. P.), 282 53d south to 59th.

Montana (L. V.), 1230 Ashland Ave. east to Lincoln Ave.

Montana (W. D.), 130 Station west to Western Ave.

Montgomery (L.), Blanchard Ave. northwest to Archer Ave.

Moore (N. D.), 366 Division south to Elm.

Moore (W. D.), S. Wood west to California Ave.

Moore Pl. (W. D.), 2029 16th south to 19th.

Moorman (W. D.), Ellen southeast to N. Paulina.

Morgan, N. (W. D.), 281 Randolph north to Chicago Ave.

Morgan, S. (W. D.), 281 Randolph south to limits.

Morgan Pl. (W. D.), 143 S. Morgan west to Aberdeen.

Morris (L.), Stewart Ave. to Wallace.

Mosspratt (S. D.), 923 31st south to Springer Ave.

Mound Ave. (L.), School west to Stewart Ave.

Mozart (W. D.), 933 North Ave. north to Palmer Ave.

Muskegon Ave (H. P.), 8318 Baltimore Ave. south to 106th.

Myrtle (L. V.), Bryn Mawr north to Olive.

Myrtle (W. D.), 24 Birch south to Ashland.

Myrtle Ave. (H. P.), I. C. R. R. west to Lake Ave.

Myrtle Ave. (H. P.), 64th south to 67th.

Myrtle Ave. (W. D.), 1773 Milwaukee Ave. north to Diversey.

Napoleon Pl. (S. D.), 2744 Wentworth Ave. west to Wallace.

Nassau (W. D.), 1326 Jackson south one block.

Nebraska (W. D.), 309 Throop west to Ashland Ave.

Nebraska Ave. (W. D.), 1051 Bloomingdale Road north to Palmer Pl.

Nellie Ave. (L. V.), 2056 Paulina east to the lake.

Nelson (L. V.), 1590 Western Ave. east to Soult.

Nevada (L. V.), 386 Evanston Ave east to the lake.

Newberry Ave. (W. D.), 270 Taylor south to 18th.

Newport Ave. (L. V.), Evanston Ave. east to the lake.

Newton (W. D.), 14 Iowa north to Division.

Nineteenth (S. D.), 1900 State west to the river.

Nineteenth (W. D.), 669 S. Union west to Crawford Ave.

Nineteenth Pl. (W. D.), 359 Johnson west to Brown.

Ninetieth (H. P.), the strand west to St. Lawrence Ave.

Ninetieth Pl. (H. P.), I. C. R. R. west to St. Lawrence Ave.

Ninety-first (H. P.), Green Bay Ave. west to St. Lawrence Ave.

Ninety-second (H. P.), Harbor Ave. west to Cottage Grove Ave.

Ninety-second Pl. (H. P.), Yates Ave. west to Luella Ave.

Ninety-third (H. P.), Harbor Ave. west to Cottage Grove Ave.

Ninety-fourth (H. P.), Commercial Ave. west to Stony Island Ave.

Ninety-fifth (H. P.), the lake west to Michigan Ave.

Ninety-sixth (H. P.), 7th Ave. west to Michigan Ave.

Ninety-seventh (H. P.), 8th Ave. west to Michigan Ave.

Ninety-eighth (H. P.), Avenue E west to Michigan Ave.

Ninety-ninth (H. P.), the lake west to State.

Nixon (W. D.), 572 Polk south to Taylor.

Noble (W. D.), 443 Kinzie north to North Ave.

Noble Ave. (L. V.), Western Ave. east to Clark.

Normal Parkway (L.), C., R. I. & P. R. R. west to Wright.

Norman Ave. (W. D.), 1083 North Ave. north to Bloomingdale Road.

North (L. V.), C. & N.-W. Ry. east to Clark.

North Ave. (N. D.), the river east to the lake.

North Ave. (W. D.), the river west to limits.

North Ave. (L. V.), Front east to Clark.

North Branch (N. D.), 45 Hawthorne Ave. northwest to Blackhawk.

North Grove (N. D.), 711 Larrabee west to Orchard.

North Park Ave. (N. D.), 38 Menomonee north to Fullerton Ave.

North Pier (N. D.), Michigan east to the lake.

North Pl. (**W**. D.), 65 Armitage Ave. northwest one-half block.

North Water (N. D.), 18 Wells east to the lake.

Norton (W. D.), 145 Gurley south to Polk.

Norwood Ave. (W. D.), N. Kedzie Ave. west to N. Homan Ave.

Notre Dame (H. P.), 100th southwest to 104th.

Nursery (N. D.), Lewis northwest to Ward.

Nutt (W. D.), 319 16th south to 18th.

Nutt Ave. (H. P.), 71st south to 87th.

Nutt Ct. (W. D.), 137 19th south to 20th

Oak (N. D.), 88 Hawthorne Ave. east to the lake.

Oak (L.), C. & G. T. R. R. west to Reese Ave.

Oak (L.), School west to Stewart Ave.

Oak Ave. (S. D.), 3612 Vincennes Ave. west to Stanton Ave.

Oak Pl. (L. V.), 1430 Belmont Ave. north to School.

Oak Grove Ave. (L. V.), 1102 Racine Ave. east to Clark.

Oakdale Ave. (L. V.), 1524 Oakley Ave. east to the lake.

Oakenwald Ave. (H. P.), 24 42d south and west to Lake Ave.

Oakland Pl. (L. V.), 1499 George north to Wellington Ave.

Oakley Ave., N. (W. D.), 952 Lake north to Berteau Ave.

Oakley Ave., S. (W. D.), 952 Lake south to limits.

Oakwood Ave. (S. D.), the lake west to Cottage Grove Ave.

Oakwood Boul. (H. P.), 3922 Cottage Grove Ave. west to Grand Boul.

O'Brien (W. D.), 497 Jefferson west to Halsted.

Ogden Ave. (W. D.), 486 Randolph southwest to Crawford Ave.

Ogden Pl. (W. D.), 125 Ogden Ave. west to S. Wood.

Oglesby Ave. (H. P.), 61st south to 71st.

Ohio (N. D.), Kingsbury east to the lake.

Ohio (W. D.), 214 N. Desplaines west to 48th.

Olga (L. V.), 1240 Nellie Ave. west to Grace.

Olive (W. D.), 976 Taylor south to 12th.

Olive (L. V.), 3902 Clark east to Southport Ave.

Olivet Pl. (W. D.), 11 Walker Ct. west one-half block.

100th (H. P.), the lake west to Willett Ave.

101st (H. P.), the lake west to Willett Ave.

102d (H. P.), the lake west to Willett Ave.

103d (H. P.), Avenue C west to State.

104th (H. P.), Avenue C west to State.

105th (H. P.), Indiana Boul. west to Indiana Ave.

106th (H. P.), Indiana Boul. west to Ill. Cent. R. R.

107th (H. P.), Avenue G west to Michigan Ave.

108th (H. P.), Avenue E west to Ill. Cent. R. R.

109th (H. P.), Avenue E west to Willett Ave.

110th (H. P.), Avenue E west to State.

111th (H. P.), First Ave. west to State.

111th Pl. (H. P.), Michigan Ave. west to State.

112th (H. P.), First Ave. west to State.

112th Pl. (H. P.), Michigan Ave. west to State.

113th (H. P.), First Ave. west to State.

113th Pl. (H. P.), Michigan Ave. west to State.

114th (H. P.), Avenue F west to Ill. Cent. R. R.

115th (Il. P.), Avenue F west to Halsted.

116th (H. P.), Avenue F west to State.

117th (H. P.), Ill. & Ind. Line west to Michigan Ave.

118th (H. P.), Ill. & Ind. Line west to State.

119th (H. P.), Ill. & Ind. Line west to State.

O'Neil (W. D.), 911 S. Halsted west one block.

Ontario (N. D.), Kingsbury east to the lake.

Ontario (W. D.), 400 46th west to 48th.

Ontario Ave. (H. P.), 130 81st south to Harbor Ave.

Orchard (N. D.), 230 Clybourn Ave. north to Dewey Ct.

Orchard (H. P.), I. C. R. R. west to Lake Ave.

Osborne (W. D.), 541 Indiana north to Ohio.

Osgood (W. D.), 114 Centre north to Fullerton Ave.

Oswego (W. D.), 573 Kinzie north one-half block.

Otis (N. D.), 203 Division north to Vedder.

Otto (L. V.), 1664 Robey east to Halsted.

Owasco (W. D.), 213 S. Western Ave. west to 46th.

Oxford Ct. (S. D.), 3838 Stanton Ave. west to Grand Boul.

Pacific Ave. (S. D.), 148 Jackson south to Taylor.

Packers' Ave. (L.), 42d south to 47th.

Page, N. (W. D.), 607 Kinzie north to Ferdinand.

Page, S. (W. D.), 651 Lake south to Madison.

Palatine (W. D.), 641 S. Homan Ave. west to Central Park Ave.

Palmer (L. V.), Sulzer north to Balmoral Ave.

Palmer Ave. (W. D.), 1191 N.

California Ave. west to Thomas Ave.

Palmer Square (W. D.), Humboldt Boul. west to Kedzie Ave.

Park (W. D.), 631 N. Wood northwest to N. Robey.

Park Ave. (W. D.), 31 S. Ashland west to city limits.

Park Ave. (L. V.), 1890 Diversey Ave. north to Surf.

Park Front (N. D.), Wells east to Clark.

Parmelee (W. D.), 1119 S. Hoyne Ave. west to California Ave.

Parnell Ave.(S. D.), 539 29th south to 39th.

Paulina, N. (W. D. and L. V.), 626 Lake north to Tuttle Ave.

Paulina, S. (W. D. and S. D.), 626 Lake south to 39th.

Pearce (W. D.), 235 S. Desplaines west to Halsted.

Pearl (N. D.), 378 Garfield Ave. north to Webster Ave.

Pearl (L. V.), Olive south to Bryn Mawr.

Pearl (L.), Belt R. R. south to 79th.

Pearson, E. (N. D.), 220 State east to the lake.

Pearson, W. (N. D.), 222 Market east to Wells.

Peck Ct. (S. D.), Michigan Ave. west to State.

Penn (N. D.), 175 Division north to Vedder.

Peoria, N. (W. D.), 239 Randolph north to Milwaukee Ave.

Peoria, S. (W. D.), 239 Randolph south to Harrison.

Peoria, S. (L.), 50th south to limits.

Perry (N. D. and L. V.), 754 Clybourn Ave. north to Leland Ave.

Perry Ave. (W. D.), 1693 Milwaukee Ave. north to Fullerton Ave.

Perry Ave. (L.), 65th south to 79th.

Peterson (W. D.), 859 N. Robey west to Hoyne Ave.

Peterson Ave. (L. V.), N. Western Ave. east to N. Clark.

Phillips (W. D.), 258 N. Halsted west to Sangamon.
Phinney Ave., N. (W. D.), Kinzie north to Chicago Ave.
Phinney Ave., S. (W. D.), 1539 Van Buren north to Colorado Ave.
Pier (S. D.), 3813 Lake Ave. east to the lake.
Pierce (H. P.), 4224 St. Lawrence Ave. west to Grand Boul.
Pierce Ave. (W. D.), 807 N. Kedzie Ave. west to Homan Ave.
Pierce (L.), Stewart Ave. west to Wallace.
Pine (N. D.), North Water north to Oak.
Pine (L. V.), N. Robey east to Ashland Ave.
Pine Grove Ave. (L. V.), Cornelia northwest to Graceland Ave.
Pitney Ct. (S. D.), C. & A. R. R. southeast to 31st.
Pittsfield Ave. (L.), 60th south to 62d.
Pleasant (N. D.), 191 Division north to Vedder.
Pleasant Ave. (L. V.), Fullerton Ave. north to Fisher Ave.
Pleasant Pl. (W. D.), 1233 N. Western Ave. west to Perry Ave.
Plum (W. D.), 220 Loomis west to Laflin.
Plymouth Pl. (S. D.), 86 Jackson south to 14th.
Poe (N. D.), 26 Maud Ave. northwest to Clyde.
Point (W. D.), 663 Armitage Ave. northwest to California Ave.
Polk (S. D.), 426 State west to the river.
Polk, W. (W. D.), the river west to S. Albany Ave.
Poplar Ave. (S. D.), 28th to 31st.
Portland Ave. (S. D.), 381 22d south to 43d.
Post (S. D.), Ashland Ave. southeast to the levee.
Potomac Ave. (W. D.), 599 N. Lincoln west to California Ave.
Powell Ave. (W. D.), 1617 Milwaukee Ave. north to Fullerton Ave.

Powell Ave. (H. P.), 99th south to 114th.
Powell's Park (W. D.), 1087 N. Western Ave. west to Powell Ave.
Prairie Ave. (S. D.), 9 16th south to 87th.
Pratt (W. D.), 292 S. Halsted west to Morgan.
Pratt Pl. (W. D.), 219 S. Hoyne Ave. west two blocks.
Primrose (L. V.), Peterson Ave. north to Fisher Ave.
Prince Ave. (W. D.), 779 N. Central Park Ave. west to Crawford Ave.
Prindiville (W. D.), 1834 Milwaukee Ave. southwest to State.
Prospect Pl. (S. D.), 3570 Cottage Grove Ave. west to Vincennes Ave.
Pulaski (W. D.), 1149 N. Hoyne Ave. west to Leavitt.
Pullman (H. P.), 104th southwest to 115th.
Purple (S. D.), 251 19th south to Archer Ave.
Putnam (W. D.), Erie north to Chicago Ave.
Quarry (S. D.), the river southeast to Stearns.
Quincy (S. D.), 220 State west to the river.
Quincy, W. (W.D.), 167 S. Clinton west to Halsted.
Quinn (S. D.), 2733 Archer Ave. southeast to 31st.
Racine Ave. (N. D.), 550 Clybourn Ave. north to Belmont Ave.
Railroad Ave. (W. D.), 64 12th south to 14th.
Railroad Ave. (L.), railroad crossing west to Wentworth Ave.
Railroad Ave. (H. P.), 71st south to 83d Pl.
Raleigh Ct. (W. D.), 675 13th south one block.
Randolph (S. D.), Michigan Ave. west to the river.
Randolph, W. (W. D.), the river west to Union Park.
Ravenswood Park (L. V.), Grace north to limits.

Rawson (W. D.), the river west to Elston Ave.

Ray (S. D.), 2924 Park Ave. west to Prairie Ave.

Raymond (W. D.), 787 N. Robey west one-half block.

Rebecca (W. D.), 603 S. Morgan west to California Ave.

Redfield (W. D.), McHenry west to Elston Ave.

Reese (N. D.), 275 Larrabee southwest to Division.

Reese Ave. (L.), see Crawford Ave.

Reynolds Ave. (H. P.), 78th south to 82d.

Rhine (W. D.), 1257 N. Leavitt west to Milwaukee Ave.

Rhodes Ave. (S. D.), 53 31st south to 35th.

Rice (W. D.), 353 N. Wood west to Lincoln.

Rice Pl. (W. D.), 1016 22d south one block.

Richmond (W. D.), 1184 Chicago Ave. north to Division.

Richmond Ave. (L. V.), 2023 Milwaukee Ave. north to Belmont Ave.

Ridge Ave. (H. P.), 82 Roberison Ave. south to Jackson Park Terrace.

Ridge Ave. (L. V.), 2599 Evanston Ave. northwest to limits.

Ridgeway Ave. (W. D.), Kinzie north to North Ave.

Ridgewood Ct. (H. P.·, 262 54th south one block.

Ritchie Pl. (N. D.), 231 Goethe north to Banks.

River (S. D.), Rush Street bridge southwest to Water.

Roberts (N. D.), 1 Erie north to Chicago Ave.

Robertson Ave. (H. P.), 4324 Grace Avenue to I. C. R. R.

Robey, N. (W. D. and L. V.), 772 Lake north to limits.

Robey, S. (W. D. and S. D.), 772 Lake south to limits.

Robinson (S. D.), 31st northwest to Illinois & Michigan Canal.

Rockwell, N. (W. D.), 1142 Lake north to Armitage Ave.

Rockwell, S. (W. D. and S. D.), 1142 Lake south to 51st.

Rokeby (L. V.), 1500 Addison Ave. north to Graceland Ave.

Root (L.), 4134 State west to Halsted.

Rosalie Ct. (H. P.), 57th south to 59th.

Roscoe (L. V.), N. Western Ave. east to Evanston Ave.

Rose (W. D.), 390 Chicago Ave. north to Cornell.

Rosebud (W. D.), 625 Bloomingdale Road northwest to N. Western Ave.

Rosemont Ave. (L. V.), Evanston Ave. east to the lake.

Rosenmerkel (L.), Stewart Ave. west to Wallace.

Rubens Ave. (L. V.), Grand Ave. north to Ernst Ave.

Ruble (W. D.), 153 16th south to 21st.

Rumsey (W. D.), 499 Indiana north to Division.

Rundel Pl. (W. D.), 73 S. Morgan west to Centre Ave.

Rupp Ave. (H. P.), 87th south to 95th.

Rush (N. D.), the river north and northwest to Elm.

Rush (L.), 417 39th south one block.

Sacramento Ave., N. (W. D.), 1392 Lake north to Central Park Boul.

Sacramento Ave., S. (W. D.), 1392 Lake south to 83d.

Saginaw Ave. (H. P.), 526 87th south to 95th.

Samuel (W. D.), 540 Chicago Ave. north to Division.

Sangamon, N. (W. D.), 259 Randolph north to the river.

Sangamon, S. (W. D.), 259 Randolph south to Harrison.

Sangamon (L.), 52d south to limits.

Sanger (S. D.), 2447 Archer Ave. southeast to 26th.

Sawyer Ave. (W. D.), 12th south to 69th.

Schell Ave. (H. P.), 71st south to 84th.

Schick Pl. (N. D.), 64 Clybourn Ave northeast to Cleveland Ave.

Schiller (N. D.), 357 Sedgwick east to the lake.

School (W. D.), 93 S. Canal west to Desplaines.

School (L. V.). Western Ave. east to Evanston Ave.

School (L.), 358 Root south to 63d.

Schuyler (W. D.), Thomas Ave. west to 1st Ave.

Schuyler (W. D.), Milwaukee Ave. west one block.

Scott (N. D.), 407 State east to the lake.

Scovel Ave. (H. P.), 99th south to 114th.

Sebor (W. D.), Ellsworth west to S. Halsted.

Second Ave. (H. P.), 176 95th south to 101st.

Sedgwick (N. D.), 85 Erie north to limits.

Sedgwick Ct. (N. D.), 328 Division south to Elm.

Seeley Ave. (W. D), 804 Madison south to Avon Pl.

Selden (W. D.), 485 S. Wood west one block.

Seminary Ave. (N. D.), 52 Maud Ave. north to Eddy.

Seminary Pl. (L. V.), 436 Racine Ave. to Seminary Ave.

Seneca (N. D.), 361 Illinois north one block.

Seneschalle (L.), 440 Root north one-half block.

Seventeenth (S. D.), 1700 State west to Grove.

Seventeenth, W. (W. D.), Arthur west to Washtenaw Ave.

Seventh Ave. (H. P.), 47 96th south to 100th.

Seventieth (H. P. and L.), Yates Ave. west to Centre Ave.

Seventy-first (H. P. and L.) the lake west to Ashland Ave.

Seventy-first Pl. (H. P.), Stony Island Ave. west to Woodlawn Ave.

Seventy-second (H. P. and L.), 71st southwest and west to Ashland Ave.

Seventy-second Pl. (H. P.), Stony Island Ave. west to Woodlawn Ave.

Seventy-third (H. P. and L.), Lake Ave. west to Ashland Ave.

Seventy-fourth (H. P. and L.), Lake Ave. west to Ashland Ave.

Seventy-fourth Pl. (H. P.), B. & O. R. R. west to Jefferson Ave.

Seventy-fifth (H. P. and L.), Lake Ave. west to Reese Ave.

Seventy-sixth (H. P.), Lake Ave. west to Halsted.

Seventy-sixth Ct. (H. P.), 7642 Coles Ave. west to Railroad.

Seventy-seventh (H. P. and L.), Lake Ave. west to Ashland Ave.

Seventy-seventh Ct. (H. P.), 7742 Coles Ave. southwest to Railroad Ave.

Seventy-eighth (H. P. and L.), Lake Ave. west to Ashland Ave.

Seventy-eighth Pl. (H. P.), 7826 Coles Ave. southwest to Railroad Ave.

Seventy-ninth (H. P. and L.), the lake west to Hyman Ave.

Seward (W. D.), 77 16th south to Lumber.

Seymour Ave. (W. D.), 973 Kinzie north to Armitage Ave.

Shakespeare Ave. (W. D.), 1161 N. California Ave. west to Humboldt Park.

Shaughnessy (N. D.), 9 Goethe north one block.

Sheffield Ave. (N. D. and L.), 472 Hawthorne Ave. north to Belmont Ave.

Shelby Ct. (W. D.), 109 19th south one block.

Sheldon (L. V), Grace north to Graceland Ave.

Sheldon, N. (W. D.), 467 Randolph north to Arbor Pl.

Sheldon, S. (W. D.), 467 Randolph south to Madison.

Sheridan (S. D.), 1273 33d south to Douglas Ave.

Sheridan Ave. (W. D.), Kinzie north to Fullerton Ave.

Sheridan Ave., S. (W. D.), 1456 Fillmore south to 12th.

Sheridan Ave. (H. P.), 61st south to 67th.

Sheridan Pl. (S. D.), 2014 Wentworth Ave. west one-half block.

Sherman (S. D.), 164 Jackson south to Stowell.

Sherman (L.), 39th south to limits.

Sherman Ave. (H. P.), 420 83d south to 78th.

Sherman Pl. (L. V.), 674 Orchard southeast to Clark.

Sherman Pl. (N. D.), 132 Pine west one-half block.

Shober (W. D.), 562 Division north to Wabansia Ave.

Sholto (W. D.), 368 Harrison south to 11th.

Short (S. D.), 2731 Cologne southeast to Fuller.

Sibley (W. D.), 522 Harrison south to Taylor.

Sidney Ave. (H. P.), 78 44th south to 45th.

Sidney Ct. (L. V.), 1934 Wrightwood Ave. northwest to Diversey.

Siebens Pl. (N. D.), 305 Larrabee northwest to Hinsche.

Sigel (N. D.), 46 Cleveland Ave. east to Wells.

Silver (W. D.), 280 Harrison south to Gurley.

Sinnott Pl. (W. D.), 70 N. Centre Ave. west to Elizabeth.

Sixteenth (S. D.), the lake west to the river.

Sixteenth (W. D.), the river west to limits.

Sixth Ave. (H. P.), 94th southeast to Indiana Boul.

Sixtieth (H. P. and L.), 6000 Stony Island Ave. west to Kincaide Ave.

Sixtieth Ct. (L.), Wentworth Ave. west to Wallace.

Sixty-first (H. P. and L.), 6100 Stony Island Ave. west to Central Park Ave.

Sixty-first Ct. (L.), Wallace west to Halsted.

Sixty-first Pl. (H P.), Madison Ave. east to I. C. R. R.

Sixty-second (H. P. and L.), I. C. R. R. west to Central Park Ave.

Sixty-second Pl. (H P.), I. C. R. R. west to Madison Ave.

Sixty-third (H. P. and L.), 6300 Stony Island Ave. west to limits.

Sixty-fourth (H P. and L.), 6300 Stony Island Ave. west to limits.

Sixty-fifth (H. P. and L.), Sheridan Ave. west to limits.

Sixty-fifth Terrace (H. P.), Stony Island Ave. west to I. C. R. R.

Sixty-sixth (H. P. and L.), Stony Island Ave. west to limits.

Sixty-sixth Ct. (H. P.), Stony Island Ave. west to Halsted.

Sixty-seventh (H. P. and L.), Stony Island Ave. west to limits.

Sixty-eighth (H. P. and L.), the lake west to Homan Ave.

Sixty-ninth (H. P. and L.), the lake west to Homan Ave.

Slade (S. D.), 1328 31st northwest one and one-half block.

Sloan (W. D.), 273 Elston Ave. west to Noble.

Smart (W. D.), 657 Kinzie north to Austin Ave.

Smith Ave. (N. D.), 129 Blackhawk north to North Ave.

Smith Ave. (S. D.), Rockwell west to Kedzie Ave.

Snell (W. D.), 341 Chicago Ave. south to Huron.

Snow (W. D.), N. Leavitt northeast to river.

Snyder (L.), 4056 Stewart Ave. west to Halsted.

Sobieski (W. D.), 257 Webster Ave. north to Fullerton Ave.

Soult (L. V.), 1492 Wellington Ave. north to Noble.

South Ave. (L. V.), Front east to Clark.

South Chicago Ave. (H. P.), 67th southeast to 95th.

South Park Ave.(S. D.),1 22d south to 87th.

South Park Ct. (H. P.), 16th south to 61st.

South Water (S. D.), the lake west and southwest to Lake.

Southport Ave. (N. D.), 95 Clybourn Pl. north to Belmont Ave.

Spaulding Ave. (W. D.), 1554 Madison south to 69th.

Spears Ave. (L.) Archer Ave. southeast to 47th.

Spring (S. D.) 1612 State west to Wentworth Ave.

Springer Ave. (S. D.), 3224 Laurel west to Waterville.

Springfield Ave. N. (W. D.), Kinzie north to Humboldt Ave.

Springfield Ave. S. (W. D.), 2008 Harrison south to 61st.

Spruce (W. D.), 242 Loomis west to Laflin.

Stanton Ave. (S. D.), 137 35th south to 39th.

Starr (N. D.), 481 Sedgwick east to Franklin.

State N. (N. D.), the river north to North Ave.

State (S. D.), the river south to 65th.

State Ct. (L. V.), Belmont Ave. south two blocks.

Station (W. D.), 1319 N. Leavitt northwest to Fullerton Ave.

Stave (W. D.). 601 Armitage Ave. northwest to California Ave.

St. Clair (N. D), 217 Michigan north to Superior.

St. Elmo (L. V.), Wood east to Lincoln Ave.

St. George's Ct. (W. D.), 191 Stave northeast to Milwaukee Ave.

St. Hedwigs (W. D.), 331 Webster Ave. north to Pulaski.

St. Helen's (W. D.), 112 Stave southwest one-half block.

St. James Pl. (L. V.), 1202 Clark northeast to Lake View Ave.

St. John's Pl. (W. D.), 546 Lake north to Arbor Pl.

St. Louis Ave. N. (W. D.), 1700 Lake north to Chicago Ave.

St. Louis Ave. S. (W. D.), 1684 Madison south to 68th.

St. Mary (W. D.), 166 Stave southwest one-half block.

Stearns (S. D.), 2860 Halsted southwest to Main.

Stein (W. D.), 75 Redfield north-west one block.

Stephens (W. D.), 1260 Jackson south to Van Buren.

Stephenson (W. D.), Lumber south to west 14th.

Stewart Ave.(W. D. and S. D.), 73 12th south to 87th.

Stone (N. D.), 613 Division north to Banks.

Stone Ave. (L.), Morgan west to Centre Ave.

Stony Island Ave. (H. P.), 147 56th south to Lake Calumet.

Storms (H. P.), P. F. W. & C. Ry. south to 87th.

Stowell (S. D.), 536 Clark west one and one-half blocks.

String (W. D.), 131 16th south to 22d.

Sullivan (N. D.), 310 Sedgwick west to Hurlbut.

Sullivan Ct. (S. D.), 2973 Lyman southeast one block.

Sultan (L.), 405 43d south to Goshen.

Sulzer (L. V.), Western Ave. east to the lake.

Summerdale Ave. (L.V.), Robey east to Southport Ave.

Summers Ave. (W. D.), 1575 Bloomingdale Road north to Armitage Ave.

Summit (S. D.), R. R. southeast to 3600 Archer Ave.

Summit Ave. (L.), 83d southwest to 87th.

Summer (W. D.), 730 15th south to 16th.

Sunnyside Ave. (L. V.), Western Ave. east to Clark.

Superior (N. D.), Roberts east to the lake.

Superior W. (W. D.), 298 N. Halsted west to 48th.
Superior Ave. (H. P.), 83d south to 93d.
Surf (L. V.), 60 Evanston Ave. east to the lake.
Surrey Ct. (L. V.), 262 Fullerton Ave. north to Dunning Ave.
Swift (W. D.), 1371 S. Kedzie Ave. west to Crawford Ave.
Swift (L. V.), 1074 Ridge Ave. north to Francis.
Swift Pl. (S. D.), 2844 Wentworth Ave. west to Stewart Ave.
Talman Ave. N. (W. D.), 1170 Lake north to North Ave.
Talman Ave. S. (W. D.), 1286 12th south to 15th.
Taylor (S. D.), 504 State west to the river.
Taylor W. (W. D.), the river west to Lawndale Ave.
Tell Ct. (N. D.), 541 Sedgwick east to Wells.
Tell Pl. (W. D.), 748 Milwaukee Ave. west to Ashland Ave.
Temple (W. D.), 323 Chicago Ave. south to Huron.
Tenth Ave. (H. P.), 45th south one block.
Terrace Ct. (S. D.), 3136 Lowe Ave. west one block.
The Strand (H. P.), 85th south to Harbor Ave.
Third Ave. (H. P.), 142 95th south to 102d.
Thirteenth (S. D.), Indiana Ave. west to State.
Thirteenth W. (W. D.), 303 Blue Island Ave. west to Boulevard.
Thirteenth Pl. W. (W. D.), 897 S. Rockwell west to California Ave.
Thirtieth (S. D.), the lake west to Halsted.
Thirtieth W. (W. D.),1431 S.Western Ave. west to Kedzie Ave.
Thirty-first (S. D.), the lake west to Illinois and Michigan Canal.
Thirty-first W. (W. D.), Illinois and Michigan Canal west to Crawford Ave.

Thirty-second (S. D.), Cottage Grove Ave. west to Hoyne Ave.
Thirty second W. (W. D.), 1523 S. Western Ave. west to Rockwell.
Thirty second Ct. (S. D.), 3166 Lake Park Ave. west to Cottage Grove Ave.
Thirty-third (S. D.), the lake west to Oakley Ave.
Thirty-third Ct. (S. D.), 3228 Halsted west to Archer Ave.
Thirty-fourth (S. D.), 3400 Cottage Grove Ave. west to Rockwell.
Thirty-fourth Ct. (S. D.), 3428 Halsted west to Robey.
Thirty-fifth (S. D.), the lake west to Illinois and Michigan Canal.
Thirty-fifth Ct. (S. D.), 3528 Halsted west to Western Ave.
Thirty-sixth (S. D.), 3600 Lake Ave. west to Kedzie Ave.
Thirty-sixth Pl. (S. D.), 3634 Vincennes Ave. west one block.
Thirty seventh (S. D.), the lake west to Illinois and Michigan Canal.
Thirty-seventh Ct. (S. D.), 3728 Indiana Ave. west to Robey.
Thirty-eighth (S. D.), 3800 Cottage Grove Ave. west to Illinois and Michigan Canal.
Thirty-eighth Ct. (S. D.), 3824 Portland Ave. west to Wood.
Thirty-ninth (S. D.), Lake Ave. west to Illinois and Michigan Canal.
Thirty-ninth Pl. (S. D.), 3930 Wabash Ave. east one-half block.
Thomas (W. D.), 485 N. Wood west to Humboldt Park.
Thomas Ave. (W. D.), 127 Palmer Pl. north to Belmont Ave.
Thome Ave. (L. V.), Clark east to Southport Ave.
Thompson (W. D.), 777 N. Leavitt west to California Ave.
Thorndale Ave. (L. V.), Evanston Ave. east to Sheffield Ave.
Throop (W. D.), 438 Madison south to 87th.
Tilden (W. D.), 207 S. Morgan west to Centre Ave.

Tinkham Ave. (W. D.), Kinzie north to North Ave.

Todd (S. D.), 2100 Grove northwest one block.

Torrence Ave. (H. P.), 742 95th south to 99th.

Tower Pl. (N. D.), 379 Chicago Ave. north to Pearson.

Town (N. D.), 249 Blackhawk north to North Ave.

Townes Ct. (N. D.), 194 North Ave. south one-half block.

Townsend (N. D.), 55 Erie north to Division.

Tracy Ave. (L.), 423 43d south to 57th.

Tremont (W. D.), 265 Spaulding Ave. west to Homan Ave.

Tremont (L.), Stewart Ave. west to Wallace.

Troy N. (W. D.), Kinzie north to Chicago Ave.

Troy S. (W. D.), 240 Colorado Ave. south to 31st.

Trumbull Ave. S. (W. D.), 426 Colorado Ave. south to 27th.

Trumbull Ave. N. (W. D.), Kinzie north to Chicago Ave.

Truro (W. D.), 761 S. Albany Ave. west to Kedzie Ave.

Trustee (W. D.), 551 Kinzie north to Austin Ave.

Tucker (S. D.), 895 35th south to 39th.

Turner (L. V.), N. Hoyne Ave. east to N. Robey.

Turner Ave. (W. D.), 1702 12th south to 24th.

Tuttle Ave. (L. V.), C. & N. W. R. R. east to N. Clark.

Twelfth (S. D.), Indiana Ave. west to the river.

Twelfth W. (W. D.), the river west to city limits.

Twentieth (S. D.), the lake west to Grove.

Twentieth W. (W. D.), Blair west to Albany Ave.

Twenty-first (S. D.), the lake west to Stewart Ave.

Twenty-first (W. D.), S. Jefferson west to St. Louis Ave.

Twenty-second (S. D.), the lake west to the river.

Twenty-second (W. D.), the river west to Ogden Ave.

Twenty-second Pl. (S. D.), 2233 Archer Ave. east to Wentworth Ave.

Twenty-third (S. D.), the lake west to Archer Ave.

Twenty-third (W. D.), 1071 Kedzie Ave. west to Hamlin Ave.

Twenty-third Pl. (S. D.), Wentworth Ave. west to Archer Ave.

Twenty-fourth (S. D.), the lake west to Butler.

Twenty-fourth (W. D.), 1129 S. Kedzie Ave. west to Crawford Ave.

Twenty-fourth Pl. (S. D.), Archer Ave. east to Wentworth Ave.

Twenty-fifth (S. D.), the lake west to Sanger.

Twenty fifth (W. D.), California Ave. west to city limits.

Twenty-fifth Ct. (W. D.), California Ave. west to Sacramento Ave.

Twenty-fifth Pl. (S. D.), Halsted east to Wentworth Ave.

Twenty-sixth (S. D.), 2600 Cottage Grove Ave. west to Halsted.

Twenty-sixth (W. D.), 1251 S. Western Ave. west to Crawford Ave.

Twenty-seventh (S. D.), the lake west to Quarry.

Twenty-seventh (W. D.), 1311 S. Kedzie Ave. west to Crawford Ave.

Twenty-eighth (S. D.), the lake west to Halsted.

Twenty-eighth (W. D.), 1357 Sacramento Ave. west to Whipple.

Twenty-ninth (S. D.), the lake west to Halsted.

Twenty-ninth (W. D.), 1381 S. Western Ave. west to California Ave.

Twomey (N. D.), 288 Sedgwick northwest one block.

Tyson Ave. (L. V.), 324 School north to Cornelia.

Uhland (N. D.), 151 Clybourn Ave. southwest to N. Halsted.

Ullman (S. D.), 971 31st south to 39th.

Union N. (W. D.), 155 Randolph north to Erie.

Union S. (W. D.), 155 Randolph south to Lumber.

Union Pl. (W. D.), 1057 Congress south to Harrison.

Union Park Pl. (W. D.), 522 Lake north to Arbor Pl.

University Pl. (S. D.), 3432 Cottage Grove Ave. west to Rhodes Ave.

Upton (W. D.), 1486 Milwaukee Ave. southwest to Western Ave.

Utica (W. D.), 1510 Fillmore south to 12th.

Van Buren (S. D.), Michigan Ave. west to the river.

Van Buren W. (W. D.), the river west to 46th.

Van Buren (L. V.), Bryn Mawr north to Peterson Ave.

Van Horn (W. D.), 577 Laflin west to Washtenaw Ave.

Vedder (N. D.), 525 Halsted east to Division.

Vermont Ave. (S. D.), 31st south to 33d.

Vernon Ave. (S. D. and H. P.), 68 29th south to 73d.

Vernon Park Pl. (W. D.), 201 Center Ave. west to Loomis.

Victor (L. V.), Swift southeast and east to Evanston Ave.

Vilas Ave. (L. V.), N. Leavitt east to Wright.

Vincennes Ave. (S. D. and H. P.), 3500 Cottage Grove Ave. southwest to 51st.

Vincennes Ave. (L.), State and 68th southwest to 87th.

Vine (N. D.), 215 Division north to Rees.

Virginia (W. D.), 181 Rebecca southwest to 16th.

Wabansia Ave. (W. D.), McHenry west to limits.

Wabansia Ave. E. (N. D.), the river northeast to Clybourn Ave.

Wabash Ave. (S. D.), S. Water south to 87th.

Wade (W. D.), 123 Elston Ave. northwest to Crittenden.

Waldo Pl. (W. D.), 21 S. Desplaines west to Halsted.

Walker Ct. (W. D.), 508 18th north one-half block.

Wall (S. D.), 947 31st south to Springer Ave.

Wallace (S. D.), 2399 Archer Ave. southeast to 87th.

Wallace Ave. (W. D.), 453 Humboldt Boul. north to Avondale Ave.

Walleck Pl. (W. D.), C., B. & Q. R. R. south to 18th.

Waller (W. D.), 370 12th south to 14th.

Walnut (W. D.), 21 N. Ashland Ave. west to Western Ave.

Walnut (L. V.), N. Robey east to N. Clark.

Walsh Ct. (W. D.), 727 S. May west to Centre Ave.

Walter (H. P.), stock yards track south to 40th.

Walton Pl. (N. D.), 330 Clark east to the lake.

Ward (N. D.), 666 Clybourn Ave. northeast to Fullerton Ave.

Ward (L. V.), 1036 Dunning north to Diversey.

Ward (S. D.), Bross Ave. south to 39th.

Ward Ave. (L.), 39th south to 50th.

Ward Ct. (W. D.), 401 Lumber west to Jefferson.

Warren Ave. (W. D.), 77 Ogden Ave. west to limits.

Warsaw Ave. (W. D.), 1707 N. California Ave. west to Thomas Ave.

Washburne Ave. (W. D.), 15 Waller west to S. Oakley Ave.

Washington (S. D.), Michigan Ave. west to the river.

Washington (W. D.), the river west to S. Halsted.

Washington Boul. (W. D.), S. Halsted west to city limits.

Washington (L. V.), Robey east to Ravenswood Park.

Washington Ave. (H. P.), 4842 Lake Ave. south to 59th.

Washington Pl. (N. D.), 292 Clark east to Dearborn Ave.

Washtenaw Ave. S. (W. D.), 1138 Wilcox Ave. south to Archer Ave.

Washtenaw Ave. N. (W. D.), 1206 Lake north to Armitage Ave.

Waterville (S. D.), 1077 32d southeast to Fox.

Waubun Ave. (L. V.), 1860 Surf north to Belmont Ave.

Waver (S. D.), 2420 Archer Ave. west one block.

Waverly Pl. (W. D.), 439 Madison north to Washington.

Wayman (W. D.) 86 N. Jefferson west to N. Halsted.

Weage Ave. (W. D.), 723 N. Kedzie Ave. west to Homan Ave.

Webb Ave.(L.), see Spaulding Ave.

Webber Ave. (L. V.), 3692 N. Robey east to Clark.

Webster Ave. (N. D.), the river east to Lincoln Park.

Webster Ave. (W. D.), 945 Elston Ave. west to Leavitt.

Webster Ave. (L. V.), Western Ave. east to Clark.

Webster Ave. (L.), 69th south to 84th.

Weed (N. D.), 334 Hooker northeast to Hawthorne Ave.

Weed Ct. (N. D.), 256 Clybourn Ave. northeast one-half block.

Wellington Ave. (L. V.), C. & N.-W. Ry east to the lake.

Wellington Pl. (H. P.), 46th north one-half block.

Wells N. (N. D.), the river north to Lincoln Park.

Wendell (N. D.), 187 Sedgwick east to Wells.

Wentworth Ave. (S. D.), 259 16th south to 85th.

Werder (W. D.), 627 N. Rockwell west to California Ave.

Westcott Ct. (L.), 80th west one-half block.

Wesson (N. D.), 39 Chicago Ave. north to Division.

West Ct. (L. V.), 1833 Belmont Ave. south one-half block.

West Water N. (W. D.), 5 Randolph north to Indiana.

West Water S. (W. D.), 5 Randolph south to Madison.

Western Ave. N. (W. D. and L. V.,) 1012 Lake north to limits.

Western Ave. S. (W. D. and L. V.), 1012 Lake south to 87th.

Wharf (W. D.), Lumber southeast to the river.

Wharton Ave. (H. P.), 498 51st south to 67th.

Wheaton (W. D.), 575 N. Kedzie Ave. west one block.

Wheelock Ave. (L.), 75th south two blocks.

Whipple (W. D.), 170 Colorado Ave. south to 28th.

Whitehouse (W. D.), 1431 S. Kedzie Ave. west to Crawford Ave.

Whitehouse Pl. (S. D.), 3000 Wentworth Ave. west to Stewart Ave.

Whiting (N. D.), 276 Market east to Wells.

Wieland (N. D.), 137 Schiller north to North Ave.

Wilcox Ave. (W. D.), 145 S. Oakley Ave. west to Sacramento Ave.

Will (W. D.), 567 Milwaukee Ave. north to Augusta.

Willard Pl. (W. D.), 361 Washington north to Randolph.

William (S. D.), Rockwell west to Kedzie Ave.

William Ave. (W. D.), 661 N. Central Park Ave. west to Hamlin Ave.

Willow (N. D.), 491 Larrabee west to Clybourn Ave.

Wilmot Ave. (W. D.), 883 N. Robey west to Hoyne Ave.

Wilson (W. D.), 29 Stewart Ave. west to S. Jefferson.

Wilson Ave. (L. V.), Leavitt east to Halsted.

Wilton Ave. (L. V.), 1426 Nellie Ave. north to Grace.

Willis Ct. (W. D.), 651 13th south to R. R. track.

Winchester Ave. (W. D.), 758 Madison south to 12th.

Winchester Ave. (L.), 46th south 87th.

Windsor Ave. (L. V.), Sheffield Ave. east to Halsted.

Winneconna (L.), Stewart Ave. southwest to Goldsmith.

Winter (L.), 39th south to 79th.

Winthrop Ave. (L. V.), Lawrence Ave. north to Thorndale Ave.

Winthrop Pl. (W. D.), 522 Polk south to Taylor.

Wisconsin (N. D.), 819 Clark west to Larrabee.

Wolcott (L. V.), 460 Belmont Ave. north to Balmoral.

Wolfram (L. V.), 1500 Ashland Ave. east to Halsted.

Wood N. (W. D.), 674 Lake north to Webster Ave.

Wood S. (W. D.), 674 Lake south to 71st.

Woodland Ave. (W. D.), Douglas Park Boul. south to 16th.

Woodland Park (S. D.), 3411 Cottage Grove Ave. east one block.

Woodlawn Ave. (H. P.), 4438 Lake Ave. south to 81st.

Woodside Ave. (L. V.), School north to Graceland Ave.

Work (L.), State west to Railroad.

Worthen Ave. (W. D.), 1256 Ogden Ave. south to 21st.

Wright (W. D.), 115 Stewart Ave. west to Morgan.

Wright (W. D.), 99 North Ave. northwest two blocks.

Wright (L.), 39th south to 87th.

Wright (L. V.), Centre north to Balmoral Ave.

Wright Ave. (L. V.), Sulzer north to Lawrence Ave.

Wright Pl. (W. D.), 143 Grand Ave. north to Huron.

Wrightwood Ave. (L. V.), Clybourn Ave. east to Lake View Ave.

Yale (L.), 63d south to 85th.

Yates Ave. (H. P.), 71st south to 75th.

1 A

Yeaton (W. D.), 513 S. Wood west to Lincoln.

York (W. D.), 171 Laflin west to Wood.

York Pl. (L. V.), 1454 Clark east to Evanston Ave.

Yorktown (S. D.), Bross Ave. south to 35th.

Zion Pl. (W. D.), 633 Throop west to Loomis.

Street Railway Routes.— The routes of the street cars cover quite conveniently a large proportion of Chicago's territory. Almost any section of the city can be reached within a half dozen blocks, by some one of the great division companies. On the South Side, the Wabash Avenue and Cottage Grove Avenue line and its connections follows more or less closely the lake coast on the extreme east to Hyde Park, and the South Side parks. The State Street cars run between this line and the Wentworth Avenue line on the west, as far south as Englewood, while the Archer Avenue line runs southwest into the lumber and packing district. In the west division, the Halsted Street cars north and south, the Milwaukee Avenue, the North Avenue to Humboldt Park; the Clybourn Avenue, the Ogden Avenue, the Indiana Street, the Lake Street, the Randolph Street, the Madison Street, the Adams Street, the Van Buren Street, the Harrison Street, and the Twelfth Street lines all cross the city in a westerly direction, commencing on the South Side. On the North Side there are the Clark Street, Wells Street, Sedgwick Street, and Larrabee Street lines running in a northerly direction, and connected by a network of other lines trending west and northwest. A traveler can start from the neighborhood of the City Hall, and find transportation any whither about the city. In this list of routes, we must not omit to mention the Lake Street elevated road, and the South Side alley elevated road, both likely soon to be completed, nor the Calumet Electric Railway, and the Chicago & Proviso Street Railway Company, who are also running electric motors. In proportion to her extent, no city in the Union has a more extended or better street car service, either in mileage or in convenience from business center to residence portion. On the main lines, all-night service is offered. We lack only the rapid transit of the elevated lines to make us happy.

Street Railway Service.— Frequent and rapid communication between the centers of trade and residence districts of cities is indispensable to their continued growth. That Chicago has kept up and is keeping up with other cities in this regard is apparent to all.

From the date of the first ordinance for a street railway on State Street, from Randolph Street to the southern city limits, on March 4, 1856 to the present time, there has been a succession of extensions until there are now 395.30 miles of street railways, horse, cable, electric, and elevated. Under an ordinance passed by the city council August 16, 1858, the CHICAGO CITY RAILWAY COMPANY laid track on State Street from Lake Street to Madison Street, and early in the spring of 1859, the track was extended to Twelfth Street, and from this beginning its lines have been from time to time extended until now they make a total length of 152.95 miles. In 1881, realizing the impossibility of serving the people by means of horse cars, 8 miles of cable track were laid on State Street from Madison to Thirty-ninth streets, which was open to

travel June 28, 1882. In the following year, track was laid on Wabash and Cottage Grove avenues, making a total of 20½ miles, operated from one power house located at Twenty-first and State streets, with 1,000 horse-power engines. The growth of business has been so great that the Company has been compelled to increase its machinery plant to 10,000 horse-power, driving 38.83 miles of cable. On the horse-car lines 2,508 horses are now in service, while the cable plants are doing the work of 7,500 horses more, with 1,250 cars.

June 1, 1868, the Board of Trustees of the village of Hyde Park passed an ordinance granting the right to operate over certain streets of the village to the Chicago and Calumet Horse and Dummy Railroad Company. This was practically the Chicago City Railway Company, and the track was soon laid on Fifty-ninth Street and Cottage Grove Avenue, as far north as Thirty-ninth Street. The system of transfers established by this company has been of much importance and has added greatly to the comfort and convenience of passengers. The longest ride over the line is about thirteen miles for a single fare of 5 cents. The Chicago City Railway Company which operates the South Side cable system, during 1890 carried 68,734,969 passengers, producing a revenue to the company of $3,436,748; of this $2,311,455 was earned by the cable cars, and $1,125,293 by the horse cars. The cost of operating the road was $2,297,657, leaving for net earnings $1,139,097. The cost of operating per mile per car was by cable 9.650 cents, by horses 21.985 cents. Number of miles run by cable, 12,740,480; number of miles run by horses, 4,859,200.

NORTH CHICAGO STREET RAILROAD COMPANY.—The first franchise granted for a street railroad on the

North Side was on May 23, 1859, and construction was soon begun on Wells Street from North Water Street to Chicago Avenue. The street was at that time planked and a T rail was laid thereon. Soon after a track was laid on Clark Street as far north as Division Street. In 1864 a steam dummy was started on Evanston Avenue, running from Diversey Street to Graceland Cemetery, a distance of about three miles. This continued to 1881, when horses were substituted. When the present management took control of the North Side system in 1886, there were thirty-five miles of track in operation and 1,850 horses; now there are 80.3 miles of track and 1,420 horses, with 3,200 horse-power supplied by engines driving 56,500 feet of cable. In 1890, a storage electric motor was given a trial which bids fair to be a great success. This machine may be adopted on some of the roads ere long.

In 1862, the West Side Railroad Company had about five miles of track, some twenty cars, and 120 horses and mules. In 1887 there were 4,327 horses in use. In the spring of 1887 they began to lay cable track on West Madison Street and Milwaukee Avenue, starting the same in August, 1890, displacing 600 horses on Madison Street, 350 horses on Milwaukee Avenue. These horses were immediately transferred to the shorter lines, increasing the number of cars and giving the people improved service. The power used at present is 2,000 horse-power at the Rockwell Street station, and 2,000 horse-power at the Cleaver Street station, and 500 horse-power at the Jefferson Street power house. The earnings of the North Chicago Street Railway Company in 1890 were $1,-972,172; expenses $1,103,276; net earnings $868,899; car mileage for the same year 6,774,103. Number of passengers carried 39,481,445; number of trips made 1,080,975. Several important extensions of the North Side system are being pushed forward at this time.

West Chicago Street Railroad Company.—This company operates the West Side horse and cable system of railways, including the lines of the Chicago Passenger Railway Company. The West Side cable system consists of two lines: the Madison Street line, which runs directly west, and the Milwaukee Avenue line, which runs northwest. Both lines connect with the downtown loop. The power for the operation of the system is supplied from three distinct power houses, all of which are supplied with the best machinery that could be obtained. The principal power house is located at Madison and Rockwell streets. It contains two 1,200 horse-power engines, and one of these is going night and day, while the other is held in reserve in case of an accident. The cable running west to Fortieth Street is driven at the rate of 14 miles an hour, while the one running east is driven 10½ miles an hour; the speed of either of them, however, can be increased at will. There is in addition a Corliss engine to propel a loop rope in the power house, by means of which the cars can be reversed at Rockwell Street. The power house itself is an attractive structure, lighted by electricity, and surmounted by a smoke stack 178 feet high.

The Milwaukee Avenue Line.—The Milwaukee Avenue power house is located at the corner of Cleaver Street. It is supplied with two Corliss engines of 1,200 horse-power each. Those two engines operate the entire Milwaukee Avenue system, which extends from Jefferson to Washington streets, to Armitage Avenue. The west-end rope is driven at the rate of 12 miles an hour, while the east-end rope is moved at the rate of 10½ miles, as with the Madison Street cables. Their speed, however, can be increased or lessened at will.

The tunnel loop is operated · from the third power house. This house is located at the corner of Jefferson and Washington streets, and is where the company's offices are to be found. This station is furnished with two 500-horse power Wetherell-Corliss engines, which are used to operate the Washington Street Tunnel loop. The cars of both the Madison Street and Milwaukee Avenue lines are delivered to the cable at this station, and by it they are drawn through the tunnel, and around the loop. The service of this particular cable is very exacting. At times the heavily loaded trains are but a few seconds apart, yet there is seldom, or ever any cause for complaint, so perfect are all the details. The dynamos for lighting the tunnel are also located at this point, as it is also the base of an electric signal system which extends along the several cable lines. By this system the conductor or gripman can communicate with the power-house or offices at any time, which is an adjunct of almost incalculable advantage in keeping the tracks clear, and stopping the machinery in case of an accident.

The gross receipts of this company for 1890, were $3,663,381; operating expenses, $2,202,767; net income, $1,460,613; fixed charges, $755,749. The number of passengers carried during the year, was 75,152.694. The cost of carrying each passenger, averaged 2.93 cents. The number of miles traveled by the cars, was 12,-215,903, an increase of 15.57 per cent. over the previous year.

Blue Island Avenue, the great southwestern thoroughfare of the city, will also be cabled by this company during the next year. The company are also at work on a tunnel under the south branch of the Chicago River, between Jackson and Van Buren streets, which will be used for cable car purposes when completed, which will be early in 1892.

CALUMET ELECTRIC STREET RAILWAY.—The first electric street railway within the limits of Chicago, started October 2, 1890, and is now in operation, running from the South Chicago Rolling Mills by way of Eighty-ninth Street, Mackinaw Avenue, Harbor Avenue, Ninety-third Street, and Stony Island Avenue to Ninety-fifth Street. The construction of two additional miles is now under way on Ninety-third Street, from Stony Island Avenue to Cottage Grove Avenue and north to Eighty-seventh Street. These lines are but the beginning of an extensive system at South Chicago to connect the manufacturing and residence suburbs which now lack proper means of communication. The Rae electric system is used, the power-house being located alongside the Chicago & Western Indiana Railroad. The generating plant consists of one 65,000 Watt rail generator, driven directly by 125-horse power engine.

THE SOUTH CHICAGO CITY RAILWAY COMPANY propose to change their plant from horse to electric power this year. On July 10, 1885, their road was completed on One Hundred and Sixth Street, from Torrence Avenue to Ewing Avenue to Ninety-second Street, a distance of three miles. In 1886 an extension was completed on Ninety-second Street from Harbor Avenue to Commercial Avenue, and on Commercial Avenue to One Hundred and Fourth Street, on One Hundred and Fourth Street to Torrence Avenue, and south to One Hundred and Sixth Street, about three miles. In 1890, two miles of old track was taken up and relaid entirely new.

THE CICERO AND PROVISO ELECTRIC STREET RAILWAY have recently completed about five miles of track on West Madison Street, West Forty-eighth Street, and West Lake Street. The Sprague overhead system is used.

ELEVATED ROADS.—Surface street railways for a time meet the requirements of cities, but as the population of cities increases, and the limits of the city are extended, they are gradually overtaxed, and the time consumed in transit becomes a practical bar to their further extension. These difficulties are now being seriously felt in Chicago.

CHICAGO & SOUTH SIDE RAPID TRANSIT COMPANY.—Profiting by the experience of New York, it was decided, by the proprietors of this road, that instead of constructing the road through the public streets, thus subjecting the company to suits for damages from all abutting owners, they would endeavor to acquire a right of way through private property by condemnation or by friendly purchase, thus fixing, and limiting at the outside, and for all time to come, the maximum cost. Having decided upon this course, the ground was carefully examined, with a view of locating where the line would be easily accessible, while doing the least damage to property, and the location was selected between Wabash Avenue and State Street, hence it is called the "Alley Elevated Road." A north and south alley runs nearly all the way between these streets, and a strip of land parallel with and adjoining the alley was acquired at a moderate cost. The company began to secure the right of way soon after the authorization by the City Council, but it was not until December,

1889, that these preliminaries were sufficiently advanced to permit the erection of the iron superstructure, and, since that time, some two miles have been substantially completed, and the right of way secured for the third mile. The company hopes to open the first section of its road to the public during the present year.

LAKE STREET ELEVATED RAILWAY COMPANY.—This company secured its right of way on Lake Street, from Market Street, west, and is now negotiating for a loop line east of Market Street.

The structure consists of latticed iron columns, set at the curb line of the street, connected by girders six feet deep. The cross-girders are connected by a girder under each rail. At present two tracks are laid, but two additional tracks can be added at any time without any change of the present structure. Construction of foundations began September 21, 1889, and has been pushed, since then, as fast as the obstacles, which always beset new undertakings, could be overcome.

The western, northwestern, and southwestern terminals of this road are still a matter of doubt. The motive power will be twenty-eight ton engines, provided with drop-pans and anti-friction journals, being used, as far as practical, all night.

Streets, Mileage of.—The mileage of the streets laid out within the City of Chicago at the first of the present year is as follows: Old city, including sections 25, 35, and 36, 40, 13; sections 25, 40, 13, and annexed parts of former town of Cicero, 853.-87 miles; former city of Lake View, 131.53 miles; former town of Jefferson, 242.28 miles; former village of Hyde Park, 541.94 miles; former town of Lake, 347.09 miles; Gano, Washington Heights, West Roseland, and part of Calumet, 119 miles; total, 2,235.71 miles. Boulevards laid out, 50 miles; viaduct approaches, 1.15 miles; grand total, 2,286.86 miles. At the present ratio, about fifty miles of street frontage per year is covered with buildings. This ratio will unquestionably increase from year to year. If this result is obtained it will require but another decade for Chicago to rank as the first city in America.

Studios.—There are about 500 professional artists in Chicago, and the majority of these have handsome, and many magnificent, studios.

On the seventh floor of the new Athenæum Building are fourteen excellent studios, fitted up for the use of the Society of Artists. In the Howland Block, on Dearborn Street, are the studios of several very prominent artists; and there are other studios in the Lakeside Building, and·in many other business blocks.

Sub-Treasury.—The Chicago branch of the United States Treasury does an immense business. The receipts for the fiscal year ending June 30 were $77,584,354.60, and the disbursements $76,321,587.76. The increase in receipts over the year previous was $10,535,920.56, and the increase in disbursements $12,101,-128.61. This money came from the internal revenue and customs departments, post offices, in a number of Western States, and other minor departments of the Government. Of the money paid out, about $8,000,000 went to pensioners.

Suburban Rapid Transit.—All the suburbs of Chicago, whether those villages now inside the limits, or those at greater distances, are easily reached by rail. An almost countless series of suburban trains are always speeding in and out of the city, and many outlying towns can be reached from the City Hall in

less time than many parts of the city proper. In the villages themselves but little has been done, however, in the way of rapid transit, except by the people of the towns lying west of the center of the city. An electric railroad—"The Cicero and Proviso" —has been constructed, and, affording easy connections with the city, and between the villages of Austin, Oak Park, River Forest, and Ridgeland, is well patronized and extremely profitable.

Summer Gardens. — Closely entwined with Chicago's growth and manners are many customs that did not come over in the "Mayflower," and in tracing their origin we find them of decided Teutonic color. Among these is the German's habit of seeking the public parks, with his entire family, on Sunday. It is a mighty poor holiday for him if the good wife and children are not by to help him enjoy it; but if he can't go to the park, then he goes to the nearest "summer garden," consisting, in the majority of cases, of a few square feet of land attached to some saloon, in which are several evergreen trees in boxes, some plants, and a band. As a usual thing, these bands are not ordinary players, because a German is a born musician. Here he sits and drinks his beer, and laughs and chats with his wife and his neighbors, and smokes his pipe, and lets the little ones taste the beer and get stifled in the smoke. There are more pretentious places, but the same causes and conditions underlie them all.

Swedenborgian (New Jerusalem) Churches.—The following is a list of the names and locations of those in Chicago:

New Church Temple, Van Buren street, east of Wabash Ave.

German Congregation, 410 W. Chicago Ave.

Tax-payers' Association. — This is an organization of many of the leading and representative citizens, who meet the first Friday of each month, at Farwell Hall. The one object of the association is to see that no abuses exist in the assessment levy and collection of taxes. The association has been instrumental in having rebates from special assessments refunded to many tax-payers, who would otherwise have remained in ignorance that the city owed them anything.

Telegraph Offices.—The two great telegraph lines in the United States practically monopolize the business, and the Western Union controls the Atlantic and Pacific Company, so the two virtually form but one line. The main office of the Western Union is on Washington street, corner of La Salle. During the day and early evening all the principal hotels, exchanges, railway stations, and many prominent points throughout the city have instruments in active operation. In messages transmitted over these telegraph lines the "body" words of the message, only, are charged for, the date, address, and signatures of messages being transmitted free. Figures are always to be written out in words. Whatever the rate for transmission may be, for every additional word about two-thirds of the rate for each of the first ten words is charged; but nothing less than ten words is ever charged. Another and lower rate is made for cross-city messages. In cable messages to Great Britain, Ireland, France, the Channel Islands, and Germany, each word written by the sender for transmission is counted as one word, including the place from, the date, and signature, if the sender chooses to write one, or all of these usual addenda. In messages going to all places beyond Great Britain and France, Germany excepted, also excepting the "place to," in the addresses of messages to South America, words containing ten or less than ten letters, are counted as one word, and words containing more than ten letters are counted ten letters, and the fraction thereof as one word, and charged for. The extra charge thus made applies only to the lines beyond the countries named. The ten-letter limit does not affect the charges between America and Great Britain, Ireland, and France.

Telephones.—Chicago, like the capital of the nation, is a "city of magnificent distances," and its business men are incessantly seeking "short cuts," to compass the labor constantly increasing, as the trade and manufactures are augmented. If it was a street-car, they took it; or a telegraph line, they connected with it, or run a private wire. But the telephone is the thing that has found more favor in the eyes of the business men of this city than any other invention. When a man can talk with his neighbor in his office, without going outside of his own, it is indeed a boon, and eagerly seized upon by every man who can pay the extortionate prices demanded by a grasping monopoly. It would be safe to say that there are more telephones in use here than in any other city of the Union, in proportion to the number of inhabitants. It really doubles the working time of one-tenth the population, by saving that which was formerly wasted in traveling from one part of the city to another in doing business.

Temperance Temple.—The Woman's Temperance Temple, now partially completed, will be one of the notable buildings of Chicago. It is located on the southwest corner of La Salle and Monroe streets. Its foundations measure 190 feet on the former street, and 96 feet on the latter street. It is a steel, fire-proof building, the first two stories being faced with a rich, dark-red granite, and the remaining stories, to the cornice, with a fine pressed brick, made to order, of a new and corresponding tint. The architecture is described as French Gothic. The La Salle Street front bears a very striking resemblance to the Adams Street front of the Pullman building. Its general ground-plan is somewhat in the shape of the letter H. The building consists of two immense wings, united by a narrower middle portion, called a vinculum. In this wing there will be a central court, seventy feet long and thirty feet deep, on the La Salle Street front, and. a similar court, eighteen feet deep, on the west side of the building, designed to admit light and promote ventilation, as well as a feature of beauty. The La Salle Street front is made continuous to a lofty stone arch, which spans the court, and forms the main entrance. The four corners presented to La Salle Street have a rounded-turret treatment, and the intermediate windows in the front of each wing are grouped under a broad arch on the next story. The steep roof is broken into terraces, marking the three stories above the cornice, each of which has its strikingly beautiful Gothic windows. From the roof of the vinculum rises a graceful, gold-bronze fleche, to the height of seventy additional feet, surmounted with a symbolical figure of a woman, with face upturned, and arm outstretched as if in prayer. The architectural effect of the whole design, therefore, is exceedingly temple-like.

The building will cost $1,100,000, and the ground is almost equally as valuable. It will be completed May

1, 1892, the same day on which the Masonic Temple is to be completed. That two such temples should be completed the same day, is somewhat remarkable.

This enterprise is the undertaking of the Woman's Temperance Building Association, of which Mrs. Matilda B. Carse is the head. It will be devoted to the temperance work, and also be used for office and business purposes.

Temperature. —The temperature of Chicago is not only very variable from day to day, but has a range during the year of from 15° to 101°. Not infrequently it will vary in one day 20°, and it behooves strangers to be prepared for these changes. Chicagoans, somewhat acclimated and proverbially rash, rarely take measures to protect themselves; hence, the large percentage of pulmonary diseases found in the death-rate (See *Vital Statistics*). The following data are from observations taken by the Signal Service Department of the Government: The mean temperature, for the past year, was 48.8°. This is about the average for the past ten years. The maximum for the year was 96° (August 2d), and the minimum 5° below zero (January 22d), being a range of 101°. Rain or snow fell upon 136 days, to the amount of 32.66 inches. The greatest atmospheric pressure, 30.74 inches, occurred on January 3d; the least, 29.29 inches, on January 12th; being a range of 1.45 inches. The mean was 30.048. The mean relative humidity was 74.8.

Tenement-Houses. — A tenement-house in Chicago is defined by law as: "Every house, building, or portion thereof, which is rented, leased, let, or hired out to be occupied as the home, or residence of more than three families, living indepen-

249   TEN—TER

deutly of one another, and doing
their cooking on the premises; or by
more than two families upon a floor,
so living, and cooking, but having a
common right in the halls, stairways,
yards, water-closets, or privies, or
some of them." The special laws relating to them provide for a fire-
escape for each separate family, for
the proper ventilation of sleeping-
apartments and halls, and for many
other things necessary to cleanliness
and health. The law has done some
good, but still there are many tenement-houses in the city that should
not be allowed to exist; they are
overcrowded and exceedingly filthy.
Especially is this true of those in the
famous "Levee" district. As an evidence of the number of tenement-
houses, the Health Department, in its
report of 1890, says: "During the year
the Tenement-house and Factory-in-
spection Department examined 23,142
buildings and houses, containing
121,938 persons; 22,877 workshops,
with 259,051 employés; served 12,-
675 notices; abated 12,178 nuisances;
3,110 cases of defective plumbing;
and 1,406 cases of defective drainage."

**Territorial Growth of Chi-
cago.**—Chicago became the county
seat of Cook in 1831, and in 1833 its
inhabitants voted to assume the
functions of an incorporated town.
The land commissioners had defined
the boundaries as State, Halsted,
Madison, and Kenzie streets—one-
half of one square mile—but the
newly organized town at once extended itself to Jackson Street on the
south, and Ohio Street on the north,
this first annexation adding about
three-eighths of one square mile.
The second annexation in 1835,
carried the town lines to Twelfth
Street on the south, and Chicago
Avenue on the north—a very considerable addition—Halsted Street

remaining the western boundary.
Then came the incorporation of the
City of Chicago, in 1837, with
boundaries extended to Twenty-
second Street on the south, Wood
Street on the west, and North Avenue on the north. The first city
annexation, in 1847, carried the
western line to Western Avenue, and
made Fullerton (east of Sedgwick)
the north line. The second city
annexation in 1853, carried the Fullerton Avenue line from the lake
to the north branch of the river;
made Thirty-first Street the south
line east of Halsted, and swept in
Canalport. The third city annexation, in 1863, further carried the
Fullerton Avenue line to Western
Avenue, and made Thirty-ninth
Street the south boundary. The
fourth city annexation, in 1869,
added a strip of two miles, on the
west, to Crawford Avenue. At this
time the city embraced about forty-
four square miles of territory, and in
this shape the city map remained
until the annexation proceedings of
the last three years, which began,
apparently, with the feeble cry of
Section 36, in the town of Jefferson,
and which, with a history that need
not be here reviewed, has culminated
in the sweeping work of June 29,
1889. On that day, by a vote of the
citizens, the city of Lake View, and
the towns of Hyde Park, Lake,
Jefferson, and Cicero, aggregating
128.24 square miles of territory, and
about 220,000 people, were annexed to,
and became part of Chicago, thus constituting a city extending twenty-
four miles from north to south, and
from four to four and one-half miles
from east to west. During the year
1890 there were annexed to the city
four suburbs—South Englewood, area
2.92 square miles; population, 3,000.
Gano, 1.80 square miles; population,
2,600. Washington Heights, 2.8
square miles; population, 3,315.

West Roseland, 1.80 square miles; population, 792; making a total annexation for the year of 9.32 square miles, with a population of 9,900. It will thus be seen that the territorial growth of Chicago has reached 181.70 square miles in 1891. Of this area 5.14 square miles are water, 176.56 land. The city is divided into thirty-four wards.

Theatres.—A feature of Chicago and notably so, is her amusements. This city now divides the honors with New York as a theatrical center. Stock companies and combinations are organized here. New plays receive their first production, and talent frequently makes its debut on the stages of the home theatres. In point of numbers, Chicago has more theatres and amusement-buildings than any other city of its size in the world. It is needless to say the character of the buildings and the quality of the amusements offered are the best that the age can produce.

The following is a list of the theatres in Chicago, the principal ones being treated of elsewhere, under separate heads:

Academy of Music, 83 South Halsted Street.

Alhambra, 1920 State Street.

Auditorium, corner of Wabash Avenue and Congress Street.

Chicago Opera House, 118 Washington Street, near Clark.

Clark Street Theatre, 43 North Clark Street,

Columbia Theatre, 108 Monroe Street.

Criterion Theatre, 274 Sedgwick Street.

Grand Opera House, 87 South Clark Street.

Halsted Street Theatre, 229 South Halsted Street.

Havlin's Theatre, 1840 Wabash Avenue.

Haymarket Theatre, 167 West Madison Street.

Hooley's Theatre, 149 Randolph Street.

Madison Street Theatre, 85 Madison Street.

Olympic Theatre, 51 South Clark Street.

Park Theatre, 325 State Street.

Paris Gaieties, 131 Michigan Ave.

People's Theatre, 339 State Street.

Standard Theatre, 169 South Halsted Street.

Waverly Theatre, 454 West Madison Street.

Windsor Theatre, 468 North Clark Street.

Timmerman's Opera House, corner Sixty-third Street and Stewart Avenue.

The Fair Sex—Nowhere in all the world has the intermingling of the strength, beauty, and intellect of the nations of the earth produced so perfect an *ensemble* as in the ladies of Chicago. They excel all their sisters in the fairness of their features, the perfection of their forms, and the vigor of their mental operations. In the cosmopolitan city of Chicago we have representatives of every race under the sun, and in the Chicago woman we have the perfected type of the whole. Notwithstanding slurs of envious, neighboring cities, the Chicagoenne is refined, dainty, and high-minded; as tasteful in her dress and appearance as a Parisienne. She is a quick-witted and brilliant conversationalist, an unequaled hostess; and, above all, a loyal wife and tender mother. She is first at the bedside of the sick and in comforting the distressed. She can also assist her husband in his business.

Theosophical Society.—This organization has, for its platform, three planks: First, to form the nucleus of a Universal Brotherhood of Humanity, without distinction of race, creed, or color. Second, to promote the study of Aryan and other Eastern literature, religions, and sciences. Third, to investigate unexplained laws of Nature, and the psychical powers of man. The parent society has its headquarters in India, with sections and branches throughout the whole world. The Chicago Theosophical Society has its headquarters at Room 30, 26 Van Buren Street, in the Athenæum building. The Chicago branch of the Theosophical Society meets here, every Saturday evening, at 8:00 P. M. Ramayana Theosophical Society, another branch of the parent society meets at 619 Jackson Boulevard, third flat, every Sunday afternoon, at 3:00 P. M. These meetings are open to all who are interested in Theosophical subjects.

Thieves in Chicago make up in industry what they lack in numbers and only the most unrelaxed watchfulness and care will suffice to protect you from the pickpocket, the hotel thief, the burglar, or most annoying and ubiquitous of all, the sneak-thief. Highway robbery is of comparatively rare occurrence, and the victims are usually belated diners-out much the worse for wine. Good bolts and bars in plenty will help to keep the burglar on the wrong side of the door; but watchfulness is an indispensable adjunct since the skill and ingenuity of the professional "Cracksman," exceed those of the most accomplished locksmith or safe-maker. Sneak-thieves usually obtain admittance to houses by making some plausible excuse and left alone in the hallway by the servant while she seeks an answer to their queries, they are off with all the hats, coats, and other portable articles within reach

before her return. They are always on the watch for a street door which is not protected by a chain and bolt, and are not infrequently in league with ostensible beggars who examine and report upon the fashioning of bolts and bars, or note their absence. It is a good rule never to leave one's hat or coat in a hallway, especially in a boarding or lodging-house. Another rule worth observing is never to deliver money or clothing upon a message from some member of the household, delivered by a stranger, as this is a common trick with sneak-thieves. It is not unjust to say, that except in cases where clews are apparent, or the value of the goods stolen sufficiently great to induce the offer of a reward, that a visit paid to the detective office is not likely to result in the recovery of stolen property or the detection of the thieves.

Thirteen Club, The, meets on the 13th of each month in room 13 of the Grand Pacific, and is sociable and charitable in purpose.

Tracy.—This beautiful suburb is only forty minutes ride from the city, by the Rock Island Road. It lies about one hundred feet above Lake Michigan, on a ridge crowned with fine oaks, has perfect drainage, pure spring water, and the best of society.

Titles.—All the abridged compilations of evidence as to the ownership of land, under the laws of Illinois, with any clouds or defects, in the shape of liens or encumbrances, which make up a record of title, are abstracts of title, in Western parlance. James H. Rees, as far as 1836, commenced making these abstracts of record, he being "Surveyor of the town of Chicago." Associating a lawyer, named Edward A. Rucker, with himself, about the year 1849, as Rees & Rucker; he inaugurated the present system. In 1852 Mr. Rucker retired and, Mr. Rees associated with himself his chief clerk, Samuel B. Chase, and soon after his two brothers, Horace G. and Charles Ç. Chase, were admitted into the firm. Mr. Rees retired, and the style of the firm name was changed to Chase Bros., and so remained until the great fire of 1871. Another set of these "tract indices," as these books were named, were opened in 1852 by Hasbrook Davis and J. Mason Parker, they did not make many abstracts, however, having prepared the books to sell, which they soon did to Thos. B. Bryan, who then sold a half interest to John Borden. Bryan & Borden at first leased their books to William W. Page, John G. Shortall, and Henry H. Handy, then they sold them to Greenebaum & Guthman. The business was continued under this title until they sold the books to John G. Shortall and John N. Staples, who made abstracts under the firm name of John G. Shortall & Co.; this was succeeded by Shortall & Hoard. Mr. Louis D. Hoard was an ex-county recorder for the County of Cook. About a month before the fire the books were leased to Henry H. Handy and Francis Pasdeloup. A third set of books were started by Fernando Jones & Co., who were succeeded by Jones & Sellers, Mr. Alfred H. Sellers being the active manager, until the fire. Besides these firms, there were quite a number of persons who could make up reliable abstracts from the public records and tract indices. One of the most reliable of these was A. T. C. Mueller, under the firm name of Mueller & Hawley, did a great deal of good work, that is now accepted as trustworthy. The fire also

shelved this firm. A. D. Wilmanns, until the close of the war, also furnished his customers with abstracts from the public indices. Part of this time he had the use of the Chase Brothers' books. During this period he was associated with Francis Pasdeloup, as Wilmanns & Pasdeloup. Just before the fire, a new firm, Handy & Pasdeloup, leased the Shortall & Hoard books, but the fire fiend nullified the lease. All the parties mentioned made abstracts which are good to-day in the real estate offices. There were a few other parties whose work on this line failed to inspire the necessary confidence in the public mind or the professional examiners.

It really seemed, on the morning of October 11, 1871, as if the whole chain of titles from the Government had ceased to exist. All the public records were destroyed, and the whole matter rested on the accuracy and amount of salvage of the work of the private abstract makers. But no firm had been able to save all their records. When they endeavored to continue business on their own account, as before the fire, they found it an impossibility, and the only possible way out was a compromise and combination, in order to make up a full set. The general public, with this experience of monopolies, thought they scented a trust, and kicked accordingly. But the pool of books was formed and then leased to Handy, Simmons & Co., who thus signed the abstracts then issued. This firm was succeeded by Handy & Co., and later were merged into "The Title Guarantee and Trust Co," which now controls all the books of abstracts for ante-fire dates in the county, and they have built for their special use a building amply supplied with vault-room, light, etc., on the old site on Washington Street. After the fire, Wilmanns & Pasdeloup, and, on the death of the latter, Wilmanns & Thielcke (Mr. Thielcke had been with Chase Bros. before the fire) commenced making up a set of post-fire books, running back to the memorable 9th of October, and thence onward. In 1875 they sold their books to the county, and they are now authority in the Recorder's office, under special legislative acts. In the winter of 1872-3, Charles G. Haddock, E. D. Coxe, and Frank H. Vallette began work upon a new set of books from the fire down. They issued abstracts signed Haddock, Coxe & Co., but this has been changed to Haddock, Vallette & Rickards. Mr. Rickards bought Mr. Coxe's interest. After the purchase of the Wilmanns & Thielcke books by the county, Gillmore, Pollock & Co. used these books for a year or more in making abstracts. In 1878, Otto Peltzer, who had published "Peltzer's Atlas of Chicago," and whose work for the county since 1853, as a professional draughtsman, had rendered him familiar with·land titles and records, resigned his position as Deputy Recorder and Superintendent of the County Abstract Department. He and a number of experts, formerly employed in the Recorder's office, united their efforts, hiring the use of Haddock,·Coxe & Co.'s books for six years, afterward using the county indices. Mr. Peltzer not only issued abstracts, ᵉ but wrote out a professional opinion of the title. So well was this done, and so sound was his judgment on the validity of title, that the increasing patronage has forced him, since 1888, to take up this line of work altogether, to the exclusion of the abstract making. The very latest new-comer in the abstract of title business, styles itself "The Cook County Abstract Company." This firm commenced operations in May, 1888, and is winning for itself busi-

ness. This list gives a full summary of all persons whose signatures, either individually or in firms, are likely to be found on any title records of Cook County, either before or since the Great Fire of 1871. It is not necessary for us to discuss the absolute necessity of a good title to every buyer of real estate.

Traits of the Native Chicagoan.—The native of Chicago is not the lean, sad, intense, subjective Yankee, nor the dilatory, fat, demonstrative dullard of the Susquehanna on the Hudson Valley; but he is always·florid, plethoric, laborious, well-fed, jolly, and complacent. A driving worker in day-light, a good sleeper of night, open, loquacious, communicative, generous, and gregarious. He is prone to do things in partnership, and loves to promote his particular trade, however small, by a show of promoting the city at large. If even he can not "see it," he is unwilling to have the fact suspected for the honor of commercially glorifying the city, is something in which the humblest Chicagoan desires to have a share. Not in prolix disquisition and droning precept, but in practical habit of thought and work, he comprehends division of labor, mutual dependence, and co-operation of effort. Whatever he has to do, he must first try the expediency of the idea by framing it into a co-operative plan. If it will not hold water on the joint stock principle, he accepts that proof of its unsoundness, and invents something else that will. Let this propensity stand on its own exalted footing. It has had an illustrious test. It is this, brought to settled habit long before the Great Fire, which accounts for the possibility of the following fact viz.: That a visitor to Chicago now, who had no knowledge of the place, would refuse to believe that a conflagration in 1871, had destroyed the greater part of the city which existed at that time.

The habits of the genuine Chicagoan are characteristic. He dines at noon, whether he is a banker or laborer, and eats three hearty meals a day; but not to collide with Eastern ways too directly, he calls his supper "dinner," and his dinner "lunch." The latter, if possible, he takes at a public house, during a period of ten minutes. He invariably wears a moustache, generally shaves his chin, gloves his hands only on dress occasions, keeps the sidewalk in business hours, unless to ride a mile, owns his horse and buggy for other times, if his income at all exceeds his subsistence; is a literary client of a daily paper; will forgive anything but diluted affectation; values his priest for his parochial energy and success; will apologize for profanity in his presence by swearing that he had never been so provoked in his life; and either expressly or tacitly connects with all manner of speech, an indication that he "means business."

Tremont House.—This is another grand architectural pile, and, in this respect, surpasses many other hotels. The interior is furnished most luxuriantly, and this, with its superb cuisine, makes it the headquarters for a large number of the substantial people who visit Chicago. The Tremont is now on the American plan, with rates ranging from $3 to $4 per day. The location is very convenient and central. It occupies the southeast corner of Lake and Dearborn streets. Proprietors, Alvin Hulbert and W. S. Eden.

Turners.—There are several "Turnvereins," or Turners' societies, in Chicago; all in a flourishing condition, and with a large and steadily increasing membership. The German inhabitants are particularly fond of the Turnverein, and other nationalities are beginning to evince interest in similar athletic societies. The "Turn Verein Vorwaerts" meets in a well-equipped hall, at No. 251 West Twelfth Street; the North Side Turnverein has a splendid home at 259 North Clark Street; the Lake View Turnverein meets on Lincoln Avenue, and several other Turner societies have headquarters in different parts of the city.

Typewriters.—The invention of various typewriting machines has brought this form of writing into very general use. Legal documents, authors' copy, business letters, etc., are now commonly typewritten. In nearly every office, where much writing is to be done, one or more machines are used. They are generally operated by young women, who are much more expert than men. In almost every large business building may be found an office, where typewriting is done for all customers who may come in. The usual rate is 5 cents per 100 words.

Uhlich Evangelical Orphan Asylum is at Burling and Center streets.

Undertakers.—For the information of strangers in Chicago, it may be said, that, in case of death, any undertaker will do all that is necessary, and required by law, in regard to death reports, burial permits, and the like, in addition to performing his usual offices.

Union Club, on the North Side, at Dearborn Avenue and Washington Park Place, own and occupy a club house, whose massive construction, original design, and model interior is a triumph of architectural splendor.

The club membership consists of gentlemen of affluence, who are recognized as the substantial citizens of Chicago. The design of the interior is modeled somewhat after the Colonial, or old English type, when the fire-places were capable of receiving the huge old back-log, and the hearth-stone was the gathering place for good cheer.

Union League Club occupies one of the handsomest buildings in the city. Architecturally, it is a grand pile. Its interior, of course, is on a scale of elegance, commensurate with the wealth and taste of its members, who are gentlemen of prominence in the community. The location is central, being just opposite the south end of the Custom House. The club was organized in 1879.

Union Park.—In 1853 Reuben Taylor took the initiatory step toward establishing this park, and this is how it was: Standing at the door of his old homestead, which stood a little north of what is now Park Avenue, he observed, one day, a surveying party dividing the site of Union Park into lots. He went over to Billy Carpenter's grocery store, near by, and complained about cutting the land up so. Mrs. Carpenter, who was leaning over the counter, overheard the conversation, and remarked: "If I was a man I would have a park there." Uncle Reuben and uncle Billy took kindly to the idea, and the former posted down to Hayes and Johnson's office to see what could be done. He found that they would sell it to the city for a park, at a reduced figure. He went home, drew up a petition, secured a number of signers, and sent it to the Common Council, and he and Mr. Carpenter went down to lobby it through. Opposition came from the

Randolph street Aldermen and others, and the fight waxed hot. Finally after six months of discussion the Randolph street Aldermen agreed to support the measure if they would extend the boundaries named in the petition so as to take in the "forks of the road," which meant the point where Lake and Washington streets "forked" on Randolph. This was done, and an ordinance passed only to be vetoed by Mayor Gray. But the measure had got such headway that the Council passed it over the veto, and the city purchased of Hayes, Johnson and others for $60,-000 eighteen acres. The park is laid out with walks and drives in all manner of pretty shapes; the center is occupied by a pond in the shape of three partially formed circles, which at a point is spanned by a handsome stone bridge, and at the north end a rustic bridge and grotto underneath leads out to a diminutive island. A swan, duck, and other water-fowl float gracefully over the surface. The beautiful grass plats are studded with trees, fountains, rustic seats and arbors, and toward the south side is the grand observatory. It is a favorite haunt of promenaders and driving parties. Recently this park has passed into the hands of the Park Commissioners, since then it has undergone many alterations and improvements. On the northeast corner of the park stand the headquarters of the West Park Board.

Union Park Congregational Church is located on the corner of Ashland Avenue and Washington Boulevard, just opposite the west side of Union Park. It is built of rough-dressed cream sandstone, in Gothic style of architecture, with a towering spire 175 feet high. It is one of the largest churches in the city, and with its park surroundings

UNION STOCK YARDS, NEAR FORTIETH AND HALSTED STREETS.

makes a handsome addition to the attractiveness of the locality, which is generally very fine. The pulpit is at all times ably filled.

Union Stock Yards. — This place is justly celebrated as the greatest meat mart in the world. The yards are located on South Halsted Street, about six miles southwest of the City Hall, and may be reached from any part of the city in a variety of ways. From the center of the city, the State Street cable line and the South Halsted Street car line are the most direct and available routes. If one desires rapid transit to this celebrated headquarters of the bovine and swine, take a Chicago, Rock Island & Pacific railway train at the Van Buren Street depot, or a Pittsburg & Fort Wayne railway train at the Union depot, Canal and Adams streets, or an Illinois Central train at the Central depot Lake Front. In fact the railroad facilities of this place are admirable. No less than twenty of the great trunk lines, fed by a thousand branches either reach here direct or via the Belt railroad. The Union Stock Yards Company figure among its assests no less than 150 miles of railway, and it is a system that connects all the systems. There is not a minute in the day or night that trains are not arriving or departing to and from all points of the compass, freighted either with live-stock or the equivalent in meat.

This institution covers 400 acres of land, with pens, buildings, railroad yards, etc. This practically amounts to a good-sized town with twenty miles of streets, twenty miles of water troughs; fifty miles of feeding troughs, and about seventy-five miles of water and drainage pipes. A number of artesian wells, 1,230 feet deep supplement the supply of water from the city pipes. The yards can

17

accommodate over 20,000 cattle, 120,-000 hogs, and 15,000 sheep, and it is frequently the case that they are taxed to their fullest capacity. As the live-stock trains arrive, the Company take charge of the stock, and its location, name of the firm to whom consigned, with description and all necessary data are registered in the office of the Company. The Stock Yards plant represents an investment of $4,000,000 and the adjacent packing houses $10,000,000. The statistics of these yards seem almost incomprehensible. During the year 1890, 3,484,280 cattle, 175,-025 calves, 7,663,828 hogs, 2,182,667 sheep, and 101,566 horses were received, the total value of which was $3,207,981,448. Of the above receipts the neighboring packing houses took and slaughtered 2,219,321 head of cattle and 5,733,082 hogs. The shipment of live-stock from the yards was 1,260,309 cattle; 61,466, calves; 1,985,700 hogs; 929,854 sheep, and 94,362 horses. Astounding as these figures are they will continue to grow larger and larger until the limits of the great western and northwestern territory are reached which will not be for a hundred years to come. The secret of Chicago's greatness to a great extent will be discovered by a careful study of these figures and facts and the many things that grow out of them.

As a historical item, it is stated that in the fall of 1832, G. W. Dole slaughtered the first lot of cattle ever packed in Chicago. They numbered 209 head, and cost $2.75 per hundred weight. About 359 hogs, costing $3 per hundred weight, were slaughtered, and packed at the same time. The average weight of cattle received in this market during the past year was 1,100 pounds per head ; hogs. 240 pounds per head, and sheep, 99 pounds per head.

The stock, as a rule, is consigned

to commission men, who at once take charge of it. These salesmen have their separate localities in the yards, and endeavor to keep them permanently. The pens are arranged in divisions known by letters, and the pens within a division are numbered. For illustration : In division A, pen 20, are sixty cattle consigned to John Doe. These cattle are owned by John Smith in Texas, and his agent, John Doe, sells them to the best possible advantage. But the buyers, representing the great packing houses, are there in force, and sales are readily effected at the market price, which frequently fluctuates, perhaps several times a day. Now the buyers, sellers, their hosts of clerks, the owners of stock, visitors, and the stock yards officials, and the innumerable employés, make up a scene of activity that is duplicated no where else in the world.

There is an exchange, bank, hotels, restaurants, and many other things connected with the Union Stock Yards, but these properly come under the head of Packing Town (which see).

Union Veteran Club, 163 Washington Street, is republican in politics, but reserves the right to act independently, when the interests of Union veterans are at stake.

Unitarian Churches.—The following is a list of the names and locations of those in Chicago :

All Souls, Oakwood Boulevard, southeast corner Langley Avenue.

Church of the Messiah, Michigan Avenue and Twenty-third Street.

Third, northwest corner Laflin and West Monroe streets.

Unity, southeast corner Walton Place and Dearborn Avenue.

United Hebrew Relief Association manages and supports the Michael Reese Hospital, assists those of the Hebrew faith that require it, and provides hospital facilities for the sick and disabled.

United States Marine Hospital receives all American seamen free, and others upon payment of a small sum. Their building and grounds are six miles from the city on the lake shore, north.

Unity Church was organized in 1857, and is probably the largest Unitarian congregation in the city. The church, both exterior and interior, shows that the contributions were quite liberal, as it is substantially built, and finished handsomely. The location is Dearborn Avenue facing Washington Square or Walton Place. Rev. T. G. Milsted is pastor.

Unity Club meets for the purpose of discussing literary and art subjects. It has no permanent location

Universalist Churches.—The following is a list of the names and locations of those in Chicago:

Church of the Redeemer, northeast corner Robey Street and Warren Avenue.

Church of Our Father, Grant Place and Larrabee Street.

St. Paul's, Prairie Avenue and Thirtieth Street.

Englewood, Sixty-third Street.

University of Chicago.—This magnificent college, now fast arising upon the site donated by Marshall Field, offers as thorough and as valuable educational advantages as Harvard, Yale, or Princeton. Dr. W. R. Harper of Yale, is president, and the most learned professors of every science have been brought together as his assistants.

In every branch and department the university will be second to none

TRANSPORTATION BUILDING.

At the southern end of the Architectural Court. 250 x 960 feet. Cost, $300,000. Architects, Adler & Sullivan, Chicago.

in the world, while the new plan of lecture courses, suggested by Dr. Harper, will be entirely and radically different from all previous systems.

October, 1892, is the time set for the opening of the college doors, and at least 1,000 students are already enrolled among the different classes.

Veterinary College.—Chicago has the best veterinary college in the United States. Its faculty numbers sixteen. It has 245 graduates now in active lucrative practice in the ninth year of its existence. It is located at 2537 and 2539 State Street. It opened its first session in the fall of 1883 with eight students, and closed its eighth in the Spring of 1891 with 167. It has always been the intention of the faculty to make the course of instruction as scientific as possible, and still eminently practical, and whatever they do, they intend to keep up with the progress of the times, no matter how rapid. There is so much governmental enactment now going on, relating to inspection of cattle and meat, both for inter-state and foreign trade, that special pains are taken to qualify students for this important branch of professional work. The building is lighted on all sides, and steam-heated. It is built of brick, three stories in height. The lecture room will seat 300 students.

Virginia Hotel.—Chicago is noted all over the world for the excellence of her hotels. The most public spirited of her citizens have taken pride in putting a part, at least, of their money into accommodations for the guests who come thither from all over the universe. A genius came here at an early day from Virginia, who knew how to build reapers, his name was Leander J. McCormick, he manufactured

first-class machines, and he is the owner of a number of the most substantially built, and best cared for business blocks in Chicago, namely: —"The Oxford," "The Major," "The Ceylon," "The Ely," and "The Victoria Hotel."

Mr. McCormick has just completed one of the finest hotels ever put up in Chicago—"The Virginia." It is located on the corner of Ohio and Rush streets, 200 feet on Ohio Street and 109 on Rush Street, and is a ten-story brick building, exclusive of the basement, which is ten feet high, five feet being above grade. It is built with the design of affording all the light and air possible. It rises to an elevation of 140 feet above the pavement. It is built after the Chicago construction—of iron and steel, pressed and hollow brick. The partitions and arches are of hollow tile, while all the material in this country and Mexico—architectural terra cotta, marble, onyx, Vert Island stone, marble mosaic, and plate glass — are drawn upon freely to make a beautiful as well as convenient building for the use of its guests. It stands just where the overflow of business north from the south side center is checked by the distinctive residence portion of the north side.

It is only a few moments of easy walking to the heart of the city. It towers above the immediate surroundings, and from the north, south, and east windows of its upper stories gives magnificent lake views. The main entrance is from Ohio Street, the ladies' entrance is from Rush Street. From the first glimpse of the interior a succession of artistic surprises is in store for the happy guest who seeks to make his home at the Virginia Hotel, and, by the way, it is named in compliment to the native State of the McCormicks. "The Mother of Presidents" may also claim to be the foster mother of agriculture. It is superfluous to say that the artistic and architectural beauties of this travelers' palace is amply supplemented by all the modern accessories and conveniences of first-class hotel life. The building throughout is absolutely fire-proof, and has.450 rooms. The upper rooms, because of their fine lake views, are the most desirable, and, from the unexcelled elevator service, they are just as convenient of access as the lower stories. It is conducted on the "American" plan, having the very best of everything, and everything the best of its kind. Every traveler who has a chance to stop at "The Virginia" during the World's Fair will find that he has all the comforts of a finely ordered home, and the conveniences of co-operative service, for which hotel living is peculiarly desirable. Those who go there will find the term "guest" has its original meaning—one whose comfort and well being are to be specially cared for. In no other country in the world is the science of hotel keeping so fully understood and applied, and "The Virginia" is a perfect type of its class.

Victoria Hotel.—This magnificent hostelry, located on Michigan Avenue and Van Buren Street, is one of the newest and most conspicuous of the lake front hotels. It was completed in May, 1891; contains 275 rooms, and is conducted on the American plan. Mr. J. M. Lee is the proprietor.

Vital Statistics.—This is a division of the Health Department under an official known as the Registrar of vital statistics; salary $1,200 per annum; office, basement of the City Hall. His calculations, based upon a population of 1,200,000—less

than the school census of July 1880—and the additions since annexed to the city, give a death rate, for the year 1890, of 18.22, a slight increase over the previous year, caused by influenza. However, this is much lower than that of the other principal cities in the Union. The total number of deaths for the year was 21,856. There were 1,282 deaths by violence; 9,954 of children under 5 years of age; 2,606, over 60, seven of whom were over 100 years old.

There was not a death from smallpox during the year. The grippe directly caused but 112 deaths, but pneumonia, and other complications with the influenza, swelled the number of victims of this class of diseases. Pneumonia carried off 2,073; consumption, 1,972; bronchitis, 1,189; typhoid fever, 1,009; accidents, 999; diphtheria, 881; croup, 380; scarlet fever, 193; malarial fever, 121; whooping cough, 201; murder, 77; suicide, 206; delirium tremens, 114; hydrophobia, 2. The total of deaths from tubercular diseases was 2,231.

Wabash Avenue.—This avenue, lying next east of State Street, was long the finest residence thoroughfare in the city, and had the advantage of being early laid out in a style appropriate to a high degree of elegance. The march of improvement, however, fixed a different destiny for it, and the fire of 1871 hastened the change. Many of the homes which still remained such were swept out of existence in the great destruction, and the remainder, lying north of Twenty-second Street, were almost without exception invaded by trade during the hurrying week which followed. It was at first believed quite generally that Wabash Avenue would at once become the favorite seat of the first-class retail and wholesale trade; and building commenced very promptly and vigorously to this end. It was soon stayed, however, and the class of business referred to has now settled back in almost its former quarter— the showy stores on State Street and well down town, and the more than substantial ones at the foot of Wabash and Michigan avenues. There they established the foundation of a grand wholesale traffic district, which has extended gradually southward and made Wabash Avenue all that it aspired to be. But the process was slower than was first calculated upon, and the character of the architecture and the traffic which it accommodates is less brilliant, though not, perhaps, less rich. Wabash Avenue can boast some splendid business architecture which extends in two almost continuous lines as far south as Twelfth Street. The famous Auditorium building, the Libby Prison War Museum, Havlin's Theatre, and many other places of amusement are on this avenue. South of that dividing line the former residences of the aristocracy still remain—some of them occupied as shops, but most of them given over to that close follower-up of retreating aristocracy, the genteel boarding-house keeper. This is the rule to Twenty-second Street, south of which the avenue is an elegant residence thoroughfare, and will remain such—though less so than Michigan Avenue and one or two other avenues to the east—through a long period of Chicago's future.

Waldheim Cemetery.— Located ten miles west of the City Hall. Take train at the Grand Central depot via Chicago & Northern Pacific Railroad. Funeral train leaves at 12.01 P. M. daily, including Sundays, running direct to the new cemetery station, immediately adjoining Waldheim, Forest Home, and Jewish cemeteries. Here are interred

the anarchists executed for connection with the Haymarket bomb-throwing. (See *Haymarket Massacre*.) A number of burying-grounds are located in this vicinity.

Ward Boundaries.—First Ward, bounded by the river, Lake Street, and Twelfth Street.

Second Ward, bounded on the north by Twelfth Street, on the south by Twenty-sixth Street from the lake to Clark Street, and by Sixteenth Street from Clark Street to the river, and on the west by the river from Twelfth Street to Sixteenth Street, and by Clark Street from Sixteenth Street to Twenty-sixth Street.

Third Ward, bounded by Twenty-sixth Street, Thirty-third Street, the lake, and Wentworth Avenue.

Fourth Ward, bounded by Thirty-Third Street, Thirty-Ninth Street, the lake, and Stewart Avenue.

Fifth Ward, commencing at Sixteenth and Clark streets, thence west to the river, thence southwest to South Halsted Street, thence south to Thirty-third Street, thence east to Wentworth Avenue, thence north to Twenty-sixth Street, thence east to Clark Street, thence north to place of beginning.

Sixth Ward, commencing at South Halsted Street and the south branch of the river, thence southwest along the river to Illinois & Michigan Canal, thence southwest to Thirty-ninth Street, thence east to Stewart Avenue. thence north to Thirty-third Street, thence west to South Halsted, thence north to place of beginning.

Seventh Ward, commencing at the river and West Twelfth Street, thence west to Johnson Street, thence south to West Twenty-second Street, thence east to South Halsted Street, thence south to the river, thence northeast to the place of beginning.

Eighth Ward, commencing at West Twelfth Street, corner of Johnson Street, thence west to Throop Street, thence south to the river, thence west to South Halsted Street, thence north to West Twenty-second Street, thence west to Johnson Street, thence north to place of beginning.

Ninth Ward, commencing at Centre Avenue, corner of West Taylor Street, thence west to South Wood Street, thence south to Illinois & Michigan Canal, thence northwest along the canal and the south branch of the river to Throop Street, thence north to West Twelfth Street, thence east to Centre Avenue, thence north to place of beginning.

Tenth Ward, commencing at South Wood Street, corner of West Taylor Street, west on West Taylor Street to Campbell Avenue, thence south to West Twelfth Street, thence west to West Forty-sixth Street, thence south to Egan Avenue, thence east to Illinois & Michigan Canal, thence northeast to South Wood Street, thence north to place of beginning.

Eleventh Ward, commencing at North May Street, corner of West Ohio Street, west on West Ohio Street to North Paulina Street, thence south to West Taylor Street, thence east to Sibley Street, thence north to West Harrison Street, thence east to Throop Street, thence north to West Van Buren Street, thence east to Centre Avenue, thence north on Centre Avenue and Ann Street to West Lake Street, thence east to North May Street, thence north to place of beginning.

Twelfth Ward, commencing at Washington Boulevard, corner North Paulina Street, west on Washington Boulevard to North California Avenue, thence north to West Lake Street, thence west to West Forty-eight Street, thence south to West Twelfth Street, thence east to Campbell Avenue, thence north to West

Taylor Street, thence east to Paulina Street, thence north to place of beginning.

Thirteenth Ward, commencing at Washington Boulevard, west on Washington Boulevard to California Avenue, thence north to West Lake Street, thence west to West Forty-eighth Street, thence north to West Chicago Avenue, thence east to North Paulina Street, thence south to place of beginning.

Fourteenth Ward, commencing at West Chicago Avenue, corner North Ashland Avenue west on West Chicago Avenue to West Forty-eight Street, thence north to West North Avenue, thence east to North Ashland Avenue, thence south to place of beginning.

Fifteenth Ward, commencing at the river and West North Avenue, west on West North Avenue to North Kedzie Avenue, thence north to West Belmont Avenue, thence east to North Western Avenue, thence south to the river, thence southeast to place of beginning.

Sixteenth Ward, commencing at North May Street corner West Ohio Street, west on Ohio Street to North Paulina Street, thence north to West Chicago Avenue, thence northeast to North Ashland Avenue, thence east to the river, thence southeast to North Carpenter Street, thence south to West Chicago Avenue, thence west to North May Street, thence south to place of beginning.

Seventeenth Ward, commencing at West Lake Street and the river, west on Lake Street to North May Street, thence north to West Chicago Avenue, thence east to North Carpenter Street, thence north to the river, thence southeast to place of beginning.

Eighteenth Ward, bounded by West Van Buren Street, West Lake Street, the river; and on the west by Center Avenue and Ann Street.

263   WAR—WAS

Nineteenth Ward, commencing at West Van Buren Street and the river, west on Van Buren Street to Throop Street, south on Throop Street to West Harrison Street, west on West Harrison Street to Sibley Street, south on Sibley Street to West Taylor Street, east on West Taylor Street to Center Avenue, south on Center Avenue to West Twelfth Street, east on West Twelfth Street to the river, and north on the river to the place of beginning.

Twentieth Ward, bounded by Division Street, Fullerton Avenue, North Halsted Street, and the river.

Twenty-first Ward, bounded by North Avenue, Fullerton Avenue, North Halsted Street, and the lake.

Twenty-second Ward, bounded by Division Street, North Avenue, North Halsted Street, and the lake.

Twenty-third Ward, bounded by Division Street, North Wells Street, and the river.

Twenty-fourth Ward—Bounded by Division Street, North Wells Street and the Lake.

Twenty-fifth Ward—Commencing at Fullerton Avenue and Lake Shore, north on Lake Shore to Church Road, thence west to North Clark Street, thence southeast to Graceland Avenue, thence east to Fullerton Avenue, thence south to Fullerton Avenue, thence to place of beginning.

Twenty-sixth Ward—Commencing at Fullerton and Racine avenues, north to Graceland Avenue, thence west to North Clark Street, thence northwest to Church Road, thence west to Western Avenue, thence south to Chicago River, thence southeast to Fullerton Avenue, thence east to place of beginning.

Twenty-seventh Ward—Commencing at Belmont and North Western avenues, north to city limits, thence west and south on city limits, West North Avenue, thence east to Kedzie Avenue, thence north to Bel-

mont Avenue, thence east to place of beginning.

Twenty-eighth Ward—Commencing at Thirty-ninth Street and Western Avenue, north to Illinois & Michigan Canal, thence southwest to Thirty-ninth Street and Crawford Avenue, thence north to North Avenue, thence west to city limits, thence south to Thirty-ninth Street, then east to place of beginning.

Twenty-ninth Ward—Commencing at Forty-seventh and State streets north to Thirty-ninth Street, thence west to city limits, thence south to Forty-seventh Street, thence east to place of beginning.

Thirtieth Ward—Commencing at Sixty-third and State streets north to Forty-seventh Street, thence west to city limits, thence south to Sixty-third Street, then east to place of beginning.

Thirty-first Ward — Commencing at Eighty-seventh and State streets, north to Sixty-third Street, thence west to city limits, thence south and east to place of beginning.

Thirty-second Ward — Commencing at Fifty-fifth Street and lake shore northwest to Thirty-ninth Street, thence west to State Street, thence south to Fifty-fifth Street, thence east to place of beginning.

Thirty-third Ward—Commencing at One hundred and thirty-sixth Street and Indiana State line north to Lake Michigan, thence northwest to Fifty-fifth Street, thence west to Stony Island Avenue, thence south to city limits, thence east to place of beginning.

Thirty-fourth Ward — Commencing at One hundred and thirty-sixth Street, and west line, Section 36, north along Stony Island Avenue to Fifty-fifth Street, thence west to State Street, thence south to city limits, thence to the place of beginning.

Washingtonian Home, 566 to

to 572 West Madison Street is a reformatory for inebriates and had its origin with the Good Templar lodges of Cook County.

Washington Park Club is the aristocratic racing association of Chicago. The race course is one of the finest and most liberally managed in this country. The club house at the course is a palatial affair, while the whole plant of grand stands, booths, betting-stands, club and other stables are on the most magnificent and appropriate scale. It is located at South Park Avenue and Sixty-first Street. The summer meeting which opens with "Derby Day," is a great event in turf circles.

Water-Works System. — The earliest effort, of which there is any record, to provide a public water supply for the citizens of Chicago, was November 10, 1834, when the Board of Trustees paid $95.50 for the digging of a well in Kinzie's Addition, located at what is now the intersection of Cass and Michigan streets. The settlers soon realized that the lake was the most suitable source of water, and for some years private enterprise reaped a financial harvest in operating water-carts for the supply of lake water to the citizens. This improved mode of procuring water was soon superseded by a more substantial and convenient means. In January, 1836, the State Legislature passed a law incorporating the Chicago Hydraulic Company. The Act of Incorporation contained about the same conditions for the preservation of the water from pollution and the protection of the works, as are now in force. The works were put in operation in the spring of 1842, having a reservoir, about two miles of wood pipe, and a twenty-five horse power engine drawing water from

the lake. The cost of that plant was $24,000. In December, 1841, the City Council contracted with the Hydraulic Company to supply the city with water for the extinguishment of fires. The pump-house was located at the corner of Lake Street and Michigan Avenue, supplying but a very small portion of the South and West Divisions of the city. There was no supply from this source to the North Division, and at least four-fifths of the then territorial limits of the city was supplied with water for domestic and other purposes from the river, or by the water-cart system from the lake. The works of the old Hydraulic Company were operated with varying success, until the Act of the Legislature of February 15, 1851, providing for the present works. The new works was commenced in 1852. The oldest and largest pumping station in the city is the North Side pumping station, situated at the foot of Chicago Avenue. At first the water was taken from an inlet basin, on the lake shore, separated from the lake by a semi-circular break-water, with an opening to the southeast, and was distributed through the three reservoirs, serving the three divisions of the city, and situated respectively at La Salle and Adams streets, Chicago Avenue and Sedgwick Street, and Morgan and Monroe streets. The first two were built in 1853, and the latter in 1854, and each held about two or three day's supply. The first iron distribution pipe was laid in Clark Street in 1852, and was four inches in diameter.

The event which exerted the greatest influence by far on the development of the water supply system, not alone in Chicago, but also of other large lake cities, was the successful completion of the first lake tunnel. The plan of the work determined upon consisted of a land shaft at the western, and a lake shaft at the eastern extremity, to be permanent, and three intermediate lake shafts for expediting the construction, to be removed on the completion of the work. The tunnel proper to be two miles in length, beginning on the lake shore, near the pumping works, and extending out in an east-northeasterly direction. The shafts to be protected by cribs, or hollow pentagonal break-waters, from storms, vessels, and ice. The horizontal diameter of the tunnel was fixed at five feet, and the vertical two inches greater for convenience for drawing the centers during construction. The size was determined upon for two reasons :

First. It was sufficient to deliver a supply for 1,000,000 inhabitants, at the rate of fifty gallons per day for each person, the average quantity used at that time.

Second. Experience in Europe had shown that while it was possible to make small tunnels in the most troublesome ground, the attempt to make large ones had sometimes failed, and that others had been attended with enormous difficulty. The work was commenced at the land shaft March 17, 1864. From the bottom of the shaft a drift, at first only intended to be temporary, was made about fifty feet westward, with a chamber at the end, with fixtures for mounting a transit. The regular tunnel work was commenced May 26, 1864. The formal celebration of the completion of the tunnel, and introduction of pure lake water by appropriate public ceremonies, took place March 25, 1867. The actual cost, including all preliminary and other expenses of whatever nature chargeable to the lake tunnel up to April 1, 1867, was $457,844.95.

In 1869 the system of water-pipe tunnels, under the Chicago River, was originated. Before that, the pipes, at the intersection of the river, were laid on the bottom of the latter, and on August 18, 1869, the large main, thus crossing the river at Chicago Avenue, was broken by a vessel dragging her anchor. This accident deprived the West Side of water for three days, and gave impetus to the change of system. Early in 1869 the buildings and water-tower, forming the bulk of the North Side pumping station of to-day, were finished. The Great Fire of 1871 did serious damage to the works. The loss to buildings and machinery was estimated at $75,-000. In eight days, however, the damage was repaired and the engines resumed work.

On July 12, 1872, work was begun on a new lake tunnel, seven feet interior diameter, from the crib to the North Side station, this was finished on July 3, 1874; and on October 12th, of the same year, an extension of the same, also seven feet in diameter, under the land, to a new pumping station at Ashland Avenue and Twenty-second Street, was also completed.

On September 19, 1876, the Board of Public Works was succeeded by the Department of Public Works, with a single responsible head.

Late in December, 1881, the old five-foot lake tunnel was pumped dry and thoroughly examined by city officials. A deposit, from four to seven inches in depth, was found on the bottom, but the brick-work did not show a single flaw.

On July 21, 1884, two new engines were put in operation at the West Side pumping works; they were counterparts of the two older engines. The total pumping capacity of the West Side station was raised, by this addition, from 15,000,000 gallons to 60,000,000 gallons per twenty-four hours, and that of both works combined to 134,000,000 gallons per twenty-four hours.

During 1887, a shore inlet tunnel,

seven feet in diameter, and 1,500 feet long, with an inlet shaft protected by a crib opposite the North Side pumping station, was completed, to be used when the supply should be endangered by ice or otherwise at the lake crib two miles out. During the same year two new engines were added to the North Side works, giving an additional amount of 12,000,-000 gallons of water per day.

At the close of the year, 1887, a contract was entered into for the construction of a new tunnel, to be eight feet in diameter, and to extend four miles out into the lake, and the work was begun on a shore shaft at the foot of Peck Court. The land ramification for this tunnel connects the shore shaft with the two new pumping stations—the South Side pumping station, at Indiana Avenue and Fourteenth Street, and the Central Pumping station, on Harrison Street, between Desplaines and Halsted streets.

The chief event of the year 1889, was the annexation of the suburban towns of Hyde Park, Lake, Jefferson, and Lake View, a territory with an area of 128 square miles and a population of 220,000 souls, whereby the water-works system of the city acquired two pumping stations with an aggregate engine capacity of 72,000,-000 gallons per twenty-four hours; one lake tunnel, six feet in diameter and 8,000 feet long, with a submerged inlet for Hyde Park and Lake; one lake tunnel, in process of construction, six feet in diameter, for Lake View and Jefferson; and about 330 miles of water pipe.

The city at present is supplied with 22 pumping engines of various types and power, representing a total engine capacity for delivering daily 260,000,000 gallons of water. From measurements obtained there was pumped during the year a daily average of over 154,000,000 gallons.

Windsor Theatre.—This well-known theatre, situated on North Clark Street, near Division, is one of the handsomest in the city, and the only first-class house on the North Side. It is one of a chain of theaters operated under the management of M. B. Leavitt, among which are the Bush Street Theatre, San Francisco, and the Broadway Theatre, Denver, Colorado.

Mr. Leavitt is one of the foremost theatrical managers of the day, controlling, in addition to his theatres, a number of first-class combinations and circuits, which enable him at all times to command the best attractions obtainable. With these advantages the "Windsor" is always provided with first-class attractions, which will compare favorably with those presented by any house in the city.

The Windsor is provided with all modern improvements, heated by steam and lighted by electricity. Mr. Ben Leavitt is local manager, and gives the comfort and convenience of his patrons his personal attention. An evening spent at this cozy theatre will never be regretted.

Western Society for the Suppression of Vice uses its endeavors to the enforcement of laws for the suppression of obscene literature, etc.

West Side Club have an elegant building at 451 Washington Boulevard. It is a social organization.

West Side Free Dispensary.—A clinical annex to the College of Physicians and Surgeons, gives gratuitous treatment to deserving poor.

Woman's Christian Association was incorporated in 1871, with the object to promote the welfare of women. It keeps an employment bureau, a boarding house for young women and a free dispensary. It is located at 184 Dearborn Street.

Woman's Exchange has for its object the providing of a place for the reception and sale of articles made by women.

Woman's Hospital of Chicago is located at 118 35th Street. It is devoted .to the treatment of the diseases and accidents peculiar to the female sex.

Woman's Medical College.— This college located directly opposite Cook County Hospital, is a handsome four story and basement brick structure. It is spacious and well lighted, and has ample accommodations for all the work at present required of it. It has lately been made a Department of the Northwestern University, thus giving the students access to the extensive physiological and pathological laboratories to be endowed and erected by the friends of the university, at a cost of not less than $100,000. This will give a chance for study on special lines without being obliged to cross the ocean. The faculty is very full and complete on all lines, and embraces forty-six physicians, who have, many of them, made honorable names for themselves in their profession. Of these, nineteen are ladies. It is to be presumed, when the college has been in existence a little longer, all its chairs will be supplied from its own graduates; Charles Warrington Earle, A. M. M. D., is now president.

Woodlawn is an ideal town, and is noted for its beautiful situation, being almost surrounded by Chicago's finest parks. It has a perfect drainage system, and many fine houses. It is on the Illinois Central R. R., eight and one-half miles from City Hall.

World's Columbian Exposition.—Three years ago, the United States, as a representative nation of the New World, began to consider the propriety of celebrating the four hundredth anniversary of the discovery of America, by inviting the nations of the Old World to visit her shores. The closing decade of the most remarkable century in the Christian era, coinciding with the anniversary of an event unequaled in the history of this sphere, suggests the uniting of all mankind in a celebration of peace. The land where necessity and courage has fostered industry and wealth presents a fitting scene for such a gathering. Columbia, the youngest of the continent of the civilized world, should act the part of hostess at the celebration of her four hundreth birthday, by extending the material evidences of the progress of the human family. And such a commemoration should be called the World's Columbian Exposition. The unanimous and enthusiastic endorsement by the citizens and press of the United States of an undertaking so grand, prompted the United States Government to legalize the holding of a World's Fair in celebrating the four hundreth anniversary of the discovery of America by Columbus; and on April 25, 1890, President Harrison approved the Act of Congress, which is as follows:

"Be it enacted by the Senate and House of Representatives of the United States of America, in Congress assembled, that an exposition of arts, industries, manufactures, and products of the soil, mine, and sea shall be inaugurated in the year eighteen hundred and ninety-two, in the City of Chicago, in the State of Illinois, as hereafter provided."

The Act provides for a national supervisory body, known as the World's Columbian Commission, to be appointed by the President, composed of two commissioners and two alternates from each State and Territory and the District of Columbia, and eight commissioners and eight alternates at large—the commissioners and alternates from the States and Territories to be appointed upon nomination by their respective Governors.

Immediately upon passage of the Act, the work of organizing and preparation was commenced, and resulted in the election of officers of the World's Columbian Commission as follows: President, Thomas W. Palmer of Michigan; First Vice-President, Thomas M. Waller of Connecticut; Director-General George R. Davis of Chicago.

The World's Columbian Exposition Association of Chicago organized as follows: Officers: President, Lyman J. Gage; First Vice-President, Thomas B. Bryan: Second Vice-President, Potter Palmer; Secretary, Benjamin Butterworth; Assistant Secretary, J. H. Kingwell; Treasurer, Anthony F. Seeberger; Auditor, William K. Ackerman.

A number of changes have been made among the officials since 1890. Harlow N. Higinbotham is now President; Ferd. W. Peck and R. A. Waller, First and Second Vice-Presidents; Howard O. Edmonds, Secretary; Anthony F. Seeberger, Treasurer; and William K. Ackerman, Auditor.

The Executive Committee is composed of members of both National and local boards. The following are the members: Harlow N. Higinbotham, President; Ferd. W. Peck, First Vice-President; R. A. Waller, Second Vice-President; Henry B. Stone, Edwin Walker, Wm. D. Kerfoot, Charles H. Schwab, A. H. Revell, Edward P. Ripley, George R. Davis, Chas. L. Hutchinson, James W. Ellsworth, Robert C.

Clowry, John J. P. Odell, Thies J. Lefens, Lyman J. Gage, and William T. Baker.

WORLD'S CONGRESS AUXILIARY, as suggested by a letter of the Secretary of State, is an authorized adjunct of the World's Fair, and aims to supplement the Exposition, which will mark the material progress of the world, by a portrayal of the wonderful achievements of the present age in science, literature, education, government, jurisprudence, morals, charity, religion, and other departments of human activity, and as the most effective means of increasing the fraternity, progress, prosperity and peace of mankind. Virtually it will be a series of congresses, at which the greatest thinkers of the world will discuss the various themes indicated.

During the Exposition, the Auxiliary will have the use of a magnificent permanent art palace, which the Chicago Art Institute is erecting on the lake front. This will have two large audience-rooms, each of 3,500 capacity, and many smaller rooms. Here, fully one hundred congresses in all will be held.

The President's proclamation was issued December 24, 1890, and therein he officially announces that the Exposition shall be opened on the first day of May, 1893, and shall not be closed until the last Thursday in October of the same year. All the nations of the earth are invited to participate. It is also stated in the proclamation that "satisfactory proof has been presented to me that provision has been made for adequate grounds and buildings for the uses of the World's Columbian Exposition, and that a sum of not less than $10,000,000, to be used and expended for the purpose of said Exposition, has been provided in accordance with the conditions and requirements of the Act."

The broad and patriotic spirit which prompts the gathering of the people of the nations to unite with the citizens of the United States in celebrating the four hundredth anniversary of the discovery of America, in this city, in the year 1893, displays a progress in the development of a universal civilization, and a recognition of the equal rights of the whole human family. In our midst will mingle the great of all lands—the statesman, the scholar, and citizen, representing every grade of government, civilization, and culture—all standing side by side upon the sacred soil of the great republic.

The magnitude and importance of this great event of the century can not be estimated or measured upon the basis of a circumscribed boundary of a city, State, or nation, but must encompass the land and water of continents, and dispense its benefits, its privileges, and blessings to all mankind. The products of all climes, from sea and land, from the barbarous tribes to the civilized nations of the earth, representing antiquity, progress, civilization, and culture, with the works of the arts and sciences, the wonderful achievements of inventive minds, and the high attainments reached in the products of skilled labor, the exhibit of the treasures and resources from the inexhaustible store-houses of nature, will contribute to the bewildering and amazing achievements and possibilities of mankind. It may be assured that the exhibits at the Columbian Exposition will cover a wider range, and be far more numerous and valuable, than were ever before gathered together. The whole world is enthused with the mighty project, and every nation will participate with the grandest exhibits of the customs, condition, and progress of its people.

All the European nations will give unqualified support and co-operation; all South and Central America, and Mexico, are preparing a magnificent exhibition of their splendid resources; even the far-away lands of Asia, Africa, and the Pacific Isles are roused to interest, and will send strange and wondrous attractions to this great Exposition.

The plans of these various countries contemplate the erection of buildings of the finest character in which to make their headquarters. The style of architecture will be characteristic of the country represented. It will thus be seen that, in addition to the buildings constructed by the Exposition, there will also be a magnificent display of architecture from every nation of the world.

The millions of money to be expended, and the mental and physical forces requisite to perfect preparation for receiving the world's inhabitants, with their varied exhibits, are of gigantic proportions, and can only bring compensation by a universal dissemination of a higher civilization, the elevation and well-being of mankind, a recognition of the dignity of skilled and honorable labor, the establishment of broader principles of fraternal intercourse, and a closer brotherhood of nations.

The site of the Exposition is to be that portion of the South Park system known as Jackson Park and the Midway Plaisance, within easy distance of the business center, and accessible by complete transportation facilities. Jackson Park has a frontage of a mile and a half on Lake Michigan, and contains 553 acres of ground, while the Midway Plaisance—which connects Jackson and Washington parks—is nearly a mile long, and 600 feet wide, making an additional area of eighty acres. On Jackson and Washington parks, previous to the selection of the Exposition site, $4,000,000 was expended in laying out and beautifying the grounds, and the Park Commissioners will expend $1,000,000 more on further ornamentation of this already attractive location.

Large as the area of Jackson Park may be, it will require the greatest care and closest calculation to make the space adequate for the thousands of exhibitors who will display their varied resources. When the Exposition was first planned, it was thought that about 125 acres would be placed under roof. But the enormous size of the great buildings makes this calculation utterly inadequate, for the Government structures, with those of Illinois, will alone cover nearly 160 acres. The dimensions of the great buildings are indicated in the following table:

Buildings.	Dimensions in feet.	Area in acres.
Manufactures and Liberal Arts................	787x1,687	30.5
Administration..........	262x262	1.6
Mines....................	350x700	5.6
Electricity	345x690	5.5
Transportation	256x960	5.6
Transportation Annex...	425x900	8.8
Woman's.................	199x388	1.8
Art Galleries...........	320x500	3.7
Art Gallery Annexes (2)	120x200	1.1
Fisheries......	165x365	1.4
Fishery Annexes (2)......	135 diam.	.8
Horticulture............	250x998	5.7
Greenhouses (8).........	24x100	.5
Machinery...	492x846	9.6
Machinery Annex.......	490x550	6.2
Machinery Power-house.	{ 490x461	2.1
Machinery Pump'g Works	77x84 }	
Agriculture.............	500x800	9.2
Agriculture Annex......	300x550	3.8
Agriculture Assembly Hall..............	125x450	1.3
Forestry............. ..	208x528	2.5
Sawmill.................	125x300	.8
Dairy...................	100x200	.5
Live Stock (2)...........	65x200	.9
Live Stock Pavilion.....	280x440	2.8
Live Stock Sheds	....	40.0
Casino	140x260	.8
Music Hall.............	140x260	.8
United States Government	345x415	3.3
United States Government Battleship.......	69.25x348	.3
Illinois State...........	160x450	1.7
Illinois State Wings (2)..	....	.3
Total		159.5

The Exposition buildings, not including those of the Government and Illinois, have also a total gallery area of 45.9 acres—a total floor space of about 200 acres. The Fine Arts Building has 7,885 lineal feet, or 145,852 square feet of wall space.

These buildings will surpass those of any previous World's Fair in numbers, size, and splendor. They will have a total frontage of more than two miles, and will be, in the main, sixty feet high, with numerous domes, towers, and turrets for architectural effect. The annexes will be scarcely less magnificent than the main buildings themselves. The live-stock sheds, which will cover an immense area, will not mar the general architectural effect, while the power-houses, pumping-works, etc., will be exhibits in themselves.

There will be several smaller Exposition buildings in addition to those named. Among them will be a reproduction of the Spanish Convent of La Rábida, in which a complete collection of Columbus relics and antique exhibits will be gathered.

The total cost of the Exposition structures alone is estimated at about $8,000,000. This does not include the cost of the State, foreign, or private buildings.

An estimate of the grand total of all appropriations, made and expected, by the United States, the Exposition Company, the States and Territories, corporate bodies, trades associations, manufacturers, and foreign nations, reaches a total of $32,000,000, with a prospect that the amount will exceed that sum. Despite the enormous expenses of this colossal undertaking, the finances of the Exposition are in a very satisfactory condition. At the inception of the enterprise, Chicago provided $10,000,000—$5,000,000 in subscriptions to the capital stock of the Exposition, and $5,000,000 in bonds voted by the city council. Subscriptions to the capital stock are continually being made, and now aggregate about $6,000,000.

The immense sums expended must, necessarily, result in developing everything great and beautiful in art, architecture, and floral and landscape decorations, in the preparation for so great an event. Among the most interesting and delightful views which will greet the visitor in reaching the Exposition grounds by steamer, a distance of six miles from the embarking point at the Lake Front Park, there will be constantly in view the towers and gilded domes of the Fair buildings, and when abreast of the site, a grand spectacle of surpassing magnificence will be presented—the vast extent of the beautiful park, the windings of the lagoon, and the superb array of scores of great buildings, elegant and imposing in their architecture, and gay with myriads of flags and streamers floating from their pinnacles and towers.

In the northern portion of the grounds will be seen a picturesque group of buildings constituting a veritable village of palaces.

Here, on a hundred acres or more, beautifully laid out, will stand the headquarters of foreign nations and of a number of the States of the Union, surrounded by lawns, walks, and beds of flowers and shrubbery; these buildings will vary greatly in size and style of architecture, and, located on wide curving avenues, will include some of the most ornate, costly, and palatial structures of the Exposition.

In the western part of the group stands the Illinois Building, 450x160 feet in size, and costing $250,000. It is severely classic in style, with a dome in the center, and a great

porch facing southward. A tenth part of the space in the building is devoted to the State Woman's Exhibit. In this portion of the park, too, stands the Fine Arts Building, a magnificent palace, 320 by 500 feet, and costing $670,000. Just south of the foreign and State buildings may be observed a considerable expanse of lagoon, with an outlet to the lake, and encompassing three islands. On the shores of this lagoon stands the United States Fisheries Building, 365 feet | in length, and flanked with a curved arcade, connecting it with two round pavilions, in which are aquaria and tackle exhibits. The glass fronts of the aquaria are 575 feet in length, and the water capacity is 140,000 gallons. Salt-water fish will be shown in tanks of water brought from the Atlantic Ocean.

Across the calm lagoon, to the south, is the United States Government Building, 345 by 415 feet, and having a dome 236 feet high. It is classic in style, covers 6.1 acres, and cost $400,000. In it is a very complete exhibit from the several Federal departments—War, Treasury, Agriculture, Interior, Post-office, and Navy; from the Smithsonian Institution, and the National Museum. On the lake shore, east of the building, and, in part, in the intervening space, the Government will have a gun battery, life-saving station complete with apparatus, a light-house, war balloons, and a full-size model of a $3,000,000 battleship of the first class. This will be constructed on piling alongside a pier, being thus surrounded by water, and apparently moored at a wharf. The ship will be 348 feet long, sixty-nine feet amidships, and will be an exact reproduction of the war-ship *Illinois*, with guns, turrets, torpedo-tubes, torpedo-nets, booms, boats, anchors, a "military mast" seventy-six feet high, and a full complement of seamen and marines, detailed from the Navy Department. The visitor arriving by steamboat will pass very near, and obtain an excellent view of the shore portion of the Government exhibits. He will also see, anchored near by, a Columbus fleet, a reproduction as near as may be of the one with which the great navigator sailed from Palos. The *Santa Maria*, an exact image of Columbus' flag-ship, will arrive from Spain, where it has been built by the citizens of Palos, and will remain here throughout the Fair.

A Government revenue cutter and one or two torpedo-boats will also be anchored off the shore.

Steaming by the Government exhibits, the visitor comes abreast of the largest building of the Exposition—that of Manufactures and Liberal Arts. It measures 1,687x787 feet, and cost $1,500,000 to erect.

This building is the largest in the world, and the largest under roof ever erected. It is three times larger than the Cathedral of St. Peter, in Rome, and four times larger than the Coliseum. Twenty such buildings as the Auditorium could be placed upon the floor.

Surrounding it on all sides is a porch two stories in height, affording a delightful promenade and a view of the other buildings of the lagoon, alive with row-boats, gondolas, and electric pleasure craft, and of the grounds generally. Its style is that of the French renaissance.

Two parallel piers extend from the shore about four hundred feet where, taking out-curves, they partially inclose a circular harbor, from the center of which rises, on a forty-foot pedestal, a commanding statue of the Republic, sixty feet in height, or 100 with the pedestal. The main pier extends out into the lake for 1,500 feet, deflecting to the north-

ward, and having at its extremity an immense Greek pavilion 200 feet in diameter. Here visitors may sit and enjoy the cooling lake breezes, listening to the finest music, and obtaining a magnificent view of the great Exposition buildings and other shore attractions. Upon leaving the pier, the visitor gazes upon an avenue, or court, several hundred feet wide, extending westward across the park, and presenting a spectacle of marvelous architectural grace and beauty. At the shoreward end of this grand avenue are a casino and a music-hall, each 140x260 feet, and connected by a peristyle. Two thousand five hundred people can sit in the audience-room of the music-hall, while the Casino contains restaurant and resting rooms. The peristyle is crowned with a group of statuary emblematic of the progress of the world, and forty-eight columns representing the States and Territories. The Convent of La Rábida, previously mentioned, is a short distance south on the shore.

To the left, on the great avenue, is the Agricultural Building, 800x500 feet, with an annex 550x300—both costing $620,000.

The building is most richly ornamented, and is adorned with many groups of statuary of heroic size. Between this and the huge Manufactures Building juts a branch of the lagoon. All down this grand avenue, encompassing a beautiful sheet of water, stand imposing buildings, and the gaze of the visitor sweeps along the majestic façades until it rests upon the Administration Building, which terminates the vista nearly a mile away. Upon traversing this "Long Walk," as it may be called, after the famous way from Windsor Castle to Ascot, the visitor will find it a veritable Bois de Boulogne in point of beauty of effect produced by landscape, archi-

WOMAN'S BUILDING.

Near the Sixtieth Street entrance of the Park. 199 x 388 feet. Architect, Miss Sophia B. Hayden.

ELECTRICITY BUILDING.

South front on the great quadrangle, and north front facing the lagoon. 345 x 700 feet. Cost, $375,000.

tecture, and gardening. Passing the Agricultural Building the visitor comes to the great Machinery Hall, which lies to the westward of it, and is connected with it by a horseshoe arcade, doubling a branch of the lagoon. This building is 492x846 feet in size, and is rich in architectural line and detail. Its cost, together with its enormous annex, was $1,200,000.

Opposite Machinery Hall, and to the north, stands the Exposition Administration Building. This is one of the most imposing, and, in proportion to its size, the most expensive one of the large structures. Richard M. Hunt, of New York, president of the American Institute of Architects, is the designer, and he made it stately and simple, yet exceedingly striking in appearance, and an excellent representative of Italian renaissance. It is 262 feet square, 277½ feet to the top of the outer dome, and cost $550,000. It is adorned with scores of statues and other works of art. In it are the offices of the National Commission and local directory, and the headquarters of all the numerous officials connected with the management and regulation of the Exposition.

To the northward of the Administration Building, on either side and facing the grand avenue, are two more immense buildings, for the electrical and the mining exhibits. These buildings are about equal in size—about 350x700 feet each—and are of French renaissance. North of these buildings, and in the main lagoon, is an island of sixteen acres in area. This is devoted to floriculture and horticulture, except the extreme north end, where the Japanese exhibit is situated. Much of the island is a "forest primeval," pathless, and untransformed by art, where the visitor may hunt the fra-

grant wild flower or the saucy chipmunk, and generally commune with nature in her native haunts.

Proceeding from the Administration Building still farther westward, the traveler arrives at the railway facilities for the arrival and departure of visitors. Six parallel tracks will sweep into the grounds in a huge circle at the extreme southwest portion, entering and leaving at nearly the same point. Around this loop the trains, in arriving and departing, sweep at intervals of a few minutes, and the depot accommodations are so extensive and well arranged that there will be almost no confusion or crowding. Within this loop made by the railway tracks is the main power-house, from which power will be furnished to such buildings on the grounds as require it.

To the southward of the line of buildings which are arranged along the south side of the grand avenue is a vast open expanse devoted to the live stock exhibit. Here an immense stock pavilion, 280x440 feet, and row on row of sheds, covering forty acres, contain the blooded stock of every land. Over toward the shore is the dairy exhibit, 100x200 feet, and the splendid Forestry Building, made entirely without iron, and 208x528 feet.

The visitor has thus far, in his tour of inspection, traversed the lake shore or hypotenuse of the triangle and across the southern end of the base. It remains only to turn toward the north and note the structures arranged along the perpendicular. The first one arrived at is the Transportation Building. This structure, 256x960 feet, and costing, with an annex 425x900, $370,000, contains exhibits of every appliance and vehicle for carrying purposes, from a cash-carrier to a balloon, and from a baby wagon to a mogul engine.

18

North of this is the Horticultural Building, 250x998 feet, and costing $300,000. Under the dome grow the tallest palms, bamboos, and tree-ferns, and the interior courts are planted with every kind of flowers and shrubs.

Still farther north, and directly opposite the park entrance of the Midway Plaisance, is the Woman's Building—one of the chief objects of interest upon the grounds. It is 199x388 feet, two stories high, and cost $138,000. The architect was Miss Sophia Hayden of Boston.

Here the lady managers have their headquarters, and here is collected a wonderful exhibit, illustrating the progress and attainment of women in the various branches of industry. The Act of Congress authorizing the holding of the Exposition also created a Board of Lady Managers, and the board has rendered valuable assistance to the National Commissioners. In addition, it holds and exercises as a dual function, the guardianship of women's special interests.

The Lady Managers have invited the women of all countries to participation in the Exposition, and numerous foreign committees, composed of women, are in successful co-operation with the official board.

Passing the Woman's Building, the visitor can turn toward the north-east, and inspect the foreign and State buildings, in the northern portion of the park, or he can turn to the west into Midway Plaisance. This beautiful parkway is occupied throughout its entire length by special Exposition features, largely of a foreign character, such as the "Bazaar of all Nations," "Street in Cairo," "Street in Constantinople," "Moorish Palace," "Maori Village," "Algerian Village," "Dahomey Village," etc., to which concessions have been granted. Villages of American Indians will also be located here, and panoramas, cycloramas, etc., will claim attention.

Almost innumerable structures and exhibits, such as reproductions of famous buildings, etc., mostly novel and striking in character, greet the eye on every side, while traversing the park.

All of the important buildings stand on terraces four feet above the general park level, thus greatly improving the general landscape effects and rendering their own appearance more imposing.

From scores of domes and towers flags and streamers are floating, and both exteriors and interiors are warm with a liberal display of color. The beautiful park with its magnificent array of architecture assuredly presents one of the finest spectacles ever seen by the eye of man.

TRANSPORTATION.—The Exposition is located within easy distance of the center of the business portion of Chicago, and accessible by means of the most complete transportation facilities.

All public passenger railways, whether steam, cable, electric, or horse, as well as the great number of steamboats on Lake Michigan, will deliver passengers conveniently near the numerous entrances to the grounds. With these unlimited facilities, it is estimated that more than one hundred and fifty thousand people per hour can be carried to and from the grounds. An intra-mural elevated railroad conveys visitors to all parts of the grounds, making it easy to go from one point to another without walking. The distances on the grounds are so great that visitors will find this arrangement to be a great source of convenience and comfort. Other means of transit will also be provided inside of the grounds. One of these, and in fact the most attractive of all, will be the means of water transit through the lagoons, canal, and basin. The waterways inside the grounds cover an area of about eighty-five acres. Here will be provided launches and small craft of all kinds. One can board these boats and travel a distance of nearly three miles, passing on the route all of the principal buildings and points of attraction. It will be one of the grandest sights of the world, and one to leave an everlasting impression on the minds of those who view it.

An enormous attendance is anticipated, and it is the intention to provide not only ample transportation facilities, but every accommodation on the grounds for the convenience and comfort of visitors, no matter how numerous they may be. Police regulations will be as perfect as can be made.

DEDICATION. — The Exposition buildings, as provided in the Act of Congress, were dedicated on October 21, 1892, the four hundredth anniversary of the landing of Columbus, with appropriate and impressive ceremonies. The Exposition will be formally opened to the public on May 1, 1893, the intervening time being reserved for the reception and placing of exhibits.

The Exposition will close October 26, 1893.

FOREIGN COUNTRIES AT THE FAIR.

Country	Amount
Argentine Republic	$ 100,000
Austria	102,300
Belgium	57,000
Bolivia	30,700
Brazil	600,000
Bulgaria	
China	500,000
Chile (informal)	
Columbia	100,000
Costa Rica	150,000
Denmark	67,000
Danish West Indies	
Ecuador	$ 125,000
Egypt (informal)	
France	579,000
Algeria	
French Guiana	
Germany	690,200
Great Britain	291,990
Bahamas	
Barbadoes	5,840
Bermuda	2,920
British Guiana	25,000
British Honduras	7,500
Canada	100,000
Cape Colony	50,000
Ceylon	65,600
Fiji	
India (informal)	
Jamaica	24,333
Leeward Islands	6,000
Malta	
Mashonaland	
Mauritius	
New Foundland	
New South Wales	243,325
New Zealand	27,500
South Australia	
Straits Settlements	
Tasmania	10,000
Trinidad	15,000
Victoria	97,330
West Australia	
Greece	57,900
Gautemala	200,000
Hawaii	
Hayti	25,000
Honduras	20,000
Hungary (informal)	
Italy	
Erythria	
Japan	630,765
Korea	
Liberia	
Madagascar	
Mexico	50,000
Morocco	150,000
Netherlands	
Dutch Guiana	10,000
Dutch West Indies	5,000
Nicaragua	30,000
Norway	56,280
Orange Free State	7,500

Paraguay	$ 100,000	Spain	$ 14,000
Persia		Cuba	25,000
Peru	140,000	Porto Rico	
Portugal (informal)		Switzerland	23,160
Madeira		Sweden	53,600
Roumania		Transvaal	
Russia	46,320	Turkey	
Salvador	12,500	Uruguay	24,000
San Domingo	25,000	Venezuela	
Servia		Total	$5,880,463
Siam		Fifty nations; thirty-three colonies.	

The amounts appropriated by various States and Territories, and by the foreign nations, must be of special interest to all friends of the great Exposition.

The following tabulated statement shows the amounts contributed by each State, and the amount expected, in addition; also, the dimensions and cost of the buildings of each State. In the preceding statement are shown the sums contributed by foreign nations.

STATES.	Appropri-ations.	From other sources.	Total ex-penditure.	Dimensions of build-ings in feet.	Cost of buildings, including donated material.	Appropri-ations expected.
Alabama	None.	$ 20,000	$ 20,000		$ 15,000	
Arkansas	"	by sub. 40,000	40,000	60 x 80	18,000	
California	$300,000	by sub. 250,000	500,000	110x500	75,000	
Colorado	100,000	by Co's. 50,000	150,000	55 x125	35,000	$ 50,000
Connecticut	None.	by Co's. 50,000	50,000	58 x 60	15,000	50,000
Delaware	10,000	by sub.	10,000		8,000	15,000
Florida	None.	150,000	150,000			
Georgia	"	by sub. 100,000	100,000		(?) 50,000	
Idaho	20,000	by sub. 50,000	70,000			80,000
Illinois	800,000	by sub. None.	800,000	160x450	250,000	
Indiana	75,000	10,000	85,000	100x170	75,000	75,000
Iowa	130,000	Something.	130,000	80 x100	50,000	
Kansas	None.	100,000	100,000		20,000	100,000
Kentucky	100,000	75.000	175,000	75 x 90	35,000	
Louisiana	36,000					
Maine	40,000	None.	40,000	65 x 65	22,000	Something.
Maryland	60,000	"	60,000	80 x120.	35,000	
Massachusetts	150,000	"	150,000		65,000	
Michigan	100,000	21,000	121,000	100x140	50,000	
Minnesota	50,000	100,000	150,000		25,000	
Mississippi	None.	25.000	25,000		15,000	
Missouri	150,000	by sub. None.	150,000	90 x110	100,000	

STATES.	Appropriations.	From other sources.	Total expenditure.	Dimensions of buildings in feet	Cost of buildings, including donated material.	Appropriations expected.
Montana.......	$ 50,000	None.	$ 50,000	64 x124	$ 15,000	Something.
Nebraska.....	50,000	"	50,000	60 x100	15,000	....
Nevada	None.	Something.	....	None.	....	Something.
New Hampshire	25,000	$ 20,000	45,000	... .	10,000	....
New Jersey....	70,000	None.	70,000	40 x 60	40,000	....
New York....	300,000	"	300,000	Wing, 16x20 97 x193	100,000	....
North Carolina.	25,000	20,000	45,000	....	10,000	Something.
North Dakota.	25,000	....	25,000	....	.... ..	"
Ohio..........	125,000	None.	125,000	....	50,000	....
Oregon	None.	Something.	....	None.	....	Something.
Pennsylvania ..	300,000	None.	300,000	....	80,000	....
Rhode Island..	50,000	"	50,000	....	15,000	....
South Carolina.	None.	50,000	50,000	....	10,000	Something.
South Dakota..	"	25,000	25,000	50 x 70	10,000	....
Tennessee	"	Something.	....	....	20,000	$ 25,000
Texas.........	"	300,000	300,000	65 x250	100,000	....
Vermont......	15,000	10,000	25,000	....	10,000	....
Virginia	25,000	50,000	75,000	....	15,000	25,000
Washington ..	100,000	Something.	100,000	138x216	50,000	50,000
West Virginia.	40,000	None.	40,000	38 x 76	20,000	....
Wisconsin	65,000	15,000	80,000	....	30,000	Something.
Wyoming....	30,000	Something.	30,000	None.	....	....
TERRITORIES.						
Alaska.........	None.	... .	....	None.	....	....
Arizona	30,000	....	30,000	Joint bldg.	15,000	....
New Mexico..	25,000	10,000	35,000	"	....	....
Oklahoma	None.	Something.	....	"	....	....
Utah...	"	50,000	50,000	....	... .	....
Total.......	$3,441,000	$1,591,000	$5,062,000	About 10 acres under roof.	$1,573,000	$370,000

Young Men's Christian Association.—This Association, in Chicago, has its headquarters at the Association building, 148 Madison Street. It has branches at 1225 West Madison Street, 653 South Canal Street, 9140 and 9142 Commercial Avenue, 3042 Archer Avenue, and Larrabee Street, corner of Grant Place. The reading-room of the main building is an attractive, well-lighted, and cheerful room, supplied with easy chairs. Convenient racks hold the papers donated to their files, including the leading secular and religious newspapers, whether daily or weekly, in company with publications on science, art, mechanics, education, architecture, etc. In this room is also placed a comfortable and ample writing table, and a request at the desk will furnish any writing material needed. On the library tables can be found choice literary, illustrated, scientific, and humorous periodicals. A large collection of cyclopedias, dictionaries, books of theology, science, biography, fiction, poetry, history, and travel make up the library. Books of special interest and importance to young men can be heard of by asking the Assistant Secretary,

The parlor is arranged with taste, is furnished with comfortable sitting facilities, and is intended for conversation, reading, leisure, or musical pastime. The amusement room is well supplied with numerous games of skill, in such large variety as to supply the wants of a large number at once. Among them are checkers, crokinole, chess, faba bags, baseball, croquet, authors, etc. Many features connected with this Association make membership both desirable and valuable to young men, especially those who are here alone struggling to commence life. Among these may be noted: homelike place, boarding-house register, informal receptions, trades' receptions, members' receptions, good company, friendly counsel, employment bureau, general information, writing conveniences, care in sickness, twelve members' parlors, parlor games, reading-rooms, current literature, educational classes, entertainments, practical talks, reference library, literary society, physical instruction, gymnasium, medical examination, twenty-four healthful baths, toilet conveniences, summer athletics, outing club, gospel meetings, training classes, Bible classes, prayer meetings, teachers' meetings. A young man can become an associate member who is over sixteen years of age, and whose moral character is satisfactory. The active membership are also young men over sixteen years of age who are members of some evangelical church. Whether the membership be regular or associate it takes a fee of $5. Special junior tickets, neither active nor associate, require an annual fee of $3, in advance, for certain limited privileges in this department. A young man may obtain membership, regardless of church connection or belief. The paid membership of the Chicago Association is nearly six thousand. It is the second in the world in the number of its departments, in its membership. and in the amount of money received annually for current expenses. The State Executive Committee has its headquarters at 148 Madison Street. Six secretaries are employed in the Illinois State work, and the annual expenditure by the State Committee, in the supervision of the State associations, is over $12,000. There is also a Young Women's Christian Association, with headquarters at room 30, 184 Dearborn Street. They have a boarding-house at 288 Michigan Street, where young women are boarded at a nominal cost.

Young Men's Hebrew Charity Society gives a "charity ball" annually, the proceeds of which are distributed among the various charities in the city, without regard to sect.

Zion Congregation Cemetery.—Located at Rosehill. (See *Rosehill Cemetery.*)

Zoological Gardens.—(See *Lincoln Park.*)

MINNEAPOLIS, ST. PAUL &

SAULT STE. MARIE RAILWAY

THE FAVORITE
ROUTE
BETWEEN

THE GREAT
NORTHWEST
AND EAST.

THE ONLY LINE RUNNING

Through Sleeping Cars
To Boston

Palatial Dining Cars Attached to all Through Trains.

SOLID TRAINS TO MONTREAL.

Equipment the Best.　　Rates always the Lowest.

OVER 100 MILES SHORTER

**BETWEEN PRINCIPAL POINTS IN THE EAST AND THE
GREAT NORTHWEST.**

For rates, maps, time tables, and other information, apply to
Company's Ticket Agents:

GUARANTY BUILDING,
MINNEAPOLIS, MINN,

185 E. 3D STREET,
ST. PAUL, MINN.

19

QUEEN ᴬᴺᴰ CRESCENT ROUTE

SHORTEST AND QUICKEST LINE FROM

CINCINNATI TO POINTS SOUTH.

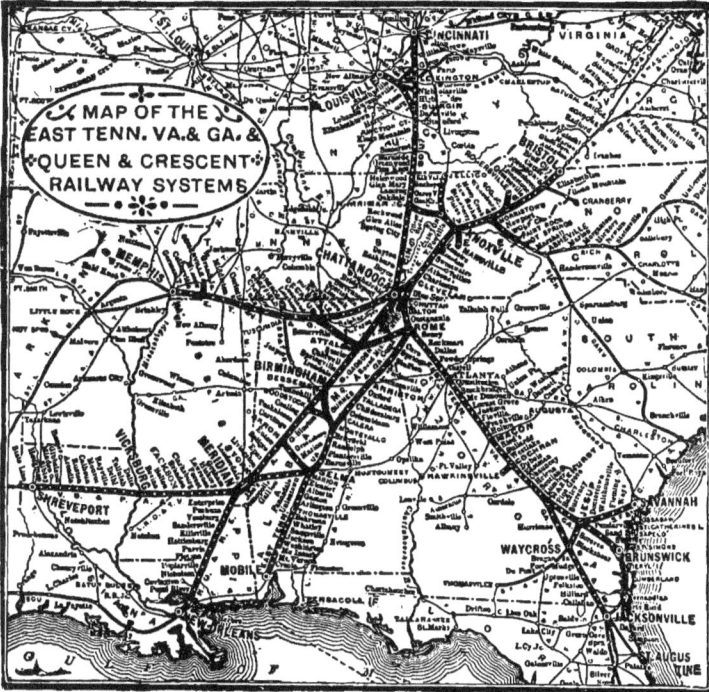

The only line running Solid Vestibuled Trains south of the Ohio River. The Florida Limited leaves Cincinnati daily via Lexington, Chattanooga, Macon, Atlanta, Jacksonville to St. Augustine, Florida.

The Queen & Crescent Special leaves Cincinnati daily via Lexington, Lookout Mountain, Birmingham, Meridian to New Orleans.

Through cars from Cincinnati via Knoxville, Ashville, and Hot Springs to Charleston, S. C.

Shortest and Quickest Line, Cincinnati to Florida and Southeastern Points. Shortest and Quickest Line via New Orleans or Shreveport to Texas, Mexico, and California.

Personally conducted Excursions to Texas, Mexico, and California, leave Cincinnati Thursday, January 21st, and every other Thursday thereafter.

For further information, address

H. A. CHERRIER, Northwestern Passenger Agent.
193 Clark Street, CHICAGO.

D. MILLER, Traffic Manager.   **D. G. EDWARDS,** General Passenger Agent.
CINCINNATI.

MINNETONKA BEACH, MINN.

HOTEL LAFAYETTE.

Largest and Finest Summer Resort House in the Northwest. Every room faces the lake. Reached during the summer season, from St. Paul and Minneapolis, by hourly trains on the Great Northern Railway.

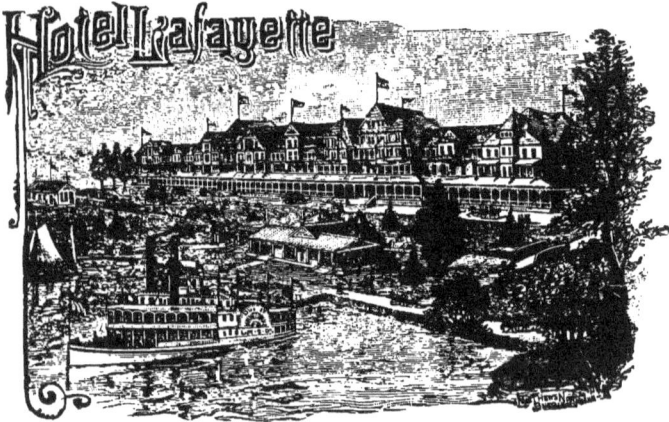

The Great Northern Railway Line

FROM

ST. PAUL AND MINNEAPOLIS

TO ALL THE

Leading Pleasure, Health, Fishing, and Hunting Resorts

IN THE NORTHWEST. DIRECT LINE TO

Litchfield, Osakis, Alexandria, Devils Lake,

Great Falls, Helena Hot Springs (Hotel Broadwater),

AND OTHER RESORTS.

Principal Route to Minnesota, Dakota, Montana, and Pacific Coast points. For tickets, publications, etc., apply to any railway or steamship ticket agent, or address

F. I. WHITNEY, General Passenger and Ticket Agent, Great Northern Railway.

A. L. MOHLER, General Manager, **P. P. SHELBY,** General Traffic Manager,

ST. PAUL, MINN.

284

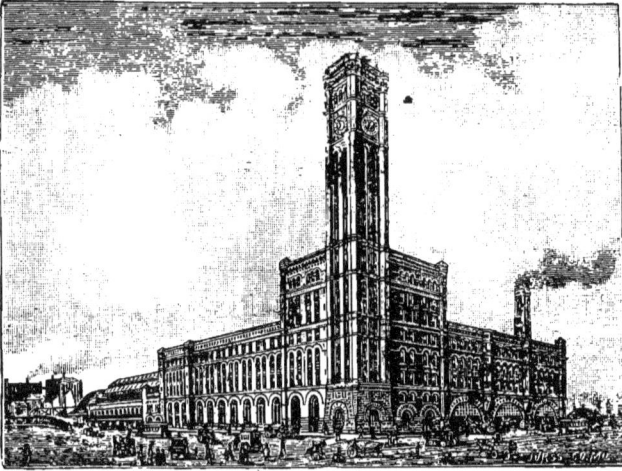

Grand Central Passenger Station, Chicago, Ill.

NORTHERN PACIFIC RAILROAD
AND WISCONSIN CENTRAL LINE

Reach the . .

Grandest Resorts in North America————

YELLOWSTONE PARK.—$120.00 from St. Paul, Minneapolis, or Duluth, Minnesota ; $140.00 from Chicago, Illinois, covering all expenses west of St. Paul, Minn.

PUGET SOUND, WASHINGTON.—$80.00 from St. Paul, Minneapolis, or Duluth, Minnesota: $100.00 from Chicago, Illinois, to Tacoma and Seattle, Washington. PORTLAND, OREGON, OR VICTORIA, B. C., and return; tickets good for six months, with stop-over privileges. Passengers are allowed choice of route, returning, when securing tickets.

CALIFORNIA.—$95.00 from St. Paul, Minneapolis, and Duluth, Minnesota; $115.00 from Chicago, Illinois, to San Francisco, California, and return.

ALASKA.—$175.00 from St. Paul, Minneapolis, and Duluth, Minnesota ; $195.00 from Chicago, Illinois, covering rail passage to and from Tacoma, Washington, and all expenses north of that point.

Train Service.—Through Sleeping Cars are run via Wisconsin Central and Northern Pacific lines from Chicago, Illinois, to points in Minnesota, North Dakota, Montana, Idaho, Oregon, and Washington. Dining Cars are carried on all through trains. Double daily passenger train service between St. Paul and Portland, April 3d to Oct. 30th

DESCRIPTIVE PUBLICATIONS.

Send to the following address for illustrated publications concerning the resorts above named; also for maps, time-cards, and any information desired in reference to rates, tickets, routes, etc.:

J. M. HANNAFORD,
Gen'l Traffic Manager,

CHAS. S. FEE,
Gen'l Pass'r and Ticket Agent,

ST. PAUL, MINN., U. S. A.

THE GREAT SOUTHWEST SYSTEM

Connecting the Commercial Centers and Rich Farms of

MISSOURI,

The Broad Corn and Wheat Fields and Thriving Towns of

KANSAS,

The Fertile River Valleys and Trade Centers of

NEBRASKA,

The Grand, Picturesque, and Enchanting Scenery, and the Famous Mining Districts of

COLORADO,

The Agricultural, Fruit, Mineral, and Timber Lands, and Famous Hot Springs of

ARKANSAS,

The Beautiful Rolling Prairies and Woodlands of the

INDIAN TERRITORY,

The Sugar Plantations of

LOUISIANA,

The Cotton and Grain Fields, the Cattle Ranges and Winter Resorts of

TEXAS,

Historical and Scenic

OLD AND NEW MEXICO,

And forms with its Connections the Popular Winter Route to

ARIZONA AND CALIFORNIA.

For descriptive and illustrated pamphlets of any of the above States, Hot Springs, Ark., San Antonio, Mexico, etc., address any Missouri Pacific Railway or " Iron Mountain Route " Agent.

JNO. E. ENNIS,

District Passenger and Land Agent, 199 S. Clark Street, CHICAGO, ILL.

S. H. H. CLARK,   **H. C. TOWNSEND,**

1st Vice-President and General Manager,   General Passenger and Ticket Agent,

ST. LOUIS, MO.

The

Chicago

Athenæum

Or, as it is well called, "The People's College," fulfills in this city almost the same beneficent purpose in useful education that the "Cooper Union" does in New York. It is now in its 21st year, having been organized by some of the most prominent and public-spirited citizens of Chicago, in the same month of the "Great Fire" of '71. This honored institution now occupies a spacious and elegant building of its own, at 18 to 26 Van Buren Street, near the Lake Front. The property cost nearly $300,000. No expense has been spared in making the numerous class-rooms and lecture-hall attractive and comfortable. The scope of educational work is broad and the instruction thorough. All studies are elective. The school now employs an efficient corps of thirty-three instructors. Students may take a full preparatory course in the common English branches, or a full Business and Short-hand course, or an Academic course to fit for college, or a course in higher Mathematics, Architectural or Mechanical Drawing, Civil Engineering and Surveying, or in Elocution and Oratory, and Parliamentary Practice, or in Vocal and Instrumental Music.

The Athenæum day departments are open the entire year with the exception of three weeks, and the evening classes five times a week during nine months of the year.

Teachers of the public schools, or those who desire to prepare for teachers' examination, may here receive the needed instruction in Mathematics, Science, Literature, the classics, or modern languages.

Evening lectures are given during the fall and winter on popular science, travel, etc.

As a further aid to its students a choice Reference and Circulating Library and Reading-room is maintained.

Great attention is also given to Physical Culture. The largest and best equipped Gymnasium in the city, under an experienced director, is here provided, in which daily drill classes for ladies and gentlemen are conducted.

Thus generously provided in all departments, and ably sustained by its influential Board of Directors, the Chicago Athenæum is destined to become one of the most attractive institutions for mental and physical culture of any city in the land.

The list of officers and directors is a sufficient guarantee of its high standard and useful aims.

☞A catalogue of the school, or any special information desired, may be obtained by addressing the Superintendent.

Board of Directors

LYMAN J. GAGE	A. C. BARTLETT
FRANKLIN H. HEAD	J. J. P. ODELL
H. H. KOHLSAAT	JOS. SEARS
CHAS. J. SINGER	WM. R. PAGE
HUGH A. WHITE	GILBERT B. SHAW
EDW. B. BUTLER	ALEX. H. REVELL
HENRY BOOTH	HARRY G. SELFRIDGE
FERDINAND W. PECK	JOHN WILKINSON

Officers

FERDINAND W. PECK	President
WM. R. PAGE	1st Vice-President
HARRY G. SELFRIDGE	2d Vice-President
JOHN WILKINSON	Rec. Sec'y and Treas.
EDWARD I. GALVIN	Superintendent

Winter Resorts of the South

TAKE THE

MONON ROUTE

LOUISVILLE, NEW ALBANY & CHICAGO RY. CO.

Two trains each way daily—

Chicago to Indianapolis and Cincinnati,

Chicago to Lafayette and Louisville,

Affording you choice of routes beyond. Pullman Safety Vestibuled Coaches on all night trains. Parlor Chair Cars on Day Trains.

The only line serving meals in a regular Dining Car, Chicago to Cincinnati.

Compartment Car in addition to the regular Pullman Sleepers on the " Electric," Chicago to Cincinnati.

For rates, schedules, etc., apply to

F. J. REED, CITY PASSENGER AGENT,
73 CLARK STREET, CHICAGO.

W. H. McDOEL,   **JAMES BARKER,**
GENERAL MANAGER.   **GENERAL PASSENGER AGENT.**
GENERAL OFFICES, MONON BLOCK, CHICAGO.

295

"LAKE SHORE ROUTE"

Lake Shore &
Michigan Southern Ry.

**THE ONLY DOUBLE TRACK
LINE BETWEEN**

CHICAGO,

CLEVELAND,

BUFFALO,

NEW YORK, and

BOSTON.

olid Vestibule Trains run daily between Chicago and
lew York, making the trip of nearly One Thousand
Miles in twenty-five hours.

The Service on the "Lake Shore"
is Unequaled.

OHN NEWELL,   **A. J. SMITH,**
Pres't and General Manager,   Gen'l Pass. and Ticket Agent
CLEVELAND, OHIO.

20

CHOICE

☀

INVESTMENTS

We call special attention to our desirable improved Business and Flat Property located in different sections of the· city. These vary in prices from $10,000 to $1,000,000, paying from 5 to 10 per cent.

Hotels and apartment houses to lease.

We have choice Real Estate Mortgages for sale and money to loan on good city property in sums of $3,000 to $50,000.

We have the finest South Side, Kenwood, and Hyde Park residence property offered for sale in Chicago.

Large list of Residences to rent.

B. A. ULRICH.   **A. L. ULRICH.**   **RUSSELL ULRICH.**

B. A. ULRICH & SONS
ESTABLISHED 1868
REAL ESTATE AGENCY
88 & 90 WASHINGTON ST.
CHICAGO.

Telephone 2972.

297

D. P. ERWIN, President.   F. W. JEWELL, Vice-Pres. and Manager.

"THE DENISON"
HOTEL

INDIANAPOLIS, IND.

This is the largest and best appointed Hotel in Indianapolis.
Has accommodations for nearly five hundred guests
and is located in the very heart of the
business center of the city.

Lighted throughout with electricity, and heated by steam.
The Cuisine is unexcelled.

RATES SAME AS ALL FIRST-CLASS HOTELS.

This House is conducted on the . .

American Plan . .

And is strictly first-class in every particular, and has
splendid Sample Rooms for Commercial Travelers.

ERWIN HOTEL CO., PROPRIETORS.

NORTH **E**AST **W**EST **S**OUTH

GEO. H. HEAFFORD, General Passenger Agent.
J. H. HILAND, General Freight Agent.
CHICAGO, ILL.

CHICAGO CITY TICKET OFFICE,

207-209 CLARK STREET.

F. A. MILLER, ASSISTANT GENERAL PASSENGER AGENT.

CHICAGO'S

GREATEST

TWO-CENT

NEWSPAPER

THE

CHICAGO

HERALD

THE HERALD'S NEW BUILDING.

Is housed more palatially than any other newspaper in the world, and its new home embodies so many out of common features as to make it

ONE OF THE SIGHTS OF THE CITY

THE VISITORS' GALLERY overlooks ten of the finest newspaper presses possible to make, and is open to everybody, every day and every night, all day and all night.

300

NEW ROUTE
NEW TRAIN
ELEGANT
EQUIPMENT

VIA THE

CENTRAL
I.C. R.R.
ROUTE.

ILLINOIS CENTRAL R.R.

CHICAGO
TO
ST. LOUIS

THE DIAMOND SPECIAL

SOLID TRAIN

LEAVES CHICAGO DAILY AT 9.00 P. M.

STOPPING AT VAN BUREN STREET, 22D STREET,
39TH STREET, AND HYDE PARK.

The Van Buren Street stop is for the special accommodation of hotel patrons,
being within easy walking distance of all the down-town hotels.

PURITAN
PILGRIM
PLYMOUTH
AND
PROVIDENCE

Of the FALL RIVER LINE

THE FAMOUS BUSINESS AND PLEASURE ROUTE BETWEEN

NEW YORK AND BOSTON
ARE THE

Four Leading Steamboats of the World

And are conceded to be the largest, handsomest, and most perfectly equipped vessels of their class ever constructed. They steer by steam, are lighted throughout by electricity, and in every detail of equipment more than meet all possible conditions of the demands of first-class travel.

The Long Island Sound Route of the Fall River Line is one of the most attractive highways of travel to be found anywhere.

Tickets by this route are on sale at all of the Principal Ticket Offices in the United States.

J. R. KENDRICK,
General Manager, Boston.

GEO. L. CONNOR,
General Passenger Agent, Boston.

S. A. GARDNER,
Superintendent, New York.

O. H. TAYLOR,
Asst. Gen'l Passenger Agent, New York.

LINDELL HOTEL

ST. LOUIS, MO.

Ranks among the best hotels in the world.

Located in the very heart of the business center of the City.

Cuisine unexcelled.

Accommodations the best.

HULBERT, HOWE & CHASSAING,

PROPRIETORS.

BURNET HOUSE

CINCINNATI, OHIO.

THE BURNET HOUSE HOTEL CO.

Strictly First-class . . .

T. W. ZIMMERMAN,

Treasurer and Manager.

305

McCoy's

NEW EUROPEAN HOTEL

COR. CLARK AND VAN BUREN STREETS,

Chicago, Ill.

Rates, $1.00 per day And Upwards.

FIRE-PROOF BUILDING.

This is one of the largest, best appointed, and most liberally managed hotels in Chicago; its location being central, and accommodations unexcelled. There are 250 elegantly furnished East, South, and West front rooms; also passenger elevator; and fire alarm bells in each room.

The restaurant which is operated in connection with the "McCoy" is one of the finest in the city.

WM. McCoy,

OWNER AND PROPRIETOR.

THE TEXAS & PACIFIC
RAILWAY COMPANY

WITH ITS CONNECTIONS

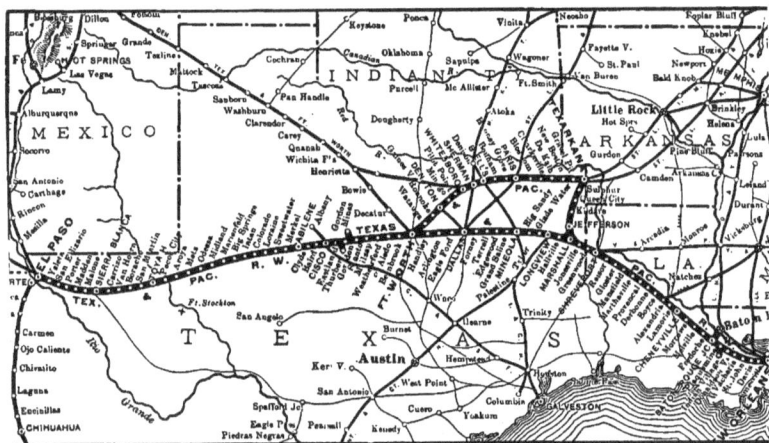

Forms THE DIRECT LINE to · ·

Paris, Sherman, Dallas, Ft. Worth, Abilene, El Paso, and all principal towns in Northern Texas, Eastern Louisiana, Old and New Mexico, Arizona, and California.

PULLMAN PALACE BUFFET SLEEPERS · ·

Through between St. Louis and El Paso, and New Orleans and Denver, WITHOUT CHANGE.

For Tickets or any Information, apply to

JOHN E. ENNIS,
Passenger Agent,
199 South Clark Street, CHICAGO, ILL.

GASTON MESLIER,
General Passenger and Ticket Agent,
DALLAS, TEXAS.

Fashionable

Tailoring

HENRY

Merchant Tailor

129 AND 131 LA SALLE STREET

CHICAGO, ILL.

Tacoma Building.)

THE CHICAGO CARPET COMPANY

Wabash Ave. and
Monroe St.

The largest stock of Carpetings to be found in the Country. Our furniture stock is always full of Novelties from all the markets of the world.

Carpetings, Furniture Draperies

Houses decorated according to period by skilled artists. Special designs furnished for Furniture, Draperies, and Decorations.

Drapery Fabrics in endless variety. All styles of Laces for windows from the finest Brussels to the cheapest Nottingham

The public can not afford to place orders before looking over our large stocks.

Chicago Carpet Company

J. C. Carroll, President.

Houston, East & West Texas and Houston & Shreveport R'ys.

Houston, Texas, to Shreveport, La., - - **232 Miles.**

The attention of the farmer, mill man, and miner is called to the territory along and adjacent to this line. This is the BEST WATERED section of the State; running streams the year round. Yellow Pine, Walnut, Oak, Ash, and Magnolia abound in virgin forests. Iron Ore is found in large quantities. Lubricating Oil is also found in paying quantities and being shipped to Northern markets. The saw mill industry is large, and mills increasing in number and size, finding ready markets for their production. This is a fine section for the farmer; lands are cheap, and produce cotton, corn, sorghum, small grain, and all kinds of vegetables. Stock of all kinds do well. The towns and country are well supplied with churches and schools.

Further information will be cheerfully furnished on application to

M. G. HOWE, Receiver H., E. & W. T. Railway; General Manager H. & S. Railway.
R. S. COLLINS, General Freight and Passenger Agent,
HOUSTON, TEXAS.

MENGER HOTEL

SAN ANTONIO,
TEXAS.

H. D. KAMPMAN,
Proprietor.

H. W. BROWDER,
Chief Clerk.

THE CHICAGO TIMES

Chicago's Greatest

Newspaper

LARGEST CIRCULATION OF ANY DEMO-
CRATIC NEWSPAPER IN THE

West

PRICE $8.00 PER YEAR, POST PAID

DELIVERED BY CARRIER, 17 CENTS PER WEEK

TIMES BUILDING, CHICAGO

THE NORTH-WESTERN LINE

C. & N. W. RY

SOLID VESTIBULED TRAINS

Between Chicago and St. Paul, Minneapolis, Council Bluffs, Omaha, Denver, and Portland.

FREE RECLINING CHAIR CARS

Between Chicago and Council Bluffs, Omaha, Denver, and Portland.

THROUGH SLEEPING CARS

Between Chicago and St. Paul, Minneapolis, Duluth, Council Bluffs, Omaha, Sioux City, Denver, Portland, and San Francisco.

SUPERB DINING CARS.

ALL AGENTS SELL TICKETS VIA THE

CHICAGO & NORTH-WESTERN RAILWAY.

H. NEWMAN,
3d Vice-President.

J. M. WHITMAN,
General Manager.

W. A. THRALL,
Gen'l Pass'r and Tkt. Agt.

322

MIDLAND HOTEL,

KANSAS CITY, MO.

ABSOLUTELY FIRE-PROOF THROUGHOUT.

Table and service unsurpassed. Centrally located.

OPERATED ON BOTH THE

AMERICAN AND EUROPEAN PLANS.

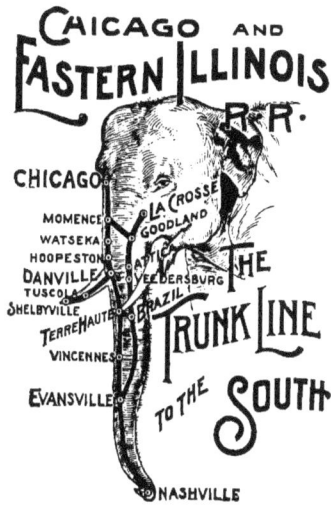

Perfect Passenger Service

No change of cars of any class between

CHICAGO AND KANSAS CITY,
CHICAGO AND ST. LOUIS,
ST. LOUIS AND KANSAS CITY,
BLOOMINGTON AND KANSAS CITY.

All trains arrive at and depart from Union depots in Chicago, Bloomington, East St. Louis, St. Louis, Kansas City, and Denver.

Palace Reclining Chair Cars (free of extra charge),
Ladies' Palace Day Cars (free of extra charge),
Pullman Compartment Sleeping Cars,
Palace Dining Cars, Pullman Parlor Cars,
Pullman Palace Buffet Sleeping Cars.

Solid vestibuled trains. All cars equipped with Westinghouse Automatic Air Brake and Blackstone Platform and Coupler. The Wharton Safety Switch is used exclusively on this line. The time of express trains is exceptionally fast over a roadway matchless for safety, speed, and comfort.

C. H. CHAPPELL,
General Manager, Chicago.

JAS. CHARLTON,
General Passenger and Ticket Agent, Chicago.

CALIFORNIA . .

All the principal Winter Resorts of California are
reached in the most comfortable manner over the
Atchison, Topeka & Santa Fé R. R.

· The Santa Fé Route

**Pullman Vestibule Sleeping Cars leave Chicago daily and run via Kansas
City to San Francisco, Los Angeles, and San Diego without change.**

Excursion Tickets and detailed information can be obtained at the following offices
of the Company: 261 Broadway, New York; 332 Washington Street, Boston; 29 South
Sixth Street, Philadelphia; 136 St. James Street, Montreal; 68 Exchange Street, Buffalo;
148 St. Clair Street, Cleveland; 58 Griswold Street, Detroit; 40 Yonge Street, Toronto;
165 Walnut Street, Cincinnati; 101 Broadway, St. Louis; 212 Clark Street, Chicago.

JOHN J. BYRNE,
Assistant Passenger Traffic Manager,
CHICAGO, ILL.

GEO. T. NICHOLSON,
General Passenger and Ticket Agent,
TOPEKA, KAN,